Ctrl + Alt + (shift) + Tab

Pro Excel Financial Modeling

Building Models for Technology Startups

■ ■ ■

Tom Y. Sawyer

D1708224

day rate
source track,
qualification
   market
   due diligence
   database
   CRM
   metrics
   template

presentable to LP's
SBA

tools credibility
qualification
   report

Apress®

Pro Excel Financial Modeling: Building Models for Technology Startups

Copyright © 2009 by Tom Y. Sawyer

ISBN-13 (pbk): 978-1-4302-1898-2

ISBN-13 (electronic): 978-1-4302-1899-9

Printed and bound in the United States of America 9 8 7 6 5 4 3 2 1

Lead Editors: Mark Beckner, Matthew Moodie
Technical Reviewer: Debra Dalgleish
Editorial Board: Clay Andres, Steve Anglin, Mark Beckner, Ewan Buckingham, Tony Campbell, Gary Cornell, Jonathan Gennick, Michelle Lowman, Matthew Moodie, Jeffrey Pepper, Frank Pohlmann, Ben Renow-Clarke, Dominic Shakeshaft, Matt Wade, Tom Welsh
Project Manager: Kylie Johnston
Copy Editor: Heather Lang
Associate Production Director: Kari Brooks-Copony
Production Editor: Katie Stence
Compositor and Artist: Kinetic Publishing Services, LLC
Proofreader: Martha Whitt
Indexer: Becky Hornyak
Cover Designer: Kurt Krames
Manufacturing Director: Tom Debolski

Distributed to the book trade worldwide by Springer-Verlag New York, Inc., 233 Spring Street, 6th Floor, New York, NY 10013. Phone 1-800-SPRINGER, fax 201-348-4505, e-mail orders-ny@springer-sbm.com, or visit http://www.springeronline.com.

For information on translations, please contact Apress directly at 2855 Telegraph Avenue, Suite 600, Berkeley, CA 94705. Phone 510-549-5930, fax 510-549-5939, e-mail info@apress.com, or visit http://www.apress.com.

Apress and friends of ED books may be purchased in bulk for academic, corporate, or promotional use. eBook versions and licenses are also available for most titles. For more information, reference our Special Bulk Sales–eBook Licensing web page at http://www.apress.com/info/bulksales.

The source code for this book is available to readers at http://www.apress.com.

This book is dedicated to my father, Tom Y. Sawyer, the last of the old-time country lawyers.

Contents at a Glance

Contents

■CHAPTER 9   Operating and Capital Expenditures Models 169

■CHAPTER 10   Statements of Profit and Loss and Cash Flow 193

■CHAPTER 11   Modeling Valuation and Investment with the FIN Model 215

■CHAPTER 12   Financial Reporting and Analysis Using the FIN Model 243

About the Author

▆**TOM Y. SAWYER** has a proven track record as a principal architect, leader, and strategist for successful business and technology ventures. Tom provides management and technology consulting services to technology-focused enterprises, specializing in early-stage organizational strategies, product development, and financial projections. A serial entrepreneur, he founded and sold an Internet data storage dot com, served as president of a regional Internet Service Provider where he negotiated the strategic sale of the company, and served as the first president of a software company that, today, is the largest enterprise software and consulting company in the moving industry. He served as chief technology officer of a GPS/GIS–centric engineering technology services company serving the utility industry. Tom gained Fortune 100 senior management experience as the director of information technology for the Martin Marietta Space Launch Systems Titan IV missile program, where he received the Outstanding Achievement Award for Information Technology Management. Prior to his Fortune 100 career, he served in progressively more responsible financial management and financial planning positions in banking, technology services, and computer manufacturing. He holds a BSBA degree in finance from the University of Florida.

About the Technical Reviewer

DEBRA DALGLEISH is owner and lead consultant at Contextures Inc., which specializes in Microsoft Office programming and development. Located in Mississauga, Ontario, Canada, Contextures serves local and international clients in financial, pharmaceutical, service, and manufacturing industries.

Self-employed since 1985, Debra has extensive experience in designing complex Excel and Access applications, as well as sophisticated Word forms and documents.

She has written three books, published by Apress, to help users master and troubleshoot Excel pivot tables: *Beginning Pivot Tables in Excel 2007*, *Excel 2007 Pivot Tables Recipes*, and *Excel Pivot Tables Recipe Book*.

In recognition of her exceptional technical contributions to the Excel community, Debra has been honored to receive Microsoft's Excel MVP award each year since 2001. You can find a wide variety of Excel tutorials and sample files on her Contextures web site: `www.contextures.com`. For daily computer tips, please visit the Contextures Blog: `blog.contextures.com`.

Acknowledgments

I would like to thank my wife, Melanie Sawyer, for hours of proofreading, brutal honesty, and sack lunches; Ken Palmer for great accounting advice; Mark Beckner for getting me started; Scott Jones and Larry Hower for the book's technical case concepts; Lee Whitney for sage advice; and the gang at Ryan and Whitney for ongoing harassment and other annoyances.

Introduction

This book outlines smart business strategies for building a technology startup and provides a comprehensive guide to building a financial model of the company. I wrote this book to share my entrepreneuring experience and to help the entrepreneur avoid many of the obstacles and hazards that I encountered while leading and participating in early-stage companies. This book is important because it combines logical business thinking and strategies with a step-by-step methodology for planning and modeling a technology company. It practically demonstrates the creation of operational and financial models that describe the workings of the company in quantitative terms. This book shows you how to take a business idea for a company and break it down into basic functional and operational components that can be modeled. The resulting model describes the business in quantitative terms and generates operational scenarios and financial projections that are needed to assess the value of the proposed enterprise.

Who This Book Is For

The ideal reader of this book is the technology entrepreneur, the business or technology student, the owner of an early-stage business, or anyone with an interest in the mechanics of planning, organizing, and developing financial projections for business enterprises. This book is also for anyone interested in using Microsoft Excel to develop operational and financial models of business enterprises.

How This Book Is Structured

This book presents a structured and logical exploration and development of a business strategy combined with the development of operational and financial models. The book takes you through the progressive creation of operational models that reflect primary functions of the business leading to the creation of financial models that develop standard financial statements.

The first three chapters of the book form an introduction to the remaining chapters, each of which takes you through a step-by-step process of building the next logical model in a sequence required to complete the entire company business model.

Chapter 1 begins with a high-level discussion of business principles and practical suggestions for the entrepreneur and concludes with a discussion of concepts for developing financial models.

Chapter 2 describes, in greater detail, the structure and methodology and best practices for building a financial model for a technology company.

Chapter 3 outlines the business case for Green Devil Control Systems (the Company), our business case company and new-breed, green technology company. We will analyze and model the Company throughout the remainder of this book.

Chapter 4 kicks off the planning process with the development of organizational concepts and the forecasting of staffing and related costs.

Chapter 5 opens our examination of Company target market assumptions with the creation of a sales and revenue forecast.

Chapter 6 develops the cost of goods sold for various product and service options of the Company and, combined with the sales and revenue forecast developed in Chapter 5, provides for a forecast of margin contribution from the sale of products and services.

Chapter 7 assesses the life cycle cost of the sales and marketing function, modeling the fixed and variable costs associated with selling the Company's products and services.

Chapter 8 plans for the application of the resources and schedule needed to develop, test, manufacture, and distribute the Company's products and services to market.

Chapter 9 budgets for capital expenditures and other operating expenditures that are associated with the core operations of the Company, product development, and sales and marketing.

Chapter 10 is the first of our financial modeling chapters covering the concepts of profit and loss and cash flow in detail and developing profit and loss financial reports.

Chapter 11 explores Company valuation and investment strategy utilizing the forecasts and assumptions developed in previous chapters.

Chapter 12 rounds out and completes our financial discussion with the creation of a Company Balance Sheet and the application of financial ratio analysis to our modeling results.

Prerequisites

The financial models and examples used in the book were developed using Microsoft Excel 2007. This book is written for readers who are familiar with Microsoft Excel at an intermediate or advanced level. The use of Microsoft Excel for financial modeling is emphasized rather than how to use Microsoft Excel in a generic sense.

Downloading the Code

The source code for this book is available to readers at www.apress.com in the Downloads section of this book's web page. Please feel free to visit the Apress web site and download all the code there. You can also check for errata and find related titles from Apress.

Contacting the Author

You are very welcome to contact me by e-mail at tom@tomysawyer.com, or feel free to visit my web sites: www.tomysawyer.com and www.tomsawyerbizcoach.com.

■■■

CHAPTER 1

Business Thinking and Financial Modeling for Technology Startups

Y our financial model is a key management tool. If built correctly, it will provide invaluable assistance in understanding, managing, and presenting your business idea. It can assist you in the simple budgeting of cash, or it can serve as the primary basis for a valuation of your company.

In this chapter, I will explain several concepts related to technology startups. We will discuss questions that entrepreneurs get from investors. We will explore strategies and principles that create success and credibility, and we will view the early-stage enterprise through the lens of *value*. We will discuss the financial model, a tool that assists the entrepreneur in planning and in articulating his or her success strategies.

I have combined thoughts and strategies for startup company success with a financial modeling tutorial. There is not always a clear correlation between business thinking and the actual financial model, but where possible, I have tried to link business thinking with the mechanics of the model. There is an important reason for this link: The *story* of your company as set forth in your business plan and the quantitative outputs of your financial model must be consistent.

Analyzing, Demonstrating, and Explaining the Value of the Financial Model

This book emphasizes business thinking about your company as you design your financial model. Business thinking will enhance the probability that your model will provide a meaningful analysis of your company, helping you explain your success strategies to a potential investor. Your model should be designed to drive out the value proposition of your company, to uncover the *profit engine* of your enterprise.

Building a business requires focus, thought, understanding, and a clear business idea. Can you articulate and quantify the value proposition for your business idea? Can you demonstrate how you are going to achieve traction and prove that you have it? What's traction? Your company is demonstrating *traction* when it is executing your operating plan, essentially as you planned it, and when your business idea has credibility with employees, investors, partners, and customers. Everyone knows traction when they see it.

Implicit in any well-designed model are the answers for most, if not all questions that the entrepreneur must answer when pursuing the resources necessary to do business. I always say, "If you can model it, you can explain it." Many subjects are qualitative in nature, and they cannot be directly represented on a spreadsheet, subjects like the vision of the company, staff qualifications, market assessments, or the company mantra. For each qualitative subject, however, there is usually some form of representation in the model. Once you explain your strategy for penetrating a market, your model should show the quantification of your strategy. Your company story should be represented by the model and vice versa. Assumptions, for example, about the number of units sold and the associated cost of goods sold should make sense based on your qualitative explanation of the market opportunity.

Make sure that you have a thorough understanding of your business idea and have done sufficient market research prior to any serious modeling exercise. You remember "garbage in, garbage out," right?

■Note Financial models are not about absolute values; they are about relationships. A good financial model demonstrates the relationships and the business tradeoffs that compose the profitability potential of the business idea. If you understand the relationships, the drivers of revenue, drivers of cost, and critical success factors, you understand the core of the business.

Many believe that sales, profit, and profitability projections shown in financial models are the keys to success in attracting investors. The truth is that investors will come up with their own projections. Investors want to understand the assumptions, the structure, and the relationships within the model. If assumptions, structure, and relationships pass the test, the entrepreneur has demonstrated complete understanding of the business side of the enterprise.

Most sophisticated potential investors are more interested in the soundness and logic of your thought process than your absolute projections. The further out in time the model projects, the weaker the validity of the forecast. However, in the short term, the model can be extremely valuable as a tool to forecast cash needs.

Attracting the Resources You Need to Grow Your Business

To state the obvious, business ventures require resources. There is a high probability that you will need to borrow or raise money at some point in the life cycle of your early-stage venture. One day, you will find yourself making a pitch to a relative, a banker, an angel investor, or a venture capitalist seeking the funding you need to build or grow your business. The question may not be asked explicitly, but investors will be calculating the value of your business as part of their assessment of your proposition. You must be able to explain the logic, rationale, and workings of your venture with sufficient clarity to enable the investors or lenders to make a determination of value. The investors must be able to arrive at an understanding of your company's value if you are to attract the resources you need to do business.

Don't underestimate the value equation in attracting talent and employees. High-quality employees make similar calculations of value to determine if they are willing to invest their time and energy, and sometimes reputations, by coming to work for your venture.

The financial model provides you with a powerful tool for articulating your business idea and assisting the investor in determining a value profile for your company. In the following sections, I will cover two important topics that are directly related to establishing the value of your company:

- The big three questions—the *big* questions that investors ask entrepreneurs
- Strategies that build value and credibility

The Big Three Questions

I have attended meeting after meeting in which the technology entrepreneur failed to convince potential investors to invest in a company. In most cases, the presentation failed to prove to the investor that the entrepreneur had a firm grasp on the business model needed to take the idea to market and profitability. Technology was rarely the showstopper. The problem repeatedly centered on the business model: the business assumptions that failed the investor's sniff test.

"What we've got here is failure to communicate."

—Donn Pearce, Cool Hand Luke

The investor is looking for entrepreneurs that have a clear sense of their opportunity and how to build the business. A good entrepreneur understands both the technical and business opportunity and how to flesh out the numbers behind it. The entrepreneur inevitably encounters *three fundamental questions* from potential investors and lenders. The questions follow:

- Cool idea; how do you make money with it?
- How much do you need and when?
- What do you think your company is worth?

These questions, which I call *the big three*, represent the starting point from which the investor or lender proceeds to assess the risk/opportunity profile of your company. These questions are actually pretty straightforward. They are the same questions anyone asks when they are thinking about purchasing virtually anything. Does it work like you say it does? How much do you want for it? What makes you think it's worth that?

What about an exit strategy? Isn't that a major question? My prejudice is that too much thinking about exit strategy is counting the chickens before they hatch. Concentrate instead on validating and building value and answering the big three questions. The exit strategy will become apparent. If the investor insists on a strategy, offer a big smile and say, "It will probably be a strategic sale, but there is always the possibility of an IPO."

How you'll make money with your idea, team, market opportunity, and the product/value proposition must be justified and explained. Risk is a major factor in any value assessment. Where is the risk in the overall business and technology model, and how may it be quantified or mitigated? Risk is the dark side of critical success factors. What is the risk that the venture's critical success factors will not be realized?

Technology differentiation or business model differentiation is also important. Internal processes for development, tools, code review, and the philosophy around development must support cost estimates to build the technology and product introduction schedules.

How much cash is needed and when? Investors prefer to fund growth in sales and building out of capability rather than early-stage research and development.

From the earliest idea scratched on a napkin through the various stages of growth, a fundamental question is repeatedly asked about early-stage companies looking for resources, "How much is it worth?" The entrepreneur will attempt to *answer* this question, but the investor will *determine* the answer, and the answer, over the life cycle of the endeavor, will greatly influence the prospects for success.

To survive due diligence by a sophisticated investor, all of these questions must be answered. A complete, well-designed financial model will not only facilitate the answers but will also provide the entrepreneur with a tool to examine "what ifs" with various assumptions and scenarios.

Note The perceived value of the early-stage venture is the primary determinant of its ability to attract the resources needed to grow the business.

Strategies That Build Value and Credibility

As you are engaged in business thinking about your technology idea, keep the following strategies and concepts in mind. I have worked with a large number of startups and have found these strategies to be invaluable as a framework for success. Each venture is different, but these strategies universally apply. I categorize the strategies into three groups as follows:

- Performance and execution:
  - Get there fast.
  - Take early action.
  - Use a feedback loop and respond rapidly.
  - Use prototypes for simultaneous research and selling.
  - Be agile with technology and development.
  - Remember that cash is king.
  - Keep good books.
- People and process:
  - Secure the team.
  - Skin in the game.
  - Seal the deal.
  - Plan for growth. Can the business scale?
- Ownership and control:
  - Know what you own.
  - Own your technology.

Performance and Execution Strategies

Performance and execution strategies are about action. Successful implementation of these strategies builds credibility that the company can perform. Investors closely watch execution and are excited by rapid progress and momentum. The old adage that "actions speak louder than words" is what these strategies are about.

Getting There Fast

"Get there fast" is the tag line for my consulting company and my primary business mantra. Successful entrepreneurs run their companies with a sense of urgency. This sense of urgency drives them to get operational quickly and to be early to market. They beat their competitors to the punch and quickly get prototypes in front of key customers while driving relentlessly toward positive cash flow. They react quickly and execute with a minimum of mistakes. The person who has the capability to operationally execute in this manner has the right stuff to be an entrepreneur.

Excellent execution is critical, especially if your concepts can be copied and replicated. If an innovation cannot be patented or kept secret, your best protection is to be early to market and to create competitive barriers like building a strong brand name or having an excellent reputation for customer support.

■Note My favorite image of the entrepreneur is Wile E. Coyote from the *Looney Tunes* cartoons. He is so focused on catching the Road Runner that he will run over the edge of a cliff and up an invisible stairway into the air. He keeps going up as long as he doesn't stop and look down. If he looks down, he falls. Don't look down!

Startups are risky business at best. Starting with a conservative idea is better, if that is possible. Ventures that are not capital intensive and have high enough profit margins to fund internal operations are definitely preferred. The entrepreneur should be looking for projects that can generate cash and break even quickly.

Think simple. Simple operational models have much lower risk profiles. Try to find models of operation that can be implemented quickly and that don't have high fixed costs so that cash crunches don't occur when schedules slip.

Ideally, offer high-value products that can support the costs of direct selling. Early-stage companies cannot afford to give away margin by relying on indirect sales channels or to severely discount or lose lead to gain future business. If your idea cannot generate cash and strong margins right away, take another look at the idea.

Taking Early Action

Startups must quickly develop market intelligence sufficient to guide them through key decisions in product specification and product positioning so that dollars spent and product development effort expended result in early business success. They must take early action to interview, understand, and gather requirements from representative companies in their target markets. This is why it is important that one of the founders or entrepreneurs have relevant industry experience. Industry credentials of the founders jump-start the connection with relevant and important sources of market information. A preexisting rotating file of industry experts that can be called and interviewed is invaluable. Industry experts should be interviewed with questions like, "If we built a product with this form, feature, and functionality, would you be interested in buying it? Why? How much would you pay for it? Why?"

■Note I was the first president of a software company that developed front and back office systems for the moving industry. Jim, the owner, was a subject matter expert in moving industry software and operations and was well known and highly respected in the industry. I had free rein to put together the working infrastructure, processes, and procedures for the software company. We designed the software with heavy guidance from Jim. After two and a half years, I stepped aside, and Jim stepped in as president. Leveraging his industry ties, his company is now the leading provider of software systems to the moving industry.

Using the Feedback Loop and Responding Rapidly

Startups must clearly identify opportunities, clearly understand and validate their value proposition, and develop offerings that deliver value. There are many unknowns, and the company must, from the beginning, implement a hot feedback loop method of doing business that generates a continuous stream of market intelligence. The company must be able to rapidly and intelligently respond and adjust to this market information feed. The feedback loop taps into representative market prospects for information and the company responds by fine tuning its offering to assure maximum price performance and acceptance. The company's ability to tap into and correctly respond to this early customer feedback loop is a critical success factor.

Herein lies a critical balancing act: the ability to parse clues from the field and respond with enhancements and improvements while simultaneously maintaining the vision for the company. The entrepreneur must be able to correctly interpret the data from the field, including sometimes ignoring it. For instance, the original market studies that tested the idea of copy machines provided resounding feedback that everyone was perfectly satisfied using carbon paper.

The true test of an entrepreneur's ability to execute is the ability to balance the vision of the company with very real market data feedback. This ability to make the right decisions and to spend money wisely often makes the difference between success and failure.

Successful entrepreneurs spend their time on operational analysis, not strategic planning. Be mindful of the marginal cost and value of pure research. It is better to get out there with a product or idea than to spend endless hours in marketing research. Where new ideas and technologies are involved, many critical uncertainties cannot be solved through market research. Concentrate on questions and issues that you can reasonably expect to resolve yourself.

Using Prototypes for Simultaneous Research and Selling

Strategies that emphasize the use of working prototypes work well and can accelerate product development. When prototypes are placed in the hands of customers, real-time marketing information is garnered, software is tested and improved, customer relations are built, and often the customer is paying along the way. If customers like your prototype, they are the source for the first orders for the product.

■Note Users of prototypes, beta customers, or early-stage strategic partners should be directly representative of the larger market or market niche that is ultimately targeted.

Building a prototype and getting it into the hands of a customer yields real-world, specific, and actionable information. The use of a prototype also uncovers key information about the way your customer utilizes and views competitive products. Prototypes are the best way to garner specific customer feedback on form, feature, functionality, and performance. Prototypes and beta partners can help you build early strategic partnerships and relationships and help you gain your first paying customer.

Being Agile with Technology and Product Development

There was a time in my career (showing my age) when there was genuine concern that the state of technology could not support some of the newer ideas for products and services. Standards were few, and major players had not yet emerged. Those days are long gone. There will always be complex engineering problems that require difficult development and tradeoff decisions between development environments and vendors, but for the most part, the tools are there to do pretty much anything you can imagine.

A company's ability to rapidly, and with agility, develop products is a key indicator of its ability to perform and execute. Product development, especially the development of new products by early-stage technology companies, is a huge undertaking. Product development cost is another key metric for investors. Companies that can optimize resources and develop products at lower costs are demonstrating critical business capabilities that may become a significant competitive advantage.

Companies must demonstrate their ability to hire the right talent at the right time during the evolving stages of product development. Early, visionary, and pathfinder developers are needed. They must have the ability to work quickly and innovatively in unstructured and rapidly changing environments. The company must demonstrate an uncanny ability of understanding real customer requirements and build product functionality that meets these requirements.

I cannot emphasize enough the requirement that technology be developed utilizing a formal methodology. There is usually tremendous pressure to get something out there in the form of a working prototype. I agree with this philosophy as long as the development is being managed using industry-standard methodologies for development, configuration management, and documentation.

As the company grows and expands its products and services, the requirement for a standard software development life cycle becomes more critical. The ability to demonstrate industry-standard software development methodologies brings great value to a technology venture, adding credibility to claims of scalability.

Most investors assume that the technology will work as advertised. They prefer to invest in building out a product from the working prototype phase and funding resources to generate sales and growth. Funding early-stage technology research and development is considered high risk.

Remembering That Cash Is King

Repeat after me, "Cash is king!" The single most important status that an early-stage company can attain is cash flow positive. The smart entrepreneur knows to focus on cash, not profits or market share or anything else. He has the wits and creativity to operate without much of it.

■**Caution** If the market does not pay for your business and you can't develop positive cash flow, your idea probably is not good enough.

Smart entrepreneurs use their energy to figure out ways to self-finance rather than scheming to raise money. They are cash fanatics, working cash forecasts with a very sharp pencil.

Their financial models are their primary cash forecasting tool, providing analysis of margin contributions, cash flows, and break even points.

In my experience, cash constraints are the number one problem of startups. Cash-strapped startups make several common mistakes:

- They buy business, deeply discounting their products or services and taking on customers that put them under with their demands and unwillingness to pay. Resources and energy can drain quickly when these types of relationships are in play.

- They try to leverage themselves into indirect sales channels and through strategic partnerships hoping to avoid the cost of direct selling. This can be a critical error, giving away control of the sales process.

- They take on investors too soon and find that investor expectations and oversight limit their flexibility and ability to operate.

- To save money they outsource the *family jewels*, key functions or technology that they cannot afford to have controlled by outsiders. This always has a dampening effect on the value of the venture.

■**Note** As an entrepreneur, you should go as far as you can on your own resources. Every milestone you achieve on your own dime is worth significantly more to you as a founder than are subsequent milestones financed by others. You will never have more leverage (ability to increase your personal net worth) than when you are working on your own dime.

Figure 1-1 shows a cash curve generated by a financial model. A *cash curve* shows a company's cumulative need for cash based on operational projections. When the company breaks even, that is, when total operating expenses are covered by cash inflows, the cumulative need for cash has peaked. Note that the bottom of the cash curve coincides directly with the point of cash flow positive. This is the point of maximum financing needs.

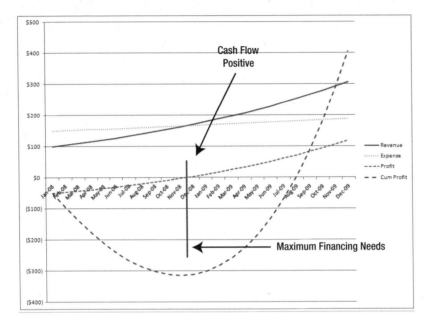

Figure 1-1. *Model-generated cash curve showing cumulative cash (financing) needs at the point of reaching cash flow positive*

Keeping Good Books

Keep excellent records and books. I have seen many investors go cold when they found that the books of the company consisted of a bank account and a couple of spreadsheets. It is important to establish a standard set of books and to keep them updated. It is critical to maintain clear records of ownership and copies of all operating and employment agreements. One of the items on any investor's due diligence checklist is a review of financial records and all operating agreements.

People and Process Strategies

The following strategies are about people and motivation. Early-stage companies are, at first, nothing more than their people. These strategies are about attracting and securing the team that is needed to execute the business plan. Often, for early-stage technology companies, the right person for the job is more motivated by the excitement of the challenge or upside potential than by just having a job. Early-stage companies get into trouble when they don't formalize agreements and set expectations with their early-stage hires.

Securing the Team

Your team is critical. At very early stages, all company value is a combination of your idea and your team. Investors will balk if they aren't impressed with the team, even if the startup is targeting a great market with a strong technology. At least one person on the team should have strong and relevant technical expertise, and another, relevant business and market expertise. Most of the entrepreneurs that I have worked with had a combination of technical expertise directly related to their business idea and excellent sales skills. Forget the dream team; you probably can't afford them. The challenge is to find and motivate diamonds in the rough. Personality, work ethic, and common sense are most important.

Skin in the Game

Investors will require that the founders and key employees demonstrate a firm commitment to the venture. Having such a firm commitment is typically called *putting skin in the game*. Investors expect full-time commitment (no part-time job situations) and financial risk on the part of the entrepreneurs. Financial risk is clearly demonstrated by cash investment in the company and, to a lesser extent, by deferred or reduced compensation. The venture should provide enough financial incentive to compensate the entrepreneur to devote time exclusively to it.

Sealing the Deal Early

A mentor of mine once gave me sage advice: Seriously think through and plan out all of your partnership and employee agreements and terms for offering equity and compensation before you get started. Once the eagle flies, that is, once there is success or the smell of success in the air, the pencils will get sharpened, and you will have a much harder time negotiating deals with key players.

I no longer believe in *sweat equity*, the idea that employees can earn ownership in the company by working at lower-than-market rates. If the employee does not bring critical skills to the table, their compensation should be limited to salary and benefits. Stock should be exclusively owned by the founders, cash investors, and individuals who bring specific, unique, and highly valuable expertise to the table.

■**Note** Today, it is practically impossible to set up any type of plan for employees to earn equity that is not treated as compensation and subject to taxation.

Key personnel that have access to trade secrets and developers that have intimate knowledge of your technical solutions should sign nondisclosure agreements at a minimum and noncompete agreements where they are applicable.

Planning for Growth

As the company moves from early stage into full-scale operations, a new type of management and operational team should join the company. The company must prove that it can scale into a full operating capability at an appropriate time in its development.

Entrepreneurs dream of exit strategies, but exit strategies usually imply that the founders must leave. Is this strategy built into the operational plan of the company? The founder brings unique capabilities to the table; can these capabilities be translated into repeatable performance without that individual?

The operational plan should acknowledge a transition from startup into operational status and demonstrate the costs and tradeoffs that are involved.

Ownership and Control Strategies

Many technology startups are highly leveraged when it comes to ownership and control. Close examination of their operations often reveals that critical functions and processes have been outsourced to save money. Many learn the hard way that outsourcing the family jewels can be precarious. Just because you own it, does not necessarily mean that you control it. Just because you control it, does not necessarily mean that you own it.

Knowing What You Own

When you purchase real estate, the seller must provide proof of title, in other words, proof of ownership for what is being sold to you. An investor in a high-tech startup is going to ask the same basic question of your company, "What do you actually own?" The answer to this question is not as cut and dried as in a real estate transaction. Ownership in this context has many dimensions, but it is critical in establishing the ultimate value of your company. Investors will investigate the multiple dimensions of ownership to determine what they are buying when they invest in your company.

WHAT, EXACTLY, ARE YOU SELLING?

A company asked me to consult with them concerning an exit strategy. The owners were thinking about exiting their business, and they wanted to begin a valuation process for their company. They had been in business for five years and sold nutritional health products and vitamins. After careful questioning, I discovered that their products were completely generic and that they had no patents or significant trade secrets related to the formulation or production of their products (all formulation, production, and shipping was outsourced). What they actually owned was their brand name and an excellent reputation for customer support.

What at first appeared to be a company with a unique product line turned out to be a marketing company with a recognizable brand and a loyal customer following. There is a huge difference between the value of a company that owns a unique product line and a marketing company that sells generic products. Which do you think is worth more?

Surprisingly, a number of entrepreneurs believe they can leverage their company into existence with minimal expense through outsourcing. They don't realize that a key component of their value proposition is their control over and protection of the attributes that make their company unique, that differentiate them from others.

Startups must own and control a central core of expertise in areas that are critical to their success. They must own and control a capability, technology, or ability to execute that is unique and separates them from their competition. Technology, operational capability to execute, and qualities that differentiate are critical attributes: they cannot be outsourced and must be kept under the control of the company. When building your company, keep a sharp eye on the ownership and control dimensions related to your company.

There are a number of dimensions of ownership:

- *Financial*: Financial ownership is generally the most straightforward type of ownership. It generally consists of ownership shares in the company. As long as you own 51 percent of the company, you have ownership and control.

- *Operational*: Operational ownership means operational control over or the ability to influence operational outcomes through discrete actions. For example, if I outsource key components of my software development, I have less operational control over the development process than I do over a developer who is an employee.

- *Market*: How can you control and own your market? Many products and concepts are hard to prove, but once proven, easy to replicate. Make sure you are protected by sustainable barriers to entry. Your best bet is quickly establishing brand recognition and a reputation for being the best at what you do. A direct sales model gives you control over your sales cycle. Indirect channels can be problematic unless you are well established and have created a pull for your product.

- *Relationships*: Can you own and control relationships? Being responsible for the satisfaction of your customers and the performance of your products and services requires that you own or take responsibility to listen to them carefully and respond to them in meaningful ways. Companies that do not own and control their relationships do not last for very long. A competitor who will take ownership of your relationship with your customer is always waiting in the wings.

- *Intellectual property*: The various ways to own and control intellectual property fall into the following categories:

  - *Patents*: My experience is that investors have varying views on the value of patents. Having them is a plus, but you have to think downstream before spending a great deal of time and effort. The primary question I ask regarding patents is, "Can I foresee the need, and do I have the resources to defend this patent? Is it worth it?" This is definitely a question for specialized legal counsel.

  - *Trade secrets*: Make sure your employees understand your company's definition of a trade secret and that they understand that their nondisclosure agreements do not permit the dissemination of this information. For instance, your customer lists, your financial records, and your internal processes for product development and customer support all are trade secrets. Make sure that your employees know this and document that this data has been presented to them.

  - *Copyrights and trademarks*: Copyrights and trademarks should be pursued on all applicable materials and marks of the company.

Owning Technology

Do you own and control your core technology? Are there critical components that are licensed from third parties? How much of your core is under the direct supervision of your employees, and how much is outsourced? Today, you can theoretically outsource 100 percent of your development. Many startups make the mistake of outsourcing critical components of their technology, secure that they are covered by ironclad performance and confidentiality agreements. My experience is that you are significantly increasing your risk profile by letting key pieces of your product development wander outside of your immediate control.

■Tip I can't say this enough: Never, never outsource the family jewels—those components or capabilities that differentiate you from the pack and make your company unique.

Partnering and outsourcing key components of your technology development process work better once you are established; I do not recommend these for the early-stage enterprise.

A LESSON ON OWNING YOUR TECHNOLOGY

My partner and I approached a large cable company that owned sophisticated document management software. We had a plan to modify their software and provide sophisticated online backup of PC files over the Internet. It took us a year to get their attention and negotiate a performance-based software usage license, but it finally happened. I raised working capital from angels based on our idea and the license agreement. I paid the cable company $100,000 to prototype the modifications. When the prototype was finished, my partner and I demonstrated the prototype to a large storage technology company. They paid us $150,000 to work with them exclusively and signed a letter of intent to work with us to the tune of $1.5 million.

When I excitedly presented the news to my partner at the cable company, his face went white. The next day, their legal team called us to announce that we were in violation of our performance agreement and that our license was rescinded. They did, however, offer us $500,000 for our company. We were young and dead broke. We sold our company, gave the investors all their money back plus 30 percent, and continued entrepreneuring. (By the way, the prototype was worthless—wrong architecture—and would have never worked.)

Common Ways of Getting Stuck

It is common for early-stage companies to lose momentum and get bogged down early in their product introduction cycles. They waste time and money frozen in the headlights as they make multiple attempts to attract the generic customer base that lies beyond their initial beta partners and the market's early adopters. They struggle with various sales and marketing techniques and positioning and repositioning their product. At this stage, it is common to see companies adding form, feature, and functionality to their products in an attempt to find the magic formula to move the product off the dime. This floundering, what I call *wobbling*, is usually the result of several common mistakes:

- The companies did not fully validate their value proposition. Their market research was faulty. Prior to beginning development, they did not have a full understanding of the true value of their product from the customers' point of view.

- They have underestimated the high cost of overcoming customer inertia and do not realize that their value proposition may not be compelling enough to cause potential customers to switch to their product.

- They have not identified the actual economic buyer of their product and service, the person or organization that is the true decision maker and catalyst for the sale.

- They adopted the "build it and they will come" philosophy of product development, assuming that their better mousetraps would be immediate successes.

- Working with early adopters during the prototype phases of product development, they have not considered the needs and requirements of the greater market population, those companies that are not early adopters.

This list of common errors results from two fundamental weaknesses that get my vote for best venture killers in the universe:

- Not clearly understanding your value proposition
- Not identifying your true economic buyer

Now that we have discussed strategies, let's discuss the concept of value. What happens to the value of a company as it accomplishes its goals?

CLOSE, BUT NO CIGAR

My client developed a state-of-the-art, GPS-based data collection system that not only collected geo-referenced field data but transmitted the data in real time back to the home office. This provided the field data collection project manager with real-time field productivity data and other operational visibility. An early product release was used to complete a large data collection project, and it worked perfectly, as advertised. When the client performed an analysis assessing the benefits of real-time data, they decided that, though they liked the idea, the benefits were not great enough to change their current way of doing business. *Close, but no cigar.* They had to reposition their product offering, shifting and improving their value proposition. We will discuss value propositions in greater detail in Chapter 8.

Looking at Startups from the Perspective of Value

In the world of startups, all aspects of analysis, presentation, and positioning of the company lead to a determination of the value of the enterprise.

The Value-Based Enterprise Perspective

Once I understood that the perceived value (value profile) of my company was a major factor in my ability to acquire resources, I changed my perspective and the way I looked at my company. I began viewing accomplishments, or the attainment of operational milestones, in terms of their contribution to the value profile of my company. I began to view the progress of my company as a series of value events. I define a *value event* as any event in the development of a company that adds value, real or perceived, to the company.

Here are some examples of value events:

- Filing a provisional patent application
- Having a key developer join the company as an employee
- Reaching the beta stage of product development
- Having a strategic partner agree to beta and field test a product
- Making your first arms-length sale of the product
- Reaching cash flow positive

As the company executes its operating plan and achieves objectives, it builds credibility and its value grows. As its value grows, it becomes more attractive to investors, and the cost of raising money from them goes down. When employees embrace the value event perspective of performance, rather than the traditional view of completing milestones, a cognitive shift takes place resulting in increased productivity and a new emphasis on increasing the value of the venture rather than just completing projects. Since most entrepreneurial staff members are inherently in it for the payoff, an emphasis on progress as value events can motivate and help guide the operating decisions of the company as they keep the company valuation always in mind.

■**Note** As the value of your venture increases, the cost of acquiring resources decreases. For example, as the venture begins to sell in the commercial market and sales forecasts firm up (value event); the company has more negotiating power with the suppliers of components.

Four Primary Value Events

There are four value events of early-stage technology development that are critical to bringing the company into true viability and profitability. Each value event represents the passage from a development phase into operational capability.

- *Proof of product*: You have built your product and proved it in the field.

- *Proof of market*: You are selling your product at a profitable price.

- *Proof of scale*: You are positioned to grow the company to the next level.

- *Cash flow positive*: The free cash you generate is equal to or exceeds your cash needs.

As each of these phases is completed, company value and credibility increase substantially over prior periods of performance. Credibility begins subjectively with the nature of the startup team and builds objectively over time as the company begins to execute its operating plan.

Figure 1-2 shows the company's cost of resources decreasing as the company achieves value events over time. Why does the cost of resources decrease? As value events are achieved, credibility increases and, for instance, conditions for raising investment dollars become more favorable. Negotiating strength with suppliers grows. Top employees can be attracted without special incentives, because the company looks strong. In Chapter 11, we will look at company valuation and investment in detail, and I will show how investment dollars become easier (cheaper) to attract as the company accomplishes value events. Most companies' capital raising strategies are closely tied to the achievement of value events.

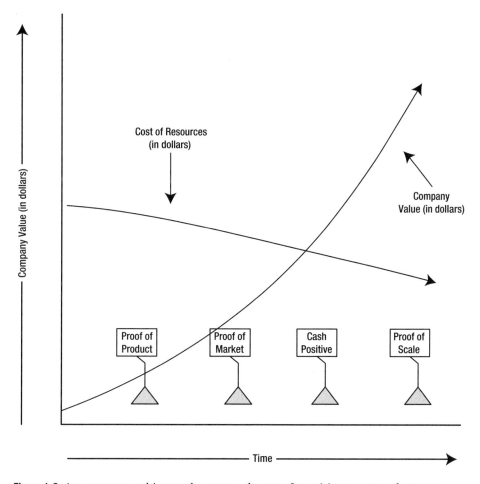

Figure 1-2. *As a company achieves value events, the cost of acquiring resources decreases.*

The following value events increase credibility by demonstrating proof of concept for the business model and the ability of the company to execute its operating plan.

Proof of Product (POP)

The technology or service of the company has been developed and beta or field tested. The first commercial version of the product is released. The company has achieved POP when

- Research and development (R&D) is complete.

- Product development is complete.

- Beta and field trials are underway.

- Commercial release 1.0 is imminent.

Proof of Market (POM)

POM is achieved when the company closes a number of initial *arms-length transaction sales*, which are sales to customers after completion of beta tests and field trials.

Arms-length customers meet the following criteria:

- They match the standard target customer profile as set forth in the sales and marketing plan.
- They are not related to the startup. They have no personal relationship to the company.
- Pricing and margin are at commercial levels as set forth in the sales and marketing plan.

Why all the fuss about arms-length transactions? Many startups go through grey area periods where they are selling to clients based on unique personal relationships, and the clients are buying at deep discounts or are early adopters. This period can be a particularly critical period for the startup as it tries to bridge the gap from its early product development and beta clients into a commercial environment. Many ventures flounder at this point, because the companies cannot lift themselves out of the custom development mode that gave them initial access to the market and into the provision of a generic commercial product to the broader market.

Proof of Scale (POS)

Rapid growth (a problem many would like to have) can present a critical challenge to an early-stage company. Investors closely assess a company's ability to grow or scale into higher levels of volume and to move from the entrepreneuring stage into full operations.

POS is achieved when the company is experiencing significant growth in sales volume and has proven its ability to acquire and manage the resources necessary to support the growth. A key criterion is the company's ability to maintain the same or better quality of support at the higher levels of volume.

Examples of critical issues encountered with rapid growth are the following:

- The company has inadequate working capital to fund resources needed for growth.
- The company suffers an inability to provide high-quality customer service at high levels of volume, resulting in a loss of reputation in the marketplace.
- The early-stage staff is not equipped in terms of experience or inclination to manage the challenges that are presented by high growth, that is, the challenges of a company that is moving past startup status.
- The company is unable to achieve profitability scaling projections at higher growth levels. Marginal costs of producing, selling, or supporting products are higher than originally forecast, thus reducing longer-range profitability.

Cash Flow Positive

Cash flow positive speaks for itself, and it speaks loudly to the value of your enterprise. Again, *cash flow positive* means that the free cash flows from operations meet or exceed cash needs for operations. The implications of this value event are significant. You have demonstrated a key component of the viability of your business.

Now that I have outlined the value concept for early-stage technology companies, it is time to think about the tool we will use to plan and articulate our success strategies, the financial model.

Thinking Critically About the Business and Financial Model

Developing a financial model is an excellent exercise in critical thinking. Modeling requires that you make specific assumptions regarding the nature of your business idea. It requires that you project operating results like sales volumes and expenses and show operating schedules in a formal way. Modeling requires that you establish and understand and then program the relationships between the moving parts of your enterprise.

A financial model lifts the operating concept out of the head of the entrepreneur and puts it on paper for all to see. It serves as a basis for analysis and is the underlying foundation for the business plan. The creation of a financial model is critical to establishing the legitimacy of your idea. As soon as you have a good feel for your major operating assumptions, you can start modeling.

I create the financial model first and then write the business plan. If I am happy with the model and it makes sense, the business plan is easy. It becomes the company story, explaining the numbers and relationships found in the model. Think of the model as the framing of a house and the business plan as the interior finish and furnishings. Be careful about doing this in reverse order. Take the time to develop the model, and the business plan will drop out naturally.

Professional investors expect a written business plan. The quality of the business plan is a clear indicator to the investor of the seriousness of the entrepreneur.

The next section is an overview of principles and functions associated with the development of financial models. I will explain the following topics as they relate to building and using a financial model:

- Design principles
- Design dimensions
- Major functions performed

Financial Model Design Principles

Most people think of financial models as a collection of spreadsheets. A financial model is more. You should think of your financial model as a computer program (created in a spreadsheet environment) and apply the rules and concepts of software development to the process of creating your model.

The principles of financial model design follow:

- *My version of the 80–20 rule*: My version as it applies to financial models is this: the last 20 percent of effort to make the model elegant by providing complex user interfaces is not worth it. The model should be useable by knowledgeable people within your organization. A financial model is an internal management tool, not a consumer product.

- *Modular, loosely coupled design*: The more modular and loosely coupled your design, the less reprogramming you will have to do. This is the case for all software development, but it is particularly important in financial models. By definition, models change a lot and are used in ways that may be different than originally anticipated.

- *Checks, balances, and diagnostics*: As you design each component of your model, you should incorporate two types of checks and balances:

- *Math checks*: Excel does not make math errors. Calculation errors will occur if your formula relationships (based on your structural design) are not correct. You must incorporate applicable math checks at the component spreadsheet level. Code included with this book will suggest contextual methodologies for math checks.

- *Sanity checks*: Subtle errors or errors that occur with certain combinations of input variables are sometimes easy to miss. Common errors occur when incorrect calculations are masked because the outputs are rolled up into greater totals. When looking at model components, you should ask yourself the question, "How do I test these calculations to see if they make sense from a business perspective?"

■**Tip** Use charts to sanity check model output. For example, I will create Line charts of line item budgets and look at them visually to see if they make sense. If rent is not going up, and that is an assumption, I have a formula problem. I might not notice the error, because it is buried in total facilities expense.

Financial Model Design Dimensions

There are four fundamental design dimensions to a financial model. What is a design dimension? A *design dimension* is an important structural or design consideration that must be addressed in order for the model to perform to expected standards. For example, under the period-of-performance design dimension, the model must accommodate the present year and five subsequent years. In order for it to support all calculation functions, the model must be designed to accommodate YR 0, YR 1, etc., data and 60 individual months (5 years) of data.

The following section will review the four fundamental design dimensions:

- Ability to generate standard financial reports

- The unique structure of your business model

- Operating variables

- Period of performance

Let's look at each of the four fundamental design dimensions in more detail.

Ability to Generate Standard Financial Reports

Your model will generate a series of analyses and reports that will ultimately roll up into three key financial reports:

- *Profit and loss statement*: A summary of revenues, costs, and expenses within an accounting period. It is also called an *income statement*.

- *Statement of cash flows*: A financial statement that provides information about a company's cash receipts, cash disbursements, and net change in cash during an accounting period.

- *Balance sheet*: A financial statement that reports the assets, liabilities, and equity of a company as of the end of a particular accounting period.

These are the primary reports used for the financial analysis of your enterprise and are usually the first reports reviewed by the financial community. The operational analysis worksheets and their lower level components roll up into these reports. It is critical that you understand the rules that govern the creation of these reports so that your model generates these reports accurately.

Your model will generate forecasts of the profit and loss statement, the statement of cash flows, and balance sheet. Forecast financial reports are called *pro forma*. If your company has any track record or actual performance, your *pro forma* will have to integrate or line up with your actual results. For instance, the profit and loss statement would show actual results through the first quarter of a year and forecasted (*pro forma*) for the remainder of the current and subsequent years.

Your model should be designed from the beginning to match with actual company financial statements. If possible your company chart of accounts should be reflected in your model design.

■**Note** You don't have to be an accountant to develop these reports, but it is a good idea to have the company accountant review your assumptions and methods regarding this dimension of the model.

The Unique Structure of your Business Model

You are modeling the unique business structure of your company. Your model will map or replicate the underlying structure of your business and show how all the moving parts fit together. The specification of this structure constitutes the primary set of critical assumptions or functional requirements for the model design.

For example, your product offering consists of a software module, a support contract for that module, and an online reporting capability. You charge a one-time fee of x for a license for the product, a yearly fee of y for a maintenance contract, and a recurring monthly fee of z for use of the online reporting. There is a specific structure to this product offering and pricing, and this structure must be replicated in your model design.

As another example, if your industry has a particular standard for collecting costs within cost centers, you should design your model to accommodate these particular cost roll up requirements.

Validate structural assumptions with your internal subject matter experts and owners of functional areas within the business. You must clearly understand the assumptions about operating structure from your internal experts before developing the model.

Operating Variables

Operating variables are the variable unit and cost data that you plug into the model. Various spreadsheets within your model serve as the user interface for the contextual input of variables. It is critical to understand what variables are to be incorporated into the model. The selection of variables determines the options for playing "what if?" The design of this portion of the model is very important. Think it through carefully. The best time to define these variables is during the previously described structural design requirements gathering process.

So, for example, using the aforementioned structure design example, you would design your model to accept the projected number of unit sales of x, y, and z over time and the projected fees charged for x, y, and z over time. Your design will provide the user with an interface to input these variables.

■**Note** There is often a time dimension to the recognition of many variable inputs. Pricing, cost, and salary assumptions will change over time, and the time dimension must be accommodated for variables.

Here's another example: the salary for a systems administrator would be input discretely as $50,000 in year one of operations, but there also has to be an assumption about how that salary might grow over the years.

Period of Performance

I never believe in forecasts beyond 18 months. Having said that, your model should accommodate at least a five-year period. I have consistently been required by investors to provide a five-year plan. You must think through the multi-year evolution of your company even if you are not confident about the operating variables, like sales forecasts, in the outlying years.

I build my models from the bottom up to accommodate monthly data. Structurally, it is easier to handle data at a more granular level and then roll it up. A monthly design allows for simpler and shorter formulas that are more easily tested for error. A more granular design gives you the flexibility you need to accommodate seasonal volumes and to forecast monthly recurring revenues with better accuracy. It is very easy to roll up monthly detail into quarterly or yearly formats.

Major Functions Performed by the Model

The subsequent chapters of this book will take you through the details of how to build a model, but for now, we will think about what we want to accomplish with the model and how best to approach it at a higher level. We have already discussed that the model will output the standard financial reports: profit and loss statement, balance sheet, and statement of cash flows.

Your model will also address the following major functional areas of your technology business:

- *Revenue sources and drivers*: What types and volumes of revenue streams are projected for your company?

- *Cost of Goods Sold*: For each unit sold or service provided, what does providing it cost?

- *Sales and marketing*: What are the costs associated with the sales and marketing of the product or service?

- *Product development*: What is the cost of the product development life cycle, including system support infrastructure and investments in development tools?

- *Staffing and personnel*: What are the compensation costs of employees and consultants, including the cost of their benefits and employment taxes?

- *Operating expenses and overhead*: What is the cost of office space, utilities, and other facilities? What is the cost of professional services like attorney fees, patent applications, or tax preparation?

- *Cash and capital*: What are the net cash requirements of the company including provision for working capital?

Here are some other questions to answer before you begin modeling:

- What are the linkages and relationships between major categories of revenue and cost?

- For each of these major categories, what are the variables that I wish to be able to test?

- What are the major phases of company growth and development, and how do I show the phases within the structure of the model?

- Do I have valid data to serve as a basis for projections? If not, when will I have it?

- Do I understand the critical success factors and relationships of the business, and can I model these relationships in a manner that will drive out the impacts of variables on them?

- What type of "what if?" capabilities will make the model a valuable tool for analysis?

- And finally, do I have enough information about the way my company will work to design a meaningful model?

■**Note** A critical success factor is an operational function or competency that a company must possess in order for it to be sustainable and profitable.

Summary

In this chapter, we have explored several key concepts related to technology startups. We have discussed common questions that entrepreneurs get from investors as well as strategies and principles that create success and credibility. You have also learned to assess the early-stage enterprise through the lens of *value*.

This chapter has emphasized business thinking about your company as you design your financial model. Your business thinking about the company will enhance the probability that your model will provide a meaningful analysis of your company, helping you explain your success strategies to a potential investor. Your model should be designed to drive out the value proposition of your company, to uncover the profit engine of your enterprise.

Developing a financial model for your technology startup accomplishes several objectives. The primary objective, an ability to clearly explain your idea in business terms, is a direct by-product of the financial modeling exercise. The model forces a business thinking process and an examination of the business concept. If you can model it, you can explain it!

The financial model is a computer program. Developing the model should be approached in the same manner that you would approach any software development project.

A well-designed financial model will allow you to drive out and understand the critical success factors in your business model. *What if* scenarios allow you to understand the magnitude of changes in revenue, cost, and profitability. Your ability to play "what if?" is dependent on a good design of the model.

The financial model will serve as a firm basis for your business plan, providing key financial information, charts, and data. You should develop your financial model first and then write your business plan.

The perceived value of your startup enterprise plays a major part in your ability to attract and retain the resources you need to implement your idea. Management should view accomplishments or the attainment of operational milestones in terms of their contribution to the value profile of the company.

Finally, remember the big three questions:

- How do you make money with it?
- How much investment do you need? Why do you need it, and when?
- What do you think your idea is worth?

■■■

CHAPTER 2

Company Business Model

I love entrepreneurs—not because they are the smartest people I have ever met, though this is often the case, but because (and I hate this overused word, but here it is) they have *passion*. They have arrived at an idea that they believe brings value to the world. Did I say "believe?" I meant *know*. They *know* their idea will bring value to the world, they *intend to make it real*, and they intend to *do it themselves*, proving any naysayers wrong. They are subject-matter experts (sometimes unacknowledged) and it is from this reservoir of expertise that their idea arises. They see a better or different way to do something, and they know they can make it happen. My experience is that the idea is their primary driver, not making money. The entrepreneur is motivated by the act of creation.

The idea, however, always requires resources to make it real, and acquisition of these needed resources is where many entrepreneurs stumble. They lack the resources to bring their ideas into reality and often do not know how to obtain these resources. They must attract a different type of visionary, the investor, who, surprisingly, has something in common with the entrepreneur. In their own way, investors are visionaries. They are envisioning the use of their investments to build something entirely new, and in my experience, they often have strong affinities toward projects that bring value to the world. Investors, however, expect a return on their investments and want to know, quantitatively, how this will be accomplished. So while the entrepreneur and the investor may have common vision, they approach the opportunity from different perspectives. Something is needed to bridge the gap between the entrepreneur and the investor. That something is the company business model.

In this chapter, we will discuss the logic and business thinking required to design and create the company business model. You will learn

- The logic and thought process behind the design of a company business model
- How to apply a project management view and a software design view in model design
- The sequence in which to create the modules
- The difference between operational models and financial models

Designing a Company

The entrepreneur turns vision into reality by introducing a product or service to the world. In order for this to happen, there must be a delivery mechanism, which is usually an organization or company. The company can take many forms and ideally takes the most efficient form needed to deliver the vision. This company must be designed in the same way the product or service it delivers is designed. How do you *design a company*? You begin by creating a business (financial) model of the company. I call it the company business model (CBM). It becomes the first prototype of the idea for the company, its first proof of concept.

▓**Note** The CBM is a prototype of the company concept and serves as a beginning proof of concept. It serves as the bridge between the entrepreneur and the investor, between vision and resources.

We will build the CBM from the initial idea of the company to a completed model within the pages of this book. Figure 2-1 provides a high-level process flow of our methodology. We start with an idea and test its feasibility. If this test is passed, we proceed to plan the CBM using both a project planning view and a software design view. The CBM consists of *operational models* that represent the workings of the company, the way the moving parts work together, and *financial models* that summarize and present the financial results of operations in standard financial formats. The rest of this chapter is devoted to a more detailed exposition of this process.

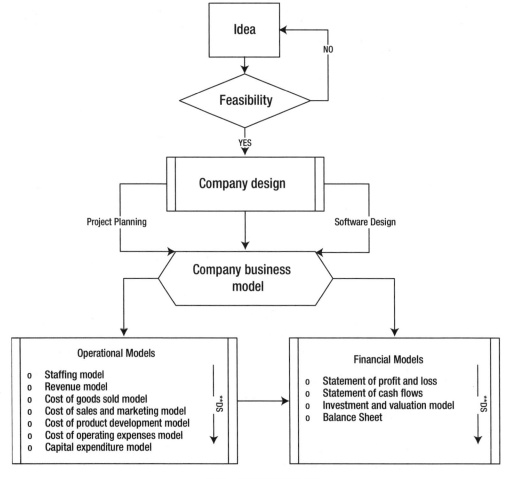

Figure 2-1. *A high-level process flow showing the thought process for building the CBM*

And now, let's begin our more detailed discussion regarding the approach to and specific methodologies for designing and creating the CBM.

Business Thinking About Financial Modeling

When I create financial models, I follow a standard methodology that draws from the best practices of two formal disciplines, project planning and the software design life cycle (SDLC). Best practices from these disciplines form the conceptual framework and point to the step-by-step process by which a CBM for a new company can be created.

At ground zero is always the *idea*. The idea must be followed by a series of steps designed to validate its feasibility (see how the founders of our business case company conducted their feasibility study in Chapter 3). If feasibility is tested and appears positive, the next step is to look at what it will take to design, build, and bring the idea to the world. In other words, it is time to design the company needed to bring the idea to fruition.

■**Caution** Be careful when testing feasibility. Make sure you aren't wearing *happy ears* when testing the waters for your idea from a market or technology viewpoint. Many entrepreneurs conduct feasibility studies that are heavily weighted toward giving them the answers they want to hear (they have happy ears). Feasibility studies must be conducted with brutal honesty.

We will approach the creation of the CBM from two perspectives: project planning and software design. Think of the company *as a project*. From a project-planning point of view, the company that we are designing has a purpose, a scope, deliverables, tasks, schedules, costs, and a work breakdown structure (WBS) or organization chart.

The CBM is created and designed using requirements and specifications that are defined during the project-planning phase. Think of the CBM as software, a computer program that models the project-based definition of the company allowing for the application of "what if" scenarios to the project definition as well as the generation of standard financial reports that are reflective of these scenarios.

The next sections present a discussion of the thought process and methodology that will be followed when developing the CBM. Read this chapter to gain a top-level view of that methodology. In the following chapters, we will discuss the details of the entire CBM, and I will explain specifically how to build it.

Applying the Project Planning View

We begin with the following idea: We are designing a company to deliver our idea to the world. We will view this company as a project and use project-planning techniques to plan this project. We will design the company to implement the plan.

Applying project planning best practices, we undertake the following steps:

1. *Define the purpose of the project (company)*: We identify the business drivers, benefits, and objectives of the company. We clarify the business idea, the product value proposition, and the major objectives that bring value to the marketplace while achieving the results that are needed to be successful.

2. *Define the scope*: We specify the scope of the company undertaking. What is the planning horizon or time frame that is covered? What are the boundary conditions or constraints on the company? For example, what products will be offered? Which markets are targeted? Are overseas markets included? What is *not included* in the scope of this company?

3. *Define naming conventions*: We determine what we will call things. What is the product name in the context of the project? What naming conventions will we use for technologies, for financial terms and reports, and for management positions and titles?

4. *Define assumptions and risks*: We list the major assumptions underlying the project plan for the company, and identify the major risk factors. What *can* go wrong? What *must* go right?

5. *Define the approach*: We agree on the approach of the company toward meeting its objectives. What are the overall time line and priority of tasks? What will be done in-house? What will be outsourced? Will the company use employees or consultants? What is the financing approach? How will money be raised to fund company operations?

6. *Define roles and responsibilities*: We also assign who does what. How will this project (the creation of this company) be managed and by whom? What is everyone's direct role and responsibility?

7. *Define company deliverables*: We determine what the company will deliver and when and how. For example, when is the first product available for sale? When does the marketing web site come on line? When and how are all patent applications filed?

8. *Define the master schedule, critical milestones, and earned value criteria*: We develop the master schedule for the company and identify the critical milestones. What is the correct order for dependent critical tasks? Define the criteria that must be met in order for a milestone to be completed (earned value criteria).

9. *Define the project work plan*: We plan out the tasks that must be accomplished to meet the schedule and milestones set forth in the master schedule, and we define the resources needed and their timing to complete each task.

10. *Define the critical path*: Finally, we sort and prioritize the sequence of tasks that must be completed on schedule for key milestones or value events to be attained on schedule.

■**Note** I define the term "critical path" differently than standard project planning lingo, where it means the longest duration path through a given work plan. For example, if an activity on the critical path is delayed by one day, the entire project will be delayed by one day (unless another activity on the critical path can be accelerated by one day). Critical path, in my terms, is that series of events or tasks that are critical to the success of the company and the attainment of critical milestones or value events.

---

11. *Define the work breakdown structure*: We derive a family tree or organizational structure that captures all the work of a project in an organized way. It is often portrayed graphically as a hierarchical tree.

Applying the Software Development View

We begin with the following idea: We are creating operational and financial models of the CBM that we are designing. This model is a computer program and will be developed using best practices from SDLC.

Applying SDLC best practices, we undertake the following steps:

1. *Initiation and planning*: Using the information from the previous planning exercise we plan for the *allocation* of cost, schedule, operating, and other assumptions into the operating components of the CBM. In other words, we organize the data developed in the planning process into groupings that can be used to design and program the various components of the model. For instance, our work breakdown structure or WBS implies or points to the definition of the organizational structure needed to develop the product. As we list the tasks required to develop the product, requirements for several types of engineers and the timing of the hires is revealed. This data is allocated for use in the staffing model.

2. *Functional requirements*: We create a list of functional requirements. Usually, this takes the form of a Functional Requirements Document (FRD). Functional requirements answer the question, "What is required of the CBM?" We derive functional requirements from the aforementioned planning data. Examples of three basic functional requirements follow:

   - Accurately create a working facsimile or model of the structural relationships among the moving parts of the company. For example, if there is a relationship between sales units and inventory balances, this relationship must exist within the model.

   - Provide "what if" capability to model the impact of variables on critical company success factors. In each component of the model, there is opportunity to provide for variable inputs of units of resources and their costs and timing. This provides the capability to test various operational scenarios within the planned structure of the company.

   - Generate standard financial reports that meet generally accepted accounting principles (are GAAP compliant) and can be analyzed by management and outside parties.

3. *Design specifications*: We develop detailed design specifications for each component of the model. Design specifications define *how* to meet the objectives of the functional requirements. Develop specifications for the model based on the functional requirements. Specifications answer the question "How does the model accomplish the 'what' of the functional requirements?" For instance, financial reporting must be GAAP compliant, which means that the cash flow statement model must perform in a certain manner. The data in the Statement of Cash Flows must be presented in a certain format, and the formulas must calculate data in a certain way. A specification for the module that develops the cash flow statement describes how this is done.

   Remember to also follow the design principles set forth in Chapter 1:

   - *Follow my version of the 80-20 rule*: The last 20 percent of effort to make the model elegant by providing complex user interfaces is not worth it.

   - *Use a modular, loosely coupled design*: The more modular and loosely coupled your design, the less reprogramming you will have to do.

   - *Design for four fundamental dimensions*: The dimensions are the ability to generate standard financial reports, the unique structure of your business model, operating variables, and period of performance.

4. *Technology selection*: We select a technology within which to develop your model. I know of no better environment for financial modeling than Microsoft Excel. The CBM in this book utilizes Microsoft Excel 2007.

5. *Building or coding software*: We now program the model based on the design specifications.

6. *Testing*: As you program the model and begin using it, test your program using checks, balances, and diagnostics. As stated in Chapter 1, use math checks and sanity checks to assure that you are not making any subtle errors.

7. *Operations and maintenance*: The primary challenge in this regard, is *configuration management*. Think through how you are going to manage different versions of the CBM. Is it as simple as saving under different file names, or do you have unique requirements that require design and programming to support version control?

Creating the Company Business Model

In the rest of this chapter, we will specifically cover the thought process and steps for building the CBM. Up to now, we have been talking concepts. It is now time to discuss actual steps and methods. Our objective is to understand the thought process, logic, and methodology that was used in building the detailed CBM as developed in the rest of this book. We utilize the planning steps and software design methodologies as a framework for explaining how the model is developed.

Taking the 35,000-Foot View

When we complete project planning, we have a top-level project perspective of the company. I call this perspective the *35,000-foot view*, and it is the starting point of our modeling process. At this point, we know something of the scope of the company vision, the type of product that will be built, and the planning horizon. We understand the value proposition and the target market. We have an idea of how the founders plan to sell the product. We have a lot of information, but how can we use it to build a CBM? Where do we start? We start at the top.

Using the Top-Down Approach

You can design anything from the bottom up or the top down. In my experience, financial modeling is a top-down process. You start at the 35,000-foot view and drive down to the level of detail or granularity needed. At first, you usually don't have enough hard data to design from the bottom up. Your data gets better as you iterate your model development from the top to the bottom. Top-down is the nature of the beast when you are modeling startups. My experience is that virtually every CBM has the same basic structure. Before we start, let's pay homage to Stephen Covey's seven habits of highly effective people and "begin with the end in mind." As previously discussed, we have three basic requirements, which, if met, define a successful CBM:

- Accurately create a working facsimile or model of the structural relationships between the moving parts of the company.

- Provide "what if" capability to model the impact of variables on critical company success factors.

- Generate standard financial reports that meet generally accepted accounting principles (are GAAP compliant) and can be analyzed by management and outside parties.

The following is the top-down approach that I use to develop financial models. I keep the preceding requirements in mind as I take each step.

Deriving the Model Structure

Where do you start in organizing or structuring the model? In my experience, there are two good starting points that provide important clues as to the ultimate structure of the model. The first, the organizational structure, provides an operational or department view. In other words, what organizationally related breakouts or roll ups of data will be needed? The second, the proposed Statement of Profit and Loss, provides excellent direction regarding the types and sources of revenues and cost of revenues and also lists all other associated (noncapital) costs of doing business. If you carefully review your organizational structure and proposed Profit and Loss Statement, the outlines of the structure of your model will become apparent.

Start with organizational structure. Design an organizational chart. Using the data I have garnered from the planning process, I organize the tasks that the company must undertake into a
work breakdown structure (WBS). The WBS becomes, or heavily influences, an organizational
chart. You cannot begin to develop a financial model if you do not have an idea of how the
company will be organized? For instance, based on the nature of the product being developed,
how will the technical side of the company be organized? You will be surprised how much is
revealed by this exercise. Is sales and marketing one organization or two? Why? You are looking
at basic functionality and basic organization at this point.

Design the company Profit and Loss Statement. The format of the Profit and Loss Statement will
serve as a guide to the operational models that you will need for the CBM. Let's look at a very
simplified profit and loss format (see Figure 2-2), so you can see why. Note the line items of the
Profit and Loss Statement and the corresponding CBM operational models that support each
line item. The profit and loss format provides a great outline for developing the operational
models you are going to need for your particular company design.

	A	B	C
1	Statement of Profit and Loss	Operational Model	Model Function
2			
3	Revenue	(REV) - Revenue Model	Forecast Sales and Revenue
4	Cost of Goods Sold	(COGS) - Cost of Goods Sold and Inventory Model	Forecast Cost of Goods Sold and Inventory
5	Net Revenue		
6	Cost of Sales and Marketing	(COSM) - Cost of Sales and Marketing Model	Forecast total cost of Sales and Marketing
7	Cost of Product Development	(DEV) - Cost of Product Development Model	Forecast total cost of Product Development
8	Cost of Salaries Wages and Benefits	(STAFF) - Staffing Model	Forecast Salary & Benefits and Consulting Costs
9	Other Operating Expenses	(OPEX) - Operating Expense Model	
10	Depreciation	(CAPEX) - Capital Expenditure Model	Forecast Capital Expenditures and Depreciation
11	Total Expenses		
12	Net Profit		

Figure 2-2. *A Statement of Profit and Loss and the CBM operational models that support each line item*

Looking downstream in our development process, we know that our CBM must create a profit
and loss statement. In order meet this requirement, we must obviously develop models that forecast
revenue; cost of goods sold; cost of sales and marketing; cost of product development; cost of salaries,
wages, and benefits; other operating expenses; and depreciation. There may be variations to this
standard list of information needs, and the source of these variations is usually discovered during
the planning of an organizational chart. For instance, if our organizational chart defined another
major department (like manufacturing), we would reflect this major cost center in the Profit and
Loss Statement, and we possibly would need to add a manufacturing model to our list of operational
models. The Profit and Loss Statement format provides an excellent guide and framework for understanding the models that we are going to need to design and build.

Developing Operational Models

Using the Profit and Loss Statement and our organizational structure as a guide, we begin the
development of *operational models*. Our operational models accurately create a working facsimile
of the structural relationships between the moving parts of the company. For instance, the Sales
and Revenue (REV) model covered in Chapter 5 creates a working facsimile of the methods and
assumptions about how the company generates revenue. The Cost of Good Sold (COGS) model,
using data from REV, develops the cost of goods sold and inventory needed to support revenue forecasted in REV. See Figure 2-5 for a listing of the *operational models* that make up the company CBM.
Note their relationships to the basic profit and loss structure.

Developing Financial and Reporting Models

We must also generate GAAP-compliant financial statements and model investment strategies for the company. Looking at this from the top down, we must develop models for the Profit and Loss Statement, Statement of Cash Flows, and Balance Sheet. We call these models Financial and Reporting (FIN) models; see Figure 2-3. The primary purpose is to utilize data from operational models to create GAAP-compliant financial reporting. The investment and valuation strategy, to have validity, is developed using the GAAP-compliant financial statements.

C	D	E	F
MODEL	WORKSHEET	DESCRIPTION	TYPE
FIN	FIN-BALANCE_CWS	Company Balance Sheet Worksheet	CWS
FIN	FIN-CASHFLOW_CWS	Company Statement of Cash Flow Worksheet	CWS
FIN	FIN-P&L_CWS	Company Profit & Loss Statement Worksheet	CWS
FIN	FIN-VALUE_CWS	Company Value and Investment Worksheet	CWS
FIN	FIN-VALUE_DB	Company Value and Investment Dashboard	CWS
FIN	FIN-MSCHEDULE_DB	Company Master Schedule	DB
FIN	FIN-STMT-ANALYSIS_DB	Financial Statements and Analysis Dashboard	DB
FIN	FIN-CHARTDAT	Financial Reporting Model Chart Data	CHARTDAT

Figure 2-3. *Financial and reporting worksheets that make up the Financial and Reporting (FIN) model*

Organizing the Sequence of the Models

You know we must develop *operational* and *financial reporting models* and that these models, used together, form the CBM and create a prototype of total company operations. In what sequence should they be developed? This is an important process question and requires some thought.

The logic of sequencing model creation is based on absolute dependencies, unfolding of company information, and iteration. Many modules have absolute dependencies on calculations from other models. For instance, cost of goods sold cannot be forecast without a sales forecast. Sequence is dictated by calculation necessities. Building the models in this recommended sequence also has the advantage of providing a top-down unfolding of the understanding of company operations. You start with the bigger picture of what is happening and drive down to lower levels of detail. Finally, building these models is an iterative process. For instance, after completing the revenue model, you will probably go back and adjust the sales and marketing staff portion of the staffing model. You may simply adjust numbers but you may also add or delete positions.

My recommendation is that the models be completed in the general sequence illustrated in Figure 2-4. Note, however, that this is not a purely serial process. For instance, REV and COGS require iterative development, as do other closely related worksheets and models.

A	B	C	D	E	F	G	H	I	J	K	L	M
Sequence of Development	DEPENDENCIES ➡	STAFF	REV	COGS	DEV	COSM	OPEX	CAPEX	FIN - P&L	FIN - CASH FLOW	FIN - VALUE	FIN - BALANCE SHEET
⬇	OPERATIONAL MODELS											
1	STAFF					X						
2	REV			X								
3	COGS		X									
4	COSM	X	X									
5	DEV	X				X						
6	OPEX	X										
7	CAPEX	X			X	X						
	FINANCIAL MODELS											
8	FIN - P&L	X	X	X	X	X	X					
9	FIN - CASH FLOW		X	X					X	X		X
10	FIN - VALUE										X	
11	FIN - BALANCE SHEET		X						X	X	X	

Figure 2-4. *Overview of model development sequence and dependencies*

Suggested Sequence of Development for the Operating Models

The following listing of modules is presented in the sequence in which I developed the CBM for this book and represents my application of the aforementioned sequencing logic:

Staffing (STAFF) model: This may not seem to be the intuitive first pick, but there is a reason for it. Once you work through the staffing model and the organizational chart in some detail, you will have a much better idea of the workings of the company. For example, thinking through the specific software positions needed and the timing of their hires requires a careful consideration of the "what" and "how" of your software development. This holds true for the entire company.

Revenue (REV) model: The sales forecast, pricing, and revenue are the basis for multiple dependent calculations in the model. When you combine the thought process of forecasting revenue with the previous staffing process, you are beginning to get a good feel for the operations of the company over time.

Cost of Goods Sold and Inventory (COGS) model: Calculations and forecasts of cost of goods sold and inventory are dependent on the sales and revenue forecasts from REV.

Cost of Sales and Marketing (COSM) model: This model forecasts total cost of sales and marketing including bonuses and commissions for sales staff and trip costs. This model is dependent on data from STAFF and REV. This model also forecasts capital expenditures needed to support sales and marketing.

Cost of Product Development (DEV) model: This model forecasts total cost of product development including bonuses and commissions for technical staff and trip costs. This model is dependent on data from STAFF and COSM. This model also forecasts capital expenditures needed to support product development.

Operating Expense (OPEX) model: This model develops other operating expenses for the company. It also uses and is dependent on operating expenditures that are generated from the STAFF model.

Capital Expenditure (CAPEX) model: This model generates the company Capital Plan and computes depreciation. Using this data, it develops a Fixed Asset Summary, which is an input to the Balance Sheet. The Capital Plan in this model is dependent on data from STAFF, COSM, and DEV.

Required Sequence of Development of the Financial Models

Unlike operational models, which can be developed in any given sequence (if you don't follow my advice and like to do things the hard way), financial models must be developed in the sequence set forth below. FIN_VALUE_CWS, the investment model, may or may not be included depending on the need, but the development of the Profit and Loss Statement precedes the Statement of Cash Flows, which precedes the Balance Sheet.

- *FIN-P&L_CWS*: This model develops the Statement of Profit and Loss. It is dependent on data from STAFF, REV, COGS, DEV, COSM, and OPEX.

- *FIN-CASHFLOW_CWS*: This model develops the Statement of Cash Flows. It is dependent on data from REV, COGS, CAPEX, FIN-P&L, and FIN-VALUE.

- *FIN-VALUE_CWS*: This model develops the company valuation and investment strategy. It is dependent on FIN-CASHFLOW_CWS.

- *FIN-BALANCE_CWS*: This model develops the Balance Sheet. It is dependent on data from COGS, CAPEX, FIN-P&L, and FIN-CASHFLOW.

Understanding the Worksheet Types and Naming Conventions

The CBM utilizes three types of worksheets (see Figures 2-5 and 2-6):

- *Calculation worksheet (CWS)*: Calculation worksheets do all the heavy lifting in the model. They are set up in a monthly format and provide for most of the calculations and variable inputs for the model. There may be more than one calculation worksheet depending on the specific model design.

- *Dashboard (DB)*: Dashboards are primarily for the summarization and display of data from calculation worksheets, although they are sometimes used for high-level data input into the calculation worksheets. The general rule is that dashboards are used to display summary data for the model.

- *Chart data (CHARTDAT)*: Chart data is preformatted data taken from the calculation worksheet or the dashboard data. Chart data may include calculations and data from other spreadsheets that is needed to present management charts relevant to the model.

See Figure 2-5 and 2-6 for a listing of calculation, dashboard, and charting worksheets that make up the CBM. Charts are not listed but are included in the model.

MODEL	WORKSHEET	DESCRIPTION	TYPE
STAFF	STAFF_CWS	Staff - Calculation Worksheet	CWS
STAFF	STAFFPLAN_CWS	Staff - Staffing Plan Worksheet	CWS
STAFF	STAFF_DB	Staff - Executive Dashboard	DB
STAFF	STAFF_CHARTDAT	Staff - Executive Chart Data	CHARTDAT
REV	REV-AR_CWS	Accounts Receivable Worksheet	CWS
REV	REV-REC-MAINT_CWS	Recurring Service Rev & Maintenance Rev Workshe	CWS
REV	REV-REVCALC_CWS	Revenue Calculation Worksheet	CWS
REV	REV-SALES-FCAST_CWS	Sales Forecasting Worksheet	CWS
REV	REV_DB	Revenue Summary Dashboard	DB
REV	REV-COGS_CHARTDAT	Revenue & COGS Chart Data	CHARTDAT
COGS	COGS-INVENTORY_CWS	Inventory and Inventory AP Worksheet	CWS
COGS	COGS-PRICE-MARGIN_CW	Product Pricing & Margin Worksheet	CWS
COGS	COGS_DB	Contribution to Margin Analysis	DB
REV	REV-COGS_CHARTDAT	Revenue & COGS Chart Data	CHARTDAT
COSM	COSM_CWS	Cost of Sales & Marketing Calculation Worksheet	CWS
COSM	COSM-BONUS_CWS	Bonus & Commission Calculation Worksheet	CWS
COSM	COSM-TRIPCALC_CWS	Trip Type Calculation Worksheet	CWS
COSM	COSM-TRIPPLAN_CWS	Trip Plan Calculation Worksheet	CWS
COSM	COSM_DB	Cost of Sales & Marketing Dashboard	DB
COSM	COSM_CHARTDAT	Cost of Sales & Marketing Chart Data	CHARTDAT
DEV	DEV_CWS	Cost of Product Development Calculation Workshee	CWS
DEV	DEV_DB	Cost of Product Development Dashboard	DB
DEV	DEV_CHARTDAT	Cost of Product Development Chart Data	CHARTDAT
OPEX	OPEX_CWS	Operational Expenditure Calculation Worksheet	CWS
OPEX	OPEX-M_CWS	Operational Expenditure Calculation Worksheet	CWS
OPEX	OPEX-Y_DB	Operational Expenditure (Yearly) Dashboard	DB
OPEX	OPEX-CAPEX_CHARTDAT	CHARTDAT-OPEX & CAPEX Chart Data	CHARTDAT
CAPEX	CAPEX_CWS	Capital Plan Calculation Worksheet	CWS
CAPEX	CAPEX-DEP_CWS	Depreciation Calculation Worksheet	CWS
CAPEX	CAPEX-FA_CWS	Fixed Assets Calculation Worksheet	CWS
CAPEX	CAPEX-FA_DB	Capital Plan and Fixed Assets Dashboard	DB
CAPEX	COGS_DB	Contribution to Margin Analysis	DB

Figure 2-5. *Listing of operating model worksheets that compose the CBM*

C	D	E	F
MODEL	WORKSHEET	DESCRIPTION	TYPE
FIN	FIN-BALANCE_CWS	Company Balance Sheet Worksheet	CWS
FIN	FIN-CASHFLOW_CWS	Company Statement of Cash Flow Worksheet	CWS
FIN	FIN-P&L_CWS	Company Profit & Loss Statement Worksheet	CWS
FIN	FIN-VALUE_CWS	Company Value and Investment Worksheet	CWS
FIN	FIN-VALUE_DB	Company Value and Investment Dashboard	CWS
FIN	FIN-MSCHEDULE_DB	Company Master Schedule	DB
FIN	FIN-STMT-ANALYSIS_DB	Financial Statements and Analysis Dashboard	DB
FIN	FIN-CHARTDAT	Financial Reporting Model Chart Data	CHARTDAT

Figure 2-6. *Listing of financial model worksheets that compose the CBM*

Defining the Period of Performance

The CBM presented in this book covers a six-year period of performance. Year zero (YR 0) represents the first year of operations and is not considered a fully integrated part of the operating model. Think of YR 0 as representing the first few months of actual company operations prior to any significant modeling or forecasting.

■**Note** Consider how you will integrate company actual operating results (of YR 0) with your financial model. If your company already has a set of books, design the model to be compatible with their formats. Financial models often become the basis for budgeting systems and must be integrated with accounting system reports. Design for this contingency.

Years one through five (YR 1 to YR 5) compose the five-year planning horizon for the model. The model is built in a monthly format (60 months). Data is combined into yearly formats when appropriate. My experience is that it is easier to design monthly and roll up data, particularly when your model has seasonal sales forecasts and is computing depreciation and recurring revenues.

Developing the Models' Design and Functionality

We have discussed structure (the models that are needed) and sequence (the order in which they should be built). Now, let's move to considerations for the design and functionality of the models themselves. We will use the Staffing (STAFF) model as the basis of our discussion. Remember that I have suggested that we start with this model because of the informational benefits derived from the analysis that is required to develop the model. See Figure 2-7 for a top-level view of the STAFF model. The following discussion and methodology is applicable to all models in the CBM.

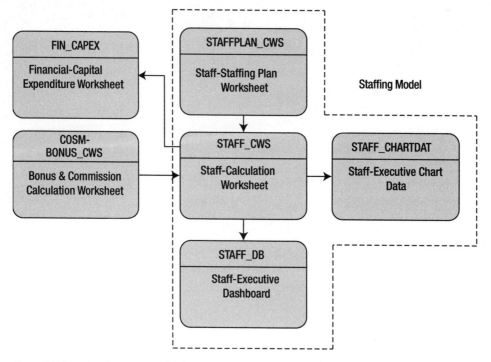

Figure 2-7. *Top-level structure of STAFF*

Reference Figures 2-7 and 2-8. The format in Figure 2-7 is used throughout this book to describe the basic design of operational and financial models. Arrows indicate general data flow relationships. In this case, STAFF_CWS is receiving data inputs from COSM-BONUS_CWS, and FIN_CAPEX is receiving data inputs from STAFF_CWS. The dotted line indicates the primary boundary of the model being described.

MODEL	WORKSHEET	DESCRIPTION	TYPE
STAFF	STAFF_CWS	Staff - Calculation Worksheet	CWS
STAFF	STAFFPLAN_CWS	Staff - Staffing Plan Worksheet	CWS
STAFF	STAFF_DB	Staff - Executive Dashboard	DB
STAFF	STAFF_CHARTDAT	Staff - Executive Chart Data	CHARTDAT

Figure 2-8. *View of Staff model worksheets, which shows the top-level structure of STAFF model*

Initiating and Planning the Model

Using the information from the previous planning exercise, we allocate cost, schedule, operating, and other assumptions to the staffing model. This means that we gather all data from our planning exercise that is relevant to designing this model. A key piece of information that we will need is the planned WBS or organizational structure. We also need to know the period of performance and have a feel for the master schedule of the primary value events that the company will strive to attain. Figure 2-9 shows the organizational chart derived from the planning exercise, and Figure 2-10 shows the master schedule developed during the planning process.

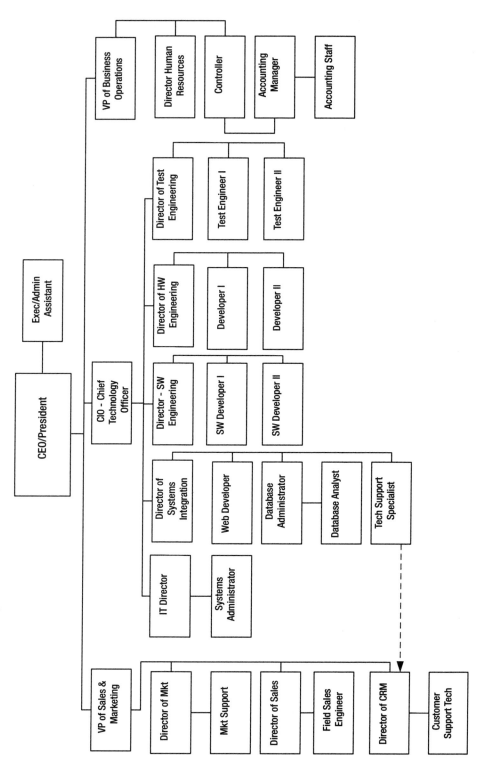

Figure 2-9. *Organizational chart derived from company project planning process*

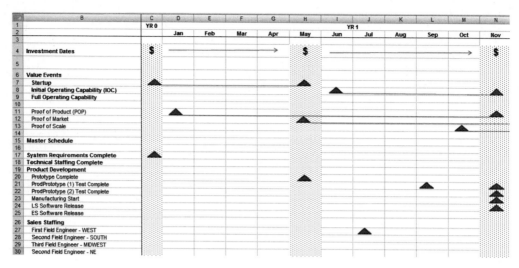

Figure 2-10. *Company master schedule derived from the planning process*

Outlining the Functional Requirements of the Model

Next, we develop the following set of functional requirements related to the STAFF model:

- Compute the total cost of salaries, wages, and benefits for the staffing requirements of the company.

- Compute the total cost of consulting services for the company.

- Provide for the ability to input headcount for employees and consultants on a monthly basis.

- Provide for the ability to input salaries for employees and consultants, and provide for a method to spread or increase these salaries over the period of performance.

- Provide for the ability to input tax rates and burdens for applicable employment taxes and benefit costs.

- Provide for the ability to add bonus and commissions computed in other modules to the baseline of costs on which taxes and benefit burdens are computed.

- Provide for the ability to calculate capital and operating expense costs for phones, computers, and office space based on headcounts.

- Roll up or summarize costs into departments or cost centers based on organizational objectives of the company.

Creating the Top-Level Model Design Specifications

Now that we have a set of functional requirements, we need to create design specifications. Design specifications describe how we are going to meet the objectives of the functional requirements. A list of design specifications based on the functional requirements follows:

- The STAFF model will be developed in Microsoft Excel. The approach will be to use calculation worksheets for primary calculations and dashboards for summarizing the data from the calculation worksheets or for spreading top-level forecasts from a yearly into a monthly format.

- Worksheets will be loosely coupled using simple linkages between them.

- Model will be designed keeping in mind that data generated will be summarized first in a departmental format and then used in the Profit and Loss Statement. This will be accomplished by formatting the calculation worksheets in a manner that can be simply linked to departmental models or the profit and loss statement format.

- User inputs of variables will be placed in logical places in the worksheet. Cells that allow input of variables will be color coded. No cells within the model will be locked.

- Spreadsheets will be organized to allow for roll up of salary and wage and consulting costs at a departmental level based on company organization. This is done by replicating the roll-up methodology for each department using departmental headcount data.

- Monthly data will be summarized into management-level reporting formats called dashboards.

- Data will be formatted into spreadsheets called CHARTDAT to be used for management charting of STAFF data.

Performing Calculations

The following is a listing of calculation specifications used in STAFF_CWS:

- Allow the headcount forecast and salary adjustment factor to spread across 60 months using a summary-level input screen.

- Allow the input of discrete baseline or target salaries for each position, which are then adjusted by a salary adjustment factor.

- Allow the input of yearly tax rates and burden rates.

- Accept bonuses and commissions calculated from a bonus and commission model.

- Calculate total taxable baseline employment costs for each department by multiplying the headcount times the adjusted salaries.

- Calculate employment taxes and benefit burdens for each department.

- Calculate total employment costs by department and in total.

Building, or Coding, the Model

Let's now look at four examples of how specifications are turned into design implementations within the STAFF model:

Input variables will be placed in logical places in the worksheet. Cells that allow input of variables will be color coded. No cells within the model will be locked. Note, in Figure 2-11, the following input variables: the Employee (Annual) and Consultant (Hourly) rates in Column B and the yes (Y) or no (N) indicators for phones (P), computers (C), and work spaces (WS) shown in Columns D, E, and F. These are logically placed alongside position titles in Column A. Input areas for the headcount are also provided. For example, Row 10 allows for headcount forecasts for the CEO/President position.

	A	B	C	D	E	F	H	I	J	K	L	M	N
1													YR 1
2	Period of Performance						Jan	Feb	Mar	Apr	May	Jun	Jul
3	Employee	Annual	Monthly	P	C	WS							
4	Consultant	Hourly	Monthly										
5													
6	VARIABLE UNITS INPUT												
7													
8	Exec												
9													
10	CEO/President	$ 175,000	$ 14,583	Y	Y		Y	1.00	1.00	1.00	1.00	1.00	1.00	1.00
11	Consultant	$ 150	$ 24,000	Y	Y		Y	-	-	-	-	-	-	-
12													
13	VP of Business Operations	$ 110,000	$ 9,167	Y	Y		Y	-	-	-	-	-	-	-
14	Consultant	$ 125	$ 20,000	Y	Y		Y	-	-	-	-	-	-	-
15													
16	VP of Sales & Marketing	$ 150,000	$ 12,500	Y	Y		Y							
17	Consultant	$ 125	$ 20,000	Y	Y		Y	-						-
18													
19	CIO - Chief Technical Officer	$ 135,000	$ 11,250	Y	Y		Y	1.00	1.00	1.00	1.00	1.00	1.00	1.00
20	Consultant	$ 125.00	$ 20,000	Y	Y		Y	-	-	-	-	-	-	-
21													
22	Exec/Admin Assistant	$ 40,000	$ 3,333	Y	Y		Y	-	-	-	-	-	-	-
23	Consultant	$ 25	$ 4,000	Y	Y		Y	-	-	-	-	-	-	-
24													
25	Total Exec							2.00	2.00	2.00	2.00	2.00	2.00	2.00
26	Total Consultant							.	.	.	.	.	.	.
27	Total Exec							2.00	2.00	2.00	2.00	2.00	2.00	2.00
28													
29	Phone Count							2.00	2.00	2.00	2.00	2.00	2.00	2.00
30	Computer Count							2.00	2.00	2.00	2.00	2.00	2.00	2.00
31	Work Space Count							2.00	2.00	2.00	2.00	2.00	2.00	2.00

Figure 2-11. *In STAFF_CWS, input variables are placed in logical locations on the spreadsheet and color coded indicating that the contents of the cells can be input by the user.*

The spreadsheet will be organized to allow for roll up of salary and wage and consulting costs at a departmental level based on company organization. See Figure 2-12, and note that the positions listed in the Sales and Mkt section mirror the organizational chart shown in Figure 2-9. Note also that the VP Sales & Marketing is shown in the Executive department (see Figure 2-11), not in the Sales and Mkt department. The spreadsheet computes total headcount and total salary, wages, and benefits for the department.

	A	B	C	D	E	F	H	I	J	K	L	M	N
1													YR 1
2	Period of Performance						Jan	Feb	Mar	Apr	May	Jun	Jul
3	Employee	Annual	Monthly	P	C	WS							
4	Consultant	Hourly	Monthly										
55													
56	Sales and Mkt												
57													
58	Director of Mkt	$ 100,000	$ 8,333	Y	Y		Y	-	-	-	-	-	-	-
59	Consultant	$ 85	$ 13,600	N	N		Y	0.50	0.50	0.50	0.50	0.50	0.50	0.50
60													
61	Mkt Support	$ 65,000	$ 5,417	Y	Y		Y	-	-	-	-	-	-	-
62	Consultant	$ 40	$ 6,400	N	Y		Y	0.25	0.25	0.25	0.25	0.25	0.25	0.25
63													
64	Director of Sales	$ 125,000	$ 10,417	Y	Y		Y	-	-	-	-	1.00	1.00	1.00
65	Consultant	$ 85	$ 13,600	Y	Y		Y	-	-	-	-	-	-	-
66													
67	Field Sales Engineer	$ 85,000	$ 7,083	Y	Y		N	-	-	-	-	-	-	1.00
68	Consultant	$ 65	$ 10,400	Y	Y		N	0.50	0.50	0.50	0.50	0.50	0.50	-
69													
70	Director of CRM	$ 90,000	$ 7,500	Y	Y		Y	-	-	-	-	-		
71	Consultant	$ 65	$ 10,400	Y	Y		Y	-	-	-	-	-	-	-
72													
73	Customer Support Tech	$ 50,000	$ 4,167	Y	Y		Y	-	-	-	-	-		
74	Consultant	$ 35	$ 5,600	Y	Y		Y	-	-	-	-	-	-	-
75													
76	Total Sales & Mkt							-	-	-	-	1.00	1.00	2.00
77	Total Consultant							1.25	1.25	1.25	1.25	1.25	1.25	0.75
78	Total Sales & Mkt							1.25	1.25	1.25	1.25	2.25	2.25	2.75
79													
80	Phone Count							1.00	1.00	1.00	1.00	2.00	2.00	2.00
81	Computer Count							1.00	1.00	1.00	1.00	2.00	2.00	3.00
82	Work Space Count							1.00	1.00	1.00	1.00	2.00	2.00	2.00

Figure 2-12. *The STAFF model showing company organization by department*

Calculate employment taxes and benefit burdens for each department. In Figure 2-13, notice that Adjusted Compensation is computed before Sales Commissions are added to calculate Tax and Burden Basis. Payroll taxes and benefits burdens are then calculated for Sales & Mkt employees. Total Consultant costs are accounted for in the total costs but are not included in the taxable basis.

	A	B	H	I	J	K	L	M	N	O
									YR 1	
1										
2	Period of Performance		Jan	Feb	Mar	Apr	May	Jun	Jul	Aug
3	Employee	Annual								
4	Consultant	Hourly								
357	Total Sales & Mkt									
358	Adjusted Compensation		$ -	$ -	$ -	$ -	$ 6,250	$ 6,250	$ 11,917	$ 11,917
359	Sales Commissions		$ -	$ -	$ -	$ -	$ -	$ -	$ -	$ -
360	Tax and Burden Basis		$ -	$ -	$ -	$ -	$ 6,250	$ 6,250	$ 11,917	$ 11,917
361										
362	Total Consultant		$ 5,200	$ 5,200	$ 5,200	$ 5,200	$ 5,200	$ 5,200	$ -	$ -
363										
364	SALES&MKT TOTAL BASIS		$ 5,200	$ 5,200	$ 5,200	$ 5,200	$ 11,450	$ 11,450	$ 11,917	$ 11,917
365										
366	Payroll Tax Calculations									
367										
368	TAXES									
369	FICA	6.20%	$ -	$ -	$ -	$ -	$ 388	$ 388	$ 739	$ 739
370	Medicare	1.45%	$ -	$ -	$ -	$ -	$ 91	$ 91	$ 173	$ 173
371	Workers Comp	0.55%	$ -	$ -	$ -	$ -	$ 34	$ 34	$ 66	$ 66
372	SUI	3.10%	$ -	$ -	$ -	$ -	$ 26	$ 26	$ 52	$ 52
373	FUI	0.80%	$ -	$ -	$ -	$ -	$ 50	$ 50	$ 95	$ 95
374	TOTAL TAXES		$ -	$ -	$ -	$ -	$ 588	$ 588	$ 1,124	$ 1,124
375										
376	EMPLOYEE BENEFITS									
377	MEDICAL INSURANCE	$ 417					$ -	$ -	$ -	$ 417
378	401 K	3.00%								
379										
380	Total Gross Benefits		$ -	$ -	$ -	$ -	$ -	$ -	$ -	$ 417
381										
382	SALES & MKT TOTAL Burden		$ 5,200	$ 5,200	$ 5,200	$ 5,200	$ 12,038	$ 12,038	$ 13,041	$ 13,458

Figure 2-13. *STAFF_CWS computes taxes and benefit burdens.*

Summarize detailed monthly data into management-level reporting formats called dashboards, as show in Figure 2-14.

	A	C	D	E	F
1		YR 2	YR 3	YR 4	YR 5
2	COMPANY TOTAL				
3					
4	EMPLOYEE FTE	26.00	34.00	44.00	44.00
5	CONTRACT FTE	0.75	0.00	0.00	0.00
6	TOTAL FTE	26.75	34.00	44.00	44.00
7	EMPLOYEE SALARY & WAGES	$ 2,009,122	$ 3,285,692	$ 4,748,412	$ 6,006,499
8	CONTRACT SALARY & WAGES	$ 40,800	$ -	$ -	$ -
9	TOTAL SALARY & WAGES	$ 2,049,922	$ 3,285,692	$ 4,748,412	$ 6,006,499
10	TOTAL TAXES	$ 188,648	$ 306,252	$ 440,997	$ 554,225
11	TAXES AS % EMPLOYEE WAGES	9%	9%	9%	9%
12	TOTAL BENEFITS	$ 202,595	$ 356,860	$ 515,903	$ 656,949
13	BENEFITS AS % EMPLOYEE WAGES	10%	11%	11%	11%
14	TOTAL PAYROLL EXPENSE	$ 2,441,165	$ 3,948,804	$ 5,705,312	$ 7,217,673
15					
16	EXECUTIVE				
17					
18	EMPLOYEE FTE	2.00	4.00	6.00	6.00
19	CONTRACT FTE	0.00	0.00	0.00	0.00
20	TOTAL FTE	2.00	4.00	6.00	6.00
21	EMPLOYEE SALARY & WAGES	$ 238,714	$ 514,355	$ 798,055	$ 999,000
22	CONTRACT SALARY & WAGES	$ -	$ -	$ -	$ -
23	TOTAL SALARY & WAGES	$ 238,714	$ 514,355	$ 798,055	$ 999,000
24	TOTAL TAXES	$ 22,104	$ 47,532	$ 73,685	$ 91,770
25	TAXES AS % EMPLOYEE WAGES	9%	9%	9%	9%
26	TOTAL BENEFITS	$ 16,702	$ 28,966	$ 52,629	$ 68,223
27	BENEFITS AS % EMPLOYEE WAGES	7%	6%	7%	7%
28	TOTAL PAYROLL EXPENSE	$ 277,521	$ 590,853	$ 924,369	$ 1,158,992

Figure 2-14. *STAFF_DB persents detailed calculations and data from STAFF_CWS in a summary fashion as a dashboard.*

Format data into CHARTDAT spreadsheets like the one shown in Figure 2-15. Use these spreadsheets to create management charts of STAFF data like the one in Figure 2-16.

	A	B	C	D	E	F	G	H	I
13	Headcount by Department								
14								YR 1	
15			Jan	Feb	Mar	Apr	May	Jun	Jul
16		Executive	2.00	2.00	2.00	2.00	2.00	2.00	2.00
17		Biz OPS	0.50	0.50	0.50	0.50	0.50	0.50	0.50
18		Sales & MKT	1.25	1.25	1.25	1.25	2.25	2.25	2.75
19		Tech Ops	10.25	10.25	10.25	11.25	12.25	12.25	12.25
20		Total Headcount	14.00	14.00	14.00	15.00	17.00	17.00	17.50

Figure 2-15. *STAFF_CHARTDAT showing headcount data from STAFF_CWS used to create headcount chart*

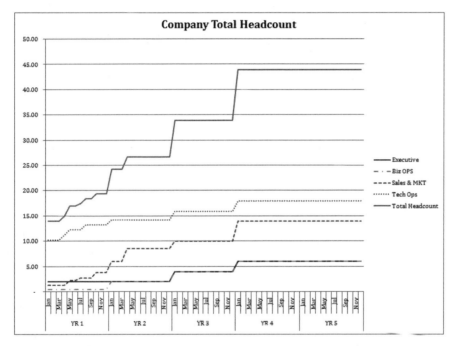

Figure 2-16. *STAFF_CHART TOT HC, the chart showing total headcount; source of data is STAFF_CHARTDAT*

Test the model using math and sanity checks to assure that you are not making any subtle errors.

■**Tip** Use Microsoft Excel's formula error function. Select Formulas from the ribbon and select Error Checking. Excel will check your spreadsheet for formula anomalies.

Perform operations and maintenance. In the case of this CBM, configuration management can be managed with systematic file saving and file-naming conventions.

Summary

In this chapter, we discussed specifics regarding planning, designing, and building the company business model (CBM). We reviewed a standard methodology for planning and designing models that draws from the best practices of two formal disciplines, project planning and the software design life cycle (SDLC). Best practices from these disciplines form the conceptual framework and point to the step-by-step process by which a CBM for a new company can be created.

Our first step is to *validate the feasibility* of the idea. If feasibility is tested and appears positive, the next step is to look to what it takes to design, build and bring the idea to the world. In other words, it is time to design the company needed to bring the idea to fruition.

We think of the company *as a project*. The company has a purpose, a scope, deliverables, tasks, schedules, costs, and a work breakdown structure (WBS) or organizational chart.

We design a company to deliver our idea to the world. Since we are thinking of the company as a project we will use project planning techniques to plan it. Then we will design the company to implement the plan.

The CBM is software, a computer program that models the project-based definition of the company allowing for the application of "what if" scenarios to the project definition and outputting standard financial reports that are reflective of these scenarios.

We create both operational and financial models of the company that we are designing. The operational models replicate the operations of the moving parts of the company. The financial models utilize the financial outputs from the operational models and present them in standard financial reports.

How will you approach the design of your CBM? How will you organize the model and in what sequence will you build it? How will you know, as you build the model, that it will provide you with the information that you need?

■■■

CHAPTER 3

The Green Devil Control Systems Business Case

This chapter will explain, in detail, a technology company business case that we will use as the basis for creating the models within this book. Green Devil Control Systems (our Company) and its products and services are fictional but are representative of early-stage technology enterprises striving to get to market today. The business case presented is designed to provide a framework in which we can review, discuss, and analyze many of the issues and challenges that face early-stage companies. In each chapter, we will review and present those parts of the business case that are relevant to the subject matter being discussed. This chapter presents a top-level overview of the Company business case, and we will discuss the following:

- Qualifications of the founders
- Formulation of the idea
- The feasibility study
- The concept of designing a company
- Formulation of planning assumptions
- Getting started

Founding Green Devil Control Systems

The two founders met in graduate school.

Founder number one rose through the ranks of the home building industry. While attending community college, he started working as a part-time electrician. He graduated with a degree in mechanical engineering and soon owned his own electrical contracting company. He then began building homes. After years of success, he turned to custom home building, becoming interested in green technologies and smart homes. He had a flair for sales and was well known in the industry, and he served on many industry committees and study groups. After more years of success, he sold his company and decided to attend graduate school to obtain an MBA before taking on his next career challenge.

Founder number two received her undergraduate and master's degrees in electrical engineering from a top engineering school. From the beginning, she had a flair for computer programming. Soon after graduation, she found herself developing embedded software for electrical control systems for a major manufacturer. She quickly rose through the ranks to become one of her company's top electrical control systems product development executives. With a passion for the outdoors, her interest in developing green alternatives to existing power systems came naturally. After ten years of intensive product development experience, she quit her job and entered graduate school for an MBA to round out her education.

During their MBA studies, these two were selected for a team to work on a case study about creating a startup company. Little did they know that they would soon be working together to start a company of their own. Over coffee, while studying balance sheets for their business case study, they began talking about their mutual interest in green technologies. A company was born.

Giving Birth to the Idea

Simply stated, the founders will design, build, and offer a product and service that will allow home-owners to control and monitor electricity usage in their homes. The founders have a common desire to bring something of value to the world and are convinced that their idea will do just that and that they possess the right mix of talent to make it happen. They believe they can deliver significant energy savings from their product and intend to create a new paradigm for energy conservation and awareness in an industry that has long needed products and technologies of this type.

Getting the Company Started

Soon after graduation, the founders rent a small office in their hometown and begin an intensive planning process for their new Company. They name the Company Green Devil Control Systems.

They decide to proceed through a logical process of planning and fact finding. They must decide, early in the game, if their idea is feasible. How will they test this? They decide to approach initial feasibility testing from three angles: market, technology, and resources. Their feasibility study asks three fundamental questions:

- Is there a potential market for the product?

- Is the technology feasible? Can it be owned, controlled, or patented?

- Are the technical resources available to bring this idea to market?

Testing Market Feasibility

Founder number one begins a market feasibility study with extensive interviews of individuals and companies that he knows in the home building industry. He prepares a presentation with an overview of the product concept and presents it to knowledgeable industry players and potential customers. He asks the question, "Would you buy this if it were offered? How much would you pay for it?"

He gathers ranges of pricing and cost data and examines the quantitative or financial aspect of the proposed value proposition. He studies the market with a sharp eye on forces that shape competition, looking for products, services, and players that could present competitive threats. He uses his industry background, connections, and know-how to gather as much information as possible to understand the market feasibility of the idea.

Assessing Technical Feasibility

Founder number two begins her feasibility study with a technology review of the product idea. She creates a functional requirements document and a preliminary design for the product. Using her own expertise and the expertise of other experts (under nondisclosure agreements), she validates the technical feasibility of the product. She examines the entire product development life cycle and assesses the feasibility of bringing the proposed technology to market. She assesses, to the extent possible, the chances of patenting the product or controlling the idea through trade secrets and technological expertise.

Validating Resource Feasibility

The founders work together and assess their ability to gather the technical team necessary to design and build the product. Their main question is not about money but expertise. Can they find and hire the right skills necessary for a project of this scope? What type of expertise are needed, and where will they hire those that have it?

Designing the Company

The feasibility studies prove positive. There appears to be a market for the idea, and the product is technically feasible. The founders' community is home to a large university providing a wealth of technical resources that can be readily accessed to form a company of this type. The next step for the founders is to design their Company.

Having read an outstanding book on financial modeling for technology companies, they begin a formal planning process. Once the planning process is completed, and using the information garnered by the process, they will develop a financial model to prototype the design for their Company. They know the financial model will put flesh on the bones of their idea and provide them with a deeper understanding of resources, relationships, and timing necessary to bring their idea to fruition. Funding requirements will be derived from the model, which will also serve as the backbone and justification for their business plan. They will develop their financial model, and using it as a baseline, write their business plan.

They proceed with a formal planning process.

The following sections explain the results from the planning process. This information forms the basis for the initial business case for Green Devil Control Systems (the Company).

Stating the Company Purpose

Green Devil Control Systems develops energy monitoring and control systems for the residential home building market.

Defining the Product

The Company builds and sells the Green Devil Energy Control System (ECS). ECS is a patent-pending, programmable hardware and software device that monitors and controls electricity usage on a circuit-by-circuit basis within the home. ECS usage will reduce electricity usage 10–35 percent annually.

Establishing the Value Proposition

The value proposition centers on four value concepts:

- Ease of setup, installation, and maintenance
- Utility cost savings that deliver a very attractive return on investment
- Attractiveness of green energy saving concepts to progressive smart-home buyers
- Added value of integrating ECS with other smart home capabilities

Identifying the Target Market

The initial target market for ECS is a subset of new housing starts, the smart homes market. Smart homes are primarily being built in the western region of the United States. They have integrated advanced networking capability to electronically control the home environment, including temperature, lighting, telecommunications, and security.

Assessing the Market

A large number of well-established electrical supply equipment manufacturers and distributors support the housing industry. The primary economic buyer or customer is the high-end home builder who is building smart homes for progressive and affluent customers. New players offering the same type of product are not known. The demand for smart homes is growing, but the pace of growth has slowed due to the recent recession in home building. The market for innovative ways to save on utility costs is an early adopter market. Government policies, in general, are highly favorable toward this type of industry. Smart home appliances and services like LANs, security systems, and smart thermostats are all complementary to the ECS product.

Developing a Marketing Strategy

The Company will position the ECS product as a green technology, a must-have feature for the progressive smart-home buyer. The founders will utilize standard branding methodologies to position Green Devil Control Systems as a standard feature for all progressive, energy-efficient homes. The Company will market ECS directly to the target buyer, the high-end home builder, using a technical and business value approach. They will also cross-market into the electrical contractor market segment that normally sells and installs electrical infrastructure. Each year they will attend two high-end home builder and home buyer trade shows and participate with a booth that portrays the Company as a sophisticated vendor of top-quality smart home infrastructure devices.

Creating the Sales Strategy

The Company will implement a direct sales strategy, selling directly to high-end home builders and developers. The Company will employ field sales engineers who are technically oriented toward electrical control devices and who can both sell and provide on-site technical support. The Company will sell into four geographical regions: West, South, Northeast, and Central. The ECS product will be presold beginning in October of YR 1. Sales regions will be implemented, and field sales engineers will be assigned to regions in the following order: West, South, Northeast, and Central.

Defining the Scope

The planning horizon for the Company is the current year plus five years. Products will be limited to versions of ECS for that period. No international sales are anticipated within the planning horizon.

Establishing Naming Conventions

Naming conventions will be developed as the financial model is developed. The primary product name, which includes any service options, is ECS.

Identifying Assumptions and Risk

Major assumption areas are the sales forecast and product pricing, the aggressive product development schedule, the ability to outsource manufacturing, and the ability to raise the necessary working capital to bring the product to market.

Major risk factors include market acceptance, market competition, and technology risks associated with product design to manufacturing. Developing the product in a timely fashion and within cost estimates is a critical success factor. Hiring qualified staff members is another critical success factor.

Developing the Production Approach

The Company will develop an initial prototype of its hardware and software followed by a production prototype. The production prototype will be thoroughly field tested and sent to labs for compliance testing. There will be two iterations of this process. Production prototypes will be converted to manufacturing designs. Manufacturing will be outsourced. Assembly and testing will be performed by the Company prior to shipment to customers.

Assigning Roles and Responsibilities

Founder number one will serve as president with primary responsibility for sales and marketing. Founder number two will serve as chief information officer and chief technology officer with responsibility for the product development and support life cycle. The founders will develop and hire the necessary staffing to implement Company strategy.

Company Deliverables

The primary Company deliverables follow:

- *Prototype development*: Low-level breadboard prototype development and testing will be completed by March of YR 1.

- *Production prototype development*: Ten production prototypes will be built and completed by May of YR 1. Five production prototypes will be used for field testing and five for compliance (lab) and safety testing.

- *Field, compliance, and safety testing*: There will be two iterations of field and compliance testing, which will include final modifications to the production prototype. Testing will be completed by September of YR 1.

- *Manufacturing design*: Manufacturing design will begin in May of YR 1 and be completed in November of YR 1.

- *Manufacturing*: Manufacturing will be outsourced and will begin in November of YR 1.

- *Product release*: The ECS product (with both software options) will be available in December of YR 1.

- *Software*: LS software and ES software will be developed in an integrated plan with product development.

Master Schedule, Critical Milestones, and Earned Value Criteria

There are clearly identified key operational milestones or value events which, when achieved, significantly increase the credibility of the Company and significantly reduce the risk profile of the venture. These value events and the dates they are planned follow:

- *Proof of product*: November of YR 1
- *Proof of market*: April of YR 2
- *Cash flow positive*: April of YR 2
- *Proof of scale*: July of YR 2

Project Work Plan

The project work plan is defined in the project master schedule.

Critical Path

The critical path of the Company is revealed by the designated value events, those value events that substantially increase the valuation of the Company, thus becoming natural points to raise investment capital.

Work Breakdown Structure

The Company will be organized into three functional organizations: Sales and Marketing, Technical Operations, and Business Development. See Figure 3-1.

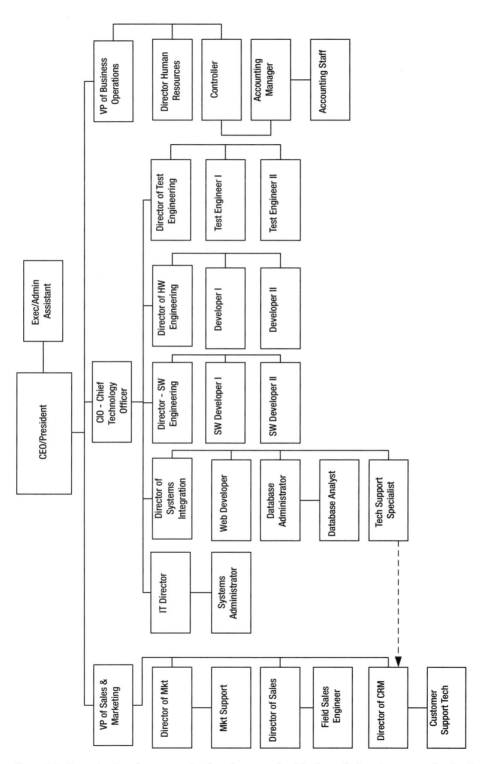

Figure 3-1. *Organizational structure developed as a result of the formal planning process for the Company*

Having completed the formal planning process, the founders are now ready to begin the creation of the company business model (CBM). They use best practices from software design life cycle (SDLC) methods to develop the model. The following chapters guide you through the detailed business thinking and development of the CBM.

Summary

In this chapter, you have witnessed the creation of an initial idea for a company and the early-stage thought process and steps necessary for the founders to get started.

The founders proceed through a logical process of planning and fact finding. They must decide, early in the game, if their idea is feasible by testing initial feasibility from three angles: market, technology, and resources. Their feasibility study addresses three fundamental questions:

- Is there a potential market for the proposed product?

- Is the technology feasible? Can it be owned, controlled, or patented?

- Are the technical resources available to bring this idea to market?

The feasibility results are positive, so they enter into a formal planning process to design the Company and bring their idea into reality. They proceed through the process, developing an initial business case for their Company. They now intend to develop a CBM based on their planning findings that will serve as the first prototype and proof of concept for their idea.

Now that the founders have developed their business case for their Company, we can peer over their shoulders as they create their CBM. As the CBM evolves, it will guide them in implementing their operating plans and allow them to hone their assumptions and strategies as they move forward. The following chapters of this book will guide you through this journey.

CHAPTER 4

■ ■ ■

The Staffing Model

In this chapter, you will learn how to plan, create, and use the Staffing (STAFF) model component of the company business model (CBM). We will begin with business thinking about staffing and how it relates to the operational implementation of your business idea. We will then plan and consider how the model will work. We will create the STAFF model to reflect your company's skill mix, organizational structure, and compensation plan.

In this chapter you will learn how to plan, create, and use the STAFF model. You will also learn how to

- Organize and develop a staffing plan.

- Model staffing cost variables including salary and the need for computers, phones, and office space.

- Compute the cost of payroll taxes and benefits

Business Thinking About Staffing: Evolution or Intelligent Design?

Don't be fooled by thinking that a great technology, a great founder, or a great market opportunity defines your company. It's the people! You can *feel it* when you walk into a business. The atmosphere from business to business varies greatly and is always palpable. The atmosphere can be animated, exciting, upbeat, positive, cynical, arrogant, dull, or even outright negative. My experience is that startup companies initially take on the personality of the founder or founders, which can be a good or bad thing. I think you know what I mean.

Developing STAFF is a great opportunity to apply business thinking to the staffing dimension of your business equation with an eye toward optimizing your greatest resource—people.

Conventional management wisdom views staffing in terms of hiring the right people needed to do a job. Management is continuously reviewing skill mix, trying to optimize and fit skills to work requirements. In this regard, a startup has a different challenge on its hands. Startups progress through distinct operational phases as they mature toward full operational viability, and "skill mix" has a different connotation as the company progresses through its phases.

These are the three phases of startup technology company development:

1. Startup

2. Initial operating capability (IOC)

3. Full operating capability (FOC)

Each operational phase requires a different breed of cat (type of employee) to excel within the dominant work environment that is characteristic of each phase. These staff characteristics I call (using a Buddhist idiom) "staff nature."

Staff nature is primarily defined as skill set but is highly influenced by temperament, preference, and orientation. For instance, there is a huge difference between the type of person you want to develop your new product and the one you want to manage a mature software configuration. Both may have similar technical backgrounds, but their views and orientations toward work could not be more different. This dimension of staffing is usually not planned for strategically.

Three types of staff nature follow:

- Visionaries

- Pathfinders

- Homesteaders

To use a Wild West analogy, the *visionaries* imagine going out west and organizing the resources for a wagon train to travel to a particular destination. The *pathfinders* are the scouts and wagon train leaders that lead and manage the wagon train over rough terrain and snowy passes to the goal. The *homesteaders* settle the land at the destination and create thriving enterprises. They are three different breeds of cat in terms of orientation, preference, and optimal value during the different phases of company development. Let's look at each phase now; see Figure 4-1.

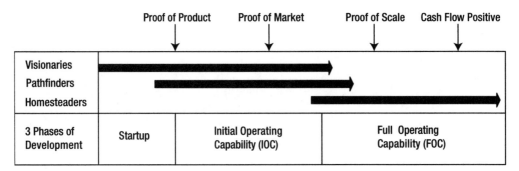

Figure 4-1. *The three phases of company development and the ideal staff natures to support each phase*

Each phase of company development requires a unique mix of resources to address the particular demands of that phase of company evolution. The following lists will give you a flavor for the *people* needs and characteristics (staff nature) needed to support the unique *product* development, *sales*, and *process* environments that are normally encountered in the evolving phases of company development.

Staffing the Startup Phase

For the startup phase, the ideal staff nature is visionary:

- *People*: Founders and one or two core technologists
- *Product*: Research and development; early prototype development
- *Sales*: Early market research, intelligence, and validation
- *Process*: Free form

Staffing the IOC Phase

Ideally, in the IOC phase, your staff will be primarily composed of pathfinders:

- *People*: Founders, initial development team, and first field sales engineers
- *Product*: Prototype rapidly evolving into first commercial release
- *Sales*: Early adopter and beta sales to get prototypes in the hands of users
- *Process*: Early/evolving definition of process and procedures

Staffing the FOC Phase

In the FOC phase, you ideally want a staff composed of homesteaders:

- *People*: Fully staffed for growing, high-quality operations
- *Product*: First commercially released versions
- *Sales*: Growing sales and brand recognition
- *Process*: Formal process and procedures

Moving Through the Phases

In my experience, entrepreneurs can explain to investors the phase of technology development they are in but, many times, cannot articulate how they will transition their team from visionaries to homesteaders. Some employees can make the transition through all stages of a company's development; many cannot. Many entrepreneurs that I have worked with have the idea that the company will evolve into the staffing mix that it needs. My experience is that failure to plan for this evolution can cause major problems along the way.

■Note One of my clients found himself stuck in a perpetual development cycle because his initial development team, a mixture of visionaries and pathfinders, could not settle on a final configuration for the product and get it to market. They were stuck in a continuous visionary development do loop. Only when a new product manager (a homesteader) was hired was the company able to get off the dime and move forward from IOC into FOC.

Your business thinking about staffing must provide a strategy for the types of positions you will need and a strategy for the evolution of staff nature that fits with the phases of company operations. Your staff's ability to successfully operate in the various stages of company evolution must be managed. Some would say this is premature hand wringing and that there are bigger fish to fry. I suggest that the operational phase shifts occur sooner rather than later.

As you develop STAFF, keep in mind the previous discussion on staff nature. Plan for the functional positions that are required and their cost, but also plan for the evolution of the staff from visionaries to homesteaders. For instance, the headcount for software developers may stay the same, but the salaries may change as you transition from pathfinder developers into homesteader developers. Your model design may handle this implicitly or explicitly. It's up to you.

Reviewing the Staffing Business Case

Green Devil Control Systems (the Company) is an early-stage technology startup that develops and sells energy monitoring and control systems, specifically the Green Devil Energy Control System (ECS). The Company completed extensive market research during the feasibility study phase of their planning (see Chapter 3 for more on this study and the analysis of market potential for the Company). The founders must now begin the design and planning process for the Company. They will begin with the modeling of a detailed staffing plan and begin the process of designing the Staffing Model component of the CBM.

Exploring the Market

In exploring the Company's market, here's what the founders decide:

> *Target market*: The initial target market for ECS is a subset of new housing starts, the smart homes market. Smart homes are primarily being built in the western region of the United States. They have integrated networking capability and advanced capabilities to electronically control the home environment including temperature, lighting, telecommunications, and security.

> *Marketing strategy*: The Company will position the ECS product as a green technology, as a must-have feature for the progressive smart home buyer.

> *Sales strategy*: The Company will implement a direct sales strategy, selling directly to high-end home builders and developers. The Company will employ field sales engineers who are technically oriented toward electrical control devices and who can both sell and provide on-site technical support.

Exploring the Product

ECS is a patent-pending, programmable hardware and software device that monitors and controls electricity usage on a circuit-by-circuit basis within a facility. ECS is installed on the facility side of the electrical breaker box. It can be purchased with Local Services (LS) or Extended Services (ES) software options.

Planning the Company's Approach

The Company will develop an initial prototype of its hardware and software followed by a production prototype. The production prototype will be thoroughly field tested and sent to labs for compliance testing. There will be two iterations of this prototyping process. Production prototypes will be converted to manufacturing designs. Manufacturing will be outsourced. Assembly and testing will be performed by the Company prior to shipment to customers.

Assessing Company Deliverables

The primary Company deliverables follow:

- Prototype development
- Production prototype development
- Field, compliance, and safety testing
- Manufacturing design
- Manufacturing
- Product release

Planning Value Events

There are clearly identified key operational milestones, or value events. When achieved, these events significantly increase the credibility of the Company and significantly reduce the risk profile of the venture. These value events and their planned dates follow:

- *Proof of product*: November of year one
- *Proof of market*: April of year 2
- *Cash flow positive*: April of year 2
- *Proof of scale*: July of year 2

Understanding the Critical Components of the Staffing Model

The following critical components must be addressed and reflected in STAFF:

- *Organization structure*: The organizational structure reflects the Company's strategy for organizing the work that must be accomplished. They must think through the best way to organize the Company in order to do the work required. The organizational structure defines the relationships between functional positions and functional teams (departments) and their reporting responsibilities. The components and dimensions of an organizational structure follow:

  - *Functional positions*: A complete listing of each functional position required to implement the business idea is incorporated in the organizational structure.

  - *Line relationships*: Operational reporting structures are defined by the organization chart of the Company.

  - *Cost structures*: Organization structures often define the cost roll-up structure of the Company.

- *Staffing plan*: STAFF provides a detailed plan of the functional positions that the Company will fill to implement their business plan. They must identify the job description and skill level of each employee that they are going to need over the full course of the business plan. They define the functional position to be filled over time as the Company evolves. STAFF provides a capability to plan for a consulting position in lieu of each functional position. The staffing plan is time phased showing the additions or reductions to headcount in functional positions over time.

- *Cost and other assumptions*: A critical part of planning is defining the cost of resources assumptions. What salaries will be required for each needed position? If consultants must be hired, what will they cost? What are your assumptions for the benefits provided and how much will they cost? What other bonus and compensation plans do you have in mind and what are your assumptions?

■**Note** There is a cost roll-up design consideration to be made here. When planning STAFF, determine the lowest level at which you need to collect employee costs. This should always be the lowest level needed for the analysis of the staffing data. For example, you may decide that it is sufficient to collect costs at the functional position level rather than at the individual employee level. Figure this out before you start programming your model.

Planning the Staffing Model

There are three steps when planning the staffing model:

1. Plan the organizational structure.
2. Create the staffing plan.
3. Define cost assumptions and key planning variables.

Planning the Organizational Structure

The Company will plan the optimal organizational structure needed to accomplish its business objectives. They will create an organizational chart (see Figure 4-2) that includes all functional positions needed for the entire life cycle of the Company. The life cycle is the five-year period of performance covered by the CBM.

Note that the organizational chart shown in Figure 4-2 defines three primary functional areas:

- *Sales and marketing*: Led by the vice president of sales and marketing
- *Technical operations*: Led by the chief technology officer
- *Business operations*: Led by the vice president of business operations

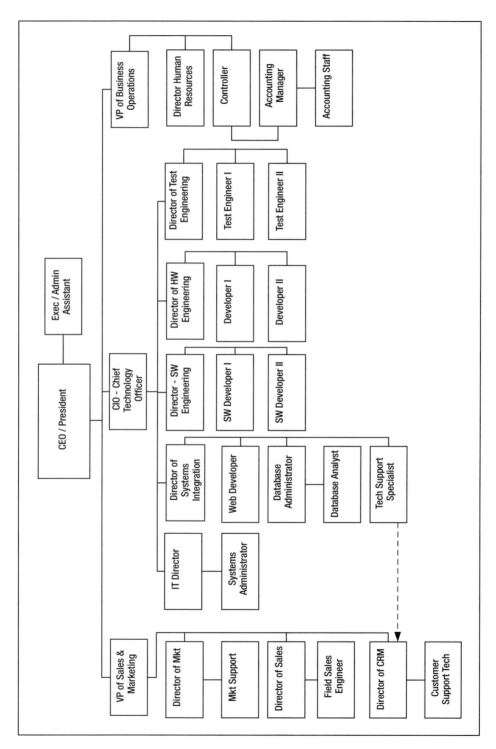

Figure 4-2. *The forecasted organizational chart that addresses all funtional positions required during the period of performance of the model.*

Creating the Staffing Plan

The Company will create a staffing plan from the organizational chart that includes:

- A listing of all functional positions organized into departments
- A time-phased projection of the number of full-time equivalents (FTE) needed to fill the positions over the period of performance of the model

---

■**Note** For the purposes of this model, a *full-time equivalent* (FTE) designates one full-time position. For example, an entry of .5 into the headcount model indicates that the position is filled half time by one person. An entry of 2.0 indicates that the functional position is filled by two full-time people or possibly four half-time people.

	A	B	C	D	E	F	G
1		YR 0	YR 1	YR 2	YR 3	YR 4	YR 5
2							
3		STAFFING PLAN					
4	**Summary Headcount by Function**						
5							
6	Executive FTE	1.00	2.00	2.00	4.00	6.00	6.00
7	Executive - Consultant	-	-	-	-	-	-
8	Executive - Total	1.00	2.00	2.00	4.00	6.00	6.00
9							
10	Business Operations - FTE	-	-	2.00	4.00	6.00	6.00
11	Business Operations - Consultant	0.25	0.50	-	-	-	-
12	Business Operations Total	0.25	0.50	2.00	4.00	6.00	6.00
13							
14	Sales & Marketing - FTE	-	3.00	8.00	10.00	14.00	14.00
15	Sales & Marketing - Consultant	-	0.75	0.50	-	-	-
16	Sales & Marketing - Total	-	3.75	8.50	10.00	14.00	14.00
17							
18	Technical Operations - FTE	1.00	9.00	14.00	16.00	18.00	18.00
19	Technical Operations - Consultant	1.75	4.25	0.25	-	-	-
20	Technical Operations - Total	2.75	13.25	14.25	16.00	18.00	18.00
21							
22	**Company - FTE**	2.00	14.00	26.00	34.00	44.00	44.00
23	**Company - Consultant**	2.00	5.50	0.75	-	-	-
24	**Company - Total**	4.00	19.50	26.75	34.00	44.00	44.00

Figure 4-3. *STAFFPLAN_CWS creates a time-phased staffing plan for each functional position defined in the organization chart.*

■Note The staffing plan in Figure 4-3 designates four departments: Executive, Business Operations, Sales & Marketing, and Technical Operations. The organizational chart shows only three line functions: Sales & Marketing, Technical Operations, and Business Operations. STAFF is grouping the top executives into an executive department to keep track of their bonus plans separately.

Defining Cost Assumptions and Key Planning Variables

The Company will develop cost assumptions (currency amounts to be input into the model) including consideration for the following:

- A salary target for each functional position and assumptions regarding changes in this range over time. A salary target (maximum salary at full operating capability of the Company) is determined for each position and adjusted on a yearly basis using a salary adjustment factor.

- Applicable employee taxes and rates.

- Employee benefits and applicable rates and burdens for each.

- Impact of other bonus and compensation plans.

■Caution Don't forget to determine the key variables that you wish to model; those variables that you wish to input and change in performing sensitivity analysis or "what ifs" in STAFF.

Using the Building Blocks of the STAFF Model

When the planning is complete, build the model (see Figure 4-4). Take into consideration the inputs and outputs from STAFF to and from other components of the CBM.

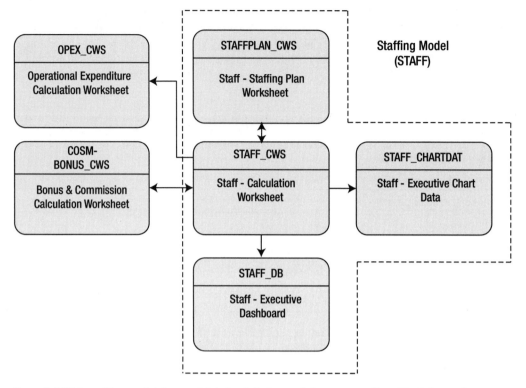

Figure 4-4. *This staffing model shows a high-level design and data-process flow. Worksheets shown within the dotted lines are primary STAFF worksheets. The arrows indicate the primary data flow direction.*

Understanding the Staffing Plan Worksheet

STAFFPLAN_CWS summarizes the monthly headcounts that are input into STAFF_CWS and allows for a top-level input of salary adjustment factors. Its primary purpose is to sanity check the headcount and salary assumptions that are input into the more detailed STAFF_CWS. To fill it in, input the salary adjustment assumptions for each functional position.

This spreadsheet is not complicated (see Figure 4-5). It provides an input screen for salary adjustment assumptions. It provides a top-down view of headcount spreads and salary adjustment assumptions, allowing the user to assess the staffing plan at a high level.

■**Note**   STAFF_CWS is linked to STAFFPLAN_CWS. When you change the salary adjustment factors in STAFFPLAN_CWS, they are automatically propagated into the Staff-Calculation Worksheet, STAFF_CWS.

STAFF uses a salary adjustment method to forecast salaries. STAFF assumes the highest level salary (target salary) the Company will pay for a position and adjusts the salaries for that position over time, growing it up to 100 percent of the maximum salary at the end of the period of performance. The logic is that it may be easier to plan for salaries as a percentage of target salary rather than inputting discrete salaries over time.

■**Note** Another way to forecast salary would be to discretely input fixed target salaries into each month of the model.

	A	B	C	D	E	F	G
1		YR 0	YR 1	YR 2	YR 3	YR 4	YR 5
2							
3		STAFFING PLAN					
4	Summary Headcount by Function						
5							
6	Executive FTE	1.00	2.00	2.00	4.00	6.00	6.00
7	Executive - Consultant	-	-	-	-	-	-
8	Executive - Total	1.00	2.00	2.00	4.00	6.00	6.00
9							
10	Business Operations - FTE	-	-	2.00	4.00	6.00	6.00
11	Business Operations - Consultant	0.25	0.50	-	-	-	-
12	Business Operations Total	0.25	0.50	2.00	4.00	6.00	6.00
13							
14	Sales & Marketing - FTE	-	3.00	8.00	10.00	14.00	14.00
15	Sales & Marketing - Consultant	-	0.75	0.50	-	-	-
16	Sales & Marketing - Total	-	3.75	8.50	10.00	14.00	14.00
17							
18	Technical Operations - FTE	1.00	9.00	14.00	16.00	18.00	18.00
19	Technical Operations - Consultant	1.75	4.25	0.25	-	-	-
20	Technical Operations - Total	2.75	13.25	14.25	16.00	18.00	18.00
21							
22	Company - FTE	2.00	14.00	26.00	34.00	44.00	44.00
23	Company - Consultant	2.00	5.50	0.75	-	-	-
24	Company - Total	4.00	19.50	26.75	34.00	44.00	44.00
25							
26	Functional - Executive						
27							
28	CEO/President	0.50	1.00	1.00	1.00	1.00	1.00
29	Consultant	-	-	-	-	-	-
30	Salary Adjustment Factor	60%	60%	70%	80%	90%	100%
31							
32	VP of Business Operations	-	-	-	-	1.00	1.00
33	Consultant	-	-	-	-	-	-
34	Salary Adjustment Factor					90%	100%
35							
36	VP of Sales & Marketing	-	-	-	1.00	1.00	1.00
37	Consultant	-	-	-	-	-	-
38	Salary Adjustment Factor				90%	90%	100%

Figure 4-5. *STAFFPLAN_CWS shows a vertical listing of functional positions organized by department and their corresponding headcount forecast and salary adjustment factors.*

Understanding the Staff Calculation Worksheet

This worksheet does the heavy lifting in STAFF. It links its Salary Adjustment Factor cells to the STAFFPLAN_CWS for salary adjustments. STAFF_CWS provides for input of headcount and salary assumptions. It calculates salaries and payroll taxes and computes the number of phones, computers, and the requirements for office space needed based on headcount projections.

Exploring the Variable Input Section of STAFF_CWS

The top portion of STAFF_CWS (see Figure 4-6) provides a visual interface for developing a monthly spread of the headcount.

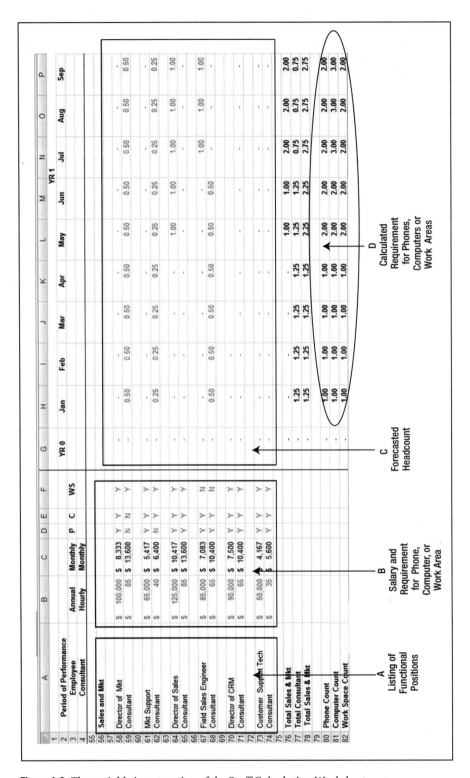

Figure 4-6. *The variable input section of the Staff Calculation Worksheet*

■**Note** STAFF_CWS links to STAFFPLAN_CWS and uses salary adjustment data and yearly assumptions for payroll tax and benefit burden amounts to calculate total cost of salaries, wages, and benefits.

The top section of STAFF_CWS is designed for the input and display of the following variables:

- A list of functional positions
- A target salary for each functional employee position, as well as consulting rate estimates and requirements for phones, computers, and office space for employees or consultants
- Forecasted headcount

■**Note** See Exercise 4-1 for how to use the SUMIF command to count phone, computer, or office space requirements.

See Exercise 4-2 for how to use FIND and REPLACE commands to speed up linking of large spreadsheets. OPEX and CAPEX models link to STAFF_CWS to access the calculated requirements for phones, computers, and office spaces. This data is needed as an input to the operating and capital expenditure plan.

Computing Salaries Using STAFF_CWS

This section of STAFF_CWS computes the salary cost for each functional slot and adjusts it for the salary adjustment percentage (see Figure 4-7). It computes consulting services expenses if the functional position is temporarily filled by a consultant.

Follow these steps to compute salaries with this worksheet:

1. *Base Compensation*: To compute base salary cost, multiply FTE units by monthly salaries.
2. *Adjustment Factor*: Note and validate the salary adjustment factor from STAFF_SP.
3. *Adjusted Compensation*: To adjust base salaries, multiply base salaries by adjustment factors.
4. *Bonus Plans*: Add commission or bonuses to base salaries.
5. *Tax and Burden Basis*: The derived tax and burden basis equals adjusted base salary plus sales commissions or bonuses.
6. *Consultant*: Compute consulting expenses by multiplying consultant FTE units by consultant monthly costs.

	A	G	H	I	J	K	L	M	N
1									YR 1
2	**Period of Performance**	**YR 0**	**Jan**	**Feb**	**Mar**	**Apr**	**May**	**Jun**	**Jul**
164	CEO/President								
165	Base Compensation	$ 7,292	$ 14,583	$ 14,583	$ 14,583	$ 14,583	$ 14,583	$ 14,583	$ 14,583
166	Adjustment Factor	60%	60%	60%	60%	60%	60%	60%	60%
167	Adjusted Compensation	$ 4,375	$ 8,750	$ 8,750	$ 8,750	$ 8,750	$ 8,750	$ 8,750	$ 8,750
168	Bonus Plans	$ -	$ -	$ -	$ -	$ -	$ -	$ -	$ -
169	Tax and Burden Basis	$ 4,375	$ 8,750	$ 8,750	$ 8,750	$ 8,750	$ 8,750	$ 8,750	$ 8,750
170									
171	Consultant	$ -	$ -	$ -	$ -	$ -	$ -	$ -	$ -
172									
173	COO - VP of BIZ OPS								
174	Base Compensation	$ -	$ -	$ -	$ -	$ -	$ -	$ -	$ -
175	Adjustment Factor	-	-	-	-	-	-	-	-
176	Adjusted Compensation	$ -	$ -	$ -	$ -	$ -	$ -	$ -	$ -
177	Bonus Plans	$ -	$ -	$ -	$ -	$ -	$ -	$ -	$ -
178	Tax and Burden Basis	$ -	$ -	$ -	$ -	$ -	$ -	$ -	$ -
179									
180	Consultant	$ -	$ -	$ -	$ -	$ -	$ -	$ -	$ -
181									
182	VP of Sales & Marketing								
183	Base Compensation	$ -	$ -	$ -	$ -	$ -	$ -	$ -	$ -
184	Adjustment Factor	-	-	-	-	-	-	-	-
185	Adjusted Compensation	$ -	$ -	$ -	$ -	$ -	$ -	$ -	$ -
186	Bonus Plans	$ -	$ -	$ -	$ -	$ -	$ -	$ -	$ -
187	Tax and Burden Basis	$ -	$ -	$ -	$ -	$ -	$ -	$ -	$ -
188									
189	Consultant	$ -	$ -	$ -	$ -	$ -	$ -	$ -	$ -
190									
191	CIO - Chief Technical Officer								
192	Base Compensation	$ 5,625	$ 11,250	$ 11,250	$ 11,250	$ 11,250	$ 11,250	$ 11,250	$ 11,250
193	Adjustment Factor	60%	60%	60%	60%	60%	60%	60%	60%
194	Adjusted Compensation	$ 3,375	$ 6,750	$ 6,750	$ 6,750	$ 6,750	$ 6,750	$ 6,750	$ 6,750
195	Bonus Plans	$ -	$ -	$ -	$ -	$ -	$ -	$ -	$ -
196	Tax and Burden Basis	$ 3,375	$ 6,750	$ 6,750	$ 6,750	$ 6,750	$ 6,750	$ 6,750	$ 6,750

Figure 4-7. *STAFF_CWS's salary computation section computes salary, consulting costs, and tax and burden basis.*

Computing Payroll Taxes and Benefit Burdens with STAFF_CWS

The next section of STAFF_CWS computes payroll taxes and benefit burdens for each department (see Figure 4-8).

The steps to do so follow:

1. *Compute payroll and other taxes*: Multiply applicable tax and burden rates by the applicable tax and burden basis.

2. *Compute the cost of medical insurance*: Multiply the forecasted monthly medical insurance per employee by the number of applicable FTE units.

3. *Compute the cost of 401K benefits*: Multiply the forecasted 401K burden (the cost to the Company to provide this benefit) by the applicable tax and burden basis. Most 401K burdens represent matching funds that employers provide for savings that employees put into their plans.

	A	G	H	I	J	K	L	M	N
1									YR 1
2	Period of Performance	YR 0	Jan	Feb	Mar	Apr	May	Jun	Jul
356									
357	Total Sales & Mkt								
358	Adjusted Compensation	$ -	$ -	$ -	$ -	$ -	$ 6,250	$ 6,250	$ 11,917
359	Sales Commissions	$ -	$ -	$ -	$ -	$ -	$ -	$ -	$ -
360	Tax and Burden Basis	$ -	$ -	$ -	$ -	$ -	$ 6,250	$ 6,250	$ 11,917
361									
362	Total Consultant	$ -	$ 5,200	$ 5,200	$ 5,200	$ 5,200	$ 5,200	$ 5,200	$ -
363									
364	SALES&MKT TOTAL BASIS	$ -	$ 5,200	$ 5,200	$ 5,200	$ 5,200	$ 11,450	$ 11,450	$ 11,917
365									
366	Payroll Tax Calculations								
367									
368	TAXES								
369	FICA	$ -	$ -	$ -	$ -	$ -	$ 388	$ 388	$ 739
370	Medicare	$ -	$ -	$ -	$ -	$ -	$ 91	$ 91	$ 173
371	Workers Comp	$ -	$ -	$ -	$ -	$ -	$ 34	$ 34	$ 66	← 1
372	SUI	$ -	$ -	$ -	$ -	$ -	$ 26	$ 26	$ 52
373	FUI	$ -	$ -	$ -	$ -	$ -	$ 50	$ 50	$ 95
374	TOTAL TAXES	$ -	$ -	$ -	$ -	$ -	$ 588	$ 588	$ 1,124
375									
376	EMPLOYEE BENEFITS								
377	MEDICAL INSURANCE					$ -	$ -	$ -	$ -	← 2
378	401 K								
379									
380	Total Gross Benefits	$ -	$ -	$ -	$ -	$ -	$ -	$ -	$ -	← 3
381									
382	SALES & MKT TOTAL Burden	$ -	$ 5,200	$ 5,200	$ 5,200	$ 5,200	$ 12,038	$ 12,038	$ 13,041

Figure 4-8. *Staff_CWS's payroll tax and benefit burden computation section*

■**Note** Medical insurance calculation is offset by three months, assuming that medical insurance will not kick in until the employee has been employed for 90 days. The 401K burden calculation is offset by 12 months, assuming that 401K benefits kick in after one year of employment.

Consulting expenses do not carry any applicable taxes or burdens and are not included in the tax and burden basis.

Understanding the Executive Dashboard

The STAFF_DB worksheet is a management summary of STAFF data (see Figure 4-9). Its primary source of data is STAFF_CWS. The STAFF_DB can be formatted and used as a high-level management report, for instance, as a display in the business plan.

	A	C	D	E	F
1		YR 2	YR 3	YR 4	YR 5
2	COMPANY TOTAL				
3					
4	EMPLOYEE FTE	26.00	34.00	44.00	44.00
5	CONTRACT FTE	0.75	0.00	0.00	0.00
6	TOTAL FTE	26.75	34.00	44.00	44.00
7	EMPLOYEE SALARY & WAGES	$2,009,122	$3,285,692	$4,748,412	$6,006,499
8	CONTRACT SALARY & WAGES	$ 40,800	$ -	$ -	$ -
9	TOTAL SALARY & WAGES	$2,049,922	$3,285,692	$4,748,412	$6,006,499
10	TOTAL TAXES	$ 188,648	$ 306,252	$ 440,997	$ 554,225
11	TAXES AS % EMPLOYEE WAGES	9%	9%	9%	9%
12	TOTAL BENEFITS	$ 202,595	$ 356,860	$ 515,903	$ 656,949
13	BENEFITS AS % EMPLOYEE WAGES	10%	11%	11%	11%
14	TOTAL PAYROLL EXPENSE	$2,441,165	$3,948,804	$5,705,312	$7,217,673
15					
16	EXECUTIVE				
17					
18	EMPLOYEE FTE	2.00	4.00	6.00	6.00
19	CONTRACT FTE	0.00	0.00	0.00	0.00
20	TOTAL FTE	2.00	4.00	6.00	6.00
21	EMPLOYEE SALARY & WAGES	$ 238,714	$ 514,355	$ 798,055	$ 999,000
22	CONTRACT SALARY & WAGES	$ -	$ -	$ -	$ -
23	TOTAL SALARY & WAGES	$ 238,714	$ 514,355	$ 798,055	$ 999,000
24	TOTAL TAXES	$ 22,104	$ 47,532	$ 73,685	$ 91,770
25	TAXES AS % EMPLOYEE WAGES	9%	9%	9%	9%
26	TOTAL BENEFITS	$ 16,702	$ 28,966	$ 52,629	$ 68,223
27	BENEFITS AS % EMPLOYEE WAGES	7%	6%	7%	7%
28	TOTAL PAYROLL EXPENSE	$ 277,521	$ 590,853	$ 924,369	$1,158,992
29					
30	BUSINESS OPERATIONS				
31					
32	EMPLOYEE FTE	2.00	4.00	6.00	6.00
33	CONTRACT FTE	0.00	0.00	0.00	0.00
34	TOTAL FTE	2.00	4.00	6.00	6.00
35	EMPLOYEE SALARY & WAGES	$ 50,000	$ 172,000	$ 279,000	$ 304,000
36	CONTRACT SALARY & WAGES	$ -	$ -	$ -	$ -
37	TOTAL SALARY & WAGES	$ 50,000	$ 172,000	$ 279,000	$ 304,000
38	TOTAL TAXES	$ 5,120	$ 16,720	$ 26,970	$ 29,220

Figure 4-9. STAFF_DB, the Staff Executive Dashboard, is the management summary of Staffing model data.

■**Note**   STAFF_DB is linked to and derives its data from STAFF_CWS.

Understanding the Executive Chart Data

STAFF_CHARDAT preformats data needed for the STAFF management and analysis charts (see Figure 4-10). Charts are defined, and the data sources for the charts are derived from linking back to the other spreadsheets in the model.

	A	B	C	D	E	F	G	H	I	J	K	L	M	N	O
3	Chart Name														
4															
5		Total FTE - Total Cost													
6								YR 1							
7			Jan	Feb	Mar	Apr	May	Jun	Jul	Aug	Sep	Oct	Nov	Dec	Jan
8		GT Headcount	14.00	14.00	14.00	15.00	17.00	17.00	17.50	18.50	18.50	19.50	19.50	19.50	24.25
9		GT COST	$ 98,067	$ 98,067	$ 98,067	$ 108,073	$ 118,570	$ 118,570	$ 119,989	$ 125,988	$ 125,988	$ 132,678	$ 133,095	$ 135,905	$ 167,865
10															
11	Headcount by Department														
12								YR 1							
13			Jan	Feb	Mar	Apr	May	Jun	Jul	Aug	Sep	Oct	Nov	Dec	Jan
14		Executive	2.00	2.00	2.00	2.00	2.00	2.00	2.00	2.00	2.00	2.00	2.00	2.00	2.00
15		Biz OPS	0.50	0.50	0.50	0.50	0.50	0.50	0.50	0.50	0.50	0.50	0.50	0.50	2.00
16		Sales & MKT	1.25	1.25	1.25	1.25	2.25	2.25	2.75	2.75	2.75	3.75	3.75	3.75	6.00
17		Tech Ops	10.25	10.25	10.25	11.25	12.25	12.25	12.25	13.25	13.25	13.25	13.25	13.25	14.25
18		Total Headcount	14.00	14.00	14.00	15.00	17.00	17.00	17.50	18.50	18.50	19.50	19.50	19.50	24.25

Figure 4-10. Using STAFF_CHARDAT, chart data is formatted and organized for the development of management and analysis charting.

■Note See Exercise 4-3 for how to create a double axis management chart to show headcount and cost of payroll on one management chart.

You can create various management charts, as shown in Figure 4-11, utilizing the base data from STAFF_CHARDAT. See Exercise 4-3 for more details on creating this type of chart.

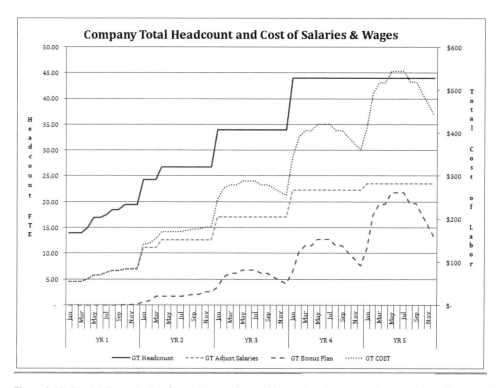

Figure 4-11. *STAFF CHART_Total FTE & Cost shows the FTE headcount and cost of labor chart (double axis) including a total headcount and total cost of salaries, wages, and benefits.*

EXERCISE 4-1. USING MICROSOFT EXCEL'S SUMIF FUNCTION TO COUNT REQUIREMENTS FOR PHONES, COMPUTERS, AND WORK SPACES

STAFF has a requirement to plan for the number of phones (cell phones or PDAs that require individual connectivity plans), office computers (desktop or laptop), and for an amount of office space or square footage needed to accommodate the headcount forecast. The requirement for each of these items is a variable cost to the Company based on the number of people that will be working for the Company. It is possible that the Company will not have to provide phones or computers or work spaces for consultants. For instance, the consultant may work from home.

- *Problem:* We have indicated with a Y (yes) or N (no) in STAFF_CWS the need for phone, computer, or work space depending on the functional position designation and whether it is filled by an employee or consultant. We want to count the number of phones, computers, and work spaces based on the input of forecasted headcount.

- *Solution:* Use the Excel SUMIF function to implement this count (see Figure 4-12). However, there is one additional complication. In many cases, the position will be filled part-time, that is, the input may be shown as a .5 instead of a 1.0. We don't want to generate count results that are fractional counts. We obviously can't purchase half a computer or half a phone; therefore, we want to round the count result up to the nearest whole number. We use the Excel ROUNDUP function to round up the results of the SUMIF count. This is good enough for our planning purposes.

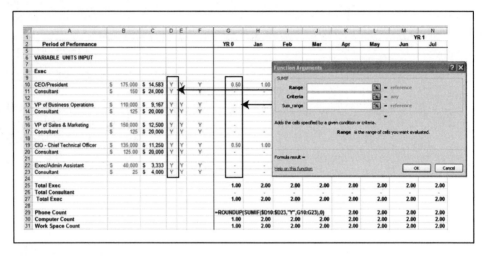

Figure 4-12. *The SUMIF input screen where you can complete the Range, Criteria, and Sum_range fields.*

1. Place your cursor in the worksheet cell in which you wish to place the first SUMIF count result. In this example, the formula is in cell G29.

2. On the ribbon's Formulas tab, select Math & Trig functions, scroll down, and select the SUMIF function.

3. Input the following variables into the formula:

    a. Select the range of cells that are the criteria for selection. In this case, the range is D10:D23, the Y and N values indicating the need for a phone.

    b. Input the criterion, which is Y, for yes.

    c. Select the sum range, the range of numbers to be summed if the criterion in the range D10:D23 is Y. In this case, the range is G10:G23. Click OK. You have created the first formula to count phones, computers, and work spaces required.

4. Prepare the formula for replication (copy) into the remaining months on the spreadsheet. The current formula is

    `=SUMIF(D10:D23,"Y",G10:G23)`

    To prepare it for copying to the 59 cells to the right, you must anchor the selection of column D by changing the column D reference to an absolute reference by inserting a dollar sign ($) as required. The formula is now

    `=SUMIF($D10:$D23,"Y",G10:G23)`

5. Modify the formula to round up SUMIF results to the nearest whole number using the ROUNDUP function. The current formula is

    `=SUMIF($D10:$D23,"Y",G10:G23)`

Modify it as follows:

```
=ROUNDUP(SUMIF($D10:$D23,"Y",G10:G23),0)
```

This allows for the rounding up of your SUMIF result to the next highest whole number with no decimal places.

You are now ready to replicate the formula for the remaining 59 months of the model by copying and pasting it to the right.

To complete this exercise, you must develop similar formulas in the two cells below your current cell and modify them to use column E and F as the *range* input. Columns E and F contain the (Y/N) selection for computers and work spaces. Remember to prepare for replication and rounding up.

You have completed the count formulas for this particular section. These formulas are replicated for each functional department.

EXERCISE 4-2. USING MICROSOFT EXCEL'S FIND AND REPLACE COMMAND TO LINK LARGE SPREADSHEETS QUICKLY

In the Staffing model, there are a large number of links between STAFF_CWS and STAFFPLAN_CWS. STAFF_CWS links its 60 monthly cells to yearly salary adjustment entries in STAFFPLAN_CWS. That's a lot of linking! The linking allows for quick spreads of salary adjustment modifications, but it is time consuming to set up.

- *Problem*: Financial models often involve large spreadsheets. Linking of cells can be time consuming and is subject to error.

- *Solution*: The Find and Replace command can be used as a powerful tool to modify formulas *en masse* when linking large spreadsheets.

In this exercise, we will use the Find and Replace command to relationally link 60 cells in STAFF_CWS, representing the 60 months of a five-year period, to five cells in STAFFPLAN_CWS, representing five yearly salary adjustment values.

1. Activate STAFF_CWS, and select the cell range G166:BO166. Press the Delete key to clear out this cell range.

2. Select cell G166. Type an equals sign indicating that you are creating a formula. Select the STAFFPLAN_CWS tab, and select cell B30. Press Enter. You are taken back to cell G166 in STAFF_CWS. You have created a link from STAFF_CWS G166 to STAFFPLAN_CWS B30 (see cell G166 in Figure 4-13).

	A	G
1		
2	**Period of Performance**	**YR 0**
164	CEO/President	
165	Base Compensation	=G10*$C10
166	Adjustment Factor	=STAFFPLAN_CWS!B30
167	Adjusted Compensation	=G165*G166
168	Bonus Plans	='COSM-BONUS_CWS'!E71
169	Tax and Burden Basis	=G167+G168
170		
171	Consultant	=G11*$C11

Figure 4-13. *Creating a link between STAFF_CWS G166 and STAFFPLAN_CWS B30*

3. Now, anchor the formula, which is =STAFFPLAN_CWS!B30, by making column B absolute. Do this by placing a dollar sign ($) in front of the "B" in the formula, resulting in the formula =STAFFPLAN_CWS!$B30. Next, copy and paste the formula in G166 across the range H166:BO166. Now, the identical formula resides in each cell of the range G10:BO10. We want to modify these formulas *en masse* to point to the correct cells in STAFFPLAN_CWS.

4. We must modify the formulas in each 12-month period to link to the appropriate year value in STAFFPLAN_CWS. Look at STAFFPLAN_CWS, and notice that the year values for YR 2 are in column D, YR 3 in column E, and so on. We will use the Find and Replace command to quickly make these changes in the formulas we just copied.

5. In STAFF_CWS, select the cell range T166:AE166 (the range of cells for YR 2). Click Find & Select. Click Find. The Find and Replace dialog box shown in Figure 4-14 will appear.

Figure 4-14. *Find and Replace dialog box*

6. We want to find all occurrences of $C in the 12 formulas in the selected range and change them to $D en masse. Type **$C** in the "Find what" field and **$D** in "Replace with", and click Replace All (see Figure 4-15). If the replacement works correctly, Excel will return a message that 12 replacements have been made, as shown in Figure 4-16. You have changed 12 formulas with one command.

Figure 4-15. *Using the Find and Replace dialog box to replace all occurrences of $C with $D*

■**Caution**   Find and Replace can be a dangerous command! *Save* before you use this command and check your results again. It will find and replace *all* occurrences. Make sure that you have given it the proper criteria and have the correct range selected. Note that you can *undo* the operation if you notice that the wrong data was changed.

Figure 4-16. *If the message does not say 12 replacements, something is wrong. We were trying to replace 12 monthly formulas.*

7. Repeat the process to change cells in the other year ranges: change YR 3 from $C to $E, YR 4 from $C to $F, and YR 5 from $C to $G.

EXERCISE 4-3. USING MICROSOFT EXCEL TO CREATE A DOUBLE-AXIS MANAGEMENT CHART

A common staffing chart used for management presentations displays total headcount and total cost of salaries and wages on one chart. One purpose of the chart is to show the relationship between the changes in headcount and the corresponding change in cost.

- *Problem*: The chart data series (data we want to chart), that is, the headcount and costs of wages, vary widely in value and are not conducive to charting together because of the wide variance in values between the headcount series and the dollar costs series. However, showing this data together on one chart is valuable because doing so clearly shows the relationship between headcount and cost.

- *Solution*: Create a double-axis chart plotting headcount on one axis and cost of salaries and wages on another. I have assumed that you have organized data that you want to chart into the STAFF_CHARTDAT file.

Follow these steps to create the chart:

1. Activate STAFF_CHARDAT, and select the data series (range B6:BJ11); see Figure 4-17.

	A	B	C	D	E	F	G	H	I	J
1								YR 1		
2			Jan	Feb	Mar	Apr	May	Jun	Jul	Aug
3	Chart Name									
4										
5	Total FTE - Total Cost									
6								YR 1		
7			Jan	Feb	Mar	Apr	May	Jun	Jul	Aug
8		GT Headcount	14.00	14.00	14.00	15.00	17.00	17.00	17.50	18.50
9		GT Adjust Salaries	$ 54,000	$ 54,000	$ 54,000	$ 59,333	$ 68,917	$ 68,917	$ 74,583	$ 78,917
10		GT Bonus Plan	$ -	$ -	$ -	$ -	$ -	$ -	$ -	$ -
11		GT COST	$ 54,000	$ 54,000	$ 54,000	$ 59,333	$ 68,917	$ 68,917	$ 74,583	$ 78,917
12										
13	Headcount by Department									
14								YR 1		
15			Jan	Feb	Mar	Apr	May	Jun	Jul	Aug
16		Executive	2.00	2.00	2.00	2.00	2.00	2.00	2.00	2.00
17		Biz OPS	0.50	0.50	0.50	0.50	0.50	0.50	0.50	0.50
18		Sales & MKT	1.25	1.25	1.25	1.25	2.25	2.25	2.75	2.75
19		Tech Ops	10.25	10.25	10.25	11.25	12.25	12.25	12.25	13.25
20		Total Headcount	14.00	14.00	14.00	15.00	17.00	17.00	17.50	18.50

Figure 4-17. *STAFF_CHARTDAT organizes and preformats your charting data as required.*

2. On the Home tab, select Insert followed by Line. Then, select the 2-D Line chart at the upper-left corner of the possible selections (see Figure 4-18). A line chart will appear within your spreadsheet, as shown in Figure 4-19.

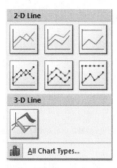

Figure 4-18. *Select the 2-D Line chart.*

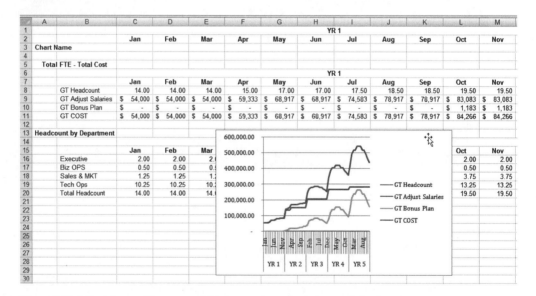

Figure 4-19. *A line chart will appear within your currently active worksheet.*

3. On the ribbon's Design tab, click Move Chart Location, select "New sheet", and click OK. A new chart sheet is inserted, and the chart will fill your screen. See Figures 4-20 and 4-21.

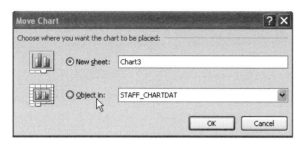

Figure 4-20. *Select "New sheet".*

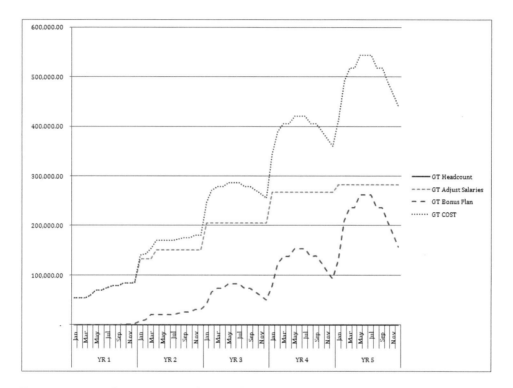

Figure 4-21. *A new sheet appears, and in it is the chart we have moved.*

4. Note that the GT Headcount line is a flat line at the bottom of the chart hugging the horizontal axis. We will select it for plotting on a secondary axis, thus making it visible. Select the Format Tab, and on the chart, select the GT Headcount line. The GT Headcount data series will become highlighted, as shown in Figure 4-22.

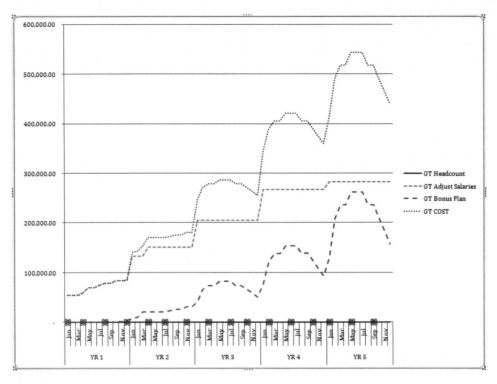

Figure 4-22. *Select the GT Headcount (series), and it will become highlighted.*

5. On the ribbon's Format tab, in the Current Selection group, click Format Selection. A Format Data Series dialog box will appear. Select Secondary Axis, and click Close (see Figure 4-23). The chart is modified to show two vertical axes, one for the headcount series and another for other cost series. (See Figure 4-24.)

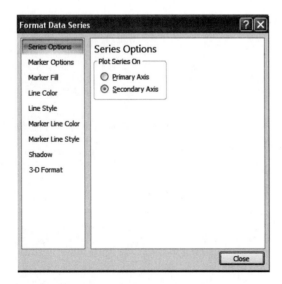

Figure 4-23. *Select Secondary Axis.*

6. Select Layout, and modify chart and axis titles as required.

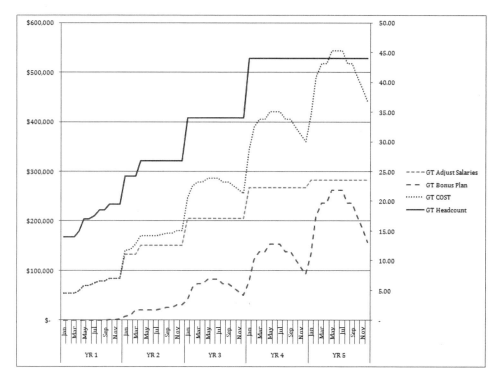

Figure 4-24. *A double-axis chart is created, ready for edit of vertical axis titles and header.*

Summary

STAFF models and documents the human resource dimension of the company business model (CBM). STAFF is developed by first determining the organizational structure that is required to implement the business strategy over the entire period of performance of the model. The organizational structure breaks the work out into functional departments and designates functional positions in each department.

The Staffing model utilizes the organizational structure and the listing of functional positions to compute the cost of salaries, wages, and benefits for the projected headcount. Costs are based on detailed assumptions of salary and benefit levels offered over the period of performance. STAFF also projects operating expenditures and capital expenditure requirements that are directly dependent on projected headcount.

When planning for staffing, you must consider the types of employee needed during each phase of the business. In the startup phase, you need visionaries. In the initial operating capability phase, you need pathfinders. In the full operating capability phase, you need homesteaders.

Here's the key question to ask yourself regarding staffing: what is your strategy for evolving your staff through the stages of company development?

■■■

CHAPTER 5

Sales and Revenue Model

In this chapter you will learn how to plan, create, and use the **Sales and Revenue (REV)** model. The REV model has been developed to demonstrate modeling of sales and revenue forecasts of Green Devil Control Systems (the Company) as set forth in its business case.

- You will learn how to model the Company's products and services and sales forecast.
- You will learn how to integrate the Company product configuration and sales forecast to develop the Company revenue forecast.
- You will learn how to develop an accounts receivable (AR) model that will be instrumental in developing cash flows in the Company's Statement of Cash Flows.

Business Thinking About Sales and Revenue

Startup technology companies struggle with sales and revenue forecasting. There are many unknowns, and many technology startups don't have time or money to fully research target markets. When thinking about sales and revenues, there are assumptions to be made and questions to be answered. As you exercise business thinking about sales and revenue, you must consider the following:

- *Value proposition*: What is the business idea?
- *Market*: What is the target market? Who is the economic buyer?
- *Product*: What products and services are offered?
- *Product availability*: When are the products and services available?
- *Sales strategy*: What is the strategy for selling into the market? What resources are being applied to the strategy and when?
- *Sales assumptions*: How much can be sold? How fast?

Validating the Value Proposition

The business idea is about delivering value, usually in the form of solving a problem or delivering a service. I will explain the value proposition in greater detail in Chapter 6 when I cover the Cost of Sales and Marketing (COSM) model. For the purposes of this chapter, we can assume that the company products and services deliver sufficient value to support sales forecast assumptions.

Analyzing the Market

The company value proposition is offered to a target market. What are the characteristics of this market? Suffice it to say that you cannot develop a sales forecast without a clear understanding of the nature and size of your market and your value proposition to this market. Who is the economic buyer? Who actually makes the decision to buy? Understanding your market and identifying the economic buyer is critical input to sales and revenue forecasting. Finally, what need is being fulfilled? Does the customer buy the value proposition?

Positioning the Product

To forecast sales and revenue, you must disaggregate (break down) products and services into components. Products and services can generate distinct revenue streams and usually have direct and identifiable variable costs associated with them. It is common for technology startups to offer product components that can be mixed and matched with different pricing scenarios to address the needs of their target markets.

Again, a primary criterion for identifying or breaking out a component is the ability to differentiate revenue streams or variable costs associated with the component. Components can also be viewed from a value proposition point of view; that is, components deliver differentiated and added value as part of the total value proposition. Components can be positioned to add incremental value to the total value proposition. Product components can be offered in different configurations and at different pricing combinations. You must understand the component structure before you can develop a sales and revenue forecasting model.

Pricing is critical to strategy. Pricing drives the customer toward the products and services that are most profitable for the company. A company may offer a wide variety of products and services. Differing products and services may deliver poor to excellent margins. Pricing strategy is utilized to drive customers toward the higher margin products and services.

Planning for Product Availability

When are the products and services commercially available? For a technology startup, this is an important question. It should be obvious that you cannot project sales or revenues until you know (or assume) the commercial release date of your products and services. Also, as products, services, and value proposition evolve over time, you must make adjustments to sales and revenue forecasts. Will version 2.0 drive more sales? What is the projected impact? Your business thinking should include considerations for the evolution of products and services over time. This evolution is a function of changing market demand and the company's ability to modify its product baseline within the constraints of its product development life cycle.

Crafting the Sales Strategy

How do you sell it? Once you have identified your target market, defined your value proposition, and defined and positioned your products and services, how do you actually close sales? The answer to this question is the foundation of your sales strategy. The sales strategy includes the entire sales and marketing life cycle from initial marketing to closing the deal. You must have a defined sales strategy in order to forecast sales. If you target a huge market with sparse sales resources, your sales forecast must reflect this fact. You must have a strategy for who will sell, how they will sell, and when they will sell. You must have a sales resource plan that is consistent with your sales forecast. Many times I have heard an entrepreneur say, "It's a billion-dollar market! All we have to do is get one percent market share!" What is your specific *boots on the ground* strategy for attaining the one percent, and when will you have it?

Making Sales Assumptions

With assumptions in hand for value proposition, market, product configuration and sales strategy, you can develop your actual sales forecast. I view sales forecasts as a continuum between opportunity and constraint. What are the most and least optimistic performances that your sales resources can deliver over time? What happens when you increase or reduce these resources? From a constraint standpoint, consider seasonality of demand and the company's ability to fulfill orders without a loss of quality. What is the potential for competitive push back and the ever-present customer inertia against change? The most important question you must be able to answer is, "What makes you think you can make this many sales in this time period?" If you can reasonably answer this question, you are ready to forecast sales.

The Products, Services, and Sales Strategy Business Case

Green Devil Control Systems is an early-stage technology startup. The Company develops energy monitoring and control systems for the residential and commercial building markets. It builds and sells the Green Devil Energy Control System (ECS). The Company founder and president has extensive experience and contacts in the home building industry. His partner and cofounder is an electrical engineer with extensive experience in electrical control systems and software.

The ECS Value Proposition

Utility and fuel costs are rising rapidly. Home and business owners are seeking ways to reduce utility costs. ECS is a patent-pending programmable hardware and software device that monitors and controls electricity usage on a circuit-by-circuit basis within a facility. ECS field tests have proved that it can reduce electricity usage by 10–20 percent annually using their Local Services (LS) software control and by 10–35 percent using the remote monitoring and advanced diagnostics and controls of Extended Services (ES).

The ECS Market

The initial target market for ECS is a subset of new housing starts, in particular, starts for *smart homes*: high-end homes that have integrated networking capability and advanced capabilities to electronically control the home environment including temperature, lighting, telecommunications, and security. Most smart homes are currently being built in the western United States, primarily in California, Nevada, and Arizona.

The ECS Product

ECS is installed on the facility side of the electrical breaker box. ECS allows for the mapping of all electric circuits extending into and utilized by the smart home. ECS is programmable and provides switching and control capabilities (like a programmable thermostat) for all individual electrical circuits. Electrical usage, down to the appliance level, can be programmed, controlled, and monitored. ECS is a network-addressable device that is designed to work seamlessly with wireless or wired local area networks (LANs) and to support Internet access.

ECS is offered with a choice of two software options. ECS can be purchased with LS or ES software.

- LS are the default software services provided with each installation of ECS and provide for a local web browser user interface to enable local setup and programming. LS provide one month of electricity usage diagnostics, require the purchase of LS software, and have a yearly software maintenance fee.

- ES provide Internet-based, secure, and remote setup, programming control, and diagnostics. ES also provide a suite of analysis tools and system setup tools for optimizing electricity usage, as well as demographic comparison data and unlimited usage data and statistics. ES require a yearly subscription.

LS and ES web browser user interfaces are highly intuitive, attractive, and easy to use.

ECS Product Availability

The Company projects initial commercial release and product availability in December of year one (YR 1).

ECS Sales Strategy

Early adopter presales will begin in October of YR 1. The western region has been chosen for initial product rollouts beginning in December of YR 1 supported by one director of sales and one field sales engineer.

ECS Sales Forecast Assumptions

To forecast sales and revenue, we must forecast the number of units that will be sold and the timing of those sales based on our understanding of market conditions. In this section, we look at the sales forecast in two dimensions:

- *Forecast of sales of units*: How many will we sell?

- *Forecast of monthly sales spread*: During the years of the forecast, how many sales units will be sold each month?

Forecasting of Sales of Units

The Company sales forecast is based on a projection of housing starts over the period of performance of the model (five years). It is assumed that all sales will be to builders of new smart homes, which constitute five to six percent of total new housing starts.

To forecast the target market, the number of housing starts is projected first, followed by the number of smart homes to be built (see Figure 5-1, from the REV-SALES-FCAST_CWS worksheet). Finally, we can derive an estimate of the percentage of target market sales by applying a percentage factor each year. This forecasting technique is simplified for the purposes of demonstrating the concept. As stated before, to give credibility to this type of forecast, you must be able to explain the specifics of how you will achieve the number of sales projected.

	A	B	C	D	E	F	G
1							
2				Top Level Sales Forecast Model			
3							
4		YR 1	YR 2	YR 3	YR 4	YR 5	Total
5							
6	Total Forecast Housing Starts	650,000	700,000	1,000,000	1,250,000	1,500,000	5,100,000
7	% Smart Homes		5%	6%	6%	6%	
8	Smart Homes Target Market		35,000	60,000	75,000	90,000	260,000
9	Yearly Target		3%	4%	5%	6%	
10	Sales Target	50	975	2,400	3,750	5,400	12,575

Figure 5-1. *REV-SALES-FCAST_CWS is an example of modeling a sales forecast based on a forecast of total housing starts.*

Forecasting the Monthly Sales Spread

After forecasting sales units, the timing or monthly spread of sales is considered. In the case of housing starts, there is a definite seasonal impact. In Figure 5-2, REV_CHART-SEASONAL charts historical housing start data. It shows that housing starts peak in June and August. Sales units in REV-SALES-FCAST_CWS (Figure 5-4) are spread to account for this seasonality.

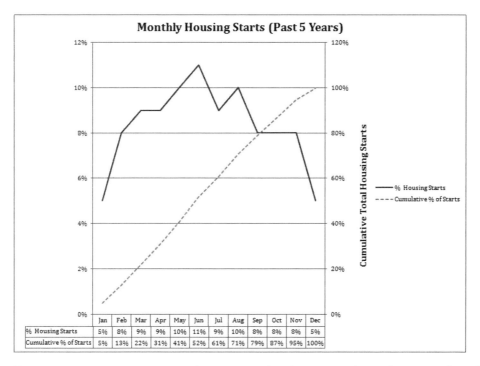

Figure 5-2. *REV_CHART-SEASONAL plots prior-year housing starts and cumulative starts from the past five years. This plot serves as a basis for spreading sales unit forecasts across the years of performance.*

Planning the Sales and Revenue Model

There are four steps to take when planning the REV model:

1. Define the product configuration and assumptions related to component revenue and costs.

2. Develop sales forecast assumptions.

3. Develop methods for forecasting revenue.

4. Develop cash collection assumptions based on revenue.

Defining the Product Configuration and Component Revenue and Cost Assumptions

Disaggregate products and services into components that may be modeled from a revenue and cost standpoint. After that, follow these steps:

1. Develop the following assumptions for each component for each year of the forecast model:

   - *List price*: List price of the product or service.
   - *Discount percent*: Percent discount assumed on each product component based on the year of sale. For example, assume a high level of discount in the first year (aggressive pricing) as the product is being introduced to the market.
   - *Sales price*: Assumed sale price after discount.
   - *Product and service options*: Options for selecting various product or services mixes.

2. Plan for the ability to change or model input parameters for the above assumptions.

Developing Sales Forecast Assumptions

Forecast sales units, and spread the sales units to create a detailed sales forecast. We should model this spreading capability to give us "what if" capability.

- Develop a method for forecasting sales by year and for modeling this forecast with the ability to consider "what if" at various levels of sales.
- Develop a method to spread the yearly forecast based on the month-to-month seasonality of other impacts to yearly sales.

Developing Methods for Forecasting Revenue

Develop pricing and revenue generation assumptions for product and services selections:

- Develop revenue generation assumptions for each component revenue source.
- Develop a method for modeling revenue sources from components.

■**Note** Software purchases generate two types of revenue: software purchase revenue and maintenance revenue. Software purchase revenue occurs once at purchase. Maintenance revenue is recurring.

Developing Cash Collection Assumptions Based on Revenue

Modeling sales forecasts also requires modeling cash collection assumptions. We must develop

- Cash collection assumptions
- A method for modeling AR and collections

Exploring the Building Blocks of the REV Model

When the planning is complete, build and test the model. The primary purpose of the REV model is to forecast company sales, revenues, and corresponding cash flow from revenues. Figure 5-3 is a high-level overview of the components and workings of the REV model. Arrows indicate primary data flow and linkages between worksheets.

■**Note** The Cost of Goods Sold (COGS) model is explained in detail in Chapter 6.

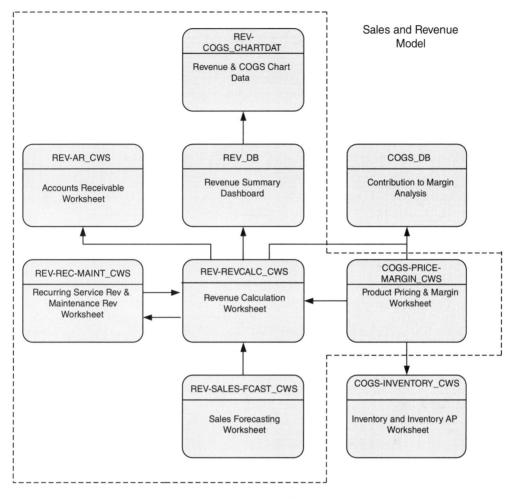

Figure 5-3. *This is the top-level design and process flow of the Sales and Revenue Model modules. The COGS model spreadsheet COGS-PRICE-MARGIN_CWS is shown within the dotted line that surrounds the key modules of the REV model because it provides important calculation information for the Sales and Revenue model. Arrows represent primary process and data flows between model components.*

The following section discusses the components of the model.

Understanding the Sales Forecasting Worksheet

The Sales Forecasting Worksheet, REV-SALES-FCAST_CWS, models the sales unit forecast and spreads the forecast across the months for each year of the period of performance of the model. This worksheet allows you to create "what if" forecasts and see the impact throughout the model. The impact from change in sales forecasts flows through the entire company business model (CBM).

■**Note** You can consider *what if* with this model, and the change in sales units will flow through the entire model. This is a powerful capability. The sales units forecast is a primary driver (critical success factor) for the CBM.

Forecasting Sales of Units

See Figure 5-4, which shows the model for total Company unit sales in REV-SALES-FCAST_CWS.

	YR 1	YR 2	YR 3	YR 4	YR 5	Total
Total Forecast Housing Starts	650,000	700,000	1,000,000	1,250,000	1,500,000	5,100,000
% Smart Homes		5%	6%	6%	6%	
Smart Homes Target Market		35,000	60,000	75,000	90,000	260,000
Yearly Target		3%	4%	5%	6%	
Sales Target	50	975	2,400	3,750	5,400	12,575

Monthly (Seasonal) Sales Spread Assumptions

	Jan	Feb	Mar	Apr	May	Jun	Jul	Aug	Sep	Oct	Nov	Dec	Total
% Housing Starts	5%	8%	9%	9%	10%	11%	9%	10%	8%	8%	8%	5%	100%
Cumulative % of Starts	5%	13%	22%	31%	41%	52%	61%	71%	79%	87%	95%	100%	

Yearly Sales Unit Forecast Spread

YR 1	Jan	Feb	Mar	Apr	May	Jun	Jul	Aug	Sep	Oct	Nov	Dec	Total
Spread										25%	25%	50%	100%
Units	-	-	-	-	-	-	-	-	-	13	13	25	51

YR 2	Jan	Feb	Mar	Apr	May	Jun	Jul	Aug	Sep	Oct	Nov	Dec	Total
Spread	3%	4%	8%	8%	8%	8%	8%	9%	10%	10%	12%	12%	100%
Units	29	39	78	78	78	78	78	88	98	98	117	117	976

YR 3	Jan	Feb	Mar	Apr	May	Jun	Jul	Aug	Sep	Oct	Nov	Dec	Total
Spread	5%	8%	9%	9%	10%	10%	10%	9%	9%	8%	7%	6%	100%
Units	120	192	216	216	240	240	240	216	216	192	168	144	2,400

Figure 5-4. *REV-SALES-FCAST_CWS is a top-level model to develop a sales unit forecast.*

Referring to Figure 5-4, the Company sales forecast is derived by multiplying the Total Forecast Housing Starts row by the % Smart Homes row, which equals the Smart Homes Target Market row. The sales forecast (Sales Target) is derived by multiplying the Smart Homes Target Market by the Yearly Target. This represents the percentage of the Smart Homes Target Market that the Company feels it can capture. As noted before, this is a simple model for the purpose of demonstrating the concept, and to use this approach, you must be able to show specifically how you will achieve the number of sales projected.

■**Note** Where do the assumptions come from? They come from market research and the entrepreneurs' feel for the market. How good are the assumptions? One measure of the entrepreneur is the ability to make this call.

Forecasting the Seasonal Sales Spread

The next portion of REV-SALES-FCAST_CWS provides a spread mechanism applied to the annual unit sales forecast, acknowledging a known seasonality factor for housing starts. In looking at past housing start data (refer to Figure 5-2), we can surmise housing starts peak in June and August and that this seasonality factor will proportionately affect sales volumes over the course of a year. Therefore, we will use the model to spread our sales unit forecasts to account for this seasonality. In Figures 5-5 and 5-6, you can see that in YR 3, YR 4, and YR 5 the projected sales units are spread using seasonal percentages. YR 2 is spread using discrete percentages that represent Company resource constraints that affect the sales process. Creating the spreadsheet in Figure 5-6 completes the modeling of the Company sales forecast.

■**Note** The decision to spread sales unit forecasts across the period of performance based on historical data is used primarily as an example. Practically speaking, many other factors influence this decision. For example, in Figure 5-2 the Cumulative % of Starts line is fairly constant in slope indicating that sales targets could be more evenly spread over the year.

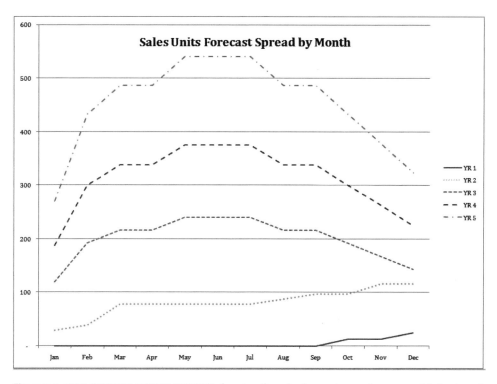

Figure 5-5. *REV_CHART-MONTH-SPREAD showing the sales forecast spread on a monthly basis each year.*

Yearly Sales Unit Forecast Spread					
YR 1	Jan	Feb	Mar	Apr	May	Jun
Spread						
Units	0	0	0	0	0	0
YR 2	Jan	Feb	Mar	Apr	May	Jun
Spread	3%	4%	8%	8%	8%	8%
Units	26	35	70	70	70	70
YR 3	Jan	Feb	Mar	Apr	May	Jun
Spread	5%	8%	9%	9%	10%	10%
Units	120	192	216	216	240	240
YR 4	Jan	Feb	Mar	Apr	May	Jun
Spread	5%	8%	9%	9%	10%	10%
Units	188	300	338	338	375	375
YR 5	Jan	Feb	Mar	Apr	May	Jun
Spread	5%	8%	9%	9%	10%	10%
Units	270	432	486	486	540	540

Figure 5-6. *Spreading the sales forecast across the period of performance using the seasonal monthly spread percentages completes the modeling of the sales unit forecast.*

Understanding the Product Pricing and Margin Worksheet

The Product Pricing and Margin Worksheet, COGS-PRICEMARGIN_CWS, breaks down Company products and services into components. The product offering is segregated into three parts providing two purchase options (as described in the "Considering the ECS Product" section earlier). Under both options, the original sale is an ECS unit, and the buyer is a home builder or contractor. So this worksheet allows for the input of differing pricing and product mix options on a yearly basis.

Under the first option, the home builder purchases and installs the ECS and loads the LS software. This provides the homeowner with a working ECS unit that is locally programmable. Under the second option, the home builder purchases and installs ECS and registers the unit by opening an ES account. The homeowner becomes a recurring customer of ES, paying for recurring ES service on a yearly basis and utilizing ES to remotely monitor and control the ECS device.

- *Option One*: Purchase ECS with LS software. This option generates three revenue streams:
  - Revenue from the purchase of ECS
  - One-time revenue from a software license for LS
  - Annual maintenance revenue for the LS software
- *Option Two*: Purchase ECS with ES. This option generates two revenue streams:
  - Revenue from the purchase of ECS
  - Annual subscription revenue for ES online services

■**Note** The selection of the LS versus ES option (the number of each option selected each year) is modeled by filling in the % Accepting Service row, in the COGS-PRICEMARGIN_CWS Worksheet, under the ES section for each year (see cell C20 in Figure 5-7). This selection is used to compute the number of ES versus LS customers. The relative number of ES customers should grow over the years, since it is the premier product choice.

The COGS-PRICEMARGIN_CWS Worksheet shown in Figure 5-7 provides the component breakdowns necessary to model the two options. It also provides the ability to model various pricing levels for each option on a yearly basis. You would expect to see pricing firm up and discounts decrease in this type of model as the Company matures and gains greater market share and brand recognition. This worksheet also models the cost of goods sold and profit margin, which will be discussed in greater detail in Chapter 6.

A	B	C	D	E	F	G	H
1		c	d	e	f	g	h
2		List Price	Discount	Sale-Price	COGS	Gross Margin $	Gross Margin %
3	YR 1						
4	Hardware						
5	Green Devil Energy Control System (ECS)	$ 5,000.00	60%	$ 2,000.00	$ 750.00	$ 1,250.00	63%
6	Test - Assembly, Packaging, Shipping	nc			$ 150.00	$ (150.00)	
7	Documentation	nc			$ 7.50	$ (7.50)	
8	Software/Media	nc			$ 1.50	$ (1.50)	
9	Total	$ 5,000.00		$ 2,000.00	$ 909.00	$ 1,091.00	55%
10							
11	Local Services (LS)						
12	Software - Local Services (LS)	$ 250	60%	$ 100.00		$ 100.00	100%
13	Yearly Maintenance (% List)	10%		$ 25		$ 25.00	$ 1.00
14							
15	Option 1 ES+ LS	$ 5,250.00		$ 2,100.00	$ 909.00	$ 1,191.00	57%
16							
17	Extended Services (ES)						
18	Account Setup	$ 25	90%	$ 2.50		$ 2.50	100%
19	Yearly Access Fee	$ 225.00	60%	$ 90.00		$ 90.00	100%
20	% Accepting Service	25%					
21							
22	Option 2 ES+ LS	$ 5,250.00		$ 2,092.50	$ 909.00	$ 1,183.50	57%

Figure 5-7. *COGS-PRICE-MARGIN_CWS provides component breakdowns necessary to model two product options. It also provides the ability to model pricing levels on a yearly basis.*

Exploring the Revenue Calculation Worksheet

The Revenue Calculation Worksheet, REV-REVCALC_CWS, shown in Figure 5-8, computes revenues, costs of goods sold, and profit margins by month by utilizing the sales unit forecast from REV-SALES-FCAST_CWS and pricing and option data from COGS-PRICEMARGIN_CWS. Monthly spreads from this worksheet are utilized by REV-REC-MAINT_CWS to calculate recurring maintenance revenue based on the number of LS option selections. Recurring ES subscription revenue is computed based on the number of ES option selections. The recurring revenue calculations derived from REV-REC-MAINT_CWS are combined with all other revenue calculations to create a master monthly revenue calculation for the model. This master monthly revenue calculation is graphically presented in Figure 5-9, REV_CHART-REVCHART.

A	B	N		O		P		Q	
2		Oct		Nov		Dec		Jan	
3									
4	Green Devil ECS								
5									
6	Units	$	13	$	13	$	25	$	29
7	List Price	$	65,000.00	$	65,000.00	$	125,000.00	$	159,500.00
8	Discount %		60%		60%		60%		25%
9									
10	Sale Revenue	$	26,000.00	$	26,000.00	$	50,000.00	$	119,625.00
11									
12	Cost of Goods Sold								
13									
14	Energy Monitor	$	9,750.00	$	9,750.00	$	18,750.00	$	19,575.00
15	Packaging	$	1,950.00	$	1,950.00	$	3,750.00	$	4,785.00
16	Documentation	$	97.50	$	97.50	$	187.50	$	195.75
17	Software/Media	$	19.50	$	19.50	$	37.50	$	39.15
18									
19	Total COGS	$	11,817.00	$	11,817.00	$	22,725.00	$	24,594.90
20									
21	Gross Margin $	$	14,183.00	$	14,183.00	$	27,275.00	$	95,030.10
22	Gross Margin %		55%		55%		55%		79%
23									
24	Software Options								
25									
26	% Accepting Service		25%		25%		25%		40%
27	Single User License Units		9.00		9.00		18.00		17.00
28	On-Line Service Units		4.00		4.00		7.00		12.00
29									
30	Single User License								
31									
32	List Price	$	2,250.00	$	2,250.00	$	4,500.00	$	4,250.00
33	Discount		60%		60%		60%		25%
34	License Revenue	$	900.00	$	900.00	$	1,800.00	$	3,187.50
35	Maintenance Revenue	$	225.00	$	225.00	$	450.00	$	425.00

Figure 5-8. *REV-REVCALC_CWS computes revenue, costs of goods sold, and profit margins by month by combining the sales unit forecast from REV-SALES-FCAST_CWS with pricing and option data from COGS-PRICEMARGIN_CWS.*

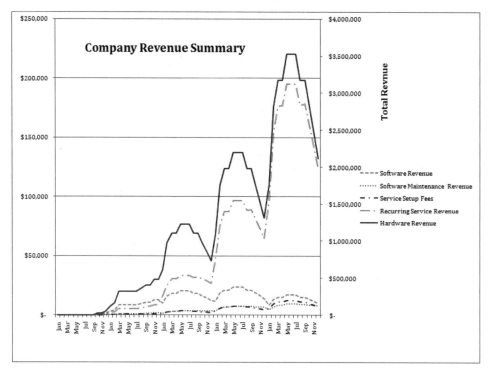

Figure 5-9. *REV_CHART-REVCHART shows the revenue forecast derived from REV-REVCALC_CWS.*

■**Note** Pay attention to the seasonal trends in revenue reflecting monthly spread assumptions from REV-SALES-FCAST_CWS, the Sales Forecasting Worksheet.

Exploring the Recurring Service Rev and Maintenance Rev Worksheet

REV-REC-MAINT_CWS calculates recurring revenue derived from both installation options:

> *Option one:* This option provides recurring revenue via yearly software maintenance fees. As shown in Figure 5-10, if LS are selected, the customer purchases a copy of the LS software. A yearly maintenance fee is charged for this software, as set forth in COGS-PRICEMARGIN_CWS. This fee is a percentage of the list price of the LS software, as modeled within COGS-PRICEMARGIN_CWS. The top half of REV-REC-MAINT_CWS performs a calculation of the recurring maintenance revenues that are generated by an increasing installed base of users.

	C	D	E	BG	BH	BI	BJ	BK	BL	BM
1										
2							YR 5			
3		Units	YR 0	Jun	Jul	Aug	Sep	Oct	Nov	Dec
130	Apr	438.00								
131	May	486.00								
132	Jun	486.00		486.00						
133	Jul	486.00			486.00					
134	Aug	438.00				438.00				
135	Sep	438.00					438.00			
136	Oct	389.00						389.00		
137	Nov	341.00							341.00	
138	Dec	292.00								292.00
139										
140	Total Monthly SubContracts	Units		962	962	875	879	789	704	613
141	Yearly Subscription Fee	$		202.50	202.50	202.50	202.50	202.50	202.50	202.50
142	Total Subscription Revenue	$		194,805.00	194,805.00	177,187.50	177,997.50	159,772.50	142,560.00	124,132.50

Figure 5-10. *REV-REC-MAINT_CWS calculates recurring maintenance revenue for the LS option.*

Option two: This option generates recurring revenue through yearly subscription fees for ES services. As shown in Figure 5-11, REV-REC-MAINT_CWS, if the ES option is selected, a yearly ES subscription fee is charged for the ongoing use of the service. The fee charged for this software is modeled in COGS-PRICEMARGIN_CWS. The bottom half of REV-REC-MAINT_CWS performs a calculation of the recurring maintenance revenues that are generated by an ever-growing base of subscribers.

■**Note** Exercise 5-1 at the end of this chapter provides a detailed explanation of the calculation of recurring maintenance revenues.

	C	D	E	BG	BH	BI	BJ	BK	BL	BM
1										
2							YR 5			
3	Susbscription	Units	YR 0	Jun	Jul	Aug	Sep	Oct	Nov	Dec
47	Jun	75.00		75.00						
48	Jul	75.00			75.00					
49	Aug	67.00				67.00				
50	Sep	67.00					67.00			
51	Oct	60.00						60.00		
52	Nov	52.00							52.00	
53	Dec	45.00								45.00
54	Jan	27.00								
55	Feb	43.00								
56	Mar	48.00								
57	Apr	48.00								
58	May	54.00								
59	Jun	54.00		54.00						
60	Jul	54.00			54.00					
61	Aug	48.00				48.00	*			
62	Sep	48.00					48.00			
63	Oct	43.00						43.00		
64	Nov	37.00							37.00	
65	Dec	32.00								32.00
66										
67	Monthly Contracts	Units		271.00	271.00	253.00	259.00	246.00	235.00	222.00
68	Maintenance Fee			35.00	35.00	35.00	35.00	35.00	35.00	35.00
69	Total Revenue	$		9,485.00	9,485.00	8,855.00	9,065.00	8,610.00	8,225.00	7,770.00

Figure 5-11. *REV-REC-MAINT_CWS calculates recurring subscription revenue for the ES option.*

Understanding the Accounts Receivable Worksheet

REV-AR_CWS, the Accounts Receivable Worksheet, develops an AR schedule based on revenue forecasts generated by the model and cash collection assumptions. This spreadsheet is an AR model. In the case of this model, and for purposes of simplicity, all cash due from revenue forecasted by the REV model is assumed to be collected in 30 days. The techniques in this model can be applied to multiple revenue streams and combined into a consolidated cash and AR position.

A SHORT TREATISE ON ACCOUNTS RECEIVABLE

When a company generates sales by providing products or services, it must either collect the total amount due in the current accounting period (month) or book or acknowledge an account receivable. Accounts receivable represent money owed to the company and are considered an asset. Accounts receivable balances are shown on the company balance sheet as a current asset.

When you create a financial model, you must forecast the amount and timing of cash collections from sales. This is accomplished, in part, by creating an AR model. The AR model is critical to forecasting cash flows, because it forecasts cash collections from expected sales.

■**Note** It is possible to have rapidly growing sales and no cash. You may have heard of companies going out of business because they grew too fast. Not being able to collect cash due can be a major contributing factor.

REV-AR_CWS utilizes revenues from REV-REVCALC_CWS and applies an assumed amount of cash (previous month sales are collected 100 percent in the next month) to the outstanding balance. As shown in Figure 5-12, the application of cash to the AR balance over time changes the AR balance from period to period. The change in the AR balances from period to period is a critical component of the computation of company cash flow.

	B	C	D	E	F	G	H
1							
2		YR 0	YR 1	YR 2	YR 3	YR 4	YR 5
3							
4	Total Sales	$ -	$ 108,225	$ 4,229,369	$ 12,873,651	$ 23,331,358	$ 37,595,013
5							
6	BEG AR Balance	$ -	$ -	$ 53,055	$ 508,238	$ 779,279	$ 1,406,578
7	+Additions to AR	$ -	$ 108,225	$ 4,229,369	$ 12,873,651	$ 23,331,358	$ 37,595,013
8	-Subtractions from AR	$ -	$ 55,170	$ 3,774,186	$ 12,602,610	$ 22,704,059	$ 36,738,208
9	ENDING AR Balance	$ -	$ 53,055	$ 508,238	$ 779,279	$ 1,406,578	$ 2,263,383
10	Change to AR	$ -	$ 53,055	$ 455,183	$ 271,041	$ 627,299	$ 856,805

Figure 5-12. *REV-AR_CWS presents an AR model developed from REV-REVCALC_CWS revenue calculations and assumes a 30-day cash collection cycle.*

■**Note** Exercise 5-2 at the end of this chapter gives a detailed explanation of the development of the AR model.

Exploring the Revenue Summary Dashboard

The Revenue Summary Dashboard (Figure 5-13) is a yearly summary of revenue, costs of goods sold, and gross margin developed by the REV model. It can be used as a management report.

	B	C	E		F		G		H		I
			YR 1		YR 2		YR 3		YR 4		YR 5
2											
3	Hardware Revenue		$	102,000	$	4,026,000	$	12,240,000	$	21,955,050	$	35,235,000
4											
5	Cost of Goods Sold		$	46,359	$	827,746	$	1,911,096	$	2,825,863	$	2,695,031
6	Gross Margin $		$	55,641	$	3,198,254	$	10,328,904	$	19,129,187	$	32,539,969
7	Gross Margin %			55%		79%		84%		87%		92%
8											
9	Software Revenue		$	3,600	$	108,375	$	203,150	$	235,305	$	168,840
10	Software Maintenance Revenue		$	900	$	15,350	$	39,250	$	81,095	$	99,855
11	Total Software Revenue		$	4,500	$	123,725	$	242,400	$	316,400	$	268,695
12											
13	Service Set Up Fees		$	375	$	9,950	$	36,100	$	75,150	$	121,600
14	Recurring Service Revenue		$	1,350	$	69,694	$	355,151	$	984,758	$	1,969,718
15	Total Service Revenue		$	1,725	$	79,644	$	391,251	$	1,059,908	$	2,091,318
16											
17	Net Revenue		$	61,866	$	3,401,623	$	10,962,555	$	20,505,495	$	34,899,981
18											
19	Green Devil ECS										
20	Units		$	51	$	976	$	2,400	$	3,753	$	5,400
21	List Price		$	255,000	$	5,368,000	$	14,400,000	$	24,394,500	$	39,150,000
22	Discount %			60%		25%		15%		10%		10%
23											
24	Sale Revenue		$	102,000	$	4,026,000	$	12,240,000	$	21,955,050	$	35,235,000
25											
26	Cost of Goods Sold										
27	Energy Monitor		$	38,250	$	658,800	$	1,458,000	$	2,051,953	$	2,657,205
28	Packaging		$	7,650	$	161,040	$	435,600	$	749,286	$	5,940
29	Documentation		$	383	$	6,588	$	14,580	$	20,520	$	26,572
30	Software/Media		$	77	$	1,318	$	2,916	$	4,104	$	5,314
31	Total COGS		$	46,359	$	827,746	$	1,911,096	$	2,825,863	$	2,695,031
32											
33	Gross Margin $		$	55,641	$	3,198,254	$	10,328,904	$	19,129,187	$	32,539,969
34	Gross Margin %			55%		79%		84%		87%		92%

Figure 5-13. *REV_DB, the Revenue Summary Dashboard, is a summary report of revenue, costs of goods sold, and gross margin data generated by the REV model.*

Exploring the Revenue and COGS Chart Data

The Revenue and COGS Chart Data Worksheet, REV-COGS_CHARTDAT (see Figure 5-14), preformats data needed for REV management and analysis charts. Charts are defined, and the data ranges for the chart are derived from linking back to the other worksheets in the model.

	B		L		M		N		O
1									
2	CHART NAME								
3									
4	REVENUE SUMMARY								
5			Oct		Nov		Dec		Jan
6									
7	Hardware Revenue		$	26,000	$	26,000	$	50,000	$	119,625
8	Software Revenue		$	900	$	900	$	1,800	$	3,188
9	Software Maintenance Revenue		$	225	$	225	$	450	$	425
10	Service Setup Fees		$	100	$	100	$	175	$	300
11	Recurring Service Revenue		$	360	$	360	$	630	$	2,025
12	Total Revenue		$	27,585	$	27,585	$	53,055	$	125,563

Figure 5-14. *REV-COGS_CHARTDAT preformats data needed for REV management and analysis charts.*

EXERCISE 5-1: USING MICROSOFT EXCEL TO FORECAST RECURRING SUBSCRIPTION REVENUE

The Company offers two product options. If customers select the Extended Services (ES) option, they are signing up for an online service offered by the Company.

- *Problem*: Online service revenues are recurring in nature. The ES option is billed to the customers once yearly on the anniversary date of their initial sign-up for the services. As the number of customers grows, computing recurring revenues from this source becomes necessary.

- *Solution*: Develop a recurring revenue model that computes recurring revenues from an increasing base of ES subscribers. This model is demonstrated in REV-REC-MAINT_CWS. The following exercise demonstrates how to build a model of this type.

Create a Monthly Count of Recurring Annual ES Subscriptions

1. Go to cell D79 within REV-REC-MAINT_CWS. This is the recurring revenue model portion of this spreadsheet.

2. As shown in Figure 5-15, create a vertical column of new ES subscription units by linking from REV-REVCALC_CWS. We are creating a vertical listing of the number of new subscription units that has been forecasted within REV-REVCALC_CWS. This vertical listing of data begins in cell D79 of REV-REC-MAINT_CWS.

	B	C	D
3	YR	Subscription	Units
78	Year	Month	
79	1	Jan	='REV-REVCALC_CWS'!$E$28
80	1	Feb	='REV-REVCALC_CWS'!$F$28
81	1	Mar	='REV-REVCALC_CWS'!$G$28
82	1	Apr	='REV-REVCALC_CWS'!$H$28
83	1	May	='REV-REVCALC_CWS'!$I$28
84	1	Jun	='REV-REVCALC_CWS'!$J$28
85	1	Jul	='REV-REVCALC_CWS'!$K$28
86	1	Aug	='REV-REVCALC_CWS'!$L$28
87	1	Sep	='REV-REVCALC_CWS'!$M$28
88	1	Oct	='REV-REVCALC_CWS'!$N$28
89	1	Nov	='REV-REVCALC_CWS'!$O$28
90	2	Dec	='REV-REVCALC_CWS'!$P$28
91	2	Jan	='REV-REVCALC_CWS'!$Q$28
92	2	Feb	='REV-REVCALC_CWS'!$R$28
93	2	Mar	='REV-REVCALC_CWS'!$S$28
94	2	Apr	='REV-REVCALC_CWS'!$T$28
95	2	May	='REV-REVCALC_CWS'!$U$28
96	2	Jun	='REV-REVCALC_CWS'!$V$28
97	2	Jul	='REV-REVCALC_CWS'!$W$28
98	2	Aug	='REV-REVCALC_CWS'!$X$28
99	2	Sep	='REV-REVCALC_CWS'!$Y$28
100	2	Oct	='REV-REVCALC_CWS'!$Z$28
101	2	Nov	='REV-REVCALC_CWS'!$AA$28
102	2	Dec	='REV-REVCALC_CWS'!$AB$28

Figure 5-15. *Link to and vertically reposition the number of new subscription units from REV-REVCALC_CWS.*

3. Create a replicable formula that copies the column D units (the number of ES service units purchased each month) into the same month for all subsequent years. See Figure 5-16 for a data view and Figure 5-17 for a formula view of this spread. Create your formula by placing a formula that grabs the current month new unit count (beginning with D79 or January of YR 1) and placing it in each corresponding month for the next five years. Follow the next steps to accomplish this:

x 228 op2. 1

a. Create the formula =$D79 in cell F79. Cell F79 corresponds to the month of January in YR 1. Copy this formula, =$D79, into the following cells: R79 (January YR 2), AD79 (January YR 3), AP79 (January YR 4), BB79 (January YR 5). The range R79:BM79 now has formulas in it that replicate the data that appears in Cell D79 each January of subsequent years.

b. Copy the range R79:BM79 to create a replicable formula that can be pasted in a cascading fashion throughout the calculation matrix of the model.

	B	C	D	O	P	Q	R	S	T	U	V	W	X	Y	Z	AA	AB
3	YR	Subscription	Units	Oct	Nov	Dec	Jan	Feb	Mar	Apr	May	Jun	Jul	Aug	Sep	Oct	Nov
88	1	Oct	4.00	4.00												4.00	
89	1	Nov	4.00		4.00												4.00

Figure 5-16. *Create a replicable formula that spreads or counts the units from column D annually, that is, repeats the number in column D each year in the same month for all out years.*

	B	C	D	O	P	Q	R	S	T	U	V	W	X	Y	Z	AA	AB
3	YR	Subscription	Units	Oct	Nov	Dec	Jan	Feb	Mar	Apr	May	Jun	Jul	Aug	Sep	Oct	Nov
88	1	Oct	=REV-REVCALC_CWS1$N$28	=$D88												=$D88	
89	1	Nov	=REV-REVCALC_CWS1$O$28		=$D89													=$D89

Figure 5-17. *Formula view of Figure 5-16*

c. Cascade the formulas (see Figure 5-18) by copying them in a cascading fashion over the period of performance of the model. To do this, paste the formula range R79:BM79 into cell G80 to replicate the formula across five years beginning in February of YR 1. Next, paste the formula range R79:BM79 into cell H81 to replicate the formula across five years beginning in March of YR 1. Repeat this cascading copy process (copy the range one cell down and one cell to the right) until you have filled the entire matrix. The last copy of range R79:BM79 is into cell BM138. You will have a lot of formulas hanging over to the right of column BM as a result of this pasting exercise. To clean up the worksheet, clear out or delete all data to the right of column BM.

	B	C	D	AB	AC	AD	AE	AF	AG	AH	AI	AJ
1												
2												
3	YR	Subscription	Units	Nov	Dec	Jan	Feb	Mar	Apr	May	Jun	Jul
88	1	Oct	4.00									
89	1	Nov	4.00	4.00								
90	2	Dec	7.00		7.00							
91	2	Jan	12.00			12.00						
92	2	Feb	16.00				16.00					
93	2	Mar	32.00					32.00				
94	2	Apr	32.00						32.00			
95	2	May	32.00							32.00		
96	2	Jun	32.00								32.00	
97	2	Jul	32.00									32.00
98	2	Aug	36.00									
99	2	Sep	40.00									
100	2	Oct	40.00									
101	2	Nov	47.00	47.00								
102	2	Dec	47.00		47.00							
103	3	Jan	72.00			72.00						
104	3	Feb	116.00				116.00					
105	3	Mar	130.00					130.00				
106	3	Apr	130.00						130.00			
107	3	May	144.00							144.00		
108	3	Jun	144.00								144.00	
109	3	Jul	144.00									144.00

Figure 5-18. *Copy the formulas created in the previous steps in a cascading fashion.*

Summarize and Price Recurring Subscription Units

While completing the steps to summarize and price recurring subscription units, refer to Figure 5-19.

1. At the bottom of the cascading formula area, summarize the monthly number of subscription units from the previous section for each month of the five-year period.

2. Multiply the number of units by the corresponding annual subscription rate (linking to the annual rate in COGS-PRICE-MARGIN_CWS).

	B	C	D	BG	BH	BI	BJ	BK	BL	BM
1										
2							YR 5			
3	YR	Subscription	Units	Jun	Jul	Aug	Sep	Oct	Nov	Dec
120	4	Jun	300.00	300.00						
121	4	Jul	300.00		300.00					
122	4	Aug	271.00			271.00				
123	4	Sep	271.00				271.00			
124	4	Oct	240.00					240.00		
125	4	Nov	211.00						211.00	
126	4	Dec	180.00							180.00
127	5	Jan	243.00							
128	5	Feb	389.00							
129	5	Mar	438.00							
130	5	Apr	438.00							
131	5	May	486.00							
132	5	Jun	486.00	486.00						
133	5	Jul	486.00		486.00					
134	5	Aug	438.00			438.00				
135	5	Sep	438.00				438.00			
136	5	Oct	389.00					389.00		
137	5	Nov	341.00						341.00	
138	5	Dec	292.00							292.00
139										
140		Total Monthly SubContracts		962	962	875	879	789	704	613
141		Yearly Subscription Fee		202.50	202.50	202.50	202.50	202.50	202.50	202.50
142		Total Subscription Revenue		194,805.00	194,805.00	177,187.50	177,997.50	159,772.50	142,560.00	124,132.50

Figure 5-19. *Summarize the monthly number of subscription units and multiply the number of units by the annual subscription rate by linking to the annual rate in COGS-PRICE-MARGIN_CWS.*

Congratulations. You have completed the forecasting of recurring subscription revenue based on forecasted subscription units.

EXERCISE 5-2: USING MICROSOFT EXCEL TO MODEL ACCOUNTS RECEIVABLE (AR)

The Company model forecasts revenue from product purchase options. It is assumed that cash will not be immediately collected from sales.

- *Problem*: The Company business model requires cash flows from revenues to be projected.

- *Solution*: Develop an AR model that will project cash collections and provide downstream data for the Company statement of cash flows and the Company balance sheet.

Develop Cash Collection Assumptions

In the case of this model, it is assumed that all revenues are collected 30 days after the sale.

Develop the AR model

The AR model is simple in concept. When revenue is generated, it adds to the AR balance. When cash is collected, the AR balance is reduced. An AR model utilizes revenue inputs as the basis for creating the AR balance and cash collection assumptions for the reduction in the AR balance. Changes in the AR balance are used to compute actual cash flow.

The following are the components of the AR model. Refer to Figures 5-20 and 5-21 for a data view and a formula view of the relationships between these components.

- *BEG AR Balance*: The beginning AR balance is either zero, in the first month, or equal to the previous month's ending AR balance.

- *+Additions to AR*: Additions to AR equal the total sales in the current month (derived from REV-REVCALC_CWS).

- *-Subtractions from AR*: Subtractions are *important!* This is where cash collection assumptions show up. Note that the formulas are pointing to the previous month's additions to AR (or revenue). In other words, the assumption is that all revenue from the previous month is collected in the next month (within 30 days).

- *Ending AR Balance*: The ending AR Balance equals the beginning balance plus the additions to AR minus the subtractions from AR.

- *Change to AR*: The change to AR equals the current month's AR minus the prior month's AR.

	B	M	N	O	P	Q	R
12		Oct	Nov	Dec	Jan	Feb	Mar
13							
14	Total Sales	$ 27,585	$ 27,585	$ 53,055	$ 125,563	$ 168,863	$ 337,725
15							
16	BEG AR Balance	$ -	$ 27,585	$ 27,585	$ 53,055	$ 125,563	$ 168,863
17	+Additions to AR	$ 27,585	$ 27,585	$ 53,055	$ 125,563	$ 168,863	$ 337,725
18	-Subtractions from AR	$ -	$ 27,585	$ 27,585	$ 53,055	$ 125,563	$ 168,863
19	ENDING AR Balance	$ 27,585	$ 27,585	$ 53,055	$ 125,563	$ 168,863	$ 337,725
20	Change to AR	$ 27,585	$ -	$ 25,470	$ 72,508	$ 43,300	$ 168,863

Figure 5-20. *The Company's AR model*

	B	M	N	O	P
12		Oct	Nov	Dec	Jan
13					
14	Total Sales	='REV-REVCALC_CWS'!N41	='REV-REVCALC_CWS'!O41	='REV-REVCALC_CWS'!P41	='REV-REVCALC_CWS'!Q41
15					
16	BEG AR Balance	=L19	=M19	=N19	=O19
17	+Additions to AR	=M14	=N14	=O14	=P14
18	-Subtractions from AR	=L17	=M17	=N17	=O17
19	ENDING AR Balance	=M16+M17-M18	=N16+N17-N18	=O16+O17-O18	=P16+P17-P18
20	Change to AR	=M17-M18	=N17-N18	=O17-O18	=P17-P18

Figure 5-21. *The formulas that make up the AR model*

■**Note** The change in AR balance from month to month measures a portion of the cash flow of the Company. Changes in AR balance are used to measure the portion of cash flow that is related to cash collections for revenue.

For simplicity, this model assumes that all revenue is handled in the same way regarding cash collection. In reality, different types of revenue streams have different collection assumptions. These differences can be modeled by creating a separate AR model for each revenue stream, each having a different cash collection assumption. The results can be combined into one AR number or shown separately.

Summary

Developing a sales and revenue forecast for your company requires serious business thinking about the value proposition, sales strategy, and target market, as well as the products and services and their pricing and availability. In this chapter, we covered the product options offered by Green Devil Control Systems and developed pricing and assumptions for those various product options. We developed a sales forecasting model, and using our pricing assumptions and sales forecast, we developed a revenue forecast including forecasts for recurring revenue streams. Finally, we developed an AR model to forecast cash receipts from revenues.

A viable sales and revenue model requires an accurate understanding of the characteristics of the target market and a clear strategy for selling into the market. If this understanding is correct, you stand a good chance of developing a useable model.

Here's a key question regarding your sales and revenue forecast: what makes you think you can make this many sales in this time period?

If you can reasonably answer this question, you are ready to forecast sales.

■■■

CHAPTER 6

Cost of Goods Sold and Inventory Model

In this chapter, you will learn how to plan, create, and use the Cost of Goods Sold and Inventory (COGS) model. The COGS model is closely related to the Sales and Revenue (REV) model discussed in Chapter 5. COGS demonstrates the modeling of the cost of goods sold and inventory requirements for Green Devil Control Systems as set forth in its business case, including modeling of variable costs, contributions to margins, inventory, and accounts payable associated with inventory.

In this chapter, you will learn how to

- Model variable costs associated with products and services and forecast and assess product and services contribution to margin.

- Develop an inventory model associated with the hardware component of the product.

- Model and forecast accounts payable (AP) associated with company inventory requirements.

Using Business Thinking About COGS

The beauty of *pure* software company business models is that there is no cost of goods sold associated with the sale of the product or service. In theory, the gross margin (revenue less cost of goods sold) on a software sale is 100 percent. That's a pretty good margin. If you offer software or online services, you will sell the product or service with little, if any, variable cost associated with each sale.

If only business could be that simple. A large segment of the high-tech world either provides hardware and software or depends on a hardware component for service offerings. Any book on financial modeling for high-tech startups must address scenarios in which there are hardware components to the offering. Our business case company, Green Devil Control Systems, provides a hardware/software combination as its product offering.

Defining "Cost of Goods Sold"

"Cost of goods sold" is a self-defining term: it is the variable cost associated with a unit of sale. Simple enough, right? Wrong. The variable cost associated with a unit of sale can be composed of a number of cost components, each with a different relationship to the unit sold. To determine the cost of goods sold, you must define the cost components of any particular unit of sale and define the variable part of the relationship of each component to the sales unit. For instance, is it a one-to-one relationship? For each unit sold, is there one unit of cost? Or is the relationship proportional, or something else? Your business thinking must include an understanding and definition of the relationship of cost of goods sold to your sales units. This book is not a treatise on cost accounting, but I will cover this subject sufficiently to set you on a course for understanding a COGS model.

■**Note** *Variable cost* refers to items of cost that vary, in total, directly or proportionately with volume. For example, the costs of lemons and sugar are variable costs to the total cost of lemonade in a lemonade stand.

Defining "Inventory"

For the purposes of the business case and COGS model, we will define *inventory* as the amount of finished goods that the company has available to sell. If a product or service has a physical (hardware) component to it, there will likely be a requirement to keep an inventory of items in stock. Inventory is either self-manufactured, purchased, or a combination thereof. In any case, purchasing, stocking, or carrying inventory has a cost associated with it. Inventory and inventory management are subjects unto themselves.

Your business thinking regarding inventory should answer two fundamental questions:

- How much inventory do I need on hand to support my sales forecast? How do factors like parts availability, manufacturing cycle, and shipping time influence my need for inventory on hand?

- What is the cost of carrying the required amount of inventory?

Inventory management, which has a complete life cycle and requires much greater analysis than that posed by these questions, is outside the scope of the COGS model.

■**Note** If you want to see inventory management best practices in action, take a look at Wal-Mart's inventory and supply chain practices. Those low prices come directly from its status as one of the best inventory and supply chain management companies in the world. Google "Wal-Mart supply chain best practices."

Assessing Profitability and Contribution to Margin

Business thinking about COGS has one primary objective: assessing the profitability of products and services from a gross margin perspective.

■**Note** *Gross profit* is what remains from sales after a company pays out the cost of goods sold. Gross profit is also called *contribution margin*. Gross profit margin is expressed as a percentage and is computed by dividing gross profit by the sales price. Gross profit is a measure of the profitability of the product itself, before other company expenses are applied, and is profit before salaries, wages, and other operating expenses of the company (expenses not directly related to the production of the product).

It is important for a company to understand the contribution margin from each of its products and services. For instance, if a company is selling different options or combinations of hardware and software, which option provides the higher contribution to margin? One product option may be selling at higher volumes but not contributing sufficient margin to justify its continued existence. Business thinking about the COGS model should include creating a model that performs an analysis of margin contribution. The sales strategy should support the optimization of gross margin by emphasizing those products that contribute the most to margin or profit. You are in business to make money, right?

To understand profitability or margin contributions, you must break down the company product offering into basic components and compute the gross margin for each of the components.

THE SEARCH FOR MARGIN

A recent client engaged me to assess its profitability. Sales were growing, but the bottom line remained the same. The principals told me that their best margins were coming from Internet sales. A margin contribution analysis showed that Internet sales were discounted so heavily that, despite their rapid growth, they were contributing less to the bottom line of the company than other sales channels. So analysis revealed that this was the root cause for the poor growth in bottom-line profits.

 This example epitomizes the joke in which the consultant says, "Bad news; we are losing a nickel on each unit sold." And the owner replies, "Don't worry we'll make it up in volume."

Considering the Green Devil Control Systems Product Offering and Sales Strategy

Recall that Green Devil Control Systems is an early-stage technology startup. The Company develops energy monitoring and control systems for residential building markets. It builds and sells the Green Devil Energy Control System (ECS). The Company president is well known and has extensive experience and contacts in the home-building industry. His partner is a graduate-level electrical engineer. She has extensive experience in developing smart control systems.

Product

ECS is a patent-pending programmable hardware and software device that monitors and controls electricity usage on a circuit-by-circuit basis within a facility. ECS is installed on the facility side of the electrical breaker box.

 ECS allows for the mapping of all electric circuits extending into and utilized by the facility. It is particularly targeted for the smart home market. ECS is programmable and provides switching and control capabilities (like a programmable thermostat) for all individual electrical circuits within a facility. Electrical usage, at the appliance level, can be programmed, controlled, and monitored. ECS is a network-addressable device designed to work seamlessly with wireless or wired LANs and to support Internet access.

 ECS can be purchased with Local Services (LS) or Extended Services (ES) software options, both of which have web browser user interfaces that are highly intuitive, attractive, and easy to use. LS are the default with each installation of ECS and provide for a local web browser user interface to enable local setup and programming. LS provide one month of electricity usage diagnostics.

 ES provide Internet-based, secure, remote setup, programming control, and diagnostics. ES also provide a suite of analysis tools and system setup tools for optimizing electricity usage, as well as demographic comparison data and unlimited usage data and statistics.

Product Development

The Company product development strategy (see Figure 6-1) includes the following major milestones and value events:

- *Prototype development*: Low-level breadboard prototype development and testing will be completed by March of year one (YR 1).

- *Production prototype development*: Ten production prototypes will be built and completed by May of YR 1. Five production prototypes will be used for field testing, and five will be used for compliance (lab) and safety testing.

- *Field, compliance, and safety testing*: There will be two iterations of field and compliance testing, which will include final modifications to the production prototype. Testing will be completed by September of YR 1.

- *Manufacturing design*: Manufacturing design will begin in May of YR 1 and be completed in November of YR 1.

- *Manufacturing*: Manufacturing will be outsourced and will begin in November of YR 1.

- *Product release*: The ECS product (with both software options) will be available in December of YR 1.

- *Software*: LS software and ES software will be developed in an integrated plan along with the product development schedule.

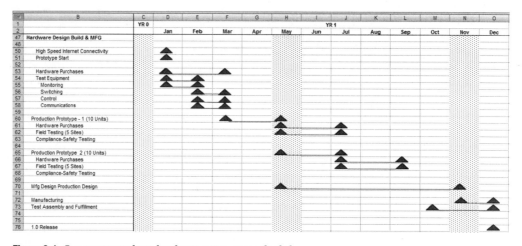

Figure 6-1. *Company product development master schedule*

Making Product Availability Fulfillment and Inventory Assumptions

The Company projects commercial release and product availability in December of YR 1. The manufacturer will ship components to the Company, where they will be inventoried, assembled, and tested prior to shipment to the customer. The Company plans to order and keep in stock (in inventory) a three-month supply of ECS units.

Product Pricing and Variable Cost

The Company projects first-year product offering price and variable costs as follows:

- The list price for the ECS product is $5,000.

- The list price for the LS software is $250.

- The list price for ES is $225 yearly with a $25 setup fee.

- The first-year cost per unit from the manufacturer is $750.

- The first-year assembly and testing cost for each unit is $150 per unit.

- The first-year documentation and software media cost is $9 per unit.

Using the COGS model, we will forecast and modify pricing and variable costs on a yearly basis.

Planning the COGS Model

The purpose of the COGS model is to forecast cost of goods sold and corresponding operating margins. COGS also models inventory and AP. The following section discusses the components of the model and how they work to develop this forecast:

- Define product configuration assumptions related to component revenue and costs.
- Develop cost of goods sold and profitability assumptions for each year.
- Develop inventory assumptions.
- Develop an inventory AP model and assumptions.

Defining Product Configuration Assumptions Related to Component Revenue and Costs

Break down the total product offering into components that may be modeled from a revenue and cost standpoint. Develop assumptions for each component for each year of the forecast model:

- *List price*: Listed price of the product or service
- *Discount percentage*: Percentage of the discount assumed on all product components based on the year of sale
- *Sale price*: Assumed sale price after discount
- *Product mix options*: Options for selecting various product or services mixes

Plan for the ability to change or model input parameters for the preceding assumptions.

■**Note** Assume a high level of discount in the first year (aggressive pricing) as the product is being introduced to the market.

Developing Cost of Goods Sold and Profitability Assumptions for Each Year

For each year of the forecast, develop price, cost of goods sold, and profitability assumptions for components of the product offering:

- Develop pricing assumptions for each product offering and pricing discount assumptions based on market acceptance assumptions. For example, you would expect early adopter sales to be deeply discounted. Assuming market acceptance, pricing could increase over time or hold steady with decreasing cost of goods sold, generating higher margins.
- Develop cost of goods sold assumptions. Will cost of goods sold increase or decrease over the years? How much and why?

Developing Inventory Assumptions

Develop assumptions for the amount of inventory that will be required to support the sales forecast. The amount of inventory required is determined by a number of factors. The primary factor is lead time consideration for supply chain events prior to the ability to ship the product. There is a supply chain behind the final availability of products. The timing of this chain and possible interruptions must be considered, versus forecast of sales demand, to determine the amount of inventory needed.

■**Note**   For our example, the Company assumes that it will purchase and have on hand (in stock) sufficient inventory to supply the next forecasted 90 days of sales.

Developing an Inventory AP Model and Assumptions

Now that we have made inventory need assumptions, that is, the amount of physical inventory that we plan to have on hand at any given time, we must plan for the payment for the inventory:

- Develop assumptions for payments for inventory purchases. In other words, how long will the Company take to pay for the purchase of inventory?

- Develop a method for modeling AP for purchased inventory. AP assumptions are determined primarily by the relationship with the vendor. Well-managed companies will negotiate the best terms possible to better manage their cash.

■**Note**   You would expect to pay a finance charge on inventory purchases that are not paid in the current month. For the purpose of this model, no finance charges are assumed.

Examining the COGS Model's Building Blocks

When the planning is complete, build and test the model. The primary purpose of the COGS model is to forecast cost of goods sold, profitability, and margin contribution of the product offering. COGS also forecasts inventory usage and develops the inventory and inventory AP models. Figure 6-2 shows a high-level overview of the components and workings of the COGS model.

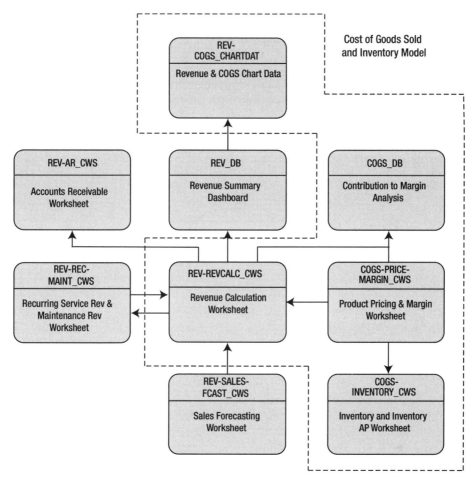

Figure 6-2. *Top-level design and process flow of the COGS model. Model components shown within the dashed line are the key components of the COGS model. Arrows indicate primary data and process flows.*

Understanding the Product Pricing and Margin Worksheet

The Product Pricing and Margin Worksheet, COGS-PRICEMARGIN_CWS, breaks down the Company product offering into components. It provides a method for modeling price and cost of goods sold, thus providing the basis for a forecast of contribution margin. The Company product offering has three components, and two purchase options are offered. The common component is the ECS device, and there are two software options available with it.

COGS-PRICEMARGIN_CWS provides the ability to model pricing, discounts, and cost of goods sold on a yearly basis for ECS, LS software, and the ES subscription service. COGS-PRICEMARGIN_ CWS, combined with unit sales forecasts from REV-SALES-FCAST_CWS, allows the Company to forecast revenues, cost of revenues, and gross margin over the period of performance of the model, taking into consideration changes in pricing and costs on a yearly basis. Referring to Figure 6-3, note the first-year pricing and cost assumptions for the Company product offering, as summarized in the next sections.

Making ECS Hardware Assumptions

The following are the assumptions for the ECS hardware:

- *List price*: The price of ECS is $5,000.

- *Discount*: All sales in YR 1 will be discounted 60 percent to provide aggressive pricing for early market penetration. Note that maintenance fees are computed as a percentage of list price, thus they carry forward any list price discount applied to the software.

- *Cost of goods sold*: The cost to purchase the ECS from the manufacturer is $750 per unit. The cost per unit to test, assemble, pack, and ship the unit to a customer is $150 per unit. Costs for documentation and other software and media are $9 per unit.

- *Gross margin*: The gross margin for the ECS unit, given the aggressive first-year pricing, is 63 percent. The total gross margin after all variable costs is 55 percent.

Making LS Software Assumptions

The following are the assumptions for the LS software:

- *List price*: The price for the LS software that comes standard with each ECS unit is $250. A yearly maintenance fee of 10 percent of the list price (when purchased) of the software will be charged on the annual anniversary date of the software purchase.

- *Discount*: All sales in YR 1 will be discounted 60 percent to provide aggressive pricing for early market penetration. Note that maintenance fees are computed as a percentage of list price, thus they carry forward any list price discount to the software.

- *Cost of goods sold*: There is no cost of goods sold for this software. The software media is included in the cost of goods sold for the ECS unit.

- *Gross margin*: The gross margin for the LS software, given no cost of goods sold, is 100 percent.

Making ES Subscription Assumptions

The following are the assumptions for the ES subscription:

- *List price*: The price for the annual ES subscription is $225. There is an additional $25 setup fee.

- *Discount*: All sales in YR 1 will be discounted 90 percent to provide aggressive pricing for early market penetration.

- *Cost of goods sold*: There is no cost of goods sold for this software, because it is downloaded with the subscription. There is no media associated with it.

- *Gross margin*: The gross margin for the ES software, given no cost of goods sold, is 100 percent.

	A	B	C	D	E	F	G	H
1			c	d	e	f	g	h
2			List Price	Discount	Sale-Price	COGS	Gross Margin $	Gross Margin %
3		YR 1						
4		Hardware						
5		Green Devil Energy Control System (ECS)	$ 5,000.00	60%	$ 2,000.00	$ 750.00	$ 1,250.00	63%
6		Test - Assembly, Packaging, Shipping	nc			$ 150.00	$ (150.00)	
7		Documentation	nc			$ 7.50	$ (7.50)	
8		Software/Media	nc			$ 1.50	$ (1.50)	
9		Total	$ 5,000.00		$ 2,000.00	$ 909.00	$ 1,091.00	55%
10								
11		Local Services (LS)						
12		Software	$ 250	60%	$ 100.00		$ 100.00	100%
13		Yearly Maintenance (% List)	10%		$ 25		$ 25.00	$ 1.00
14								
15		Option 1 ES+ LS	$ 5,250.00		$ 2,100.00	$ 909.00	$ 1,191.00	57%
16								
17		Extended Services (ES)						
18		Account Setup	$ 25	90%	$ 2.50		$ 2.50	100%
19		Yearly Access Fee	$ 225.00	60%	$ 90.00		$ 90.00	100%
20		% Accepting Service	25%					
21								
22		Option 2 ES+ LS	$ 5,250.00		$ 2,092.50	$ 909.00	$ 1,183.50	57%

Figure 6-3. *COGS-PRICEMARGIN_CWS, the Product Pricing and Margin Worksheet, provides for the modeling of price and cost of goods sold for product offerings by year.*

Understanding the Revenue Calculation Worksheet

The Revenue Calculation Worksheet, REV-REVCALC_CWS, computes revenues, cost of goods sold, and profit margins by month by combining the sales unit forecast from REV-SALES-FCAST_CWS with pricing and option data from COGS-PRICEMARGIN_CWS. See Figure 6-4.

	A	B	N	O	P	Q	R
2			Oct	Nov	Dec	Jan	Feb
3							
4		Green Devil ECS					
5							
6		Units	13	13	25	29	39
7		List Price	$ 65,000.00	$ 65,000.00	$ 125,000.00	$ 159,500.00	$ 214,500.00
8		Discount %	60%	60%	60%	25%	25%
9							
10		Sale Revenue	$ 26,000.00	$ 26,000.00	$ 50,000.00	$ 119,625.00	$ 160,875.00
11							
12		Cost of Goods Sold					
13							
14		Energy Monitor	$ 9,750.00	$ 9,750.00	$ 18,750.00	$ 19,575.00	$ 26,325.00
15		Packaging	$ 1,950.00	$ 1,950.00	$ 3,750.00	$ 4,785.00	$ 6,435.00
16		Documentation	$ 97.50	$ 97.50	$ 187.50	$ 195.75	$ 263.25
17		Software/Media	$ 19.50	$ 19.50	$ 37.50	$ 39.15	$ 52.65
18							
19		Total COGS	$ 11,817.00	$ 11,817.00	$ 22,725.00	$ 24,594.90	$ 33,075.90
20							
21		Gross Margin $	$ 14,183.00	$ 14,183.00	$ 27,275.00	$ 95,030.10	$ 127,799.10
22		Gross Margin %	55%	55%	55%	79%	79%
23							
24		Software Options					
25							
26		% Accepting Service	25%	25%	25%	40%	40%
27		Single User License Units	9.00	9.00	18.00	17.00	23.00
28		On-Line Service Units	4.00	4.00	7.00	12.00	16.00
29							
30		Single User License					
31							
32		List Price	$ 2,250.00	$ 2,250.00	$ 4,500.00	$ 4,250.00	$ 5,750.00
33		Discount	60%	60%	60%	25%	25%
34		License Revenue	$ 900.00	$ 900.00	$ 1,800.00	$ 3,187.50	$ 4,312.50
35		Maintenance Revenue	$ 225.00	$ 225.00	$ 450.00	$ 425.00	$ 575.00

Figure 6-4. *REV-REVCALC_CWS computes revenue, cost of goods sold, and profit margins by month by combining the sales unit forecast from REV-SALES-FCAST_CWS with pricing and option data from COGS-PRICEMARGIN_CWS.*

Monthly spreads are utilized by REV-REC-MAINT_CWS to calculate recurring maintenance revenue based on the number of Option 1 selections of LS. Recurring ES subscription revenue is computed based on the number of Option 2 selections of ES. The resulting calculations from REV-REC-MAINT_CWS are combined with all revenue calculations to create a master monthly revenue calculation for the model.

Understanding the Contribution to Margin Analysis Worksheet

The Contribution to Margin Analysis Worksheet, COGS_DB, computes contribution to gross margin by product offering by year. It is important to understand and to model contribution to margin. Since varying possibilities of price and cost can be selected and modeled in COGS-PRICEMARGIN_CWS, and the product option sales mix changes over time, contribution to margin also changes. Companies must have a clear understanding of where their margin is coming from and in what proportions.

In the example shown in Figure 6-5, contribution to margin is computed on the two product options that are offered. Note that the margin percentages for Option 1 and Option 2 are identical but that the absolute dollar contribution varies from month to month based on the mix of customer selection between the ES and LS options.

	A	B		N		O		P
9								
10				Oct		Nov		Dec
11								
12		Total Revenue	$	27,585	$	27,585	$	53,055
13		Total Gross Margin	$	15,768	$	15,768	$	30,330
14		Gross Margin %		57%		57%		57%
15		Option 1 Contribution	$	10,944	$	10,944	$	21,888
16		Option 2 Contribution	$	4,824	$	4,824	$	8,442
17								
18		Option 1 - ECS and LS						
19		Sale Units		9.00		9.00		18.00
20		ECS Sale Revenue		18,000		18,000		36,000
21		ECS Gross Margin $	$	9,819	$	9,819	$	19,638
22		LS Gross Margin $	$	1,125	$	1,125	$	2,250
23		Contribution to Margin	$	10,944	$	10,944	$	21,888
24		Gross Margin %		57%		57%		57%
25								
26		Option 2 - ECS and ES						
27		Sale Units		4.00		4.00		7.00
28		ECS Sale Revenue		8,000		8,000		14,000
29		ECS Gross Margin $	$	4,364	$	4,364	$	7,637
30		ES Gross Margin $	$	460	$	460	$	805
31		Contribution to Margin	$	4,824	$	4,824	$	8,442
32		Gross Margin %		57%		57%		57%
33								
34		Total						
35		Sale Units		13.00		13.00		25.00
36		Total ECS Sale Revenue	$	26,000	$	26,000	$	50,000
37		ECS Gross Margin $	$	14,183	$	14,183	$	27,275
38		Software - SVC Gross Margin $	$	1,585	$	1,585	$	3,055
39		Contribution to Margin	$	15,768	$	15,768	$	30,330

Figure 6-5. *COGS_DB computes the dollar contribution to margin by month.*

On a yearly basis (see Figures 6-6 and 6-7), Option 2 is clearly generating significantly more margin dollars than Option 1.

A	B		E	F	G	H	I	J	K	L	M
1			YR 1		YR 2		YR 3		YR 4		YR 5
2											
3	Total Revenue	$	108,225		$4,229,369		$12,873,651		$23,331,358		$ 37,595,013
4	Total Gross Margin	$	61,866		$3,401,623		$10,962,555		$20,505,495		$ 34,899,981
5	Total Gross Margin %		57%		80%		85%		88%		93%
6	Option 1 Contribution	$	43,776	40%	$2,017,773	48%	$ 4,356,747	34%	$ 4,123,888	18%	$ 3,498,588
7	Option 2 Contribution	$	18,090	17%	$1,383,850	33%	$ 6,605,808	51%	$16,381,607	70%	$ 31,401,393

Figure 6-6. *COGS_DB summarizes contribution to margin showing that Option 2 is the primary contributor to margin dollars in YR 5.*

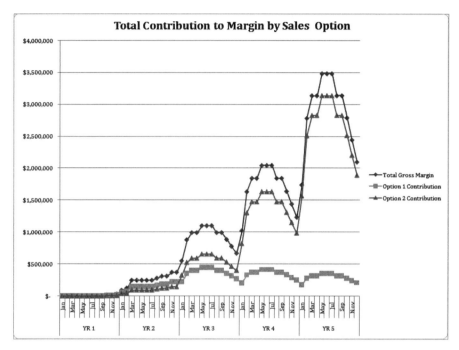

Figure 6-7. *The COGS_CHART_MARGIN chart shows that Option 2 is generating substantially more dollar margin over the period of performance of the model.*

Understanding the Inventory and Inventory AP Worksheet

We have defined inventory as the amount of finished goods that the Company has available to sell. The Company has designed its ECS product and outsourced its manufacturing. The manufacturer ships components back to the Company, where they are tested, assembled, packaged, and shipped to the customer.

Making Inventory Model Assumptions

The Company has made the following modeling assumptions regarding inventory:

- The Company will keep on hand (in stock) sufficient sales units to support the next three months of forecasted sales.

- The cost of purchasing inventory is equal to the cost of goods sold of the ECS unit as modeled in COGS-PRICEMARGIN_CWS. This price, as shown in the model, is lower in the out years. Inventory will be paid for 60 days after purchase.

- For the purposes of this model, there is no finance charge assessed with this delay in payment.

- The cost of purchasing inventory units will drop from year to year due to price breaks given by the manufacturer for higher volume production.

- The Company will use a last-in, first-out (LIFO) method to calculate the cost of inventory (see Exercise 6-1 at the end of this chapter for more on LIFO).

COGS-INVENTORY_CWS, the Inventory and Inventory AP Worksheet, is an inventory model and an AP model for the calculation of AP on inventory purchases. Figure 6-8 shows the monthly inventory model of COGS-INVENTORY_CWS. Figure 6-9 shows the yearly form of the model. There are two things to note about Figure 6-8:

- The July-ending inventory amount of 13 units is equal to the amount of forecasted sales units for August through October (the next 90 days of forecasted sales after July). The ending inventory in the model is consistent with the assumption that the Company has on hand, or in stock, sales units to support the next three months of forecasted sales.

- The cost of inventory goes down from $750 per unit to $675 per unit between December (YR 1) and January (YR 2).

■**Note** Exercise 6-1 at the end of this chapter provides a detailed explanation of the inventory model.

B	J	K	L	M	N	O	P
23 Monthly Inventory Model	Jul	Aug	Sep	Oct	Nov	Dec	Jan
24							
25 Forecasted Sales Units	-	-	-	13	13	25	29
26							
27 Cost of Inventory	$ 750	$ 750	$ 750	$ 750	$ 750	$ 750	$ 675
28							
29 Beginning Inventory							
30 Inventory - Units	-	13	26	51	67	93	146
31 Inventory - $ Cost	$ -	$ 9,750	$ 19,500	$ 38,250	$ 50,250	$ 69,750	$ 109,500
32							
33 Inventory In							
34 Inventory - Units	13	13	25	29	39	78	78
35 Inventory - $ Cost	$ 9,750	$ 9,750	$ 18,750	$ 21,750	$ 29,250	$ 58,500	$ 52,650
36							
37 Inventory Out							
38 Inventory - Units	-	-	-	13	13	25	29
39 Inventory - $ Cost	$ -	$ -	$ -	$ 9,750	$ 9,750	$ 18,750	$ 19,575
40							
41 Change in Inventory							
42 Inventory - Units	13	13	25	16	26	53	49
43 Inventory - $ Cost	$ 9,750	$ 9,750	$ 18,750	$ 12,000	$ 19,500	$ 39,750	$ 33,075
44							
45 Ending Inventory							
46							
47 Inventory - Units	13	26	51	67	93	146	195
48 Inventory - $ Cost	$ 9,750	$ 19,500	$ 38,250	$ 50,250	$ 69,750	$ 109,500	$ 142,575

Figure 6-8. *The COGS-INVENTORY_CWS monthly inventory model*

	B	C	D	E	F	G	H
1	Yearly Inventory Model	YR 0	YR 1	YR 2	YR 3	YR 4	YR 5
2							
3	Forecasted Sale Units	-	51	976	2,400	3,753	5,400
4							
5	Beginning Inventory						
6	Inventory - Units	-	-	146	528	826	1,188
7	Inventory - $ Cost	$ -	0	109,500	367,350	548,385	746,309
8	Inventory In						
9	Inventory - Units	-	197	1,358	2,698	4,115	5,862
10	Inventory - $ Cost	$ -	$ 147,750	$ 916,650	$ 1,639,035	$ 2,249,876	$ 2,884,544
11	Inventory Out						
12	Inventory - Units	-	51	976	2,400	3,753	5,400
13	Inventory - $ Cost	$ -	$ 38,250	$ 658,800	$ 1,458,000	$ 2,051,953	$ 2,657,205
14	Change in Inventory						
15	Inventory - Units	-	146	382	298	362	462
16	Inventory - $ Cost	$ -	$ 109,500	$ 257,850	$ 181,035	$ 197,924	$ 227,339
17	Ending Inventory						
18	Inventory - Units	$ -	$ 146	$ 528	$ 826	$ 1,188	$ 1,650
19	Inventory - $ Cost	$ -	$ 109,500	$ 367,350	$ 548,385	$ 746,309	$ 973,647

Figure 6-9. *The COGS-INVENTORY_CWS yearly inventory model*

Understanding the Inventory AP Model

COGS-INVENTORY_CWS is also an AP model for inventory payables based on the assumption that inventory purchases will be paid for with 60-day terms, that is, purchases in one month will be paid for 60 days following the purchase. Note that we are purchasing inventory (hardware units) 90 days in advance but paying for the units on 60-day terms.

■**Note** For purposes of the Company business model, the only company AP balances are for inventory. It is assumed that all other expenses are paid for in the month in which they are incurred. This affects the cash flow of the Company and is discussed in greater detail in Chapter 10.

A SHORT TREATISE ON AP

Money owed to a vendor or supplier for purchased items or services is called an *account payable*. When a company purchases products or services, it must either pay for them in the current month or owe the vendor or supplier. Usually, the amount owed is acceptable to the vendor and within payment terms that the vendor has allowed. If payment is made under the payment terms, the account payable is considered current. If not, it is considered past due. Accounts payable due dates and amounts are *aged* by accounting systems, showing amounts owned to vendors in 30, 60, or 90 days. This is called an *accounts payable aging*.

Accounts payable balances are carried on the company balance sheet as a current liability, meaning they are assumed to be a liability that must be satisfied (paid off) in the near term. Monies owed for loans or debt are not considered accounts payable; they are shown on the balance sheet as notes of debt payable and normally considered long-term debt.

When you create a financial model, you must forecast cash payments for purchases. This is accomplished by creating an AP model. The AP model is a critical component to forecasting cash flows.

The following image shows COGS-INVENTORY_CWS, a monthly inventory AP model. Note that the amount of payable reductions is equal to the amount of inventory purchases made two months prior. If an inventory purchase of $9,750 was made in July, according to this model, it is paid for in September.

	B	J	K	L	M	N	O
62	**Monthly Inventory AP Model**	**Jul**	**Aug**	**Sep**	**Oct**	**Nov**	**Dec**
63							
64							
65	Beginning Payable Balance	$ -	$ 9,750	$ 19,500	$ 28,500	$ 40,500	$ 51,000
66	Inventory Purchases	$ 9,750	$ 9,750	$ 18,750	$ 21,750	$ 29,250	$ 58,500
67	Accounts Payable	$ 9,750	$ 19,500	$ 38,250	$ 50,250	$ 69,750	$ 109,500
68	Payable Reductions	$ -	$ -	$ 9,750	$ 9,750	$ 18,750	$ 21,750
69	Payable Balance	$ 9,750	$ 19,500	$ 28,500	$ 40,500	$ 51,000	$ 87,750
70	Increase/Decrease In Payables	$ 9,750	$ 9,750	$ 9,000	$ 12,000	$ 10,500	$ 36,750

The following image shows COGS-INVENTORY_CWS, the yearly inventory AP model.

	B	C	D	E	F	G	H
51	**Yearly Inventory AP Model**	**YR 0**	**YR 1**	**YR 2**	**YR 3**	**YR 4**	**YR 5**
52							
53	Beginning Payable Balance	$ -	$ -	$ 87,750	$ 275,400	$ 387,585	$ 501,917
54	Inventory Purchases	$ -	$ 147,750	$ 916,650	$ 1,639,035	$ 2,249,876	$ 2,884,544
55	Accounts Payable	$ -	$ 147,750	$ 1,004,400	$ 1,914,435	$ 2,637,461	$ 3,386,460
56	Payable Reductions	$ -	$ 60,000	$ 729,000	$ 1,526,850	$ 2,135,545	$ 2,820,574
57	Payable Balance	$ -	$ 87,750	$ 275,400	$ 387,585	$ 501,917	$ 565,886
58	Increase/Decrease In Payables	$ -	$ 87,750	$ 187,650	$ 112,185	$ 114,332	$ 63,970

■**Note** Exercise 6-2 at the end of this chapter provides a detailed explanation of the AP model.

Understanding Revenue and COGS Chart Data

REV-COGS_CHARTDAT preformats data needed for COGS management and analysis charts. Charts are defined, and the data ranges for the chart are derived from linking back to other relevant spreadsheets in the model. Figure 6-10 shows COGS_CHART-INVENTORY, a charting of inventory usage and inventory AP balance. Figure 6-11 shows the format of REV-COGS_CHARTDAT.

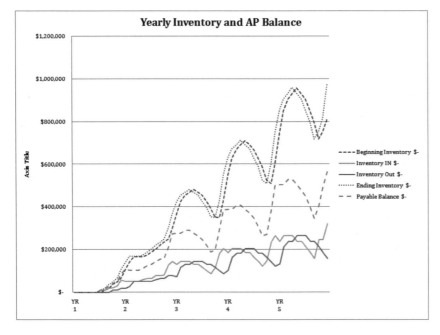

Figure 6-10. *COGS_CHART-INVENTORY is a chart showing inventory usage and inventory AP balance.*

A	B	J	K	L	M	N
46	COGS_CHART-INVENTORY					
47		YR 1				
48		Jul	Aug	Sep	Oct	Nov
49	Beginning Inventory	$ -	$ 9,750	$ 19,500	$ 38,250	$ 50,250
50	Inventory In	$ 9,750	$ 9,750	$ 18,750	$ 21,750	$ 29,250
51	Inventory Out	$ -	$ -	$ -	$ 9,750	$ 9,750
52	Ending Inventory	$ 9,750	$ 19,500	$ 38,250	$ 50,250	$ 69,750
53	Payable Balance	$ 9,750	$ 19,500	$ 28,500	$ 40,500	$ 51,000

Figure 6-11. *REV-COGS_CHARTDAT preformats data needed for COGS management and analysis charts.*

EXERCISE 6-1: USING MICROSOFT EXCEL TO FORECAST INVENTORY USAGE

The Company has outsourced its manufacturing and must purchase its sales unit inventory from the manufacturer to support its sales forecast. As you've seen, the Company has made the following modeling assumptions regarding inventory:

- The Company will keep on hand (in stock) sufficient sales units to support the next three months of forecasted sales.

- The cost of purchasing inventory is equal to the cost of goods sold of the ECS unit, as modeled in COGS-PRICEMARGIN_CWS.

- Inventory will be paid for 90 days after purchase. For the purposes of this model, no finance charges are associated with these payment terms.

- The cost of purchasing inventory units will drop from year to year.

- The Company will use a LIFO method to calculate cost of inventory.

■**Definition** *Last-in, first-out* (LIFO) refers to a method of valuing inventory in which the items acquired last are treated as the ones sold first. The Company inventory model assumes that the cost of purchasing sales units from the manufacturer for inventory decreases over the years. This inventory model uses the current period unit price of inventory to price out current period reductions in inventory, even though previously purchased inventory was purchased at a higher price. Inventory audits will adjust for this, but that subject is beyond the scope of this book.

This situation leads us to the following problem and solution:

- *Problem*: The company must project inventory usage and the cost of the usage.

- *Solution*: Develop an inventory model that is consistent with company planning assumptions for inventory and can be utilized by an AP model for downstream calculations of cash flow.

Develop the Inventory Model

This model utilizes a back-into technique (see Figure 6-14) for deriving the number of inventory units that must be purchased in support of the preceding assumption that the ending inventory must always be equal to the number of sales unit forecasted for the next three months. See Figure 6-12 for a data view of the monthly inventory model and Figure 6-13 for a formula view of the model.

B	J	K	L	M	N	O	P
23 **Monthly Inventory Model**	Jul	Aug	Sep	Oct	Nov	Dec	Jan
24							
25 **Forecasted Sales Units**	-	-	-	13	13	25	29
26							
27 **Cost of Inventory**	$ 750	$ 750	$ 750	$ 750	$ 750	$ 750	$ 675
28							
29 **Beginning Inventory**							
30　Inventory - Units	-	13	26	51	67	93	146
31　Inventory - $ Cost	$ -	$ 9,750	$ 19,500	$ 38,250	$ 50,250	$ 69,750	$ 109,500
32							
33 **Inventory In**							
34　Inventory - Units	13	13	25	29	39	78	78
35　Inventory - $ Cost	$ 9,750	$ 9,750	$ 18,750	$ 21,750	$ 29,250	$ 58,500	$ 52,650
36							
37 **Inventory Out**							
38　Inventory - Units	-	-	-	13	13	25	29
39　Inventory - $ Cost	$ -	$ -	$ -	$ 9,750	$ 9,750	$ 18,750	$ 19,575
40							
41 **Change in Inventory**							
42　Inventory - Units	13	13	25	16	26	53	49
43　Inventory - $ Cost	$ 9,750	$ 9,750	$ 18,750	$ 12,000	$ 19,500	$ 39,750	$ 33,075
44							
45 **Ending Inventory**							
46							
47　Inventory - Units	13	26	51	67	93	146	195
48　Inventory - $ Cost	$ 9,750	$ 19,500	$ 38,250	$ 50,250	$ 69,750	$ 109,500	$ 142,575

Figure 6-12. *COGS-INVENTORY_CWS, the company inventory model showing inventory units and cost of inventory*

■**Tip** To show or display formulas in a worksheet (formula view), select the Formula tab on the menu ribbon and select the Show Formulas option. All formulas will be displayed. To reverse and return to a normal (data) view, select the Show Formulas option again.

B	J	K	L	M
23 **Monthly Inventory Model**	Jul	Aug	Sep	Oct
24				
25 **Forecasted Sales Units**	='REV-REVCALC_CWS'!K6	='REV-REVCALC_CWS'!L6	='REV-REVCALC_CWS'!M6	='REV-REVCALC_CWS'!N6
26				
27 **Cost of Inventory**	='COGS-PRICE-MARGIN_CWS'!$F5	='COGS-PRICE-MARGIN_CWS'!$F5	='COGS-PRICE-MARGIN_CWS'!$F5	='COGS-PRICE-MARGIN_CWS'!$F5
28				
29 **Beginning Inventory**				
30　Inventory - Units	=I47	=J47	=K47	=L47
31　Inventory - $ Cost	=I48	=J48	=K48	=L48
32				
33 **Inventory In**				
34　Inventory - Units	=J47-(J30-J38)	=K47-(K30-K38)	=L47-(L30-L38)	=M47-(M30-M38)
35　Inventory - $ Cost	=J34*J27	=K34*K27	=L34*L27	=M34*M27
36				
37 **Inventory Out**				
38　Inventory - Units	='REV-REVCALC_CWS'!K6	='REV-REVCALC_CWS'!L6	='REV-REVCALC_CWS'!M6	='REV-REVCALC_CWS'!N6
39　Inventory - $ Cost	=J38*J27	=K38*K27	=L38*L27	=M38*M27
40				
41 **Change in Inventory**				
42　Inventory - Units	=J34-J38	=K34-K38	=L34-L38	=M34-M38
43　Inventory - $ Cost	=J35-J39	=K35-K39	=L35-L39	=M35-M39
44				
45 **Ending Inventory**				
46				
47　Inventory - Units	=SUM(K25:M25)	=SUM(L25:N25)	=SUM(M25:O25)	=SUM(N25:P25)
48　Inventory - $ Cost	=I48+J43	=J48+K43	=K48+L43	=L48+M43

Figure 6-13. *COGS-INVENTORY_CWS , the formula view of the inventory model*

■**Note** To understand this model, you have to consider that we first compute inventory *units*, and then we compute the corresponding *dollar* costs associated with units that are passing in and out of inventory.

Make Inventory Unit Calculations

The following applies to only inventory *units*:

- *Ending inventory* is the sum of forecasted sales units for the next three months. We are backing into the number of units to guarantee that the number of units in inventory will always equal the next three months' sales unit forecast.

- *Beginning inventory* is the number of ending inventory units from the previous month.

- *Inventory out* equals the number of units sold in the current month.

- *Inventory in* is backed into (see Figure 6-14). We are deriving the number of inventory units we need to purchase in order to maintain an ending inventory level that is equal to the sum of forecasted sales units for the next three months.

- *Change in inventory* is the *total* (net) of current month inventory units in and inventory units out.

	B	I	J	K
23	Monthly Inventory Model	Jun	Jul	Aug
33	Inventory In			
34	Inventory - Units	=I47-(I30-I38)	=J47-(J30-J38)	=K47-(K30-K38)
35	Inventory - $ Cost	=I34*I27	=J34*J27	=K34*K27

Figure 6-14. *In COGS-INVENTORY_CWS, the backing-into formula that derives the number of inventory units that must be purchased in order to maintain an ending unit inventory that is equal to the sum of forecasted sales units for the next three months.*

Make Inventory Dollar Value Calculations

The following applies to only inventory dollar *costs*:

- *Ending inventory* equals the previous month's inventory balance plus the change in the current month's inventory.

- *Beginning inventory* equals the previous month's ending inventory dollar balance.

- *Inventory out* equals the number of units sold (out) in the current month times the current month's cost of an inventory unit.

- *Inventory in* equals the number of inventory units (in) times the current month's cost of an inventory unit.

- *Change in inventory* equals the total (net) of current month's inventory costs in and out.

The combination of unit and dollar calculations in the inventory model is consistent with a LIFO cost accounting method for inventory.

EXERCISE 6-2: USING MICROSOFT EXCEL TO MODEL INVENTORY AP

The Company model assumes purchases of inventory from its manufacturer.

- *Problem*: The company business model requires that cash flows from revenues be projected.

- *Solution*: Develop an AP model that projects payments for inventory and provides downstream data for the company Statement of Cash Flows and the Company Balance Sheet.

Develop Cash Payment Assumptions

In the case of this model, it is assumed that payments for inventory are made in 60 days.

Develop the Accounts Payable Model

The model is a simple concept. When inventory is purchased, this adds to the accounts payable balance. When payments are made, the accounts payable balance is reduced. An accounts payable model utilizes inventory purchase forecasts from the inventory model as the basis for creating the payable balance and applies the cash payment assumption for reduction in the payable balance. Changes in the payable balance are used to compute actual cash flow in the Company Statement of Cash Flows. See Figure 6-15 for a data view of this model and Figure 6-16 for a formula view of this model.

	B	J	K	L	M
62	**Monthly Inventory AP Model**	**Jul**	**Aug**	**Sep**	**Oct**
63					
64					
65	Beginning Payable Balance	$ -	$ 9,750	$ 19,500	$ 28,500
66	Inventory Purchases	$ 9,750	$ 9,750	$ 18,750	$ 21,750
67	Accounts Payable	$ 9,750	$ 19,500	$ 38,250	$ 50,250
68	Payable Reductions	$ -	$ -	$ 9,750	$ 9,750
69	Payable Balance	$ 9,750	$ 19,500	$ 28,500	$ 40,500
70	Increase/Decrease In Payables	$ 9,750	$ 9,750	$ 9,000	$ 12,000

Figure 6-15. *The monthly AP model data view*

	B	J	K	L	M
62	**Monthly Inventory AP Model**	**Jul**	**Aug**	**Sep**	**Oct**
63					
64					
65	Beginning Payable Balance	=I69	=J69	=K69	=L69
66	Inventory Purchases	=J35	=K35	=L35	=M35
67	Accounts Payable	=J65+J66	=K65+K66	=L65+L66	=M65+M66
68	Payable Reductions	=H66	=I66	=J66	=K66
69	Payable Balance	=J67-J68	=K67-K68	=L67-L68	=M67-M68
70	Increase/Decrease In Payables	=J69-I69	=K69-J69	=L69-K69	=M69-L69

Figure 6-16. *Formula view of the monthly AP model*

Let's review the line-item components of the AP model. Referring to the Figure 6-15 data view and Figure 6-16 formula view, the following is an explanation of the line items in the AP Model and their relationship to each other:

- *Beginning Payable Balance*: The beginning balance is either zero (in the first month) or equal to the previous month's ending payable balance.

- *Inventory Purchases*: These equal the total inventory purchases (in dollars) in the current month (derived from the inventory model).

- *Accounts Payable*: This row calculates the Beginning Payable Balance plus Inventory Purchases.

- *Payable Reductions*: *Important!* This row is where the cash payment assumptions show up. Note that the formulas are pointing to inventory purchases from two months ago. In other words, the model assumes that all inventory purchased from the two months prior is paid for 100 percent in the current month.

- *Payable Balance*: This row calculates Accounts Payable minus Payable Reductions.

- *Increase/Decrease in Payables*: This row reflects the change in the payable balance from the prior month to the current month.

Note The change in AP balance (increase or decrease in payables) from month to month measures a portion of the cash flow of the Company. Changes in AP balance are used to measure the portion of cash outflow that is related to cash payments for inventory.

Summary

In this chapter, we have explored the Cost of Goods Sold and Inventory (COGS) model. I have defined cost of goods sold as a variable cost associated with a unit of sales, and we examined complexities surrounding the cost of goods sold definition. We have broken down the company product offering into components and computed gross margin or contribution to margin for differing options of the offering. We have developed a model for analyzing contribution to margin for the product offering options. The company offers a hardware and software combination and has an inventory requirement, and in this chapter, the inventory and accounts payable associated with the company's offerings are modeled and explained.

The bottom line of COGS is an analysis and understanding of the product contribution to margin. In other words, what profit does the product generate prior to other operating expenses of the company? Understanding inventory and accounts payable associated with it is also an important part of the product offering and profitability equation.

These are the overarching questions regarding the Cost of Goods Sold and Inventory model: How will you optimize product profitability? How will you manage your cost of goods sold and inventory?

■ ■ ■

CHAPTER 7

Cost of Sales and Marketing Model

Technology startup companies have two primary cost drivers: sales/marketing and technology development. The cost of sales and marketing is the cost the company incurs to implement its sales and marketing strategy. A financial model, in and of itself, cannot define or articulate strategies for selling and marketing of products and services. It can, however, model the application of resources to the implementation of these strategies. The Cost of Sales and Marketing (COSM) model quantifies and forecasts amounts and timing of resources applied to the implementation of the company's sales and marketing strategy.

In this chapter, you will learn how to plan, create, and use the COSM model, and in addition, you will learn the following:

- How to assess the need for sales and marketing resources based on a thorough assessment of the target market

- The issues to consider in crafting a compelling value proposition

- What resources are to be planned for in the COSM model

- How to develop a model to forecast and quantify the total cost of sales and marketing needed to support the sales and marketing life cycle

Business Thinking about the Cost of Sales and Marketing

Business thinking about the cost of sales and marketing begins with a definition of scope. What is included in COSM? The following definitions are provided to get you thinking:

Cost of sales and marketing: The cost of sales and marketing is the cost of resources required to support sales and marketing activities. Sales and marketing functions and resources must also be viewed within the context of a total customer support life cycle, which includes customer relationship management sales and customer support functions.

Customer relationship management (CRM): CRM is the organized management of customer relationships including processes, methodologies, and technologies that result in enhanced market intelligence flow in support of sales and marketing and increased customer satisfaction. CRM includes *customer-facing systems* and customer and technical support functions.

Business thinking on the cost of sales and marketing recognizes CRM costs as part of the total cost of sales and marketing; I therefore include CRM resources as part of the COSM model. Some technology startups make a common mistake in failing to adequately invest in the resources, processes, and company culture needed to provide a continuous, hot feedback loop of information to and from the customer. This feedback loop is critical in supporting both product development and sales and marketing. Articulating the company value proposition is also dependent on this feedback loop.

Well-designed CRM functionality provides a critical customer interface that generates feedback used to position products and services better. This is particularly important in early stages of product development and sales. Proof of product and proof of market value events are validated, in part, by tangible customer feedback and their acceptance of product form, feature, and functionality. The customers' validation and acceptance of the value proposition is substantiated by their purchases of the product at the desired pricing level.

Formal CRM is rarely implemented during very early stages in company development. It evolves over time and becomes more formalized as sales and markets mature, but the business thinking and orientation about it must be there from the beginning.

Business thinking about sales and marketing must first be strategic. The company must complete three strategic business thinking steps before it is ready to model resources in COSM:

1. Complete a market assessment.

2. Develop the value proposition.

3. Plan the sales and marketing implementation strategy.

Completing the Market Assessment

Michael Porter's Five Forces that shape competition make a good starting place for any market assessment ("The Five Forces That Shape Strategy," *Harvard Business Review*, January 2008):

Established rivals: A primary consideration when thinking about established rivals is *barriers to entry*. A successful startup will have seriously considered these barriers to entry when developing its market strategy. What will be required, in terms of investment, to be competitive in an industry that already has established players? Incumbency has its advantages—to name a few, brand recognition, economies of scale, and established distribution channels.

Suppliers: Powerful suppliers, including providers of labor, can shape sales and marketing strategies. For instance, the need to plug and play with major hardware suppliers can strongly influence sales and marketing strategies for technology products. The cost of labor to support the installed base of products can influence value propositions and increase the customer's cost to switch to your product and away from another.

Customers: Powerful customers can force down prices and demand higher quality and better service by playing competitors against one another. Your company may have to deal with a distinct customer group that has unique negotiating leverage. Price sensitivity of buyer groups must be clearly understood.

New players: New players bring new capacity and are often highly aggressive, putting pressure on prices. New players can sow a high level of uncertainty in the market with unproven claims. It is difficult to position value propositions against new and unknown players. When there are a large number of new entrants into a market space, there is impact on market share and profitability strategies.

Substitute products or services: A substitute performs the same or similar function as the company product offering but by a different means. If the function offered by the company product is already being performed in any manner by the customer, this constitutes a substitute. Substitutes are often overlooked in competitive analysis.

Other forces that should be considered in a market assessment follow:

Industry growth rate: How fast is the industry growing, and how does this growth affect potential rivalry and opportunities? Is a fast growth rate attracting lots of new entrants and competitors?

Technology and innovation: For technology startups, the states of technology and innovation in a target market are key factors in assessing opportunity. Where is the target industry on the technology adoption curve? Is the industry innovative and technologically savvy, or is it slow to adopt new technologies? Is there a new technology wave afoot in the industry that will shape product offering and positioning?

Government: What government policies, rules, or regulations affect the target market? A better way to ask the question is, how do specific government policies affect the five forces within the target market? For instance, do new government wage guidelines affect the cost of labor to build or support your product?

Complementary products and services: What other products and services, when used with the company product, add value? Is the combination of another product or service greater in value than the value of each individually? Is their sum greater than the whole related to your product offering out there?

I find that assessing a target market within the five forces framework is particularly helpful for startups because the five forces reveal the most significant aspects of the competitive environment and provide a baseline for sizing up a company's strengths and weaknesses.

The five competitive forces also reveal the drivers of industry competition. The company value proposition can be tested for validity within this framework. Company strategy can be viewed from the standpoint of positioning (aligning) with or protecting against competitive market forces. It should be clearly noted that each industry or target market has a differing competitive force profile.

The company must complete a market assessment before it develops its value proposition. Understanding the competitive forces reveals the drivers of competition in the target market. A market assessment will uncover differences in customers, suppliers, and substitutes while assessing potential new entrant rivals and incumbent competitors. This information can become the basis for articulating the superior performance that your product delivers—your value proposition.

Developing the Value Proposition

Your company must develop, as a central business skill, a capability to develop and articulate the value proposition. From the beginning think about what people, systems, processes, procedures and methods will be needed to ingrain this skill into your organization. Your COSM model should reflect planned investments for the development and ongoing support of these activities.

Developing and creating your value proposition must be done within the larger context of positioning your product in the target market. Testing the value proposition against the five forces will help determine the competitive *positioning* of the product in the market.

■**Note** Here's a product positioning analogy: Imagine the five competitive forces as a large river. Upstream lies your goal of profitability, and you must swim to get there. Each of the five competitive forces is a current running downstream. Some currents (forces) are stronger than others. How best to swim upstream? A smart swimmer finds the place in the river where the current is weakest or, given his abilities, where he can best swim upstream. That is where you must *position* yourself (*your product*) to swim upstream toward the goal.

The first rule of developing a value proposition is to *know your customer's business*. The second rule is to *substantiate your value claims*.

The heart and soul of a value proposition is the ability to substantiate your claims. This can be difficult in early stages of product development with new and untried products, but the processes and methods to substantiate performance claims must be built into company culture from the beginning. Claims should always translate into monetary terms and be explained in accessible and persuasive language. Generic performance studies have value, but performance metrics that the customers can apply directly to their business situations are invaluable.

Presenting Three Types of Value Proposition

The value proposition model developed by James Anderson, James Narus, and Wouter van Rossum is helpful in understanding the components of a compelling value proposition ("Customer Value Propositions in Business Markets," *Harvard Business Review*, March 2006). Their model defines three types of value propositions, listed below. Each type answers an increasingly probing question by the customer and correspondingly requires a different level of understanding of the customer's business.

All benefits: This is the value proposition form that I encounter most frequently in my consulting practice. It consists of a list of all the benefits that are believed to be delivered to target customers. It answers the customer question, "Why should our firm purchase your offering?" The pitfall is that the list often *asserts advantages* and features that have *no benefit* to the target customer. In fact, many of the benefits may be points of parity with the next best alternative. This type of value proposition ignores points of difference from competitors. All that is required to develop this type of value proposition is knowledge of your own product.

Favorable points of difference: This form of value proposition is developed with the understanding that the *customer has an alternative*. It answers the customer question, "Why should our firm purchase your offering instead of your competitor's?" To develop this type of value proposition, you must have a detailed understanding of your competitor's products and be able to articulate all favorable points of difference between your product and theirs. You may also define and solve the customer's problem in a different way. The pitfall to this type of value proposition is that, without a clear understanding of the customer, it may stress points of difference that have little value to the customer. This type of value proposition is a significant improvement over the *all benefits* type. An in-depth *understanding of competitor products and capabilities* is required to deliver this form of value proposition.

Resonating focus: This form of value proposition answers the customer question, "What is most worthwhile for our firm to keep in mind about your offering?" This value proposition delivers a simple, yet captivating, message of what makes the product offering superior on the few elements that *matter most* to the customer. It focuses on the one or two points of difference that deliver the greatest value to the customer. This is the gold standard of value propositions. A company that can deliver this type of value proposition has demonstrated that it *fully grasps the critical issues that face its customer*. This form of value proposition requires that you understand what the customer values. Dedicated resources are required to garner this type of customer information.

Employing a Return on Investment Model

Technology startups have classically presented their value propositions in terms of a Return on Investment (ROI) model, justifying technology product and service delivery on the basis of an acceptable return on the investment. Traditionally, the quantitative component of the ROI analysis was presented as the end product. Highly successful companies deliver more than this—they deliver this type of analysis within the context of a larger value proposition. That is, each component of the ROI equation is presented within the context of its value to the customer. The following example shows the components of an ROI model and discusses its relationship to the value proposition concepts discussed previously.

■**Note** The *return on investment (ROI)* is the ratio of money gained or lost (realized or unrealized) on an investment relative to the amount of money invested.

A classic way of viewing ROI for technology products is shown in Figure 7-1. The basic idea is that savings (D), resulting from the new technology implementation, are large enough to provide an acceptable ROI for the project investment (A + B). Savings are forecasted reductions in operating costs from the existing baseline of projected costs, line C. The project investment equals the total of nonrecurring internal process changes (A) and nonrecurring expense for hardware software and services (B). Line C represents existing and slightly improving marginal operating cost expectations assuming no major investment in new technology.

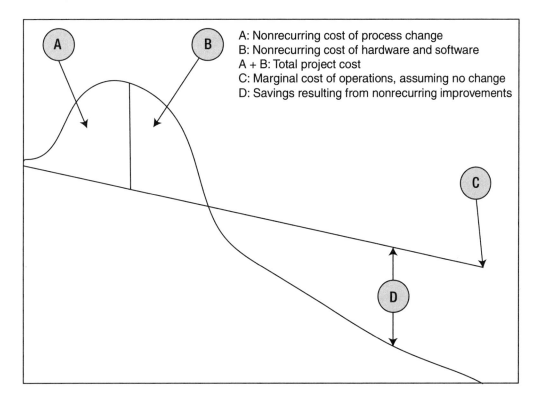

Figure 7-1. *The return on investment concept for technology implementations*

In this example, ROI is computed as follows: ROI equals savings (D) divided by total project cost (A + B).

Another way of looking at this type of return is *payback period*. In other words, how long does it take to recoup the funds outlaid for the project from operating savings? Acceptable payback periods vary over time and by projects. The customer decides what is acceptable and what is not based on internal benchmarks for return on invested capital.

A more detailed discussion of the components of the ROI equation follows, with comments regarding the relationship of the value proposition to each component.

Nonrecurring Cost of Process Change

The nonrecurring costs of process change make up the *switching costs* incurred by the customers in changing from their existing capabilities to the new technology. These costs include all hardware, software, and other costs associated with moving to the new system. In many cases, this is difficult to quantify, because people and processes are affected. Customers often view these types of costs as very high, because these costs interfere with business as usual. The customers may feel that a good alternative to these costs is to do nothing.

The value proposition shows that the switching costs incurred are offset by increases in productivity due to improved processes, better information, and better-trained employees. One objective of the value proposition is to mitigate the switching impact and emphasize the benefits to the process of switching.

Nonrecurring Cost of Hardware and Software

The nonrecurring costs of hardware and software include the nonrecurring costs of all hardware and software and fees associated with acquiring the technology for the project, including other hardware and software systems that must be upgraded in tandem. These amounts are quantifiable. The customer compares price points with alternative systems in this category. Capital expenditures may be required for this category of cost. The customer factors recurring costs for software and hardware into downstream savings calculations.

The value proposition emphasizes favorable points of difference between the selected hardware and software in terms of performance and the capability to solve high-value problems for the customer. The task of the value proposition is to emphasize that selection of your company's product delivers superior performance to alternative choices.

Total Project Cost

The total project cost is computed by combining the nonrecurring cost of process change with the nonrecurring cost of hardware and software. The total project cost is the *number* that must be sold internally to the customer in order for the project to be approved and the product purchased.

The presenters of the value proposition must understand the customers' perceived total cost of the project so that they can assist the customer with justification of the sale.

Marginal Cost of Existing Operations

The marginal cost of operations is a projection, by the customers, of the marginal or incremental costs of the current state of their operations, before implementing the technology project. The customers will compare this cost against a projected new cost profile assuming the benefits of the project are realized.

The presenters of the value proposition must clearly understand the customers' assessment of their ongoing cost of operations in order to support claims that savings will result from project implementation.

Savings Resulting from Nonrecurring Improvements

Savings are computed by subtracting forecasted operating costs after the implementation from current projected operating costs. Recurring costs associated with the technology project are included in the forecasted operating costs after project implementation.

The value proposition must include a detailed presentation of the positive impact of the project on the customers' ways of doing business. These claims must be substantiated, ideally, by empirical data that directly relates to the customers' operating environments.

Understanding Sales and Marketing Strategy

A sales and marketing strategy has two ultimate goals: communicate a compelling value proposition to your target customers and execute a sales plan that results in sales and profitability. The strategy consists of the *what, when, and how* of selling the product once the market has been assessed and the value proposition developed. The scope of the strategy, as previously discussed, should emphasize marketing and sales activities but also include CRM support of the entire customer support life cycle.

The sales and marketing strategy first takes the form of a project plan that is driven by product availability. The project plan should include the following components:

- Staffing plan

- Bonus and compensation plan

- Expense budgets

- Travel and trip plan

- Capital plan

The COSM model forecasts and quantifies the sales and marketing plan. See Figure 7-2.

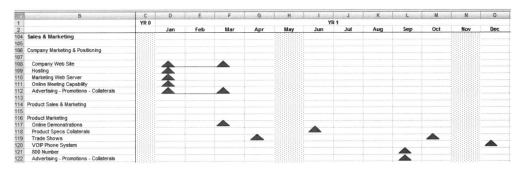

Figure 7-2. *Part of the Company Sales and Marketing Strategy project plan*

Next, we will review the company business case and its sales and marketing assumptions before planning the COSM model and explaining how it works.

Exploring the Sales and Marketing Strategy Business Case

Recall that Green Devil Control Systems (the Company) is an early-stage technology startup that develops and sells energy monitoring and control systems, specifically the Green Devil Energy Control System (ECS). The Company completed extensive market research during the feasibility study phase of their planning. See Chapter 3 for more on this study and their analysis of market potential for the Company.

Exploring the Product

ECS is a patent-pending, programmable hardware and software device that monitors and controls electricity usage on a circuit-by-circuit basis within a facility. ECS is installed on the facility side of the electrical breaker box. It can be purchased with Local Services (LS) or Extended Services (ES) software options.

Assessing the Market

The Company founders have a high level of understanding of the market that they are targeting. Nonetheless, they have carefully assessed this market from the standpoint of competitive factors, knowing that this approach helps to clarify market penetration success strategies. The following sections contain their assessment of market conditions and related strategies.

Established Rivals

There are a large number of well-established electrical supply equipment manufacturers and distributors supporting the housing industry. The strategy is to differentiate ECS from electrical control equipment by selling direct to high-end home builders, who purchase unique and innovative products for their progressive, high-end home-buying customers.

Suppliers

ECS is manufactured from the assembly of generic hardware components that are swappable, thus mitigating the influence of hardware suppliers. Unique aspects of the design are controlled in-house. There is an issue of finding reasonably priced contractors who can install electrical control equipment and set up software. The Company plans to mitigate this issue with outstanding training, technical support, and the inherent ease of use of the product.

Customers

The primary economic buyer or customer is the high-end home builder who is building smart homes for progressive and affluent customers. The strategy is to garner a premium price via presentation of ECS from a utility cost savings and a green perspective. ECS has additional value when integrated with other smart systems in the home, like automatic thermostats and security systems.

New Players

New players offering the same type of product are not known. There are a number of new players in the smart homes systems category, and these companies are being closely researched for points of difference to the product.

Substitute Products or Services

The prime substitute for ECS is to do nothing and to continue to manage electrical usage in traditional ways. The strategy is to overcome traditional means by providing documented cost savings to the customers.

Industry Growth Rate

The demand for new green smart homes is growing but is currently slowed due to the recent recession in home building.

Technology and Innovation

New technology for green homes is burgeoning as utility prices soar. The market for innovative ways to save utility costs is an early adopter market.

Government

Government policies, in general, are highly favorable toward this type of industry. Highly visible government standards and energy ratings for energy efficiency serve as a valuable benchmark for the product.

Complementary Products and Services

Smart home appliances and services, like LANs, security systems, and smart thermostats, are all complementary to the ECS product. Integrating ECS as one network component of a smart home suite of capabilities is value added.

Creating a Resonating Offer to the Customer

The Company value proposition will center on four value concepts:

- Ease of setup, installation, and maintenance
- Utility cost savings that deliver a very attractive ROI
- Attractiveness of green energy saving concepts to progressive smart home buyers
- Added value of integrating ECS with other smart home capabilities

The value proposition will be substantiated initially during field testing and compliance testing. Field testing will be conducted within new smart homes. Installation and support costs will be documented. Utility savings will be validated by running tests in parallel with standard methods. As the product is sold commercially, a formal customer data gathering program will be implemented that creates a hot feedback loop from both smart home builders and the downstream users of ECS and the ES software and service options.

Capturing the Market

With the market assessment and value proposition completed, the Company is ready to define its sales and marketing strategy.

Target Market

The Company will focus on the new smart home market exclusively because the founders have direct experience in this area, and this segment of the market is an early adopter of new home-building technologies.

Marketing Strategy

The Company will position the ECS product as a green technology, now a must-have feature for the progressive smart home buyer. The company will create market pull from home buyers by advertising in high-end housing media and becoming visible to the affluent and environmentally minded population. The Company will utilize standard branding methodologies to position Green Devil Control Systems as a standard feature for all progressive energy efficient homes. The company will also leverage governmental energy efficiency standards and achieve necessary energy efficiency standards as required to substantiate claims to the general public.

The Company will market ECS directly to the target buyer, the high-end home builder, using a technical and business value approach. The Company will also cross market into the electrical contractor market segment, which normally sells and installs electrical infrastructure. Marketing will be accomplished by a combination of Web and traditional advertising. The Company will attend two high-end home builder and home buyer trade shows per year and participate with a booth that portrays the Company as a sophisticated vendor of top-quality, smart home infrastructure devices.

The Company will utilize a sophisticated Web presence including a social networking strategy that engages progressive home buyers and builders and environmental building advocates. The Company will invest in Voice over IP (VOIP) and provide 800 numbers to enhance customer communications. The Company will also invest in sophisticated online meeting support systems.

Sales Strategy

The Company will implement a direct sales strategy, selling directly to high-end home builders and developers. The Company will employ field sales engineers who are technically oriented toward electrical control devices and who can both sell and provide on-site technical support. The Company will sell into four geographical regions: west, south, northeast, and central. The ECS product will be presold beginning in October of YR 1. Sales regions will be implemented and field sales engineers will be assigned first in the west, followed by the south, northeast, and central regions. Field sales engineers will travel extensively and sell face to face. The sales strategy specifically embraces a boots on the ground approach, since the product will initially be associated with control systems and other housing infrastructure items that have been traditionally sold in this manner.

Sales and Marketing Support Strategy

The Company will implement a sophisticated CRM support strategy that will include the hiring of a CRM director and support staff. The company will invest in CRM software and sophisticated help desk and technical support online services. The CRM function will have responsibility for the customer feedback loop from both a technical and sales support perspective. There will be a dotted-line reporting structure from technology development technicians to the director of CRM to make sure that first-rate technical support and feedback are maintained between the customer and the Company. In other words, technology technicians must provide technical support services to the director of CRM as part of their job responsibilities within technical operations.

Sales and Marketing Compensation Plan

The Company will provide a formal bonus and sales commission compensation plan. Field sales engineers will be highly compensated, primarily from performance-based incentives as provided in the bonus and compensation plan.

Staffing Plan and Organizational Structure

The Company will incrementally staff the sales and marketing function to a level of 14 employees in the first five years of operations. The vice president of sales and marketing is hired in YR 1 and is included in the executive department headcount (see Figure 7-3 for the headcount and Figure 7-4 for the organizational structure).

	B	C	D	E	F	G	H
		YR 0	YR 1	YR 2	YR 3	YR 4	YR 5
6	Headcount						
7	Director of Marketing		-	1.00	1.00	1.00	1.00
8	Marketing Support		-	-	1.00	1.00	1.00
9	Director of Sales		1.00	1.00	1.00	1.00	1.00
10	Field Sales Engineer		1.00	4.00	4.00	6.00	6.00
11	Director of CRM		-	1.00	1.00	1.00	1.00
12	Customer Support Tech		1.00	1.00	2.00	4.00	4.00
13	Headcount Sales and Mkt	-	3.00	8.00	10.00	14.00	14.00
14	Consultant HeadCount	-	0.75	0.50	-	-	-
15	Total Headcount	-	3.75	8.50	10.00	14.00	14.00

Figure 7-3. *Sales and marketing headcount plan*

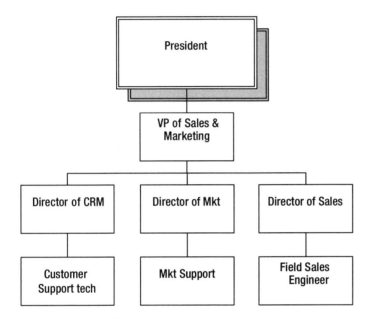

Figure 7-4. *Sales and marketing organizational chart*

Planning the COSM Model

The purpose of the COSM model is to forecast and quantify resources required to implement the Company sales and marketing strategy. The following points are the business thinking and planning considerations the Company should undertake prior to designing a COSM model:

- Review all Company business case planning assumptions regarding the sales and marketing strategy of the Company. Build a time-phased project plan that sets forth the major milestones related to sales and marketing strategy including events that require expenditures. This project plan should be tightly integrated with product release dates.

- Review and consider staffing requirements and salary ranges needed to implement the strategy. See Chapter 9 to make sure the model accommodates all planning staff requirements for sales and marketing. Pay particular attention to the timing of sales resource hires to make sure they support the sales forecast.

- Plan for the development of a sales and marketing operating expense budget model. This model should accommodate planning for operating and capital expenses required to implement the sales and marketing strategy. COSM_CWS will serve as this model.

- Plan for the development of a bonus and commission plan model to forecast and model bonus and commission compensation. Commissions and bonuses are a major variable expense of sales and marketing activities and should be modeled separately from normal expense and capital budgets. COSM-BONUS_CWS will serve as this model.

- Plan for the development of a trip expense model to forecast sales-and-marketing-related travel. Sales-related travel is a major variable expense and should be modeled separately then combined with normal expense budgets. COSM-TRIPCALC_CWS and COSM-TRIPPLAN_CWS will serve as this model.

■**Note** Metrics are a critical consideration in planning the COSM model. The main idea is that the cost of sales and marketing is measured and assessed against sales and revenue performance. In other words, is the Company investment in sales and marketing yielding the sales and revenues expected? When designing the COSM model, make sure it generates data that can be analyzed in this context.

Using the Building Blocks of the COSM Model

When the planning is complete, build and test the model. This section provides an overview of the COSM model (see Figure 7-5) and the top-level functionality of model components.

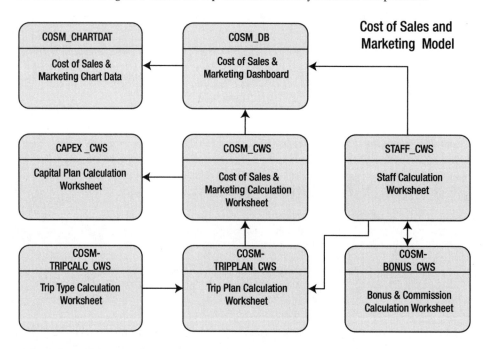

Figure 7-5. *In this top-level design and process flow of the Cost of Sales and Marketing (COSM) model, the arrows indicate major data and process flows.*

Understanding the Staff Calculation Worksheet

The Staff Calculation Worksheet (see Figure 7-6) is discussed in detail in Chapter 4. This worksheet plays an important part in the development of cost of sales and marketing. Sales and marketing staffing, salary, bonuses, and commissions are planned and calculated using this worksheet. In addition, the worksheet also forecasts requirements for phones, computers, and workspace needed for the sales and marketing staff. To utilize STAFF_CWS as input to COSM, follow these steps:

1. Begin at the Variable Inputs section of STAFF_CWS (cell A56 in Figure 7-6) and modify target salaries. Next, indicate with a "Y" or "N" if phones, computers, or workspaces are needed for each position. Note that no workspace is originally indicated for field sales engineers (as the model assumes they will work remotely).

2. In the Sales and Marketing Variable Inputs section (cell A56) of STAFF_CWS, modify headcount based on the staffing needs of the Company's strategy.

3. Go to the STAFF_CWS cell C78 and modify the adjustment to salary fields for sales and marketing positions as needed. The combination of the target annual salary and the salary modification field yields the forecasted salary for the position.

You have now planned headcounts, salaries, and phone, computer, and workspace requirements for the sales and marketing function. COSM computes salaries, taxes, benefits, and related expenses automatically.

	A	B	C	D	E	F	G	H	I	J	K	L
1												
2	Period of Performance						YR 0	Jan	Feb	Mar	Apr	May
3	Employee	Annual	Monthly	P	C	WS						
4	Consultant	Hourly	Monthly									
56	**Sales and Mkt**											
57												
58	Director of Mkt	$ 100,000	$ 8,333	Y	Y	Y	-	-	-	-	-	-
59	Consultant	$ 85	$ 13,600	N	N	Y	-	0.50	0.50	0.50	0.50	0.50
60												
61	Mkt Support	$ 65,000	$ 5,417	Y	Y	Y	-	-	-	-	-	-
62	Consultant	$ 40	$ 6,400	N	Y	Y	-	0.25	0.25	0.25	0.25	0.25
63												
64	Director of Sales	$ 125,000	$ 10,417	Y	Y	Y	-	-	-	-	-	1.00
65	Consultant	$ 85	$ 13,600	Y	Y	Y	-	-	-	-	-	-
66												
67	Field Sales Engineer	$ 85,000	$ 7,083	Y	Y	N	-	-	-	-	-	-
68	Consultant	$ 65	$ 10,400	Y	Y	N	-	0.50	0.50	0.50	0.50	0.50
69												
70	Director of CRM	$ 90,000	$ 7,500	Y	Y	Y	-	-	-			
71	Consultant	$ 65	$ 10,400	Y	Y	Y	-	-	-	-	-	-
72												
73	Customer Support Tech	$ 50,000	$ 4,167	Y	Y	Y	-	-	-	-	-	-
74	Consultant	$ 35	$ 5,600	Y	Y	Y	-	-	-	-	-	-
75												
76	Total Sales & Mkt						-	-	-	-	-	1.00
77	Total Consultant						-	1.25	1.25	1.25	1.25	1.25
78	Total Sales & Mkt						-	1.25	1.25	1.25	1.25	2.25
79												
80	Phone Count						-	1.00	1.00	1.00	1.00	2.00
81	Computer Count						-	1.00	1.00	1.00	1.00	2.00
82	Work Space Count						-	1.00	1.00	1.00	1.00	2.00

Figure 7-6. *STAFF_CWS, the Staff Calculation Worksheet, contains the variable input of the sales and marketing planning section.*

Understanding the Bonus and Sales Commission Worksheet

COSM-BONUS_CWS, the Bonus and Sales Commission Worksheet (see Figure 7-7), is a model for forecasting and planning bonuses and sales commissions. This worksheet plays an important role in developing the cost of sales and marketing. Sales commissions and bonuses are a primary incentive for sales forces and executives and a major variable cost of sales and marketing. The

COSM-BONUS_CWS Worksheet is one example of developing a model for this type of expenditure, but there are many ways to implement a model of this type. The primary functionality of COSM-BONUS_CWS is to develop commissions and bonuses at a *top level* for selected employees. The bonus calculations are then linked to and added back into the detailed compensation calculations of the staffing model (STAFF_CWS) for the purposes of computing taxes and benefits.

■**Note**   For a more detailed discussion of building this type of model, see Exercise 7-1 at the end of this chapter.

	B	E	F	G	H	I	J
2		YR 0	YR 1	YR 2	YR 3	YR 4	YR 5
9	**Bonus Pool**						
10	CEO/President	-	1.00	1.00	1.00	1.00	1.00
11	VP of Business Operations	-	-	-	-	1.00	1.00
12	VP of Sales & Marketing	-	-	-	1.00	1.00	1.00
13	CIO - Chief Technical Officer	-	1.00	1.00	1.00	1.00	1.00
14	Director of Mkt	-	-	-	1.00	1.00	1.00
15	Director of CRM	-	-	-	1.00	1.00	1.00
16	Director of Systems Int		-	-	1.00	1.00	1.00
17	Director Software Eng		1.00	1.00	1.00	1.00	1.00
18	Director Hardware Eng		1.00	1.00	1.00	1.00	1.00
19	Director of Test Eng		-	-	1.00	1.00	1.00
20	**Bonus Pool Count**	-	4.00	4.00	9.00	10.00	10.00
21							
22	**Bonus Allocation**						
23	CEO/President	$ -	$ 387	$ 11,244	$ 30,452	$ 51,264	$ 87,250
24	VP of Business Operations	$ -	$ -	$ -	$ -	$ 51,264	$ 87,250
25	VP of Sales & Marketing	$ -	$ -	$ -	$ 30,452	$ 51,264	$ 87,250
26	CIO - Chief Technical Officer	$ -	$ 387	$ 11,244	$ 30,452	$ 51,264	$ 87,250
27	Director of Mkt	$ -	$ -	$ 9,042	$ 30,452	$ 51,264	$ 87,250
28	Director of CRM	$ -	$ -	$ 10,857	$ 30,452	$ 51,264	$ 87,250
29	**Total Bonus Allocation**	$ -	$ 773	$ 42,386	$ 152,258	$ 307,582	$ 523,500
30	**Per Head Allocation**		$ 193	$ 10,596	$ 16,918	$ 30,758	$ 52,350
31							
32	**Commission Plan**						
33	Director of Sales	-	0.67	1.67	1.00	1.00	1.00
34	Field Sales Engineer		0.50	4.00	4.00	6.00	6.00
35	**Commission Plan Count**	-	1.17	5.67	5.00	7.00	7.00
36							
37	**Commission Allocation**						
38	Director of Sales	$ -	$ 1,547	$ 38,952	$ 109,626	$ 146,468	$ 249,286
39	Field Sales Engineer	$ -	$ 1,547	$ 134,223	$ 438,502	$ 878,807	$ 1,495,713
40							
41	**Total Commission Allocation**	$ -	$ 3,093	$ 173,174	$ 548,128	$ 1,025,275	$ 1,744,999
42	**Per Head Allocation**		$ 2,651	$ 30,560	$ 109,626	$ 146,468	$ 249,286

Figure 7-7. *COSM-BONUS_CWS, the Bonus and Sales Commission Worksheet, calculates bonuses and commissions for executives and sales and marketing staff.*

Understanding the Trip Type Calculation Worksheet

The COSM-TRIPCALC_CWS Worksheet (see Figure 7-8) is a model for forecasting and planning business trips for the Company. Sales-related travel is a major variable expense and should be modeled separately then combined with other expenses.

This worksheet is a straightforward model for computing the costs of various types of trips taken during the course of business for the Company. Different trip types are based on variations in airfare, lodging, per diem rates, and rental car expenses. Each trip type has a different assumption for the number of trip days and trip nights. This simple model is utilized by the Trip Plan Calculation Worksheet to compute the total cost of trips.

Note For a more detailed discussion of building this type of model, see Exercise 7-2 at the end of this chapter.

	B	C	D
2	Trip Cost Assumptions		
3		Trip Days	Nights
4	Business/Marketing	3	2
5	Airfare		$ 650.00
6	Lodging	$ 120.00	$ 240.00
7	Per Diem	$ 50.00	$ 150.00
8	Rental Car	$ 85.00	$ 255.00
9	Total Trip Cost		$ 1,295.00
10			
11	Technical/Consulting	2	2
12	Airfare		$ 650.00
13	Lodging	$ 120.00	$ 240.00
14	Per Diem	$ 50.00	$ 100.00
15	Rental Car	$ 85.00	$ 170.00
16	Total Trip Cost		$ 1,160.00
17			
18	Direct Sales Trip	4	3
19	Airfare		$ 650.00
20	Lodging	$ 120.00	$ 360.00
21	Per Diem	$ 50.00	$ 200.00
22	Rental Car	$ 85.00	$ 340.00
23	Total Trip Cost		$ 1,550.00
24			
25	Manufacturing Support	3	2
26	Airfare		$ 1,500.00
27	Lodging	$ 150.00	$ 300.00
28	Per Diem	$ 50.00	$ 150.00
29	Rental Car	$ 85.00	$ 255.00
30	Total Trip Cost		$ 2,205.00
31			
32	Training/Other	3	2
33	Airfare		$ 650.00
34	Lodging	$ 150.00	$ 300.00
35	Per Diem	$ 50.00	$ 150.00
36	Rental Car	$ 85.00	$ 255.00
37	Total Trip Cost		$ 1,355.00

Figure 7-8. *COSM_TRIPCALC_CWS calculation worksheet for trip cost by type of trip*

Understanding the Trip Plan Calculation Worksheet

COSM-TRIPPLAN_CWS, the Trip Plan Calculation Worksheet (see Figure 7-9), is a model for forecasting and planning business trips for the Company and for computing the total cost of trips. Trip cost data is accessed from COSM-TRIPPLAN_CWS and multiplied by the number of planned trips to develop a total cost of trips by department.

	B	C	L	M	N	O	P	Q	R	S
2	Trip Model		Aug	Sep	Oct	Nov	Dec	Jan	Feb	Mar
106	SALES & MKT Trip Count									
107										
108	Business/Marketing									
109	Technical/Consulting									
110	Direct Sales Trip		1.00	1.00	2.00	2.00	2.00	3.00	3.00	3.00
111	Manufacturing Support									
112	Training/Other									
113										
114	Total Trips		1.00	1.00	2.00	2.00	2.00	3.00	3.00	3.00
115										
116	SALES & MKT Trip Cost									
117										
118	Business/Marketing		$ -	$ -	$ -	$ -	$ -	$ -	$ -	$ -
119	Technical/Consulting		$ -	$ -	$ -	$ -	$ -	$ -	$ -	$ -
120	Direct Sales Trip		$ 1,550	$ 1,550	$ 3,100	$ 3,100	$ 3,100	$ 4,650	$ 4,650	$ 4,650
121	Manufacturing Support		$ -	$ -	$ -	$ -	$ -	$ -	$ -	$ -
122	Training/Other		$ -	$ -	$ -	$ -	$ -	$ -	$ -	$ -
123										
124	Total SALES & MKT Trip Cost		$ 1,550	$ 1,550	$ 3,100	$ 3,100	$ 3,100	$ 4,650	$ 4,650	$ 4,650

Figure 7-9. *COSM-TRIPPLAN_CWS, the Trip Plan Calculation Worksheet, forecasts sales and marketing department trips as well as trips for other departments.*

Understanding the Cost of Sales and Marketing Calculation Worksheet

COSM_CWS, the Cost of Sales and Marketing Calculation Worksheet (see Figure 7-10), is used to develop the operating budget and capital expenditure budget for the sales and marketing department. This simple worksheet accepts monthly inputs for expenditures and summarizes expenses in three categories: marketing expenses, direct sales expenses, and total CRM and technical support. These categories correspond with the organizational structure of the sales and marketing department.

The last section of the worksheet links to COSM-TRIPPLAN_CWS and picks up the total cost of trips forecast for sales and marketing in the trip model. There is also a section for the input of capital expenditure forecasts, and these inputs are linked into CAPEX_CWS, the Capital Plan, where they appear as sales and marketing capital expenditure inputs in the total Company capital plan.

	B	C	D	E	F	G
2		YR 0	Jan	Feb	Mar	Apr
4	**Marketing Expense**					
5						
6	Web Site Development	$ -	$ 2,500	$ 2,500	$ 2,500	
7	Web Site Hosting		$ 250	$ 250	$ 250	$ 250
8	Internet Marketing					
9	Online Meeting Support	$ 250	$ 250	$ 250	$ 250	$ 250
10	Marketing Collaterals				$ 2,500	$ 2,500
11	Advertising					
12	Entertainment	$ 690	$ 550		$ 550	
13	Membership/Affiliations		$ 35	$ 35	$ 35	$ 35
14	Trade Shows					
15	Seminars & Conferences					
16	Specialty Events					
17	Subscriptions & Dues		$ 15	$ 15	$ 15	$ 15
18						
19	**Total Marketing Expense**	$ 940	$ 3,600	$ 3,050	$ 6,100	$ 3,050
20						
21	**Direct Sales Expense**					
22						
23	Entertainment					
24	Membership/Affiliations		$ 150	$ 150	$ 150	$ 150
25	Trade Shows					
26	Seminars & Conferences					
27	Specialty Events					
28	Networking Events					
29	Subscriptions & Dues		$ 15	$ 15	$ 15	$ 15
30						
31	**Total Direct Sales Expense**	$ -	$ 165	$ 165	$ 165	$ 165
32						
33	**CRM & Tech Support**					
34	Online CRM Support System					$ 250
35	VOIP Phone System					
36	CRM Software and System					
37						
38	**Total CRM & Tech Support**	$ -	$ -	$ -	$ -	$ 250

Figure 7-10. *COSM_CWS, the Cost of Sales and Marketing Calculation Worksheet, provides an input template and summarizes operating expenses and capital expenditures for the sales and marketing department.*

Understanding the Capital Plan Calculation Worksheet

CAPEX _CWS, the Capital Plan Calculation Worksheet (see Figure 7-11), is discussed in more detail in Chapter 9. Sales and marketing capital expenditures are input into COSM_CWS. This data is linked into CAPEX_CWS, where it becomes part of the total Company capital expenditure plan.

	B	C	D	E	F	G	H	I	J
2	**Capital Plan**			YR 0	Jan	Feb	Mar	Apr	May
3		Basis of							
4		Estimate	Units						
5									
6	**Facilites**								
7	Furniture and Fixtures	FAC_CWS		$ 1,000	$ 2,000	$ -	$ -	$ 250	$ 500
8	Office Computers	FAC_CWS		$10,000	$ 25,000	$ -	$ -	$ 2,500	$ 5,000
9	**Total Facilities**			$11,000	$ 27,000	$ -	$ -	$ 2,750	$ 5,500
10									
11	**Marketing and Sales**								
12	VOIP Phone System	$ 10,000	ea	$ -	$ -	$ -	$ -	$ 10,000	$ -
13	Marketing Web Server	$ 3,500	ea	$ -	$ -	$ 3,500	$ -	$ -	$ -
14	**Total Marketing and Sales**			$ -	$ 3,500	$ -	$ -	$ 10,000	$ -

Figure 7-11. *CAPEX_CWS showing the sales and marketing department capital plan*

Understanding the Cost of Sales and Marketing Dashboard

COSM_DB, the Cost of Sales and Marketing Dashboard (see Figure 7-12), provides an important management summary, or *view*, of the cost of sales and marketing. In one view, revenue, headcount, compensation, and total cost of sales and marketing are summarized. This data is created by linking to the worksheets within COSM that we have previously discussed. The following are the component data sources that make up COSM_DB:

Sales and revenue: Source is REV_DB

Headcount: Source is STAFF_CWS

Compensation: Source is STAFF_CWS

Operating expense and capital: Source is COSM_CWS

The summary data from COSM_DB is used to perform analysis and to sanity check the relationship between sales and marketing costs and the level of sales. Here are two prime management questions: Is the relationship between sales and marketing cost and revenue generated satisfactory? Am I getting the bang for my buck out of sales and marketing that I need?

Data from COSM_DB is summarized and preformatted in COSM_CHARTDAT to generate management charts that may answer these questions.

	B	C	D	E	F	G	H
1		YR 0	YR 1	YR 2	YR 3	YR 4	YR 5
2	**Sales and Revenue**						
3	Sale Units		$ 51	$ 976	$ 2,400	$ 3,753	$ 5,400
4	Total Revenue		$ 102,000	$4,026,000	$12,240,000	$ 21,955,050	$ 35,235,000
5	Net Revenue		$ 61,866	$3,401,623	$10,962,555	$ 20,505,495	$ 34,899,981
6	**Headcount**						
7	Director of Marketing		-	1.00	1.00	1.00	1.00
8	Marketing Support		-	-	1.00	1.00	1.00
9	Director of Sales		1.00	1.00	1.00	1.00	1.00
10	Field Sales Engineer		1.00	4.00	4.00	6.00	6.00
11	Director of CRM		-	1.00	1.00	1.00	1.00
12	Customer Support Tech		1.00	1.00	2.00	4.00	4.00
13	Headcount Sales and Mkt	-	3.00	8.00	10.00	14.00	14.00
14	Consultant HeadCount	-	0.75	0.50	-	-	-
15	Total Headcount	-	3.75	8.50	10.00	14.00	14.00
16	Average Yearly Headcount	-	1	7	10	14	14
17	**Compensation**						
18	Salaries & Wages	$ -	$ 96,500	$ 512,500	$ 731,500	$ 1,073,500	$ 1,090,000
19	Commissions and Bonuses	$ -	$ 3,093	$ 189,980	$ 609,031	$ 1,127,802	$ 1,919,499
20	Taxes	$ -	$ 9,403	$ 65,471	$ 123,748	$ 202,457	$ 275,195
21	Medical Insurance	$ -	$ 3,333	$ 33,000	$ 57,475	$ 65,000	$ 102,487
22	401 K	$ -	$ -	$ 4,045	$ 22,756	$ 41,852	$ 67,265
23	Total Employee Costs	$ -	$ 112,329	$ -	$ -	$ -	$ -
24	Average Salary		$ 68,118	$ 70,690	$ 73,150	$ 76,679	$ 77,857
25	Average Comm & Bonuses		$ 2,184	$ 26,204	$ 60,903	$ 80,557	$ 137,107
26	Average Compensation		$ 70,301	$ 96,894	$ 134,053	$ 157,236	$ 214,964
27	Consultant Total Fees	$ -	$ 132,000	$ 58,800	$ -	$ -	$ -
28	**Operating Expense and Capital**						
29	Marketing Expense	$ 940	$ 96,500	$ 512,500	$ 731,500	$ 1,073,500	$ 1,090,000
30	Total Direct Sales Expense	$ -	$ 4,480	$ 18,480	$ 19,980	$ 31,980	$ 37,980
31	Total CRM & Tech Support	$ -	$ 2,250	$ 11,500	$ 6,000	$ 6,000	$ 6,000
32	Total Trip Costs	$ -	$ 12,400	$ 106,550	$ 155,760	$ 192,960	$ 229,000
33	Total Sales & Marketing Costs	$ 940	$ 115,630	$ 649,030	$ 913,240	$ 1,304,440	$ 1,362,980
34	Sales & Marketing Total	$ 940	$ 359,959	$ 707,830	$ 913,240	$ 1,304,440	$ 1,362,980
35	Total Capital Expenditures	$ -	$ 3,500	$ -	$ -	$ -	$ -

Figure 7-12. *COSM_DB, the Cost of Sales and Marketing Dashboard, summarizes COSM data and provides a single view of key metrics related to the cost of sales and marketing.*

Understanding the Cost of Sales and Marketing Chart Data Worksheet

COSM_CHARTDAT (see Figure 7-13) summarizes and preformats data used for management charts related to the COSM model.

	B	C	D	E	F	G	H	I	J
30	COSM_CHART-SAL-WAGES								
31									YR 1
32		YR 0	Jan	Feb	Mar	Apr	May	Jun	Jul
33	Salaries & Wages	$ -	$ -	$ -	$ -	$ -	$ 6,250	$ 6,250	$ 11,917
34	Commissions and Bonuses	$ -	$ -	$ -	$ -	$ -	$ -	$ -	$ -
35	Total Employee Costs	$ -	$ -	$ -	$ -	$ -	$ 6,250	$ 6,250	$ 11,917
36	Consultant Total Fees	$ -	$ 13,600	$ 13,600	$ 13,600	$ 13,600	$ 13,600	$ 13,600	$ 8,400
37	Taxes and Benefits	$ -	$ -	$ -	$ -	$ -	$ 588	$ 588	$ 1,124
38	Sales & Marketing Total	$ -	$ 5,200	$ 5,200	$ 5,200	$ 5,200	$ 12,038	$ 12,038	$ 13,041

Figure 7-13. *COSM_CHARTDAT, the Cost of Sales and Marketing Chart Data Worksheet*

EXERCISE 7-1. USING MICROSOFT EXCEL TO DEVELOP A BONUS AND COMMISSION PLAN MODEL

The Company must forecast the total cost of sales and marketing. Bonuses and sales commissions are a primary motivator of executives and sales and marketing staff. It is important that a comprehensive compensation plan be developed in order to attract the type of sales and marketing talent the Company needs to be successful.

- *Problem*: Bonuses and commissions are a significant variable cost component of the total cost of sales and marketing. Bonuses and sales commissions must be forecast at a level of detail that satisfies the need for a centralized compensation plan while, at the same time, providing data input to other components of the model.

- *Solution*: Develop an effective Bonus and Commission model.

■**Note** The model in this example is relatively simplistic and is developed to demonstrate the main concepts that must be addressed. In my experience, compensation plan models are often highly complex.

Understand the Model Functionality

The Bonus and Sales Commission Worksheet (COSM-BONUS_CWS) is the Bonus and Commission model. The idea behind this type of model is twofold:

- The Company should develop a top-level compensation plan for executives and the sales team. This plan should be consistent in fairness of application. It should also be effective and targeted in its ability to motivate desired performance from various functional positions.

- The Bonus and Compensation model should compute bonus and sales commission compensation based on performance (which is typically sales and revenue based) and allocate compensation amounts back to the cost centers to which they are directed. In other words, the compensation plan generates compensation amounts and passes it to applicable parts of the model where the bonuses and commissions are added to normal salary and wage compensation.

Understand the Model Structure

Note the structure of the model shown in Figure 7-14. The top portion of the spreadsheet computes bonuses for executives, and these are followed by sales commission computations for the sales staff.

B	C	D	F	G	H	I	J
			YR 1	YR 2	YR 3	YR 4	YR 5
Bonus and Commission Plan							
Total Revenue (Plan Basis)			$ 61,866	$ 3,401,623	$ 10,962,555	$ 20,505,495	$ 34,899,981
Bonus Basis		3%	$ 1,547	$ 85,041	$ 274,064	$ 512,637	$ 872,500
Commission Basis		5%	$ 3,093	$ 173,174	$ 548,128	$ 1,025,275	$ 1,744,999
Bonus Pool							
CEO/President			1.00	1.00	1.00	1.00	1.00
VP of Business Operations			-	-	-	1.00	1.00
VP of Sales & Marketing			-	-	1.00	1.00	1.00
CIO - Chief Technical Officer			1.00	1.00	1.00	1.00	1.00
Director of Mkt			-	-	1.00	1.00	1.00
Director of CRM			-	-	1.00	1.00	1.00
Director of Systems Int			-	-	1.00	1.00	1.00
Director Software Eng			1.00	1.00	1.00	1.00	1.00
Director Hardware Eng			1.00	1.00	1.00	1.00	1.00
Director of Test Eng			-	-	1.00	1.00	1.00
Bonus Pool Count			4.00	4.00	9.00	10.00	10.00
Bonus Allocation							
CEO/President			$ 387	$ 11,244	$ 30,452	$ 51,264	$ 87,250
VP of Business Operations			$ -	$ -	$ -	$ 51,264	$ 87,250
VP of Sales & Marketing			$ -	$ -	$ 30,452	$ 51,264	$ 87,250
CIO - Chief Technical Officer			$ 387	$ 11,244	$ 30,452	$ 51,264	$ 87,250
Director of Mkt			$ -	$ 9,042	$ 30,452	$ 51,264	$ 87,250
Director of CRM			$ -	$ 10,857	$ 30,452	$ 51,264	$ 87,250
Total Bonus Allocation			$ 773	$ 42,386	$ 152,258	$ 307,582	$ 523,500
Per Head Allocation			$ 193	$ 10,596	$ 16,918	$ 30,758	$ 52,350
Commission Plan							
Director of Sales			0.67	1.67	1.00	1.00	1.00
Field Sales Engineer			0.50	4.00	4.00	6.00	6.00
Commission Plan Count			1.17	5.67	5.00	7.00	7.00
Commission Allocation							
Director of Sales			$ 1,547	$ 38,952	$ 109,626	$ 146,468	$ 249,286
Field Sales Engineer			$ 1,547	$ 134,223	$ 438,502	$ 878,807	$ 1,495,713
Total Commission Allocation			$ 3,093	$ 173,174	$ 548,128	$ 1,025,275	$ 1,744,999

Figure 7-14. *COSM-BONUS_CWS, a model for calculating bonuses and commissions*

The various sections in this worksheet follow:

- *Total Revenue (Plan Basis)*: The plan basis (the amount on which the bonuses are calculated) is the Company's total revenue. The source of this data is REV-REVCALC_CWS. Note that most compensation plans have a wide variety of bases on which bonuses and commissions may be computed.

- *Bonus Basis and Commission Basis*: In this model, bonuses will be based on 3 percent of total revenue and commissions computed at 5 percent of total revenue. These percentages are multiplied by the plan basis to generate a bonus and commission basis, or the bonus amounts that will be allocated to the bonus pool and commission amounts that will be allocated to the sales staff. This is a simplification of the concept. Many plans have complex algorithms for developing the amounts of bonus and compensation.

- *Bonus Pool*: The bonus pool is made up of participants who fill specific functional positions. The participants will receive an allocation from the bonus basis. The model lists the functional positions that will receive a bonus and links back to the headcount data for that position in order to count the number of people that are working in that position. If a position is not filled, the pool is smaller, and the participants get a bigger share. As the pool grows, the reverse occurs. The source of headcount data is STAFF_CWS. Many compensation plans allocate various types of bonus or commissions to various functional positions within the Company, as does this model. Note in Figure 7-15 that the headcount for each functional position that participates in the pool is taken from STAFF_CWS.

- *Bonus Pool Allocation*: The Bonus Pool Allocation calculation (see Figure 7-15) is made for each functional position by first dividing the Bonus Basis (cell F50) by the Bonus Pool Count (cell F67). This computes the per-person amount of allocation for each functional position. We then multiply this result by the number of people occupying the position to allocate the bonus to the position. In the case of the bonus pool, there is a one-to-one ratio between the functional title and number of people in the position.

Note It is possible for the Bonus Pool Count to be zero. To avoid an error resulting from dividing by zero, I have used the IF function to first test to see if the Bonus Pool Count is greater than zero before I do my division. For example the formula in cell F71 is =IF(F$67>0,(F$50/F$67),0)*F56 or, stated in English, "if the Bonus Pool Count (cell F67) is greater than zero, go ahead and divide the Bonus Basis (cell F50) by the Bonus Pool Count (cell F67). If not, my result is zero."

	B	F	G
		Jan	Feb
45			
46			
47	Bonus and Commission Plan		
48			
49	Total Revenue (Plan Basis)	='REV-REVCALC_CWS'!E42	='REV-REVCALC_CWS'!F42
50	Bonus Basis	=F49*$D50	=G49*$D50
51	Commission Basis	=F49*$D51	=G49*$D51
52			
53			
54	Bonus Pool		
55			
56	CEO/President	=STAFF_CWS!H10	=STAFF_CWS!I10
57	VP of Business Operations	=STAFF_CWS!H13	=STAFF_CWS!I13
58	VP of Sales & Marketing	=STAFF_CWS!H16	=STAFF_CWS!I16
59	CIO - Chief Technical Officer	=STAFF_CWS!H19	=STAFF_CWS!I19
60	Director of Mkt	=STAFF_CWS!H58	=STAFF_CWS!I58
61	Director of CRM	=STAFF_CWS!H70	=STAFF_CWS!I70
62	Director of Systems Int	=STAFF_CWS!H93	=STAFF_CWS!I93
63	Director Software Eng	=STAFF_CWS!H105	=STAFF_CWS!I105
64	Director Hardware Eng	=STAFF_CWS!H114	=STAFF_CWS!I114
65	Director of Test Eng	=STAFF_CWS!H123	=STAFF_CWS!I123
66			
67	Bonus Pool Count	=SUM(F56:F66)	=SUM(G56:G66)
68			
69	Bonus Allocation		
70			
71	CEO/President	=IF(F$67>0,(F$50/F$67),0)*F56	=IF(G$67>0,(G$50/G$67),0)*G56
72	VP of Business Operations	=IF(F$67>0,(F$50/F$67),0)*F57	=IF(G$67>0,(G$50/G$67),0)*G57
73	VP of Sales & Marketing	=IF(F$67>0,(F$50/F$67),0)*F58	=IF(G$67>0,(G$50/G$67),0)*G58
74	CIO - Chief Technical Officer	=IF(F$67>0,(F$50/F$67),0)*F59	=IF(G$67>0,(G$50/G$67),0)*G59
75	Director of Mkt	=IF(F$67>0,(F$50/F$67),0)*F60	=IF(G$67>0,(G$50/G$67),0)*G60

Figure 7-15. *Formula view of the calculation of Bonus Allocation within COSM-BONUS_CWS*

- *Commission Plan and Commission Allocation:* Commission plan participants are the director of sales and the field sales engineer(s). The field sales engineer position is an example in which more than one person fills a position. The director of sales and field sales engineers, under the assumptions of this model, receive sales commissions because of being directly involved in selling. All other executives are compensated via the bonus plan. The source of headcount data is STAFF_CWS. This model takes a simple approach of computing a sales commission basis then allocating the commission among sales staff. Most commission plans are far more complex.

Note, in Figure 7-16, that the headcount for each functional position that participates in the pool is taken from STAFF_CWS. The Commission Allocation calculation is made for each functional position by first dividing the Commission Basis (cell F51) by the Commission Plan Count (cell F89). We use the IF statement in the same way as previously described. This computes the per-person amount of allocation for each functional position. We then multiply this result by the number of people occupying each position to allocate commissions. In the case of the commission, only one person occupies the director of sales position but multiple people may fill the field sales engineer position.

	B	F	G
45		Jan	Feb
46			
47	**Bonus and Commission Plan**		
48			
49	Total Revenue (Plan Basis)	='REV-REVCALC_CWS'!E42	='REV-REVCALC_CWS'!F42
50	Bonus Basis	=F49*$D50	=G49*$D50
51	Commission Basis	=F49*$D51	=G49*$D51
52			
84	**Commission Plan**		
85			
86	Director of Sales	=STAFF_CWS!H64	=STAFF_CWS!I64
87	Field Sales Engineer	=STAFF_CWS!H67	=STAFF_CWS!I67
88			
89	**Commission Plan Count**	=SUM(F86:F88)	=SUM(G86:G88)
90			
91	**Commission Allocation**		
92			
93	Director of Sales	=IF(F$89>0,(F$51/F$89),0)*F86	=IF(G$89>0,(G$51/G$89),0)*G86
94	Field Sales Engineer	=IF(F$89>0,(F$51/F$89),0)*F87	=IF(G$89>0,(G$51/G$89),0)*G87
95			
96	**Total Commission Allocation**	=SUM(F93:F95)	=SUM(G93:G95)

Figure 7-16. *Formula view of the calculation of Bonus Allocation within COSM-BONUS_CWS*

Use Model Outputs in the Staffing Model

Once bonuses and commissions are computed and allocated to their proper functional positions, we must link STAFF_CWS to COSM-BONUS_CWS in order to add the bonuses and commissions to the Tax and Burden Basis for each functional position. See Figure 7-17 for a data view of this linking and Figure 7-18 for a formula view. The tax and burden basis is the basis on which employment taxes and benefits are calculated for the position.

	A	W	X	Y	Z
1				YR 2	
2	**Period of Performance**	Apr	May	Jun	Jul
3	Employee				
4	Consultant				
321	**Director of Sales**				
322	Base Compensation	$ 10,417	$ 10,417	$ 10,417	$ 10,417
323	Adjustment Factor	80%	80%	80%	80%
324	Adjusted Compensation	$ 8,333	$ 8,333	$ 8,333	$ 8,333
325	Sales Commissions	$ 2,716	$ 2,716	$ 2,716	$ 2,716
326	Tax and Burden Basis	$ 11,049	$ 11,049	$ 11,049	$ 11,049
327					
328	Consultant	$ -	$ -	$ -	$ -
329					
330	**Field Sales Engineer**				
331	Base Compensation	$ 28,333	$ 28,333	$ 28,333	$ 28,333
332	Adjustment Factor	80%	80%	80%	80%
333	Adjusted Compensation	$ 22,667	$ 22,667	$ 22,667	$ 22,667
334	Sales Commissions	$ 10,863	$ 10,863	$ 10,863	$ 10,863
335	Tax and Burden Basis	$ 33,530	$ 33,530	$ 33,530	$ 33,530
336					
337	Consultant	$ -	$ -	$ -	$ -
338					
339	**Director of CRM**				
340	Base Compensation	$ 7,500	$ 7,500	$ 7,500	$ 7,500
341	Adjustment Factor	80%	80%	80%	80%
342	Adjusted Compensation	$ 6,000	$ 6,000	$ 6,000	$ 6,000
343	Sales Commissions	$ 849	$ 849	$ 849	$ 849
344	Tax and Burden Basis	$ 6,849	$ 6,849	$ 6,849	$ 6,849

Figure 7-17. *In STAFF_CWS, note that sales commissions from COSM-BONUS_CWS are added to the Tax and Burden Basis row on which taxes and benefits are calculated.*

⯑	A	W
1		
2	Period of Performance	Apr
3	Employee	
4	Consultant	
321	Director of Sales	
322	Base Compensation	=W64*$C64
323	Adjustment Factor	=STAFFPLAN_CWS!$D86
324	Adjusted Compensation	=W322*W323
325	Sales Commissions	='COSM-BONUS_CWS'!U93
326	Tax and Burden Basis	=W324+W325
327		
328	Consultant	=W65*$C65

Figure 7-18. *Formula view of STAFF_CWS showing the link back to COSM-BONUS_CWS for sales commission calculations*

EXERCISE 7-2. USING MICROSOFT EXCEL TO MODEL TRIP EXPENSES

The Company must forecast the total cost of sales and marketing. Sales-and-marketing-related travel or trip costs are a major variable cost of sales and marketing.

- *Problem*: Trip costs are related to sales and marketing milestones and to headcount. The costs of airfare, lodging, and per diem expenses are variable based on the type of trip taken. This cost and the number of trips should be modeled separately from operating expense budgets.

- *Solution*: Develop a Trip Cost model to forecast the cost of trips for the Company.

Understand the Model Structure and Functionality

The COSM-TRIPCALC_CWS and the COSM-TRIPPLAN_CWS (the trip plan calculation worksheets) are utilized together to model the cost of trips for the Company. The idea behind this type of model is simple:

- Company operations will require different types of trips taken by persons in different functional areas in the normal course of business. Trips vary in cost based on trip duration, destination, and other cost variables, such as time of year.

- The trip model forecasts costs for trip types and then forecasts the number of trips by each functional area. The two pieces of data (trip costs and number of trips) are combined to generate the total cost of trips, which is then allocated back into the operating expense budget of each functional area.

Next is a discussion of the development of the trip costs model.

Referring to Figure 7-19, note that there are differing assumptions that drive costs for business/marketing trips versus technical/consulting trips.

	B	C	D
2	Trip Cost Assumptions		
3		Trip Days	Nights
4	Business/Marketing	3	2
5	Airfare		$ 650.00
6	Lodging	$ 120.00	$ 240.00
7	Per Diem	$ 50.00	$ 150.00
8	Rental Car	$ 85.00	$ 255.00
9	Total Trip Cost		$ 1,295.00
10			
11	Technical/Consulting	2	2
12	Airfare		$ 650.00
13	Lodging	$ 120.00	$ 240.00
14	Per Diem	$ 50.00	$ 100.00
15	Rental Car	$ 85.00	$ 170.00
16	Total Trip Cost		$ 1,160.00

Figure 7-19. *The COSM-TRIPCALC_CWS worksheet, which forecasts varying costs for different types of trips*

Figure 7-20 provides a formula view of the same data.

	B	C	D
2	Trip Cost Assumptions		
3		Trip Days	Nights
4	Business/Marketing	3	2
5	Airfare		650
6	Lodging	120	=C6*$D$4
7	Per Diem	50	=C7*$C$4
8	Rental Car	85	=C8*$C$4
9	Total Trip Cost		=SUM(D5:D8)
10			
11	Technical/Consulting	2	2
12	Airfare		650
13	Lodging	120	=C13*$D$11
14	Per Diem	50	=C14*$C$11
15	Rental Car	85	=C15*$C$11
16	Total Trip Cost		=SUM(D12:D15)

Figure 7-20. *Formula view of the COSM-TRIPCALC_CWS worksheet, which forecasts varying costs for different types of trips*

Note the following regarding trip cost calculation for business/marketing trips.

- *Airfare*: Airfare (cell D5) is a one-time cost of each trip and is manually input into the model.

- *Lodging*: The cost of lodging (cell D6) is computed by multiplying the number of trip nights (cell D4) by the lodging per night cost (cell C6).

- *Per Diem*: The per diem cost is computed by multiplying the daily per diem rate (cell C7) by the number of trip days (cell C4).

- *Rental Car*: The rental car cost is computed by multiplying daily rental car cost (cell C8) by the number of trip days (cell C4).

- *Total Trip Cost*: The total trip cost is computed by summarizing all trip costs (cells D5:D8).

The following is a discussion of the development of trip forecasts and the total cost of trips for the Company.

Referring to Figure 7-21, note the structure of COSM-TRIPPLAN_CWS:

- *Total Sales & Mkt (Headcount)*: A headcount for the sales department is presented (from STAFF_CWS) as a guide for planning the number of trips.

- *SALES & MKT Trip Count*: This is the number of forecasted trips (of each type).

- *Total Trips*: This calculates the total number of monthly trips.

- *SALES & MKT Trip Cost*: The number of trips of each type is multiplied by the trip cost of each type of trip (from COSM-TRIPCALC_CWS), and the total cost of trips for the department is calculated.

	B	C	T	U	V	W
1					YR 2	
2	**Trip Model**		Apr	May	Jun	Jul
102	**Total Sales & Mkt -Employee**		8.00	8.00	8.00	8.00
103	**Total Consultant**		0.50	0.50	0.50	0.50
104	**Total Sales & Mkt Headcount**		8.50	8.50	8.50	8.50
105						
106	**SALES & MKT Trip Count**					
107						
108	Business/Marketing					
109	Technical/Consulting		1.00		1.00	
110	Direct Sales Trip		4.00	5.00	5.00	7.00
111	Manufacturing Support					
112	Training/Other					
113						
114	**Total Trips**		5.00	5.00	6.00	7.00
115						
116	**SALES & MKT Trip Cost**					
117						
118	Business/Marketing	$ -	$ -	$ -	$ -	
119	Technical/Consulting	$ 1,160	$ -	$ 1,160	$ -	
120	Direct Sales Trip	$ 6,200	$ 7,750	$ 7,750	$ 10,850	
121	Manufacturing Support	$ -	$ -	$ -	$ -	
122	Training/Other	$ -	$ -	$ -	$ -	
123						
124	**Total SALES & MKT Trip Cost**	$ 7,360	$ 7,750	$ 8,910	$ 10,850	

Figure 7-21. *COSM-TRIPPLAN_CWS, the Trip Plan Calculation Worksheet*

Figure 7-22 provides a formula view of the same data. Note the formula for calculating trip costs: trip costs are calculated by multiplying the number of trips by the cost of that type of trip, as forecast in COSM-TRIPCALC_CWS.

	B	C	T
1			
2	**Trip Model**		Apr
102	**Total Sales & Mkt -Employee**		=STAFF_CWS!W76
103	**Total Consultant**		=STAFF_CWS!W77
104	**Total Sales & Mkt Headcount**		=STAFF_CWS!W78
105			
106	**SALES & MKT Trip Count**		
107			
108	Business/Marketing		
109	Technical/Consulting		1
110	Direct Sales Trip		4
111	Manufacturing Support		
112	Training/Other		
113			
114	**Total Trips**		=SUM(T108:T113)
115			
116	**SALES & MKT Trip Cost**		
117			
118	Business/Marketing		='COSM-TRIPCALC_CWS'!$D$9*'COSM-TRIPPLAN_CWS'!T108
119	Technical/Consulting		='COSM-TRIPCALC_CWS'!$D$16*'COSM-TRIPPLAN_CWS'!T109
120	Direct Sales Trip		='COSM-TRIPCALC_CWS'!$D$23*'COSM-TRIPPLAN_CWS'!T110
121	Manufacturing Support		='COSM-TRIPCALC_CWS'!$D$30*'COSM-TRIPPLAN_CWS'!T111
122	Training/Other		='COSM-TRIPCALC_CWS'!$D$37*'COSM-TRIPPLAN_CWS'!T112
123			
124	**Total SALES & MKT Trip Cost**		=SUM(T118:T123)

Figure 7-22. *Formula view of COSM-TRIPPLAN_CWS showing the calculation of trip costs based on the number of forecasted trips*

And finally, trip costs are allocated back to the operating expense budgets for each functional department. Figure 7-23 shows trip costs in COSM_CWS, the marketing department expense budget. This data comes from the COSM-TRIPPLAN_CWS model shown in this exercise.

	A	B	S	T
2			Apr	May
33		CRM & Tech Support		
34		Online CRM Support System	$ 250	$ 250
35		VOIP Phone System		
36		CRM Software and System		
37				
38		Total CRM & Tech Support	$ 250	$ 250
39				
40		Total Trip Costs	$ 7,360	$ 7,750
41				
42		Total Sales & Marketing Costs	$24,675	$11,565

Figure 7-23. *COSM_CWS showing marketing and sales department trip costs that have been forecast in COSM-TRIPPLAN_CWS*

Summary

In this chapter, we have explored the Cost of Sales and Marketing (COSM) model. I have defined the cost of sales and marketing to include not only direct sales and marketing activities but also costs associated with customer relationships in support of the total customer support life cycle. I have explained the three steps that must be completed before modeling resources:

1. Complete a market assessment.
2. Develop the value proposition.
3. Plan the sales and marketing implementation strategy.

We have completed our market assessment within the context of the five forces that shape competition, and we developed a value proposition and analyzed three types of increasingly valuable value proposition. We also looked at ROI as a classic method for presenting the value of technology products and services.

We have reviewed the COSM model and forecast major components of sales and marketing cost:

- Staffing costs
- Bonus and sales commission costs
- Operating expense and capital expenditure costs
- Trip costs

Finally, we discussed the need to design COSM from a sales and marketing metrics point of view. The model should generate data that will assist in measuring the effectiveness of company investment in sales and marketing.

Here are the key questions regarding the Cost of Sales and Marketing model: Is the investment in sales and marketing generating expected results in sales and revenues? If not, why not?

■■■

CHAPTER 8

Cost of Product Development Model

Technology startup companies have two primary cost drivers:

- Product development
- Sales and marketing

The cost of product development is the cost the company incurs to design, build, and deliver its product to the market. A financial model, in and of itself, cannot define or articulate strategies for designing and developing products. It can, however, model the application of resources planned for the implementation of these strategies. The Cost of Product Development (DEV) model quantifies and forecasts the resources needed to the implement a company's product development strategy.

In this chapter, you will learn how to plan, create, and use the DEV model. In addition, you will learn

- About business objectives and product development strategies
- What resources are to be considered and planned for in the DEV model
- How to develop a model to forecast and quantify the total cost of product development needed to support the product development life cycle

Business Thinking About Product Development

Product development is the lifeblood and core process of a technology company. All other processes take their cues from and are dependent on, to a greater or lesser extent, product development. Failure in product development generally spells failure for the company. The objective of product development is to implement a development process that assures the product output exhibits the qualities the customer wants to see. A company that can uncover what a customer wants and design, build, and distribute a product to meet those needs at an acceptable cost will be successful.

This comprehensive process, which I will call product life cycle management (PLM), includes all aspects of product development from inception to retirement, from customer requirements and conceptual design to detail and production design, and from manufacturing to sales support and maintenance services. In today's world, product development is increasingly evolving in the direction of complex electromechanical systems that include a significant component of embedded software.

The product development implementation strategy is the key to the kingdom of technology company success.

■**Note** At best, a book on financial modeling can only present a conceptual framework for modeling product development and the costs associated with it. In practice, the product development strategy is highly complex. The financial model can only reflect and represent the product development strategy by presenting the time phasing and quantification of resources required to implement the strategy. The primary product development financial model output is the company's cost of product development, hence the title to this chapter.

In practice, product development strategy is highly complex and requires extensive and detailed attention. One example of this complexity, which is beyond the scope of this book, is the need for formal project planning. It is critical that early-stage companies utilize a formal project planning methodology and tools like Microsoft Project to develop detailed resource-loaded project plans. Project plans should be integrated with the financial model and linked so that changes in the project plan flow directly into the model. It should be noted that most early-stage companies are resource constrained and under tremendous pressure to get a product out the door. Though it may seem counterintuitive, this is precisely the time when it is most important to implement formal planning and project control methodologies. You don't have to invest in fancy collaboration systems to create a working environment that values and practices these disciplines.

To begin business thinking about product development, we must first view it at a strategic level and within a framework of business objectives and technology company critical success factors. We should also view business objectives from the traditional perspective of time, cost, and quality. In other words, the product must be developed quickly and efficiently, at a reasonable cost, and be of high quality, exceeding customer demands.

The next section will discuss top-level business objectives, strategies, and tactics for achieving them.

Product Development Objectives, Strategies, and Tactics

Each of the following subjects points to a critical product development capability and best practice that should be considered by a high-tech startup:

- Product concept and design
- Planning
- Time to market
- Product development and production
- Team
- Product life cycle
- Quality
- Development capacity
- Customers
- Suppliers
- Intellectual property

Creating Product Concept and Design

Product design must address the following to be smart, efficient, and flexible:

Objective: Develop smart product designs, and quickly develop market intelligence that guides the company through key decisions in product specification and product positioning. The objective is that dollars spent and product development effort expended result in early business success.

Strategy: Product design must clearly support *identified opportunities*, features, and functions of the product, and the product's value proposition *must be validated with potential customers*.

Tactics: A company must take early action to interview, understand, and gather requirements from representative customers in their target markets.

■**Note** It usually takes the same amount of time and talent to design a product that meets the needs of a few customers as one that will meet the needs of many. Given the limited resources of most startups, it behooves a company to leverage its resources to meet the greatest demand. This means that targeting the right market segment and meeting the requirements of that segment are the most critical decisions that the company makes.

Planning

Here are important considerations to guarantee effective product planning:

Objective: Implement a formal and proactive planning process to manage all aspects of PLM.

Strategy: Formalized planning will be a key factor in management of the product development process. Planning will be ingrained and trained into the organization and will become a critical business skill of the company.

Tactics: A company will engage in formal and proactive planning of all aspects of PLM. Plans will be developed at multiple levels and will be integrated with sales and marketing strategies.

Optimizing the Time to Market

Time to market is critical. Consider the following, and shrink your time to market:

Objective: Bring products to market fast and efficiently.

Strategy: The time to market can be critical to a product's success, and the window of opportunity may be narrow. The first to market may enjoy a significant competitive advantage. Every day that can be shaved off time to market increases sales potential. The use of prototypes can uncover key information about the way your customer views your value proposition resulting in faster, more focused product innovation.

Tactics: Production prototypes must be placed in the hands of customers at the earliest possible date. Formal informational feedback loop practices will be used to garner information from the field.

Adopting Agile Product Development and Production

Optimization of product development from a cost and production standpoint is critical. Adopt the following approach for optimal results:

Objective: Optimize product development and production costs, developing the product efficiently and at as low a cost as possible.

Strategy: Product development cost is a critical metric for technology companies. The primary strategy to accomplish this goal is to *do it right the first time*, thus reducing iterations.

Tactics: A company must adopt practices and technologies that optimize product development, which might include the following:

- Adopting concurrency as the primary environment for developing products
- Creating designs that reduce complexity and therefore reduce the need for iterations in product design
- Implementing quick response feedback loops for engineering changes
- Adopting agile and responsive change management practices
- Creating a collaborative design work environment and providing access to integrated product data and collaboration tools
- Utilizing state-of-the-art enabling technologies like CAD, CAM, CAE, and PDM
- Driving down component costs by closely managing the design-to-manufacturing process

Forming the Team

The right skills and the right time are necessary for the right team. Consider the following strategies to achieve the correct mix of talent at the right time:

Objective: Build a product development team with the right skills and utilize the right methods to achieve product development success.

Strategy: Early on, visionary and pathfinder developers are needed. They must have the ability to work quickly and innovatively in unstructured and rapidly changing environments. As the company matures, the composition of the team should evolve toward a homesteader staffing profile.

Tactics: Utilize small cross-functional teams and incentivize team members to work collaboratively. Provide them with tools and infrastructure to assist in collaboration across barriers of time, distance, and even cultural differences. Hire the right product development talent at the right times during the evolving stages of product development.

■**Note** See Chapter 4 for a more detailed explanation of visionary, pathfinder, and homesteader staff types.

Managing the Product Life Cycle

The product life cycle must be profitable. Pay attention to the following approaches to managing the full life cycle:

Objective: Design and build for a longer, more profitable product life with a goal of maximizing value throughout its life cycle.

Strategy: It is generally accepted that 70 to 80 percent of the life cycle costs of a product are determined during product development. Create designs with the full product life cycle costs in mind, including the ability to support, modify, and repair products and to take advantage of cheaper materials and components.

Tactics: Work closely with suppliers and manufacturers to design optimized life cycle cost into the product. Closely integrate product design with manufacturing design to optimize handoff to manufacturing.

Building in Quality

Quality must be understood as a fundamental assumption. Keep these ideas in mind as you manage quality throughout the entire product life cycle:

Objective: Develop products that exhibit outstanding quality and that exceed customer expectations while keeping costs in check.

Strategy: Implement rigorous quality control standard methodologies to ensure the highest quality possible for the product. Adopt a rigorous quality orientation within the company, setting quality as a top priority.

Tactics: Implement quality methodologies like Six Sigma. Place high emphasis on testing and customer feedback loops to ensure customer satisfaction with the quality of the products and services.

■**Note** *Six Sigma* refers to a set of practices first created by Motorola that attempts to systematically remove imperfections in manufacturing processes while improving quality and efficiency. Six Sigma is one of many methodologies that are utilized by companies to improve the quality of their products and services.

Sustaining Development Capacity

To achieve proof of scale, you must prove your company's development capacity. Consider these approaches that will result in scalable development capacity as you grow:

Objective: Create sustainable and scalable development capacity. Scalable capabilities can absorb large increases in volumes with small increases in marginal costs and no loss of quality.

Strategy: Build sustainable and scalable PLM capabilities into the company.

Tactics: Train and invest in all aspects of people, process, and technology necessary to scale to higher levels of output quickly and efficiently. Implement formal and scalable methodologies for planning and software and product development.

Taking Care of Your Customers

Taking care of your customers during their life cycle engagement with you is critical to success. Approach customer satisfaction using the following ideas:

Objective: Design and build customer service and satisfaction into products.

Strategy: Product design should include considerations for customer satisfaction and support.

Tactics: Products should be designed for quick updates and repair. Complementary customer support systems like customer relationship management (CRM) should be tightly integrated into PLM.

Know Your Suppliers

Suppliers can be your best friend or worst enemy. Develop supplier relationships using the following objectives and strategies:

Objective: Develop and optimize supply chain business relationships, and mitigate impact and risk associated with powerful suppliers.

Strategy: Aggressively work with suppliers to develop win-win business relationships. Powerful suppliers like to see growth potential. Make sure they understand your strategies for growth and success.

Tactics: Implement product and manufacturing design and materials sourcing strategies with suppliers that optimize the ability to produce the product at a low cost. Product design should take suppliers and supply chains into consideration to provide maximum flexibility in sourcing parts and materials to reduce cost and risk.

Capture Intellectual Property

Finally, intellectual property (IP) can be one of your most critical assets. Develop and leverage it using the following processes and ideas:

Objective: Capture IP as a formal part of the development process.

Strategy: Build comprehensive IP capture into the product design process.

Tactics: Develop methods to formally integrate technology capture into the design process. For example, within 3-D CAD design, implement a formal capture of the designer's decision criteria in selecting various design alternatives or materials. Implement policies, procedures, training, and technologies that optimize the capture of company IP during the product development life cycle.

■**Note** You really have not finished designing a product until you get it through manufacturing engineering. In other words, plan and own the entire life cycle. Product development is not something you can throw over the wall even if outsourcing is needed.

Developing the Green Devil Control Systems Product Development Strategy

Green Devil Control Systems is an early-stage technology startup that develops energy monitoring and control systems for residential markets. The Company builds and sells the Green Devil Energy Control System (ECS). The Company president has extensive experience and contacts in the home building industry. His partner is a graduate level electrical engineer, and she has extensive experience in developing smart control systems.

Product

ECS is a patent-pending programmable hardware and software device that monitors and controls electricity usage on a circuit-by-circuit basis within a facility. ECS is installed on the facility side of the electrical breaker box.

ECS allows for the mapping of all electric circuits extending into and utilized by the facility and is particularly targeted for the smart homes market. ECS provides switching and control capabilities (like a programmable thermostat) for all individual electrical circuits within a facility. Electrical usage, at the appliance level, can be programmed, controlled, and monitored.

In addition, ECS is a network addressable device. It is designed to work seamlessly with wireless or wired LANs and to support Internet access.

ECS comes with two software options: Local Services (LS) or Extended Services (ES). The LS and ES web browser user interfaces are highly intuitive, attractive, and easy to use.

The LS software is the default option installed with each ECS system and provides for a local web browser user interface to enable local setup and programming. LS provide one month of electricity usage diagnostics.

ES provide Internet-based, secure, remote setup, programming control, and diagnostics. The ES software also provides a suite of analysis tools and system set up tools for optimizing electricity usage. In addition, ES provide demographic comparison data and unlimited usage data and statistics.

ECS hardware is composed of the following integrated components (see Figure 8-1):

- *Monitoring (measuring) module*: Monitors the usage of electricity

- *Switching module*: Allows virtual switching of circuits within the home for electricity usage management

- *Control module*: Controls the unit and contains the embedded software control systems

- *Communications module*: Provides network connectivity

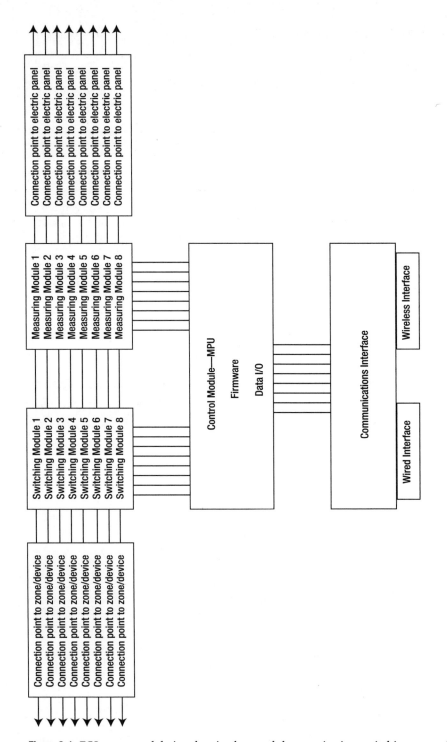

Figure 8-1. *ECS conceptual design showing key modules: monitoring, switching, control, and communications*

Scheduling Product Development

Time to market is critical for the Company, which will move quickly to build and test production prototypes and move into manufacturing status. The Company product development strategy (see Figures 8-2 and 8-3) includes the following major milestones and value events:

- *Prototype development*: Low-level prototype development and testing will be completed by March of YR 1.

- *Production prototype development*: Ten production prototypes will be built and completed by May of YR 1. Five production prototypes will be used for field testing and five for compliance (lab) and safety testing.

- *Field, compliance, and safety testing*: There will be two iterations of field and compliance testing, which will include final modifications to the production prototype. Testing will be completed by September of YR 1.

- *Manufacturing design*: Manufacturing design will begin in May of YR 1 and be completed in November of YR 1.

- *Manufacturing*: Manufacturing will be outsourced and will begin in November of Year 1.

- *Product release*: The ECS product (with both software options) will be available in December of YR 1.

- *Software*: LS software and ES software will be developed in an integrated plan with product development.

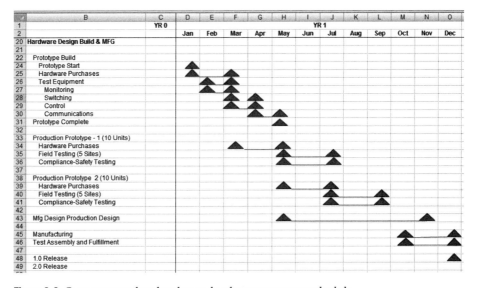

Figure 8-2. *Company product hardware development master schedule*

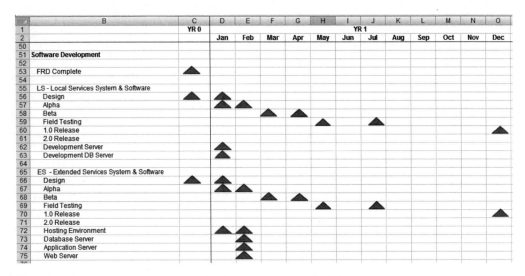

Figure 8-3. *Company product software development master schedule*

Targeting Operational Dates for Product Availability and Inventory

The Company projects commercial release and product availability in December of YR 1. The manufacturer will ship components to the Company, where they will be inventoried, assembled, and tested prior to shipment to the customer. The Company plans to order and keep in stock (in inventory) a three-month supply of ECS units.

Strategizing Product Development

The Company will follow a formal product development methodology. Product development requires the integrated development of both hardware and software. The following sections offer an overview of the Company's product development strategy.

Generating the Concept

The principals of the Company are subject matter experts in the target market and the technical configuration of the product offering. They will take early action to interview, understand, and gather requirements from representative customers in this market. Specifically, they will work closely with major electrical contractors in their target markets to introduce and test ECS.

Designing the Product

The principals of the Company, being subject matter experts in electrical control system design, will implement industry product development best practices into the design of the product. Specifically, they will tightly integrate production and manufacturing designs to ensure a smooth handoff to the manufacturing outsourcer.

Implementing Rapid Prototyping and Iterative Development Practices

The Company will implement rapid prototyping methodologies for both software and hardware. It will develop a prototype of ECS and quickly get it into the field for testing and to compliance laboratories for compliance and certification. Specifically, the Company will place production prototypes in the hands of potential customers as soon as possible and it will

- Utilize quick-response form, feature, and functionality feedback loops for product engineering changes.
- Adopt agile and responsive change-management practices to ensure that improvement suggestions from the field are rolled into product designs quickly and efficiently, thus reducing time to market.

Developing the Prototype

Prototype development will be implemented under a concurrency methodology using cross-functional work teams. The Company will build a prototype, followed by two more production prototypes that will be field and compliance tested in two test cycles. The Company will also implement the following initiatives in support of the effort:

- Implement formal project plans for software and hardware development.
- Adopt concurrency as the primary environment for developing products.
- Create designs that reduce complexity and the need for iterations in product design.
- Create a collaborative design work environment, providing ready access to integrated product data and collaboration tools.
- Utilize state-of-the-art enabling technologies like CAD.

Manufacturing and Ramping Up

The Company will begin manufacturing design, in close relationship with outsourced manufacturer candidates, concurrently with the beginning of the build of the second production prototype. Final selection of the manufacturer will be based on the demonstrated capability of manufacturer to convert production prototype designs into manufacturing designs and tooling. The Company will implement product and manufacturing design and materials sourcing strategies that optimize the ability to produce the product at low cost and with high quality. Product design will take suppliers into consideration and provide maximum flexibility in sourcing parts and materials to reduce cost and risk.

Implementing Product Testing and Quality Assurance

The Company will implement rigorous quality and product testing programs throughout the life cycle of product development. The Company will present its production prototypes to national laboratories for compliance and safety testing and will secure all certifications necessary for product introduction into national markets.

Creating the Staffing Plan and Organizational Structure

The Company will hire staff and organize itself to optimize the implementation of the aforementioned strategies. The Company will also hire resources to manage its information technology (IT) requirements, and the technical operations department will have total responsibility for these functions. The Company will apply small, cross-functional teams to the product development tasks and offer incentives to team members for working collaboratively, as well as providing the tools and infrastructure to assist in collaboration.

The Company will initially hire developers that fit the visionary and pathfinder staff profile, as described in Chapter 4. As the Company and the product baseline mature, the staff will evolve toward the homesteader profile required to manage mature product and technology baselines.

The Company will incrementally staff the technical operations department as required to support product development and information technology functions. The following is an overview of the organizational structure (see Figure 8-4) and the staff positions that are planned:

Chief technical officer. The CTO is responsible for all aspects of the IT department and reports directly to the president.

Information technology staff. These functional staff positions are responsible for Company information technology including support of business and CRM systems.

Systems integration staff. This functional area staff is responsible for integration of hardware and software product development functions and for hosted services.

Software development staff. This functional area staff is responsible for all aspects of software development in support of product development.

Hardware development staff. This functional area staff is responsible for all aspects of hardware development, manufacturing, and product fulfillment.

Test engineering staff. This functional area staff is responsible for full life cycle testing of product components.

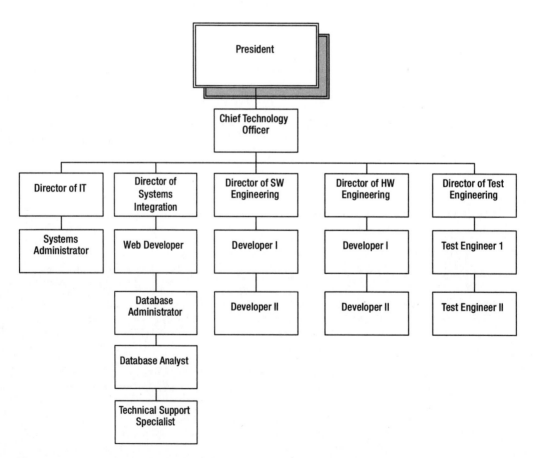

Figure 8-4. *The technical operations staff, as outlined in this organizational chart, is responsible for all aspects of Company product development and technology support services.*

Considering Other Product Development Strategies

Other product development strategies sometimes fall out of consideration because they are not in the critical path of the standard product development process. Nevertheless, these strategies are very important and add significant value to both the Company and the product and services:

IP capture: The Company will build comprehensive IP capture into the product design process. It will engage legal counsel for patent applications and implement policies, procedures, training, and technologies that optimize the capture of company IP during the product development life cycle.

Customer satisfaction: Product design will include consideration for customer satisfaction and support. Products will be designed for quick updates and repair and with complimentary support systems like CRM.

Product life cycle cost: Company product design heavily considers product life cycle costs and the ability and cost required to support, modify, and repair the product.

Scalable product development capacity: The Company specifically intends to build a sustainable and scalable product development capability. This will be accomplished through training and investment in all aspects of people, process, and technology necessary to scale to higher levels of output quickly and efficiently.

Planning the DEV Model

The purpose of the DEV model is to forecast and quantify resources required to implement the Company product development strategy. The Company should take the following steps prior to designing a DEV model:

1. Review all Company business case planning assumptions regarding the product development strategy. Build a time-phased project plan that sets forth the major milestones related to product development, including all events that require expenditures.

2. Review and consider staffing requirements and salary ranges needed to implement the strategy. See Chapter 4 to make sure the model accommodates all planning staff requirements for technical operations. Pay particular attention to the timing of technical resource hires to make sure they support the product development schedule.

3. Plan the operating expense resources needed to support the strategy (see DEV_CWS in Figure 8-10). DEV_CWS should accommodate planning for product development operating and capital expenses.

4. Plan for the development of a Bonus and Commission model to forecast and model bonus and commission compensation (see Chapter 7 for COSM-BONUS_CWS). Bonuses are a major variable expense of product development activities and should be modeled separately from normal expense and capital budgets.

5. Plan for the development of a Trip Cost model to forecast technical and manufacturing support related travel (see Chapter 6 for COSM-TRIPPLAN_CWS and COSM-TRIPCALC_CWS). Technical- and manufacturing-related travel is a major variable expense and should be modeled separately from normal expense budgets.

Exploring the Building Blocks of the DEV Model

When the planning is complete, build and test the model. The following section provides an overview of the DEV model and the top-level functionality of model components. See Figure 8-5 for an illustration of the model.

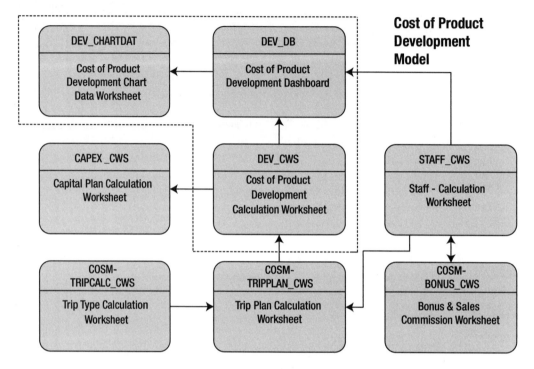

Figure 8-5. *Top-level design and process flow of the Cost of Product Development (DEV) model. The core model is within the dotted lines, and arrows represent the major data and process flows.*

Using the Staff Calculation Worksheet

The Staff Calculation Worksheet is discussed in detail in Chapter 4. This worksheet plays an important part in the development of the cost of product development. Technical operations support, including staffing salary, bonuses, and commissions, is planned and calculated using this worksheet. In addition, the worksheet also forecasts requirements for phones, computers, and work space needed for the technical operations department staff. To utilize STAFF_CWS as input to the DEV model, follow these steps:

1. Go to the Variable Inputs section of STAFF_CWS (see Figure 8-6), and modify the target salaries in the Technical Operations section of the worksheet. Indicate with a "Y" or "N" if a phone (P), computer (C), or work space (WS) is needed for each position. Note that each of the Company's positions requires a phone, computer, and work space, the assumption being that the entire staff will work within formal offices of the Company. Working from home, in this example, is not anticipated.

2. In the Technical Operations Variable Inputs section of STAFF_CWS, modify headcount based on the staffing needs of the strategy.

3. Go to the SALARY-BENEFIT $ CALC section of the worksheet (cell A160), and if necessary, modify the adjustment to salary for each position. This modification may be done universally, by year, by modifying the adjustment to salary field in STAFF_SP. The combination of the target annual salary and the salary modification field yields the forecasted salary for the position.

You have now planned headcount, salaries, and phone, computer, and work space requirements for the technical operations functions of the Company. The STAFF model computes salaries, taxes, benefits, and related expenses automatically.

	A	B	C	D	E	F	G	H	I	J	K
1											
2	Period of Performance						YR 0	Jan	Feb	Mar	Apr
3	Employee	Annual	Monthly	P	C	WS					
4	Consultant	Hourly	Monthly								
84	Technical Operations										
87	IT Director	$ 85,000	$ 7,083	Y	Y	Y	-	-	-	-	-
88	Consultant	$ 85	$ 13,600	Y	Y	Y	-	0.25	0.25	0.25	0.25
89											
90	Systems Administrator	$ 65,000	$ 5,417	Y	Y	Y	-	1.00	1.00	1.00	1.00
91	Consultant	$ 35	$ 5,600	Y	Y	Y	0.25	-	-	-	-
92											
93	Director of Systems Int	$ 110,000	$ 9,167	Y	Y	Y	-	-	-	-	-
94	Consultant	$ 85	$ 13,600	N	Y	Y	-	0.50	0.50	0.50	0.50
95											
96	Web Developer	$ 65,000	$ 5,417	Y	Y	Y	-	-	-	-	-
97	Consultant	$ 35	$ 5,600	N	Y	N	0.50	0.50	0.50	0.50	0.50
98											
99	Database Administrator	$ 75,000	$ 6,250	Y	Y	Y	-	-	-	-	-
100	Consultant	$ 65	$ 10,400	N	Y	N	-	0.50	0.50	0.50	0.50
101											
102	Database Analyst	$ 50,000	$ 4,167	Y	Y	Y	-	-	-	-	-
103	Consultant	$ 40	$ 6,400	N	Y	N	-	-	-	-	-
104											
105	Director Software Eng	$ 110,000	$ 9,167	Y	Y	Y	-	1.00	1.00	1.00	1.00
106	Consultant	$ 85	$ 13,600	N	Y	Y	0.50	-	-	-	-
107											
108	SW Developer I	$ 50,000	$ 4,167	Y	Y	Y	-	-	-	-	-
109	Consultant	$ 35	$ 5,600	N	N	N	-	-	-	-	-
110											
111	SW Developer II	$ 75,000	$ 6,250	Y	Y	Y	0.50	1.00	1.00	1.00	1.00
112	Consultant	$ 50	$ 8,000	N	N	N	-	1.00	1.00	1.00	1.00

Figure 8-6. *The Staff Calculation Worksheet, STAFF_CWS, showing the Variable Inputs section of the Technical Operations planning area.*

Using the Bonus and Sales Commission Worksheet

The Bonus and Sales Commission Worksheet, COSM-BONUS_CWS, is a model for forecasting and planning bonuses and sales commissions (see Figure 8-7). This worksheet plays an important part in developing the cost of product development. Bonuses are a primary incentive for key technology management positions. COSM-BONUS_CWS is one example of developing a model for this type of expenditure, but there are many ways to implement a model of this type. The primary functionality of COSM-BONUS_CWS is to develop commissions and bonuses at a *top level* and to allocate commissions and bonuses back into the detailed compensation calculations of the Staffing model (STAFF) for the purposes of total salaries, wages, and benefits.

■**Note** For a more detailed discussion of building this type of model, refer to Exercise 8-1 at the end of this chapter.

	B	C	D	F	G	H	I	J
2				YR 1	YR 2	YR 3	YR 4	YR 5
3	**Bonus and Commission Plan**							
5	Total Revenue (Plan Basis)			$ 61,866	$ 3,401,623	$ 10,962,555	$ 20,505,495	$ 34,899,981
6	Bonus Basis		3%	$ 1,547	$ 85,041	$ 274,064	$ 512,637	$ 872,500
7	Commission Basis		5%	$ 3,093	$ 173,174	$ 548,128	$ 1,025,275	$ 1,744,999
8								
9	**Bonus Pool**							
10	CEO/President			1.00	1.00	1.00	1.00	1.00
11	VP of Business Operations			-	-	-	1.00	1.00
12	VP of Sales & Marketing			-	-	1.00	1.00	1.00
13	CIO – Chief Technical Officer			1.00	1.00	1.00	1.00	1.00
14	Director of Mkt			-	-	1.00	1.00	1.00
15	Director of CRM			-	-	1.00	1.00	1.00
16	Director of Systems Int			-	-	1.00	1.00	1.00
17	Director Software Eng			1.00	1.00	1.00	1.00	1.00
18	Director Hardware Eng			1.00	1.00	1.00	1.00	1.00
19	Director of Test Eng			-	-	1.00	1.00	1.00
20	**Bonus Pool Count**			4.00	4.00	9.00	10.00	10.00
21								
22	**Bonus Allocation**							
23	CEO/President			$ 387	$ 11,244	$ 30,452	$ 51,264	$ 87,250
24	VP of Business Operations			$ -	$ -	$ -	$ 51,264	$ 87,250
25	VP of Sales & Marketing			$ -	$ -	$ 30,452	$ 51,264	$ 87,250
26	CIO – Chief Technical Officer			$ 387	$ 11,244	$ 30,452	$ 51,264	$ 87,250
27	Director of Mkt			$ -	$ 9,042	$ 30,452	$ 51,264	$ 87,250
28	Director of CRM			$ -	$ 10,857	$ 30,452	$ 51,264	$ 87,250
29	**Total Bonus Allocation**			$ 773	$ 42,386	$ 152,258	$ 307,582	$ 523,500
30	Per Head Allocation			$ 193	$ 10,596	$ 16,918	$ 30,758	$ 52,350
31								
32	**Commission Plan**							
33	Director of Sales			0.67	1.67	1.00	1.00	1.00
34	Field Sales Engineer			0.50	4.00	4.00	6.00	6.00
35	**Commission Plan Count**			1.17	5.67	5.00	7.00	7.00
36								
37	**Commission Allocation**							
38	Director of Sales			$ 1,547	$ 38,952	$ 109,626	$ 146,468	$ 249,286
39	Field Sales Engineer			$ 1,547	$ 134,223	$ 438,502	$ 878,807	$ 1,495,713
40								
41	**Total Commission Allocation**			$ 3,093	$ 173,174	$ 548,128	$ 1,025,275	$ 1,744,999

Figure 8-7. *COSM-BONUS_CWS, the Bonus and Sales Commission Worksheet, calculates bonuses and commissions for executives, key technology management, and sales and marketing staff.*

Using the Trip Type Calculation Worksheet

The Trip Type Calculation Worksheet, COSM-TRIPCALC_CWS, is a model for forecasting and planning business trips for the Company (see Figure 8-8). Travel related to technology, manufacturing support, and consulting is a major variable expense and should be modeled separately, since it is dependent on headcount and product development operating schedules and assumptions. An example of this type of travel would be trips made by hardware developers to visit the manufacturer for technical interchange meetings.

This worksheet is a straightforward model for computing the costs of various types of trips taken during the course of business for the Company. Different trip types are based on variations in airfare, lodging, per diem rates, and rental car expenses. Each trip type has a different assumption for the number of trip days and trip nights. This simple model is utilized by the Trip Plan Calculation Worksheet, COSM-TRIPPLAN_CWS, to compute the total cost of trips.

■**Note** For a more detailed discussion of building this type of model, refer to Exercise 8-2.

	B	C	D
2	Trip Cost Assumptions		
3		Trip Days	Nights
4	**Business/Marketing**	3	$ 2
5	Airfare		$ 650.00
6	Lodging	$ 120.00	$ 240.00
7	Per Diem	$ 50.00	$ 150.00
8	Rental Car	$ 85.00	$ 255.00
9	Total Trip Cost		$ 1,295.00
10			
11	**Technical/Consulting**	2	$ 2
12	Airfare		$ 650.00
13	Lodging	$ 120.00	$ 240.00
14	Per Diem	$ 50.00	$ 100.00
15	Rental Car	$ 85.00	$ 170.00
16	Total Trip Cost		$ 1,160.00
17			
18	**Direct Sales Trip**	4	$ 3
19	Airfare		$ 650.00
20	Lodging	$ 120.00	$ 360.00
21	Per Diem	$ 50.00	$ 200.00
22	Rental Car	$ 85.00	$ 340.00
23	Total Trip Cost		$ 1,550.00
24			
25	**Manufacturing Support**	3	$ 2
26	Airfare		$ 1,500.00
27	Lodging	$ 150.00	$ 300.00
28	Per Diem	$ 50.00	$ 150.00
29	Rental Car	$ 85.00	$ 255.00
30	Total Trip Cost		$ 2,205.00
31			
32	**Training/Other**	3	$ 2
33	Airfare		$ 650.00
34	Lodging	$ 150.00	$ 300.00
35	Per Diem	$ 50.00	$ 150.00
36	Rental Car	$ 85.00	$ 255.00
37	Total Trip Cost		$ 1,355.00

Figure 8-8. *COSM-TRIPCALC_CWS is the calculation worksheet for trip cost by type of trip*

Using the Trip Plan Calculation Worksheet

The Trip Plan Calculation Worksheet, COSM-TRIPPLAN_CWS, is a model for forecasting and planning business trips for the Company and for computing the total cost of trips (see Figure 8-9). Travel costs related to technology and manufacturing support are a major variable expense and are specifically modeled, and then the costs are included with the other related expense budgets.

	B	C	D	E	F	G	H	I	J	K	L
1									YR 1		
2	Trip Model		YR 0	Jan	Feb	Mar	Apr	May	Jun	Jul	Aug
176	**Total Technical Operations**			6.00	6.00	6.00	7.00	8.00	8.00	8.00	9.00
177	**Total Consultant**			4.25	4.25	4.25	4.25	4.25	4.25	4.25	4.25
178	**Total Technical Operations**			10.25	10.25	10.25	11.25	12.25	12.25	12.25	13.25
181	**Technical Operations Trip Count**										
183	Business/Marketing										
184	Technical/Consulting				1.00		1.00		1.00		1.00
185	Direct Sales Trip										
186	Manufacturing Support										
187	Training/Other										
189	**Total Trips**		-	-	1.00	-	1.00	-	1.00	-	1.00
191	**Technical Operations Trip Cost**										
192											
193	Business/Marketing		$ -	$ -	$ -	$ -	$ -	$ -	$ -	$ -	$ -
194	Technical/Consulting		$ -	$ 1,160	$ -	$ 1,160	$ -	$ 1,160	$ -	$ 1,160
195	Direct Sales Trip		$ -	$ -	$ -	$ -	$ -	$ -	$ -	$ -	$ -
196	Manufacturing Support		$ -	$ -	$ -	$ -	$ -	$ -	$ -	$ -	$ -
197	Training/Other		$ -	$ -	$ -	$ -	$ -	$ -	$ -	$ -	$ -
198											
199	**Total Technical Operations Trip Cost**		$ -	$ 1,160	$ -	$ 1,160	$ -	$ 1,160	$ -	$ 1,160

Figure 8-9. *COSM-TRIPPLAN_CWS, the Trip Plan Calculation Worksheet, forecasts technical operations' technical, consulting, and manufacturing support trips, as well as trips for other Company departments.*

Using the Cost of Product Development Calculation Worksheet

The Cost of Product Development Calculation Worksheet, DEV_CWS, is used to develop the operating budget and capital expenditure budget for technical operations (see Figure 8-10). This simple worksheet accepts monthly inputs for expenditures and summarizes expenses for the following categories or groupings of cost; these categories correspond with the organizational structure of Company technical operations:

Information Technology: Operating expenses related to Company IT functions including business systems

Systems Integration: Operating expenses related to systems integration of hardware and software product development functions and for hosted services

Software Development: Operating expenses related to all aspects of software development in support of overall product development

Hardware Development: Operating expenses related to all aspects of hardware development, manufacturing, and product fulfillment

Test Engineering: Operating expenses related to full life cycle testing of product components

Total Tech Ops Trips: The total cost of all technical operations department trips

Capital Requirements: The total technical operations capital expenditure requirements

The last section of the worksheet links to COSM-TRIPPLAN_CWS and picks up the total cost of trips forecasted for product development from the Trip Cost model. There is also a section for the input of capital expenditure forecasts, and these inputs are linked into the Capital Plan, CAPEX _CWS, where they appear as Technical Operations inputs in the total capital plan.

	B	C	D	E	F	G	H	I	J	K
1									YR 1	
2	Technical Operations		YR 0	Jan	Feb	Mar	Apr	May	Jun	Jul
4	Information Technology									
5										
6	Software & Licenses	$	-							
7	Hardware									
8	Maintenance Agreements			$ 500	$ 500	$ 500	$ 500	$ 500	$ 500	$ 500
9	Software Lease									
10	Hardware Lease									
11	Media and Training Materials									
12	Computer Supplies			$ 250	$ 250	$ 250	$ 250	$ 250	$ 250	
13	Training									
15	Total IT	$	-	$ 500	$ 750	$ 750	$ 750	$ 750	$ 750	$ 750
16										
17	Systems Integration									
18										
19	Software & Licenses									
20	Hosting Services			$ 2,500	$ 2,500	$ 2,500	$ 2,500	$ 2,500	$ 2,500	$ 2,500
21	High Speed Internet			$ 90	$ 90	$ 90	$ 90	$ 90	$ 90	$ 90
22	Connectivity Hardware			$ 1,000	$ 1,000	$ 1,000				
23	Maintenance Agreements									$ 250
24	Software Lease									$ 150
25	Hardware Lease									
26	Media and Training Materials									$ 500
27	Computer Supplies	$	250	$ 100	$ 100	$ 100	$ 100	$ 100	$ 100	$ 100
28	Training									
30	Total Systems Integration	$	250	$ 3,690	$ 3,690	$ 3,690	$ 2,690	$ 2,690	$ 2,690	$ 3,590
31										
32	Software Development									
33										
34	Software & Licenses			$ 5,500						
35	Hardware			$ 500	$ 500	$ 500				
36	Maintenance Agreements			$ 450	$ 450	$ 450	$ 450	$ 450	$ 450	$ 450
37	Software Lease			$ 500	$ 500	$ 500	$ 500	$ 500	$ 500	$ 500
38	Hardware Lease									
39	Media and Training Materials									
40	Computer Supplies	$	250	$ 100	$ 100	$ 100	$ 100	$ 100	$ 100	$ 100

Figure 8-10. *DEV_CWS, the Cost of Product Development Calculation Worksheet, develops and summarizes operating expenses and capital expenditures for technical operations.*

See Exercise 8-3 in the end of this chapter for a more detailed look at the development of DEV_CWS.

Using the Capital Plan Calculation Worksheet

The Capital Plan Calculation Worksheet, CAPEX _CWS, is discussed in more detail in Chapter 9 and is shown in Figure 8-11. Technical operations capital expenditures are input into DEV_CWS. This data is linked into CAPEX_CWS, where it becomes part of the total capital expenditure plan.

	A	B	E	F	G	H	I	J
1								
2		**Capital Plan**	**YR 0**	**Jan**	**Feb**	**Mar**	**Apr**	**May**
16		**Technical Operations**						
17		\						
18		**Information Technology**						
19		LAN Server	$ -	$ 3,500	$ -	$ -	$ -	$ -
20		Internet - Connectivity Equipment	$ -	$ 2,500	$ -	$ -	$ -	$ -
21		Biz Ops Application Server	$ -	$ -	$ -	$ -	$ -	$ -
22								
23		**Systems Integration**						
24		Database Server	$ -	$ -	$ 3,500	$ -	$ -	$ -
25		Application Server	$ -	$ -	$ 3,500	$ -	$ -	$ -
26		Web Server	$ -	$ -	$ 3,500	$ -	$ -	$ -
27								
28		**Software Development**						
29		Development Server	$ -	$ 3,500	$ -	$ -	$ -	$ -
30		Development DB Server	$ -	$ 3,500	$ -	$ -	$ -	$ -
31								
32		**Hardware Development**						
33		Test Hardware Products	$ -	$ -	$ -	$ -	$ -	$ -
34		Test Equipment	$ -	$ 10,000	$ 25,000	$ 10,000	$ -	$ -
35								
36		**Test Engineering**	$ -	$ -	$ -	$ -	$ -	$ -
37								
38		**Total Technical Operations**	$ -	$ 23,000	$ 35,500	$ 10,000	$ -	$ -
39								
40		**Total Capital Plan**	$11,000	$ 53,500	$ 35,500	$ 10,000	$ 12,750	$ 5,500

Figure 8-11. *CAPEX_CWS, showing the technical operations capital plan*

Using the Cost of Product Development Dashboard

The Cost of Product Development Dashboard, DEV_DB, provides an important management summary, or *view*, of the total cost of product development (see Figure 8-12). In one view, revenue, headcount, compensation, and the total cost of sales and marketing are summarized. This data is created by linking to the worksheets within COSM that we have previously discussed in Chapter 7. The following component data sources make up COSM_DB:

Sales and Revenue: Source is REV_DB

Headcount: Source is STAFF_CWS

Compensation: Source is STAFF_CWS

Operating Expense and Capital: Source is DEV_CWS

The summary data from DEV_DB is presented as an overview of the resources that are planned for the technical operations department and for product development in total.

	B	C	D	E	F	G	H
1		YR 0	YR 1	YR 2	YR 3	YR 4	YR 5
6	Headcount						
7	IT Director	-	-	-	1.00	1.00	1.00
8	Systems Administrator	-	1.00	1.00	1.00	1.00	1.00
9	Director of Systems Int	-	-	1.00	1.00	1.00	1.00
10	Web Developer	-	1.00	1.00	1.00	2.00	2.00
11	Database Administrator	-	-	1.00	1.00	1.00	1.00
12	Database Analyst	-	-	-	1.00	1.00	1.00
13	Director Software Eng	-	1.00	1.00	1.00	1.00	1.00
14	SW Developer I	-	-	1.00	1.00	2.00	2.00
15	SW Developer II	0.50	1.00	1.00	1.00	1.00	1.00
16	Director Hardware Eng	-	1.00	1.00	1.00	1.00	1.00
17	Developer I	-	1.00	1.00	1.00	1.00	1.00
18	Developer II	0.50	1.00	1.00	1.00	1.00	1.00
19	Director of Test Eng	-	-	1.00	1.00	1.00	1.00
20	Test Engineer I	-	-	1.00	1.00	1.00	1.00
21	Test Engineer II	-	1.00	1.00	1.00	1.00	1.00
22	Technical Support Specialist	-	1.00	1.00	1.00	1.00	1.00
23	Total Headcount	1.00	9.00	14.00	16.00	18.00	18.00
24	Total Consulting Headcount	1.75	4.25	0.25	-	-	-
25	Compensation						
26	Salaries & Wages	$ 6,021	$ 558,333	$ 974,500	$ 1,137,000	$ 1,265,000	$ 1,345,000
27	Commissions and Bonuses	$ -	$ 773	$ 43,428	$ 121,806	$ 205,055	$ 349,000
28	Taxes	$ 568	$ 52,748	$ 95,954	$ 118,253	$ 137,885	$ 158,040
29	Medical Insurance	$ -	$ 38,750	$ 122,375	$ 193,600	$ 276,183	$ 322,102
30	401 K	$ -	$ 1,155	$ 18,098	$ 31,083	$ 38,210	$ 44,517
31	Consulting Costs	$ 11,000	$ 362,400	$ 40,800	$ -	$ -	$ -
32	Total Employee Costs	$ 17,589	$1,014,160	$1,295,154	$ 1,601,742	$ 1,922,332	$ 2,218,659
33	Operating Expense and Capital						
34	Information Technology	$ -	$ 8,285	$ 3,420	$ 3,420	$ 3,420	$ 3,420
35	Systems Integration	$ 250	$ 40,680	$ 47,580	$ 61,080	$ 67,080	$ 67,080
36	Software Development	$ 250	$ 19,600	$ 12,600	$ 12,600	$ 12,600	$ 12,600
37	Hardware and Manufacturing	$ 250	$ 252,200	$ 7,200	$ 7,200	$ 7,200	$ 7,200
38	Test Engineering	$ 1,050	$ 8,600	$ 600	$ 600	$ 600	$ 600
39	Trip Costs	$ -	$ 23,785	$ 95,460	$ 48,120	$ 45,800	$ 41,390
40	Total Operating Budget	$ 1,800	$ 353,150	$ 166,860	$ 133,020	$ 136,700	$ 132,290
41	Product Development Total	$ 19,389	$1,367,310	$1,462,014	$ 1,734,762	$ 2,059,032	$ 2,350,949
42	Total Capital Expenditures	$ -	$ 68,500	$ 7,000	$ -	$ -	$ -

Figure 8-12. *DEV_DB, the Cost of Product Development Dashboard, summarizes DEV data and provides a single view of key metrics related to the cost of product development.*

Using the Cost of Product Development Chart Data Worksheet

The Cost of Product Development Chart Data Worksheet, DEV_CHARTDAT, summarizes and pre-formats data used for management charts related to the DEV model (see Figure 8-13).

	B	C	D	E	F	G	H	I
2	CHART NAME							
3	DEV_CHART-Operating Expense							
4								YR 1
5		Jan	Feb	Mar	Apr	May	Jun	Jul
6								
7	Information Technology	$ 500	$ 750	$ 750	$ 750	$ 750	$ 750	$ 750
8	Systems Integration	$ 3,690	$ 3,690	$ 3,690	$ 2,690	$ 2,690	$ 2,690	$ 3,590
9	Software Development	$ 7,050	$ 1,550	$ 1,550	$ 1,050	$ 1,050	$ 1,050	$ 1,050
10	Hardware and Manufacturing	$ 5,600	$ 3,100	$ 3,100	$ 600	$ 40,600	$ 40,600	$ 75,600
11	Test Engineering	$ 1,050	$ 1,050	$ 2,050	$ 2,050	$ 2,050	$ 50	$ 50
12	Trip Costs	$ -	$ 1,160	$ -	$ 1,160	$ -	$ 1,160	$ -
13	Total Inf Technology OP Expense	$17,890	$ 11,300	$ 11,140	$ 8,300	$ 47,140	$ 46,300	$ 81,040

Figure 8-13. *DEV_CHARTDAT, the Cost of Product Development Chart Data Worksheet*

EXERCISE 8-1. USING MICROSOFT EXCEL TO DEVELOP A BONUS AND COMMISSION PLAN MODEL

The Company must forecast the total cost of product development. Bonuses are a primary motivator of senior technology management. It is important that a comprehensive compensation plan be developed to attract the type of technical talent the Company needs to be successful.

- *Problem*: Bonuses are a significant variable cost component of the total cost of product development. Bonuses must be forecast at a level of detail that satisfies the need for a centralized compensation plan and, at the same time, provides data input to other components of the model.

- *Solution*: Develop a Bonus and Commission model, and utilize the model to forecast bonuses for technical management staff.

▓**Note** Refer to Exercise 7-1 for details of model functionality. Utilize the exercises in Chapter 7 as a guide for computing bonuses for senior technical staff.

EXERCISE 8-2. USING MICROSOFT EXCEL TO MODEL TRIP EXPENSES

The Company must forecast total cost of product development. Technical- and manufacturing-related travel costs are a major variable cost of product development.

- *Problem*: Trip costs are related to product development milestones and to headcount. The costs of airfare, lodging, and per diem expenses are variable based on the type of trip taken. These costs and the number of trips should be modeled separately from operating expense budgets.

- *Solution*: Develop a Trip Cost model to forecast the cost of trips for the Company.

COSM-TRIPCALC_CWS and COSM-TRIPPLAN_CWS, the trip calculation and planning worksheets, are utilized together to model the cost of trips for the Company. The ideas behind this type of model are simple:

- Company operations will require different types of trips taken by different functional areas in the normal course of business. Trips vary in cost based on trip duration and assumptions on destination and other cost variables, like time of year.

- The Trip Cost model forecasts costs for trip types then forecasts the number of trips by each functional area. The two pieces of data (trip costs and number of trips) are combined to generate the total cost of trips, which is then allocated back into the operating expense budget of each functional area.

▓**Note** Refer to Exercise 7-2 for details of model functionality. Utilize the exercises in Chapter 7 as a guide for computing trip costs for technical operations.

EXERCISE 8-3. USING MICROSOFT EXCEL TO DEVELOP THE COST OF PRODUCT DEVELOPMENT CALCULATION WORKSHEET

The Company must forecast the total cost of product development.

- *Problem*: Nonpersonnel-related technical and manufacturing expenses and capital expenditures related to product development must be forecast.

- *Solution*: Develop a Cost of Product Development Calculation Worksheet.

DEV_CWS, the Cost of Product Development Calculation Worksheet, is used to develop the operating and capital budget for technical operations. This straightforward worksheet is structured to organize costs based on the organizational structure that has been determined in this chapter. All data is manually input into the model, month by month, with the exception of trip costs, which are computed in COSM-TRIPPLAN_CWS and linked within DEV_CWS. See Figure 8-14 for a data view of DEV_CWS and Figure 8-15 for a formula view of the same spreadsheet.

DEV_CWS provides sections to input operating expenses for the major functions that operate within the technical operations department. The structure of DEV_CWS showing these functional breakouts follows:

- Information technology department operating expenses

- Systems integration department operating expenses

- Software development operating expenses

- Hardware and manufacturing operating expenses

- Test engineering operating expenses

- Total technical operations trip costs

- Total technical operations operating expenses

- Capital requirements

	B	C	D	E	F	G	H	I	J	K
1									YR 1	
2	Technical Operations		YR 0	Jan	Feb	Mar	Apr	May	Jun	Jul
4	Information Technology									
5										
6	Software & Licenses	$	-							
7	Hardware									
8	Maintenance Agreements			$ 500	$ 500	$ 500	$ 500	$ 500	$ 500	$ 500
9	Software Lease									
10	Hardware Lease									
11	Media and Training Materials									
12	Computer Supplies				$ 250	$ 250	$ 250	$ 250	$ 250	$ 250
13	Training									
15	Total IT	$	-	$ 500	$ 750	$ 750	$ 750	$ 750	$ 750	$ 750
16										
17	Systems Integration									
18										
19	Software & Licenses									
20	Hosting Services			$ 2,500	$ 2,500	$ 2,500	$ 2,500	$ 2,500	$ 2,500	$ 2,500
21	High Speed Internet			$ 90	$ 90	$ 90	$ 90	$ 90	$ 90	$ 90
22	Connectivity Hardware			$ 1,000	$ 1,000	$ 1,000				
23	Maintenance Agreements									$ 250
24	Software Lease									$ 150
25	Hardware Lease									
26	Media and Training Materials									$ 500
27	Computer Supplies	$	250	$ 100	$ 100	$ 100	$ 100	$ 100	$ 100	$ 100
28	Training									
30	Total Systems Integration	$	250	$ 3,690	$ 3,690	$ 3,690	$ 2,690	$ 2,690	$ 2,690	$ 3,590

Figure 8-14. *The data view of DEV_CWS, the Cost of Product Development Calculation Worksheet*

In each departmental section, applicable expenses for the department are manually input and then summarized (see Figure 8-15, rows 15 and 30). Total technical operations expenses are summarized at the bottom of the spreadsheet.

The Total Tech Ops Trips row is linked back to COSM-TRIPPLAN_CWS. See Figure 8-16, which is a formula view of the link for Total Tech Ops Trips. In Figure 8-16, also note the formula view of data input for capital requirements.

	B	C	D	E	F	G	H
1							
2	Technical Operations		YR 0	Jan	Feb	Mar	Apr
4	Information Technology						
5							
6	Software & Licenses	0					
7	Hardware						
8	Maintenance Agreements			500	500	500	500
9	Software Lease						
10	Hardware Lease						
11	Media and Training Materials						
12	Computer Supplies			250	250	250	
13	Training						
15	Total IT		=SUM(D6:D14)	=SUM(E6:E14)	=SUM(F6:F14)	=SUM(G6:G14)	=SUM(H6:H14)
16							
17	Systems Integration						
18							
19	Software & Licenses						
20	Hosting Services			2500	2500	2500	2500
21	High Speed Internet			90	90	90	90
22	Connectivity Hardware			1000	1000	1000	
23	Maintenance Agreements						
24	Software Lease						
25	Hardware Lease						
26	Media and Training Materials						
27	Computer Supplies		250	100	100	100	100
28	Training						
30	Total Systems Integration		=SUM(D19:D29)	=SUM(E19:E29)	=SUM(F19:F29)	=SUM(G19:G29)	=SUM(H19:H29)

Figure 8-15. *The formula view of DEV_CWS, the Cost of Product Development Calculation Worksheet*

	B	C	D	E	F
1					
2	Technical Operations		YR 0	Jan	Feb
63	Test Equipment				
64	Maintenance Agreements				
65	Software Lease				
66	Hardware Lease				
67	Media and Training Materials				
68	Computer Supplies		50	50	50
69	Training				
70					
71	Total Test Engineering		=SUM(D61:D70)	=SUM(E61:E70)	=SUM(F61:F70)
72					
73	Total Tech Ops Trips		='COSM-TRIPPLAN_CWS'!D199	='COSM-TRIPPLAN_CWS'!E199	='COSM-TRIPPLAN_CWS'!F199
74					
75	Total Tech Ops		=D71+D57+D43+D30+D15+D73	=E71+E57+E43+E30+E15+E73	=F71+F57+F43+F30+F15+F73
76					
77	Capital Requirements				
78					
79	Information Technology				
80	LAN Server			3500	
81	Internet – Connectivity Equipment			2500	
82	Biz Ops Application Server				
83					
84	Systems Integration				
85	Database Server				3500
86	Application Server				3500
87	Web Server				3500
88					
89	Software Development				
90	Development Server			3500	
91	Development DB Server			3500	
92					
93	Hardware Development				
94	Test Hardware Products				
95	Test Equipment			10000	25000
96					
97	Test Engineering				
98					
99	Total Capital Requirements		=SUM(D80:D98)	=SUM(E80:E98)	=SUM(F80:F98)

Figure 8-16. *The formula view of DEV_CWS, the Cost of Product Development Calculation Worksheet, showing link to COSM-TRIPPLAN_CWS for trip costs*

Capital plan inputs (also shown in Figure 8-16) are the source for the capital plan in CAPEX_CWS. See Figure 8-17 for a formula view of CAPEX_CWS, which links back to DEV_CWS to obtain capital expenditure entries for technical operations.

	A	B	E	F	G
1					
2		Capital Plan	YR 0	Jan	Feb
16		Technical Operations			
17					
18		Information Technology			
19		LAN Server	=DEV_CWS!D80	=DEV_CWS!E80	=DEV_CWS!F80
20		Internet - Connectivity Equipment	=DEV_CWS!D81	=DEV_CWS!E81	=DEV_CWS!F81
21		Biz Ops Application Server	=DEV_CWS!D82	=DEV_CWS!E82	=DEV_CWS!F82
22					
23		Systems Integration			
24		Database Server	=DEV_CWS!D85	=DEV_CWS!E85	=DEV_CWS!F85
25		Application Server	=DEV_CWS!D86	=DEV_CWS!E86	=DEV_CWS!F86
26		Web Server	=DEV_CWS!D87	=DEV_CWS!E87	=DEV_CWS!F87
27					
28		Software Development			
29		Development Server	=DEV_CWS!D90	=DEV_CWS!E90	=DEV_CWS!F90
30		Development DB Server	=DEV_CWS!D91	=DEV_CWS!E91	=DEV_CWS!F91
31					
32		Hardware Development			
33		Test Hardware Products	=DEV_CWS!D94	=DEV_CWS!E94	=DEV_CWS!F94
34		Test Equipment	=DEV_CWS!D95	=DEV_CWS!E95	=DEV_CWS!F95
35					
36		Test Engineering	=DEV_CWS!D97	=DEV_CWS!E97	=DEV_CWS!F97
37					
38		Total Technical Operations	=SUM(E19:E37)	=SUM(F19:F37)	=SUM(G19:G37)
39					
40		Total Capital Plan	=E38+E14+E9	=F38+F14+F9	=G38+G14+G9

Figure 8-17. *The formula view of CAPEX _CWS, showing formula links back to DEV_CWS to get capital inputs from technical operations*

Summary

In this chapter, I introduced and explained the Cost of Product Development (DEV) model. The DEV model forecasts the total cost of product development of a company. It is the quantitative representation of the planning for product development.

The cost of product development is the cost the company incurs to design, build, and deliver its product to the market. Product development is the lifeblood and core process of a technology company and all other company processes are dependent, to a greater or lesser extent, on product development. Failure in product development generally spells failure for the company. The objective of product development is to implement a development process that assures that the product delivers the functionality and qualities the customer expects. A company that can uncover what a customer wants, design a product to meet those needs, and build and distribute it at an acceptable cost will be successful.

The product development implementation strategy is the key to the kingdom of technology company success. Business thinking about product development must begin at a strategic level and within a framework of business objectives and technology company critical success factors. We should also view business objectives from the traditional perspectives of time, cost, and quality. In other words, the product must be developed quickly, efficiently, and at a reasonable cost and be of high quality that exceeds customer demands.

In this chapter, we have considered the following critical product development objectives and strategies:

Product concept and design: Designing what the customer wants

Planning: Planning as a key management discipline

Time to market: Being fast to market as a critical success factor

Product development and production: Considering product development life cycle methods and tools

Team: Building the right team at the right time

Product life cycle: Designing for optimized product life cycle cost

Quality: Considering product quality as a way of life

Development capacity: Building scalable product development capacity

Customers: Creating products that keep customers happy

Intellectual property: Capturing IP as you build the product

Here are the key questions to ask yourself regarding company product development and its cost: How will your company get to market fast with a profitable product that meets customer expectations? How much will it cost to accomplish this?

CHAPTER 9

■■■

Operating and Capital Expenditures Models

In this chapter, you will learn how to plan, create, and use the Operating Expenditure (OPEX) model and the Capital Expenditure (CAPEX) model. These models are used to forecast, respectively, general operating expenses and capital expenditures. The two models are presented together in one chapter because they present and juxtapose the concepts of expense and capital, and presenting them together allows the important linkages between them to be explained.

Companies spend money on everything from paper clips to manufacturing systems. These expenditures fall into two cost categories: expense or capital. In other words, a cash outlay is either an expensed item or a capital item.

The CBM developed in this book categorizes expenses into the following major groupings:

- Sales and marketing
- Cost of technical operations
- Salaries, wages, and benefits
- General operating

Previous chapters have modeled all the preceding categories of expense with the exception of general operating expenses and capital expenditures.

We will begin with business thinking about cash flow and then move into consideration of operating and capital expenditures. After that, we will plan and consider how the OPEX and CAPEX models work together and how they are used downstream in other financial reports to develop the business picture for a venture. We will create an OPEX model that projects general operating expenses and a CAPEX model that projects capital expenditures and computes depreciation for the company.

OPEX and CAPEX models are fairly straightforward and don't involve as much design thought as some of the previous models we have developed. We do not need to build sophisticated "what if" flexibility into these models, because these models are fed data by the "what if" models. We do, however, need solid thinking about what it is going to cost to implement the company plan. Business thinking in this chapter centers on levels of operating expenditures and capital expenditures that are required to support the operations of the venture.

Business Thinking About Cash Flow

Burn, baby, burn! When investors look at a company's outgoing cash flow, they call it the *burn rate*, the rate at which cash is being consumed by the enterprise. It is critical that management understand the burn rate and have a handle on cash needs. *Running out of cash is often the single greatest problem* that early-stage technology companies face.

Thus far, we have computed the cost of goods sold using the COGS model, the cost of sales and marketing using the COSM model, the cost of product development using the DEV model, and employee costs using the STAFF model. These are the major users of cash.

The OPEX and CAPEX models project general operating expenses and capital expenditures, which also represent a significant portion of the total cash outflow of the company. The total cash position of the company is developed from combining *all of these sources and uses of cash* into a consolidated view, the Statement of Cash Flows.

As we forecast expenditures, we are creating a forecast of cash flow. This chapter supports computing cash flows by developing operating expenditure and capital expenditure forecasts, computing depreciation, and creating a fixed asset schedule. These expenditures feed into the Statement of Cash Flows, which provides a fully adjusted and reconciled view of the true cash position of the company.

We will be unable to derive a complete picture of cash flows until we integrate all of the components that determine cash flow into the Statement of Cash Flows. This final integration of the company Profit and Loss Statement and the Statement of Cash Flows is accomplished in Chapter 10.

The Statement of Cash Flows depicts the net cash generated by a company and is organized into the three primary types of *activities* that generate or use cash. The Statement of Cash Flows is organized into three sections (see Figure 9-1), described as follows:

- *Operating activities*: Cash generated from operations is cash generated from sales less cost of goods sold and operating expenses. The net amount of cash provided (or used) by operating activities is a key figure on the Statement of Cash Flows.

- *Investing activities*: Cash generated from investing activities results from events or transactions where cash is expended or received for capital assets, such as plant and equipment assets, or computers, or other assets not generally held for resale. Investing activities have an indirect relationship to the central ongoing operations of the business.

- *Financing activities*: Cash generated from financing activities is cash that flows to and from business owners (equity financing) and creditors (debt financing). Loan repayments, dividend payments, and other like transactions are considered financing activities.

The categories of expenditures covered thus far and those that will be covered in this chapter map into Cash Flows activities like this:

- Cost of sales and marketing, cost of product development, cost of salaries, wages, and benefits, and general operating expenses (covered in this chapter) are all considered *operating activities*. They show up in the Statement of Cash Flows as outflows.

- Capital expenditures (covered in this chapter) are shown as *investing activities*. They show up in the Statement of Cash Flows as cash outflows.

- Thus far, we have not modeled any *financing activities*. When we model investments in Chapter 11, we will develop investment assumptions that will show up under financing activities.

Figure 9-1 illustrates a sample Statement of Cash Flows showing the relationship of the Profit and Loss Statement to the Operating Activities section of the statement. Expenditures for cost of sales and marketing, cost of product development, cost of salaries and wages, and general operating expenses are included in the total expenses line of the Profit and Loss Statement. Capital expenditures are shown in the Investment Activities section. The inner workings of the Statement of Cash Flows are covered in detail in Chapter 10.

Statement of Profit and Loss		Month 1		Month 2
Sales	$	15,000	$	25,000
Cost of Goods Sold (COGS)	$	3,500	$	5,000
Gross Margin	$	11,500	$	20,000
Total Expenses	$	7,000	$	8,500
Net Income	$	4,500	$	11,500
Statement of Cash Flows				
Operating Activities				
Net Income	$	4,500	$	11,500
Adjustment to Cash used by operating activities				
Depreciation	$	500	$	500
(Increase) decrease in A/R+Other Assets	$	(12,500)	$	(16,000)
(Increase) decrease in Inventory	$	(500)	$	(1,000)
Increase (decrease) in AP- COGS/Inventory	$	1,000	$	1,200
Increase (decrease) in AP- Other Expenses	$	1,625	$	2,000
Total Adjustments	$	(9,875)	$	(13,300)
Net Cash From Operating Activities	$	(5,375)	$	(1,800)
Investment Activities				
Purchase of Capital Assets and Other Assets	$	30,000	$	-
Net Cash Used in Investing	$	30,000	$	-
Financing Activities				
Members Contribution	$	50,000	$	-
Net increase <decrease> in cash	$	14,625	$	(1,800)
Cash Balance at Beg of Period	$	-	$	14,625
Cash Balance at End of Period	$	14,625	$	12,825

Figure 9-1. *Example of a Statement of Cash Flows*

This book is not meant to be a primer on accounting. In college, I changed my major from accounting to finance because I had to read one too many accounting primers. What follows is a high-level discussion of the differences between expense and capital items. Reader beware: I have generalized a good deal in this exposition. There are exceptions to all principles stated. Your accounting buddy down the hall is counting on your lack of understanding for his job security. You will, however, understand enough to go forward with the accurate handling and modeling of the different types of expenditures you will encounter.

Expense and capital expenditures are viewed and accounted for differently by generally accepted accounting principles (GAAP) and by the tax authorities. Your financial model should adhere to GAAP, as do the all the financial models in this book.

■**Note** *Generally accepted accounting principles* (GAAP) are the common set of accounting principles, standards, and procedures that companies use to compile their financial statements. GAAP are a combination of authoritative standards (set by policy boards) and represent commonly accepted ways of recording and reporting accounting information.

It is important to understand the distinction between expense and capital so that you can accurately model the flow of expense and capital through your model in accordance with GAAP standards.

Criteria for Capital Expenditures

Expenditures for an asset that has a useful life substantially beyond one year are capital expenditures. For example, purchases of database servers that have useful lives of multiple years are capital expenditures.

Capital expenditures are carried on the books as capital assets. They are accounted for on the company balance sheet, and the cash that is outlaid for them is shown as an outflow of cash in the Statement of Cash Flows.

Capital assets are depreciated. They are reduced in value over time to represent the *using up or consumption* of the useful life of the asset. If you look at a balance sheet in the year that the asset is purchased, you will see its value shown on the balance sheet at its full purchase cost. A few years later, its value on the balance sheet will have been reduced by depreciation. The lower value is then considered its *book value*.

Calculating Depreciation

Depreciation is the assumed reduction in book value of an asset due to usage, passage of time, wear and tear, technological outdating, obsolescence, or other similar factors. One common way of computing depreciation is called the *straight line method*, where depreciation is calculated by dividing the original book or purchase value of the asset by the number of periods of its useful life. For example, a server that costs $3,000 and has a useful life of five years would be depreciated at $600 per year. At the first anniversary of its purchase, its book value would show on the balance sheet as $2,400 ($3,000 − $600 = $2,400).

■**Note** Depreciation is a noncash expense. Depreciation is an accounting entry used to reduce the book value of an asset over its useful life. It does not represent cash going out the door. Depreciation is adjusted for within the Statement of Cash Flows in order to establish the actual cash position of the company.

Defining Expensed Items

An item that is not a capital item is an *expense item*. Expensed items are not carried on the books as an asset, and depreciation is not applied to them. Expensed items are assumed to have a short useful life and are effectively *consumed* when they are paid for. Expense items show up on the Profit and Loss Statement. Depreciation is included on the Profit and Loss Statement as an expense but does not represent a cash outlay.

Considering Categories of Expense

There are four primary types of expense (cost) that make up most company cost structures:

- *Fixed*: Fixed costs do not vary with changes in volume. Examples are rent or insurance payments.

- *Variable*: This type of cost varies proportionately with volume. Sales commissions would be an example.

- *Semivariable*: This type of cost includes a combination of variable and fixed costs. A semi-variable cost varies with changes in volume but does so less than proportionately. Examples are staffing costs, where there must be a minimum number on the staff but the staff may increase with increases in volume beyond a certain level.

- *Nonrecurring*: Nonrecurring costs only occur once or they occur infrequently. Tax preparation fees that occur once a year would meet this criterion.

Planning the Operating Expenditure (OPEX) Model

Developing the OPEX model requires that you plan for the forecasting of general operating expenses. Remember that general operating expenses are *not* capital items. We will address capital items in the CAPEX model. The major categories for these expenses follow:

- *Rent*: Rent for office facilities

- *Phone*: Local, long-distance, and 800 services and those very expensive cell phone plans

- *Office and administrative*: Postage, banking fees, finance charges, and miscellaneous

- *Accounting and other*: Tax preparation and general accounting services

- *Legal*: Legal services for patent preparation, corporate structure, and partnering agreements

- *Licenses and permits*: Various operating licenses and permits

- *Sales and use taxes*: Various government licenses to do various types of commerce

- *Depreciation*: Depreciation of capital assets shown as an expense (See the CAPEX model discussions later in this chapter.)

For each of these cost categories, you must ascertain the following information:

- Is the expense forecasted internally by the model, or is it a discrete (manual) input based on information external to the model?

- What type of cost is it: fixed, variable, semivariable, or nonrecurring?

- What is the estimated monthly amount of the expense? How often will it occur, and how much will it grow per year?

Planning the Capital Expenditure (CAPEX) Model

Developing the CAPEX model requires that you forecast the acquisition of capital items by all functional areas of the company. This plan is called the Capital Plan and is a time-phased listing of capital acquisitions. In addition, you must calculate depreciation on the capital assets that you plan to buy and you must create a schedule (Fixed Asset Schedule) that summarizes the capital purchases and depreciation in a format that can be used downstream in the Balance Sheet and the Statement of Cash Flows.

You will plan to develop the following primary models and modules:

- *Capital planning*: This is the master plan of all capital expenditures planned by each functional area of the company. To develop this plan, you must think through the capital purchase requirements for each functional area of the company for the entire time period that you are modeling for the company.

- *Depreciation calculation model*: You must develop a model that allows you to depreciate the capital assets that are planned for in the Capital Plan. You must figure out how you are going to compute the depreciation on your capital expenditures. For example, if you are using a straight line method, you must compute depreciation by dividing the purchase value by the number of periods over which you will depreciate the asset.

- *Keep Fixed Assets Schedule*: You must combine the Capital Plan and computed depreciation into this schedule. It will be used downstream and covered in more detail in Chapter 12 when we develop the Balance Sheet.

Building and Using the OPEX and CAPEX Models

When the planning is complete, build the models. Take into consideration the inputs and outputs from these models to and from other components of the CBM.

Figure 9-2 is a high-level component and flow chart of the OPEX and CAPEX models and shows the OPEX and CAPEX models and their data flow relationships. Two major inputs to these models are operating and capital expenditure requirements that are developed in STAFF_CWS. A primary downstream output of the model is fixed asset data from CAPEX-FA_DB that is utilized in FIN_BALSHEET_CWS to create the company Balance Sheet. OPEX and CAPEX share the chart data spreadsheet OPEX-CAPEX_CHARTDAT.

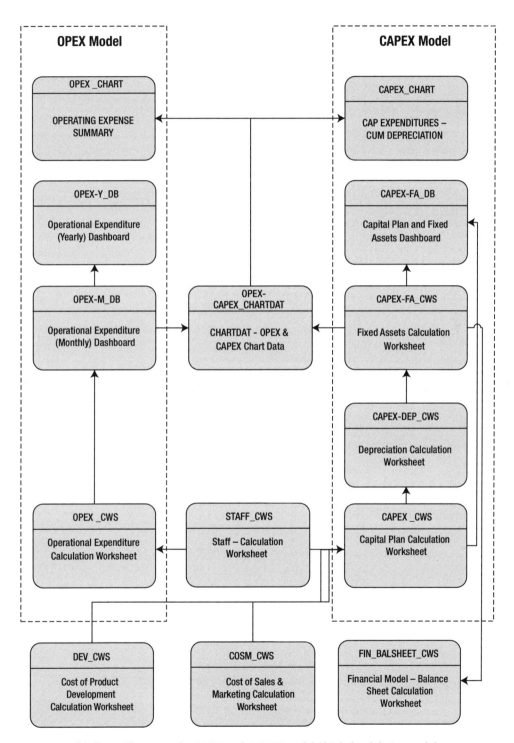

Figure 9-2. *This figure illustrates the OPEX and CAPEX models' high-level design and data process flows. Spreadsheets within the dotted lines are primary modules of models. Arrows indicate major data flows.*

Exploring the Building Blocks of the OPEX Model

The purpose of the OPEX model is to forecast general operating expenditures. The following section discusses the components of the model and how they work to develop this forecast.

Developing the Operational Expenditure Calculation Worksheet

The Operational Expenditure Calculation Worksheet, OPEX _CWS, calculates three variable expense items from requirement counts in the STAFF_CWS Worksheet. OPEX_CWS is an interim calculation spreadsheet that provides operating expense calculations (e.g., phone, work space, or rent expenses) for OPEX-M_CWS and capital requirement calculations (e.g., office computers, furniture, and fixtures) for CAPEX_CWS.

For example, a work space expense (or rent) utilized by OPEX-M_CWS is computed as follows: the count of staff requiring work space is accessed via linking from STAFF_CWS. This number is multiplied by a manually entered factor of 50 square feet per person. Other unit costs are manually entered and calculated based on counts generated in STAFFPLAN_CWS. The square footage is multiplied by $4 per square foot, yielding a monthly rent of $3,200 for 16 employees, as shown in Figure 9-3. In this model, as headcount increases, so does rent.

■**Note** OPEX _CWS is linked to STAFF_CWS to access requirement counts used in phone, computer, and work space calculations.

Practically speaking, this method of computing work space best serves as an example of how to compute work space needs in complex situations. In a one-location setting, the amount of rent paid would probably be a discrete input based on known external factors.

	A	B	C	D	E	F	G	H	I	J	K
										YR 1	
2		Cost Data	YR 0	Jan	Feb	Mar	Apr	May	Jun	Jul	Aug
21	**Work Space**										
22											
23	Executive			2.00	2.00	2.00	2.00	2.00	2.00	2.00	2.00
24	Business Operations			1.00	1.00	1.00	1.00	1.00	1.00	1.00	1.00
25	Sales & Marketing			1.00	1.00	1.00	1.00	2.00	2.00	2.00	2.00
26	Technical Operations			8.00	8.00	8.00	9.00	10.00	10.00	10.00	11.00
27	Total (Cumulative)		4.00	12.00	12.00	12.00	13.00	15.00	15.00	15.00	16.00
28	New		4.00	8.00	-	-	1.00	2.00	-	-	1.00
29											
30											
31	**Compute Phone Expense**										
32	Phone Purchase	$ 190.00	$ 760	$ 1,140	$ -	$ -	$ 190	$ 380	$ -	$ -	$ 190
33	Monthly Plan	$ 90.00	$ 360	$ 900	$ 900	$ 900	$ 990	$ 1,170	$ 1,170	$ 1,170	$ 1,260
34	Total Phone Expense		$ 1,120	$ 2,040	$ 900	$ 900	$ 1,180	$ 1,550	$ 1,170	$ 1,170	$ 1,450
35											
36	**Compute Computer Expense**										
37	New Computer Expense	$ 2,500.00	$ 10,000	$ 25,000	$ -	$ -	$ 2,500	$ 5,000	$ -	$ 2,500	$ 2,500
38	Total Computer Expense		$ 10,000	$ 25,000	$ -	$ -	$ 2,500	$ 5,000	$ -	$ 2,500	$ 2,500
39											
40	**Compute Work Space Expense**										
41	Work Space Per Employee	$ 50	$ 800	$ 2,400	$ 2,400	$ 2,400	$ 2,600	$ 3,000	$ 3,000	$ 3,000	$ 3,200
42	Cost per Sq. Ft.	$ 4.00									
43	Total WS Expense (Rent)		$ 800	$ 2,400	$ 2,400	$ 2,400	$ 2,600	$ 3,000	$ 3,000	$ 3,000	$ 3,200
44											
45	**Compute Furniture and Fixtures**										
46	Office Set Up (Desk-Chairs etc.)	$ 250.00	1,000.00	2,000.00	-	-	250.00	500.00	-	-	250.00
47	Total Furniture & Fixtures		1,000.00	2,000.00	-	-	250.00	500.00	-	-	250.00

Figure 9-3. *OPEX_CWS computes variable expenses for phones, computers, and work spaces based on requirements from the Staffing Calculation Worksheet, STAFF_CWS.*

Using the Operational Expenditure (Monthly) Worksheet

The Operational Expenditure (Monthly) Worksheet, OPEX-M_CWS, is the primary calculation spreadsheet for the development of operating expenses. It is developed by combining cost items that have been previously calculated in OPEX_CWS and cost items that are individually estimated from sources external to the model.

OPEX-M_CWS utilizes formulas that spread monthly estimates for expenditure line items and increase them by a yearly compounded growth rate. These formulas provide a quick way to spread cost estimates over multiple years, but my experience is that you will tweak these spreads to fine-tune them.

The basis for each type of cost line item is identified in the Notes column, as shown in Figure 9-4. If the amounts are precalculated in another worksheet, the worksheet name is also in the column. A monthly estimate of cost for each operating expense is included in the Month Est column. A percentage growth factor for each line item is included in the YR-Growth % column.

Note OPEX-M_CWS is linked to OPEX_CWS for calculations of cell phone and rent expenses.

	A	B	C	D	E	F	G	H	I	J	K	L
											YR 1	
		Notes	Month Est	YR-Growth %	YR 0	Jan	Feb	Mar	Apr	May	Jun	Jul
3												
4	Office and Admin											
5												
6	Rent	From OPEX_CWS	na	na	$ 800	$ 2,400	$ 2,400	$ 2,400	$ 2,600	$ 3,000	$ 3,000	$ 3,000
7												
8	Phone											
9	Local Service	Monthly est w/increase	$ 90.00	5.0%	$ 1,080	$ 90	$ 90	$ 90	$ 90	$ 90	$ 90	$ 90
10	Long Distance	Monthly est w/increase	$ 250.00	2.5%	$ 2,255	$ 250	$ 250	$ 250	$ 250	$ 250	$ 250	$ 250
11	800 Service	Monthly est w/increase	$ 350.00	15.0%	$ -	$ 350	$ 350	$ 350	$ 350	$ 350	$ 350	$ 350
12	Cell Phones	From OPEX_CWS	na	na	$ 1,120	$ 2,040	$ 900	$ 900	$ 1,180	$ 1,550	$ 1,170	$ 1,170
13	Total Phone				$ 4,455	$ 2,730	$ 1,590	$ 1,590	$ 1,870	$ 2,240	$ 1,860	$ 1,860
14												
15	Office & Admin											
16	Postage	Monthly est w/increase	$ 50.00	2.5%	$ 678	$ 50	$ 50	$ 50	$ 50	$ 50	$ 50	$ 50
17	Ofice Shipping	Monthly est w/increase	$ 125.00	2.5%	$ 1,500	$ 125	$ 125	$ 125	$ 125	$ 125	$ 125	$ 125
18	Banking Fees	Monthly est w/increase	$ 35.00	2.5%	$ 350	$ 35	$ 35	$ 35	$ 35	$ 35	$ 35	$ 35
19	Miscellaneous	Monthly est w/increase	$ 150.00	2.5%	$ 689	$ 150	$ 150	$ 150	$ 150	$ 150	$ 150	$ 150
20	Total Office and Admin				$ 3,217	$ 360	$ 360	$ 360	$ 360	$ 360	$ 360	$ 360
21												
22	Accounting & Other											
23	Accounting General	Monthly est w/increase	$ 75.00	2.5%	$ 3,500	$ 75	$ 75	$ 75	$ 75	$ 75	$ 75	$ 75
24	Accounting Tax Prep	Discrete Non-recurring	April		$ 1,500				$ 1,500			
25	Other Consulting Fees	Monthly est w/increase	$ 150.00	2.5%	$ 3,300	$ 150	$ 150	$ 150	$ 150	$ 150	$ 150	$ 150
26	Total Accounting & Other				$ 8,300	$ 225	$ 225	$ 225	$ 1,725	$ 225	$ 225	$ 225
27												
28	Legal			2.5%								
29	Corporate	Monthly est w/increase	$ 250.00	2.5%	$ 2,500	$ 250	$ 250	$ 250	$ 250	$ 250	$ 250	$ 250
30	Partnership Ageements	Monthly est w/increase	$ 250.00	2.5%		$ 250	$ 250	$ 250	$ 250	$ 250	$ 250	$ 250
31	Patent Protection	Non-recurring			$ 8,500	$ 20,000						
32	Total Legal	Discrete Estimate			$11,000	$ 20,500	$ 500	$ 500	$ 500	$ 500	$ 500	$ 500

Figure 9-4. *The Operational Expenditure (Monthly) Worksheet*

Reviewing the Operational Expenditure (Yearly) Dashboard

The Operational Expenditure (Yearly) Dashboard, OPEX-Y_DB, is a summary report of OPEX-M_DB. It is created by linking to and summarizing OPEX-M_DB and can be utilized as a management report to summarize operating expenses (see Figure 9-5).

Note OPEX-Y_DB is linked to OPEX-M_DB and summarizes the data from this more detailed spreadsheet into a summary report.

	B	C	D	E	F	G	H
1		YR 0	YR 1	YR 2	YR 3	YR 4	YR 5
5	Rent	$ 800	$ 35,400	$ 57,000	$ 72,000	$ 91,200	$ 91,200
6							
7	Phone						
8	Local Service	$ 1,080	$ 1,080	$ 1,134	$ 1,191	$ 1,250	$ 1,313
9	Long Distance	$ 2,255	$ 3,000	$ 3,075	$ 3,152	$ 3,231	$ 3,311
10	800 Service	$ -	$ 4,200	$ 4,830	$ 5,555	$ 6,388	$ 7,346
11	Cell Phones	$ 1,120	$ 15,860	$ 29,360	$ 35,700	$ 45,990	$ 44,280
12	Total Phone	$ 4,455	$ 24,140	$ 38,399	$ 45,597	$ 56,859	$ 56,250
13							
14	Office & Admin						
15	Postage	$ 678	$ 600	$ 615	$ 630	$ 646	$ 662
16	Office Shipping	$ 1,500	$ 1,500	$ 1,538	$ 1,576	$ 1,615	$ 1,656
17	Banking Fees	$ 350	$ 420	$ 431	$ 441	$ 452	$ 464
18	Miscellaneous	$ 689	$ 1,800	$ 1,845	$ 1,891	$ 1,938	$ 1,987
19	Total Office and Admin	$ 3,217	$ 4,320	$ 4,428	$ 4,539	$ 4,652	$ 4,768
20							
21	Accounting & Other						
22	Accounting General	$ 3,500	$ 900	$ 923	$ 946	$ 969	$ 993
23	Accounting Tax Prep	$ 1,500	$ 1,500	$ 1,500	$ 1,500	$ 1,500	$ 1,500
24	Other Consulting Fees	$ 3,300	$ 1,800	$ 1,845	$ 1,891	$ 1,938	$ 1,987
25	Total Accounting & Other	$ 8,300	$ 4,200	$ 4,268	$ 4,337	$ 4,408	$ 4,480
26							
27	Legal						
28	Corporate	$ 2,500	$ 3,000	$ 3,075	$ 3,152	$ 3,231	$ 3,311
29	Partnership Ageements	$ -	$ 3,000	$ 3,075	$ 3,152	$ 3,231	$ 3,311
30	Patent Protection	$ 8,500	$ 20,000	$ 5,000	$ 5,000	$ 5,000	$ 5,000
31	Total Legal	$ 11,000	$ 26,000	$ 11,150	$ 11,304	$ 11,461	$ 11,623
32							
33	Licenses and Permits	$ -	$ 300	$ 308	$ 315	$ 323	$ 331
34							
35	Sales and Use Taxes	$ -	$ 300	$ 308	$ 315	$ 323	$ 331
36							
37	Depreciation	$ 183	$ 24,338	$ 31,913	$ 36,300	$ 41,700	$ 41,517
38							
39	Total Expense	$ 27,955	$118,998	$147,772	$174,707	$210,926	$210,501

Figure 9-5. *The Operational Expenditure (Yearly) Dashboard*

Utilizing the OPEX and CAPEX Chart Data Worksheet

The OPEX and CAPEX Chart Data Worksheet, OPEX-CAPEX_CHARTDAT, preformats data needed for OPEX and CAPEX management and analysis charts. Charts are defined, and the data for each chart is accessed by linking back to relevant data source spreadsheets in the model (see Figure 9-6).

	A	B	C	D	E	F	G	H	I
3									
4	OPERATING EXPENSE SUMMARY								
5								YR 1	
6			Jan	Feb	Mar	Apr	May	Jun	Jul
7									
8		Rent	$ 2,400	$ 2,400	$ 2,400	$ 2,600	$ 3,000	$ 3,000	$ 3,000
9		Total Phone	$ 2,730	$ 1,590	$ 1,590	$ 1,870	$ 2,240	$ 1,860	$ 1,860
10		Total Office and Admin	$ 360	$ 360	$ 360	$ 360	$ 360	$ 360	$ 360
11		Total Accounting & Other	$ 225	$ 225	$ 225	$ 1,725	$ 225	$ 225	$ 225
12		Total Legal	$ 20,500	$ 500	$ 500	$ 500	$ 500	$ 500	$ 500
13		Licenses and Permits	$ 25	$ 25	$ 25	$ 25	$ 25	$ 25	$ 25
14		Sales and Use Taxes	$ 25	$ 25	$ 25	$ 25	$ 25	$ 25	$ 25
15		Depreciation	$ 1,075	$ 1,667	$ 1,833	$ 2,046	$ 2,138	$ 2,138	$ 2,179
16		Total Expense	$ 27,340	$ 6,792	$ 6,958	$ 9,151	$ 8,513	$ 8,133	$ 8,174
18									
19	CAPITAL EXPENDITURES AND DEPRECIATION								
20									
21								YR 1	
22			Jan	Feb	Mar	Apr	May	Jun	Jul
23									
24		Capital Expenditure	$ 53,500	$ 35,500	$ 10,000	$ 12,750	$ 5,500	$ -	$ 2,500
25		Cum Capital Expenditure	$ 53,500	$ 89,000	$ 99,000	$ 111,750	$ 117,250	$ 117,250	$ 119,750
26		Cum Depreciation	$ 1,075	$ 2,742	$ 4,575	$ 6,621	$ 8,758	$ 10,896	$ 13,075
27		Depreciation	$ 1,075	$ 1,667	$ 1,833	$ 2,046	$ 2,138	$ 2,138	$ 2,179

Figure 9-6. *OPEX and CAPEX chart data is formatted and organized for the development of management and analysis charting.*

■**Note** Exercise 9-2 shows how to display capital expenditures and depreciation.

The management chart, OPEX_CHART, shown in Figure 9-7, is an example of the type of management chart that can be produced from the OPEX model. This chart is a little busy, but it points out the value of charting expense data. Notice the nonrecurring blips in legal and accounting fees. Legal fees drop from an all-time high in the first month (patent work) and then recur as patents are updated. Accounting fees jump during each tax cycle. Other charges grow as you might expect over the years.

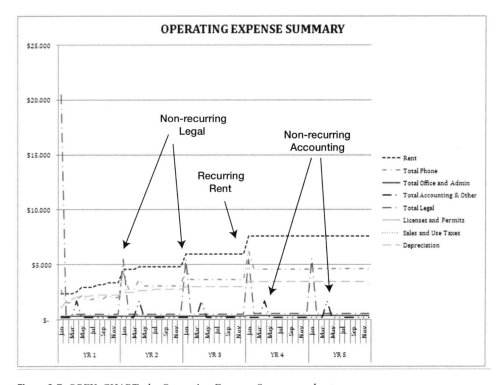

Figure 9-7. *OPEX_CHART, the Operating Expense Summary chart*

The Building Blocks of the CAPEX Model

The purposes of the CAPEX model are to forecast capital expenditures and depreciation and to develop a Fixed Asset Schedule to be used later in developing the company Balance Sheet. The following section discusses the components of the model and how they work to develop this forecast.

Understanding the Capital Plan Calculation Worksheet

The Capital Plan Calculation Worksheet, CAPEX _CWS, generates a summary of the Capital Plan from which depreciation is calculated by CAPEX-DEP_CWS. Capital expenditure requirements are linked to and originate in the STAFF, COSM and REV models. Furniture, fixtures, and office computer capital requirements are precomputed amounts that are accessed via links to OPEX_CWS (see Figure 9-8).

	A	B	E	F	G	H	I	J	K	L
1									YR 1	
2		Capital Plan	YR 0	Jan	Feb	Mar	Apr	May	Jun	Jul
6		Facilites								
7		Furniture and Fixtures	$ 1,000	$ 2,000	$ -	$ -	$ 250	$ 500	$ -	$ -
8		Office Computers	$10,000	$ 25,000	$ -	$ -	$ 2,500	$ 5,000	$ -	$ 2,500
9		Total Facilities	$11,000	$ 27,000	$ -	$ -	$ 2,750	$ 5,500	$ -	$ 2,500
10										
11		Marketing and Sales								
12		VOIP Phone System	$ -	$ -	$ -	$ -	$ 10,000	$ -	$ -	$ -
13		Marketing Web Server	$ -	$ 3,500	$ -	$ -	$ -	$ -	$ -	$ -
14		Total Marketing and Sales	$ -	$ 3,500	$ -	$ -	$ 10,000	$ -	$ -	$ -
15										
16		Technical Operations								
17										
18		Information Technology								
19		LAN Server	$ -	$ 3,500	$ -	$ -	$ -	$ -	$ -	$ -
20		Internet - Connectivity Equipment	$ -	$ 2,500	$ -	$ -	$ -	$ -	$ -	$ -
21		Biz Ops Application Server	$ -	$ -	$ -	$ -	$ -	$ -	$ -	$ -
22										
23		Systems Integration								
24		Database Server	$ -	$ -	$ 3,500	$ -	$ -	$ -	$ -	$ -
25		Application Server	$ -	$ -	$ 3,500	$ -	$ -	$ -	$ -	$ -
26		Web Server	$ -	$ -	$ 3,500	$ -	$ -	$ -	$ -	$ -
27										
28		Software Development								
29		Development Server	$ -	$ 3,500	$ -	$ -	$ -	$ -	$ -	$ -
30		Development DB Server	$ -	$ 3,500	$ -	$ -	$ -	$ -	$ -	$ -
31										
32		Hardware Development								
33		Test Hardware Products	$ -	$ -	$ -	$ -	$ -	$ -	$ -	$ -
34		Test Equipment	$ -	$ 10,000	$ 25,000	$ 10,000	$ -	$ -	$ -	$ -

Figure 9-8. *CAPEX_CWS is the Capital Plan summary derived by linking to all capital requirements sources in the CBM.*

Note CAPEX_CWS is linked to OPEX_CWS and accesses capital requirement calculations for furniture and fixtures and office computers and to the COSM and REV models for all other capital requirements.

Understanding the Depreciation Calculation Worksheet

CAPEX-DEP_CWS calculates depreciation on capital assets acquired per the Capital Plan developed in CAPEX_CWS. The formulas in this spreadsheet calculate straight line depreciation based on a variable input for the number of years that the asset is to be depreciated. For example, if you choose to depreciate the assets over five years you type **5** into the Years field (cell M2), as shown in Figure 9-9. The model will calculate straight line depreciation on a five-year basis.

Note See Exercise 9-1 for instructions on creating a straight line depreciation model.

	A	B	C	D	E	F	G	H	I	J	K	L	M	N	O	P	Q	R
1								Depreciation Calculation					Years	Months				
2								Depreciation Assumption Years				→	5.00	60.00	Note : Must be at least 1 year			
3																		
4					YR 0	Jan	Feb	Mar	Apr	May	Jun	Jul	Aug	Sep	Oct	Nov	Dec	Jan
5	CAP PLAN																	
6	Cell Ref	Year	Month															
7	E	-	YR 0	$ 11,000	$ 183	$ 183	$ 183	$ 183	$ 183	$ 183	$ 183	$ 183	$ 183	$ 183	$ 183	$ 183	$ 183	$ 183
8	F	1	Jan	$ 53,500		$ 892	$ 892	$ 892	$ 892	$ 892	$ 892	$ 892	$ 892	$ 892	$ 892	$ 892	$ 892	$ 892
9	G	1	Feb	$ 35,500			$ 592	$ 592	$ 592	$ 592	$ 592	$ 592	$ 592	$ 592	$ 592	$ 592	$ 592	$ 592
10	H	1	Mar	$ 10,000				$ 167	$ 167	$ 167	$ 167	$ 167	$ 167	$ 167	$ 167	$ 167	$ 167	$ 167
11	I	1	Apr	$ 12,750					$ 213	$ 213	$ 213	$ 213	$ 213	$ 213	$ 213	$ 213	$ 213	$ 213
12	J	1	May	$ 5,500						$ 92	$ 92	$ 92	$ 92	$ 92	$ 92	$ 92	$ 92	$ 92
13	K	1	Jun	$ -							$ -	$ -	$ -	$ -	$ -	$ -	$ -	$ -
14	L	1	Jul	$ 2,500								$ 42	$ 42	$ 42	$ 42	$ 42	$ 42	$ 42
15	M	1	Aug	$ 2,750									$ 46	$ 46	$ 46	$ 46	$ 46	$ 46
16	N	1	Sep	$ -										$ -	$ -	$ -	$ -	$ -
17	O	1	Oct	$ 2,750											$ 46	$ 46	$ 46	$ 46
18	P	1	Nov	$ -												$ -	$ -	$ -
19	Q	2	Dec	$ -													$ -	$ -
20	R	2	Jan	$ 14,000														$ 233

Figure 9-9. *CAPEX-DEP_CWS, the Depreciation Calculation Worksheet, demonstrates the cascade method of modeling straight line depreciation.*

■**Note** CAPEX-DEP_CWS is linked to CAPEX_CWS to access monthly capital expenditure totals.

Understanding the Fixed Assets Calculation Worksheet

The Fixed Assets Calculation Worksheet, CAPEX-FA_CWS, develops a Fixed Assets Schedule by combining capital expenditure and depreciation data. The Fixed Assets Schedule is used in developing the company Balance Sheet in Chapter 12 and is developed by creating a cumulative view of the book value of purchased assets as depreciation is applied to them.

The Fixed Assets Calculation Worksheet (see Figure 9-10) links to capital expenditure data from CAPEX_CWS and depreciation data from CAPEX-DEP_CWS. This schedule combines the addition of capital with accumulated depreciation to create a schedule of the ongoing book value of capital assets. This schedule is used downstream in FIN-BALANCE_CWS to create the company Balance Sheet.

	B	C	D	E	F	G	H	I	J
3		YR 0	YR 1	YR 2	⊕ YR 3	YR 4	YR 5		
4									
5	Fixed Assets	$ -	$ 11,000	$ 136,250	$ 165,000	$ 181,500	$ 208,500		
6	CAPEX	$ 11,000	$ 125,250	$ 28,750	$ 16,500	$ 27,000	$ -		
7	Cumulative Fixed Assets	$ 11,000	$ 136,250	$ 165,000	$ 181,500	$ 208,500	$ 208,500		
8	Change in Assets	$ 11,000	$ 125,250	$ 28,750	$ 16,500	$ 27,000	$ -		
9	Depreciation	$ (183)	$ (24,338)	$ (31,913)	$ (36,300)	$ (41,700)	$ (41,517)		
10	Accumulated Depreciation	$ (183)	$ (24,521)	$ (56,433)	$ (92,733)	$ (134,433)	$ (175,950)		
11		$ -							
12	Net Fixed Assets	$ 10,817	$ 111,729	$ 108,567	$ 88,767	$ 74,067	$ 32,550		
13									
14						YR 1			
15		YR 0	Jan	Feb	Mar	Apr	May	Jun	Jul
16									
17	Fixed Assets	$ -	$ 11,000	$ 64,500	$ 100,000	$ 110,000	$ 122,750	$ 128,250	$ 128,250
18	CAPEX	$ 11,000	$ 53,500	$ 35,500	$ 10,000	$ 12,750	$ 5,500	$ -	$ 2,500
19	Cumulative Fixed Assets	$ 11,000	$ 64,500	$ 100,000	$ 110,000	$ 122,750	$ 128,250	$ 128,250	$ 130,750
20	Change in Assets	$ 11,000	$ 53,500	$ 35,500	$ 10,000	$ 12,750	$ 5,500	$ -	$ 2,500
21	Depreciation	$ (183)	$ (1,075)	$ (1,667)	$ (1,833)	$ (2,046)	$ (2,138)	$ (2,138)	$ (2,179)
22	Accumulated Depreciation	$ (183)	$ (1,258)	$ (2,925)	$ (4,758)	$ (6,804)	$ (8,942)	$ (11,079)	$ (13,258)
23									
24	Net Fixed Assets	$ 10,817	$ 63,242	$ 97,075	$ 105,242	$ 115,946	$ 119,308	$ 117,171	$ 117,492

Figure 9-10. *CAPEX-FA_CWS, the Fixed Assets Calculation Worksheet, shows the monthly calculation of the fixed assets as well as the yearly roll up.*

■**Note** CAPEX-FA_CWS is linked to CAPEX_CWS for capital expenditure data and to CAPEX-DEP_CWS for depreciation data.

Reviewing the Capital Plan and Fixed Assets Dashboard

The Capital Plan and Fixed Assets Dashboard, CAPEX-FA_DB, provides a management summary of the company Capital Plan and Fixed Assets Schedule (see Figure 9-11). These two summaries are developed by summarizing data from CAPEX_CWS and CAPEX-FA_CWS.

■**Note** CAPEX-FA_DB is linked to CAPEX_CWS and CAPEX-FA_CWS and accesses and summarizes, respectively, Capital Plan data and fixed asset schedule data.

	B	C	D	E	F	G	H
26	**Software Development**						
27	Development Server	$ -	$ 3,500	$ -	$ -	$ -	$ -
28	Development DB Server	$ -	$ 3,500	$ -	$ -	$ -	$ -
29							
30	**Hardware Development**						
31	Test Hardware Products	$ -	$ -	$ -	$ -	$ -	$ -
32	Test Equipment	$ -	$ 45,000	$ -	$ -	$ -	$ -
33							
34	**Test Engineering**	$ -	$ -	$ -	$ -	$ -	$ -
35							
36	**Total Technical Operations**	$ -	$ 68,500	$ 7,000	$ -	$ -	$ -
37							
38	**Total Capital Plan**	$ 11,000	$125,250	$ 28,750	$ 16,500	$ 27,000	$ -
39							
40							
41	**Fixed Assets Summary**	**YR 0**	**YR 1**	**YR 2**	**YR 3**	**YR 4**	**YR 5**
42							
43	Fixed Assets	$ -	$ 11,000	$ 136,250	$ 165,000	$ 181,500	$ 208,500
44	CAPEX	$ 11,000	$ 125,250	$ 28,750	$ 16,500	$ 27,000	$ -
45	Cumulative Fixed Assets	$ 11,000	$ 136,250	$ 165,000	$ 181,500	$ 208,500	$ 208,500
46	Change in Assets	$ 11,000	$ 125,250	$ 28,750	$ 16,500	$ 27,000	$ -
47	Depreciation	$ (183)	$ (24,338)	$ (31,913)	$ (36,300)	$ (41,700)	$ (41,517)
48	Accumulated Depreciation	$ (183)	$ (24,521)	$ (56,433)	$ (92,733)	$ (134,433)	$ (175,950)
49		$ -	$ -	$ -	$ -	$ -	
50	**Net Fixed Assets**	$ 10,817	$ 111,729	$ 108,567	$ 88,767	$ 74,067	$ 32,550

Figure 9-11. *CAPEX-FA_DB, the Capital Plan and Fixed Assets Dashboard*

The chart shown in Figure 9-12 is an example of a management chart developed from data derived from the CAPEX model. It is an example of a combination line and bar chart used to display capital expenditures and cumulative depreciation. It can be useful to display the recurring and non-recurring aspects of capital expenditures on one chart. As before, chart data is preformatted and the charts are defined in OPEX-CAPEX_CHARTDAT.

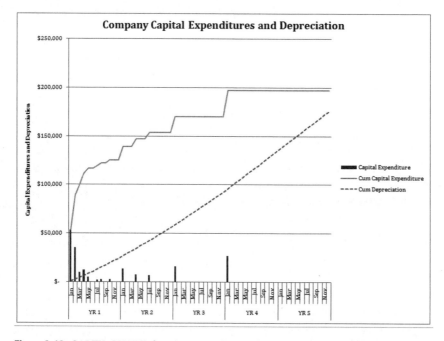

Figure 9-12. *CAPEX_CHART showing recurring and nonrecurring capital expenditure impacts*

■**Note** Exercise 9-2 explains how to show capital expenditures and depreciation using a combination chart like the one shown in Figure 9-12.

EXERCISE 9-1. USING MICROSOFT EXCEL TO COMPUTE STRAIGHT LINE DEPRECIATION

Capital expenditures must be depreciated. CAPEX is required to depreciate capital assets that are purchased per the Capital Plan. It is assumed that a straight line method will be used.

- *Problem:* The Capital Plan within CAPEX determines monthly capital expenditures for the period of performance of the model, which is 60 months. The depreciation calculation method must compute depreciation on assets beginning in the month of acquisition and provide a cumulative total of these calculations. This calculation requirement presents a dilemma of how to best accomplish this calculation in a spreadsheet format without creating highly complex and lengthy formulas. Depreciation models must have the flexibility to compute depreciation based on a variety of useful life scenarios. In other words, the depreciation model should be able to compute depreciation based on a variable useful life entry.

- *Solution:* Develop a standard straight line depreciation calculation formula that accepts a useful life (years to be depreciated) parameter as a variable. Cascade (time phase) this standard formula in a manner that allows for a cumulative depreciation calculation.

Obtain Monthly Capital Expenditures

Activate CAPEX-DEP_CWS, and link to and vertically reposition monthly capital expenditures from CAPEX_CWS. Begin by selecting cell D7 and typing =, selecting cell E40 in CAPEX _CWS, and pressing Return. This creates the link. Repeat this process to create a matrix of capital expenditures (the vertical component) and monthly depreciation calculations (the horizontal component). Assume, for the purposes of this model that, during YR 0, all purchases were made in December, in effect treating the YR 0 column as if it is a month. See Figure 9-13 for an illustration of this step.

■**Note** I entered column references from CAPEX_CWS in column A. I use these column references as a visual reference to check and make sure that my formulas are correct in the matrix.

Set the Lifetimes of Capital Assets

Create a variable input area for the input of years (which equals the useful life of the asset in years), and convert the Years value into Months. The Months calculation will be the variable input to the straight line depreciation calculation formula. I have created this area in the range M2:N2 at the top of the spreadsheet. See Figure 9-13, which demonstrates this and the previous step.

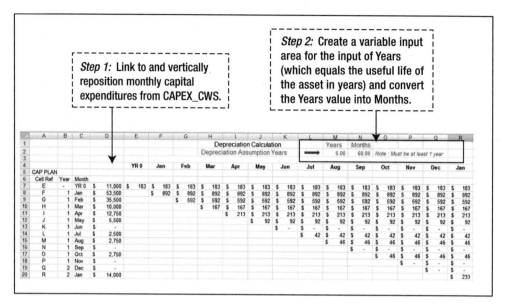

Figure 9-13. *Building the straight line depreciation model*

Create a Straight Line Depreciation Formula

Create a straight line depreciation formula that calculates straight line depreciation of the purchased asset over the period of performance of the model based on a variable Month value input.

■**Note** Creating the depreciation formula gets tricky, because the formula should only create depreciation entries for the number of months needed to fully depreciate the asset. If the capital expenditure is fully depreciated, the formula should place a zero in the remaining period of performance calculation fields.

Create a formula that can be replicated or copied in a cascading fashion over the month matrix that we have created. This formula has three parts (see Figure 9-14):

- In the first month of the calculation, reference the capital amount in column D and divide it by the number of months calculated in the months variable $N$2. This becomes the first month's (and all subsequent months') depreciation amount for the capital asset.

- In the second month, test to see if the previous monthly calculations have fully depreciated the item. Using the IF function, test if the sum of previous calculations is less than the original amount of capital expenditure. If so, keep calculating; otherwise, input zero into the field. *Note that, in the second month test, we are testing only the value in the previous month's field.*

- In the third month, use identical logic but expand the test criteria to all previous fields ($E7:F7), and anchor the test range at cell E7. This allows us to copy the formula to the right as many times as we need, and the test range will expand accordingly.

We copy the third month formula into the remaining cells to the right that make up the full period of performance. We are not yet ready to cascade-copy the formula throughout the matrix.

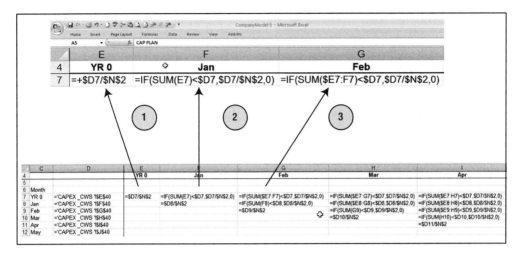

Figure 9-14. *Developing a standard straight line depreciation calculation formula: 1 is the first month's calculation, 2 is the second month's calculation, and 3 is the third month's calculation.*

Replicate the Depreciation Formula for All Months

Copy the straight line depreciation formula throughout the entire matrix. Cascade the formulas (see Figure 9-15) by copying them in a cascading fashion over the period of performance of the model. To do this, paste the formula range E7 to BM7 into cell F8 to replicate the formula across five years beginning in February of YR 1. Next, paste the formula range E7:BM7 into cell G9 to replicate the formula across five years beginning in March of YR 1. Repeat this cascading copy process (copy the range one cell down and one cell to the right) until you have filled the entire matrix. The last copy of range E7:BM7 is into cell BM67. As you copy the formulas, they will overhang the end of your matrix. Delete all columns to the right of your last month to clean up the spreadsheet (see Figure 9-15).

Summarize the Total of all Depreciation

Summarize the total of all depreciation on the last line, which is row 69. You now have a depreciation schedule for your capital assets. As your capital model changes, your depreciation schedule will change also.

Note For the purposes of this model, it is assumed that all categories of capital are depreciated over the same useful life (Months). You can see how this model may be replicated to compute straight line depreciation for individual items or groupings or items that must be depreciated over varying time periods.

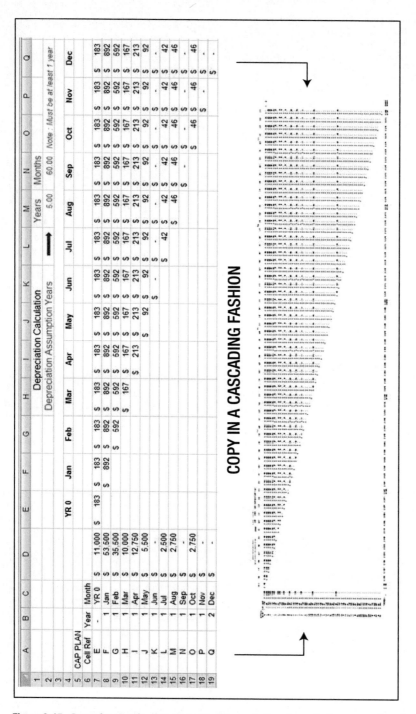

Figure 9-15. *Copy the standard straight line depreciation formula in a cascading fashion, thus building the depreciation calculation matrix.*

EXERCISE 9-2. CREATING A COMBINATION BAR AND LINE CHART TO DISPLAY CAPITAL EXPENDITURES AND DEPRECIATION

Management reviews of capital expenditures and depreciation are facilitated by reports and charts that display a combined picture, which includes capital expenditures and depreciation. Often, these charts display three data series: capital expenditures, cumulative capital expenditures, and cumulative depreciation.

- *Problem:* A line series chart is a good way to display two of the three required data series, cumulative capital expenditures and cumulative depreciation. Capital expenditures are best shown in a bar format, since they are non-recurring in nature. We need to create a combination bar and line chart to display all data required.

- *Solution:* Create a combination bar and line chart to display capital expenditure and depreciation data on one chart.

Select the Data Range for the Chart

Open OPEX-CAPEX_CHARTDAT, and highlight the data series for Capital Expenditures and Depreciation to be charted (range B21:BJ26), as shown in Figure 9-16. Note that we are not selecting the range for monthly depreciation, which was used to calculate (for chart purposes) cumulative depreciation.

	A	B	C	D	E	F	G	H	I	J
4		OPERATING EXPENSE SUMMARY								
5								YR 1		
6			Jan	Feb	Mar	Apr	May	Jun	Jul	Aug
7										
8		Rent	$ 2,400	$ 2,400	$ 2,400	$ 2,600	$ 3,000	$ 3,000	$ 3,000	$ 3,200
9		Total Phone	$ 2,730	$ 1,590	$ 1,590	$ 1,870	$ 2,240	$ 1,860	$ 1,860	$ 2,140
10		Total Office and Admin	$ 360	$ 360	$ 360	$ 360	$ 360	$ 360	$ 360	$ 360
11		Total Accounting & Other	$ 225	$ 225	$ 225	$ 1,725	$ 225	$ 225	$ 225	$ 225
12		Total Legal	$ 20,500	$ 500	$ 500	$ 500	$ 500	$ 500	$ 500	$ 500
13		Licenses and Permits	$ 25	$ 25	$ 25	$ 25	$ 25	$ 25	$ 25	$ 25
14		Sales and Use Taxes	$ 25	$ 25	$ 25	$ 25	$ 25	$ 25	$ 25	$ 25
15		Depreciation	$ 1,075	$ 1,667	$ 1,833	$ 2,046	$ 2,138	$ 2,138	$ 2,179	$ 2,225
16		Total Expense	$ 27,340	$ 6,792	$ 6,958	$ 9,151	$ 8,513	$ 8,133	$ 8,174	$ 8,700
18										
19		CAPITAL EXPENDITURES AND DEPRECIATION								
20										
21								YR 1		
22			Jan	Feb	Mar	Apr	May	Jun	Jul	Aug
23										
24		Capital Expenditure	$ 53,500	$ 35,500	$ 10,000	$ 12,750	$ 5,500	$ -	$ 2,500	$ 2,750
25		Cum Capital Expenditure	$ 53,500	$ 89,000	$ 99,000	$ 111,750	$ 117,250	$ 117,250	$ 119,750	$ 122,500
26		Cum Depreciation	$ 1,075	$ 2,742	$ 4,575	$ 6,621	$ 8,758	$ 10,896	$ 13,075	$ 15,300
27		Depreciation	$ 1,075	$ 1,667	$ 1,833	$ 2,046	$ 2,138	$ 2,138	$ 2,179	$ 2,225

Figure 9-16. *OPEX-CAPEX_CHARTDAT organizes and preformats your charting data as required.*

Insert the Line Chart

On the menu ribbon's Insert tab, click Line. In the top row of 2-D Line charts, click Line, which is the first chart type (see Figure 9-17). A line chart will appear on the active worksheet, as shown in Figure 9-18, and the Chart Tools menu will be activated on the ribbon.

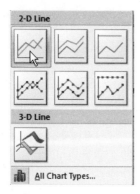

Figure 9-17. *Select the first 2-D Line chart.*

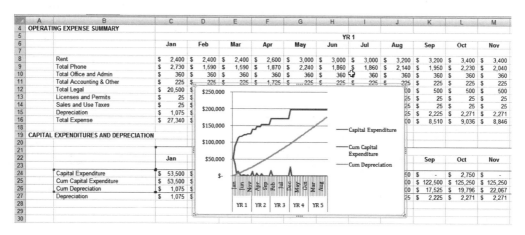

Figure 9-18. *A line chart will appear within your currently open spreadsheet.*

Move the Chart to a New Worksheet

On the ribbon's Design tab, click Move Chart Location. In the Move Chart dialogue box, select "New sheet", type in the name that you want, and click OK (see Figure 9-19). A chart sheet is inserted into a new spreadsheet (see Figure 9-20) and will fill your screen.

Figure 9-19. *Select "New sheet".*

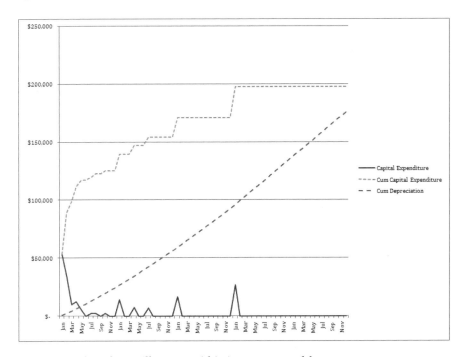

Figure 9-20. *A line chart will appear within in a new spreadsheet.*

Highlight the Capital Expenditure Series

On the chart, select the capital expenditure line. The Capital Expenditure data series will become highlighted (see Figure 9-21).

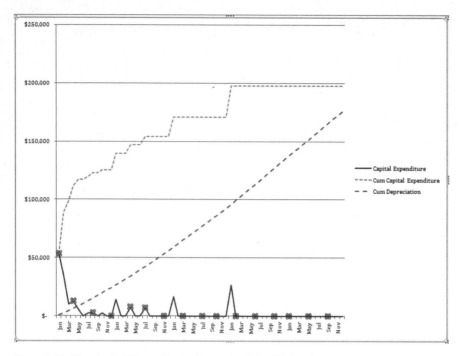

Figure 9-21. *The Capital Expenditure data series is highlighted.*

Convert the Chart to a Bar Chart

On the ribbon, click Change Chart Type. Select Column as the chart type, and use the Clustered Column chart, which is selected by default (see Figure 9-22). Click OK.

The Capital Expenditure data series will be converted to a column format (see Figure 9-23).

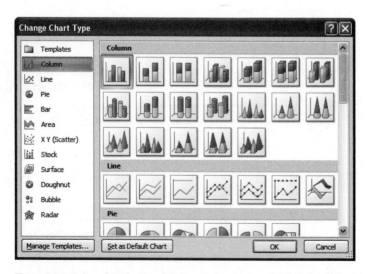

Figure 9-22. *Select the Clustered Column chart type, which is the default selection.*

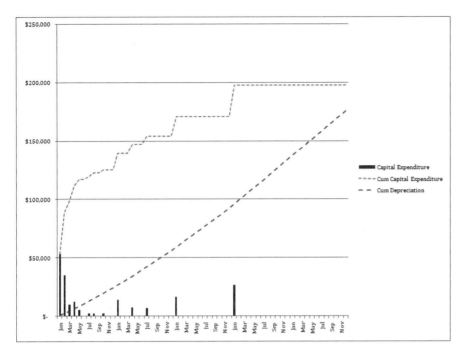

Figure 9-23. *The Capital Expenditure data series is converted to a clustered column format.*

Modify the Titles

To complete the chart, click the ribbon's Layout tab, and add a chart title and axis titles.

Summary

The Operating Expenditure (OPEX) and Capital Expenditure (CAPEX) models are used to forecast operating expenses and capital expenditures, which together compose a significant portion of cash outflows.

Investors look at a company's outgoing cash flow, or burn rate (the rate at which cash is being consumed by the enterprise), so it is critical that management understand the burn rate and have a handle on cash needs. Again, running out of cash is often the single greatest problem that early stage technology companies face.

As we forecast expenditures, we must address the accurate calculation of cash flow. The cash position of the company is developed from combining *all sources and uses of cash* into a consolidated view, the Statement of Cash Flows.

Understanding the difference between an expense and a capital item is important, since they are handled differently in the calculation of cash flows.

Here's the overarching question regarding cash flows: how will you use the CBM to manage your cash needs?

■■■

CHAPTER 10

Statements of Profit and Loss and Cash Flow

This is the first chapter of three (Chapters 10, 11, and 12) that deal with the financial and financial reporting aspects of modeling the startup technology company. In previous chapters, we have built financial models of operational components of the company and planned and quantified key operating aspects. We have modeled staffing (STAFF), operating and capital expenditures (OPEX and CAPEX), sales and revenues (REV), and cost of goods sold (COGS). We have also modeled the costs of sales and marketing (COSM) and product development (DEV).

In this chapter, we will create a consolidated view of the operations and financial performance of the company by developing two key financial statements or reports:

- Profit and Loss Statement
- Statement of Cash Flows

These financial reports are generated by consolidating outputs from operational models that we have previously developed.

This chapter focuses on company performance as presented in the Profit and Loss (P&L) Statement and the Statement of Cash Flows. In Chapter 11, we will explore, in detail, company valuation and investments. In Chapter 12, we will develop the Balance Sheet, compare the three key financial reports side by side, and discuss their relationships in more detail. We will also discuss other operating metrics that are important in assessing company performance and financial condition.

In this chapter, you will learn how to plan, create, and use key components of the Financial Reporting (FIN) model. In addition you will learn how to

- Develop a Profit and Loss Statement.
- Develop a Statement of Cash Flows.
- Reconcile the Profit and Loss Statement and the Statement of Cash Flows.
- Interpret or read the Profit and Loss Statement and the Statement of Cash Flows.

Business Thinking about Profit, Loss, and Cash Flow

Business thinking about profit, loss, and cash flow is essentially thinking about company performance. To understand company performance, you must understand and be able to read and interpret the Profit and Loss Statement and the Statement of Cash Flows. These two statements must be viewed together in order to understand the total operating performance picture. The relationship between the two financial statements must be understood while creating and modeling and interpreting them.

Both statements present a running account of operating results over a designated time or accounting period. In contrast, the Balance Sheet shows the status of the company from an asset and liability standpoint at the end of each period. As stated previously, the Balance Sheet will be covered in more detail in Chapter 12.

Understanding the Profit and Loss Statement

The Profit and Loss Statement shows operating performance by comparing revenue, cost of revenue, and gross margin against other company expenses. The resulting calculation results in a profit or loss, or as many call it, the *bottom line*. The structure of this report varies from company to company, but basically takes the form shown in Figure 10-1. The bottom line, or Net Income, is computed as follows: Sales *minus* Cost of Goods Sold *equals* Gross Margin *less* Total Expenses *equals* Net Income.

Statement of Profit and Loss	Month 1	Month 2
Sales	$ 15,000	$ 25,000
Cost of Goods Sold (COGS)	$ 3,500	$ 5,000
Gross Margin	$ 11,500	$ 20,000
Cost of Sales & Mkt	$ 1,500	$ 2,000
Cost of Product Dev	$ 1,000	$ 1,000
Cost of Sal-Wages-Benefits	$ 2,500	$ 2,500
Other Operation Expense	$ 1,500	$ 2,500
Total Operating Expense	$ 6,500	$ 8,000
Depreciation	$ 500	$ 500
Total Expenses	$ 7,000	$ 8,500
Net Income	$ 4,500	$ 11,500

Figure 10-1. *A sample P&L showing the first two months of company operation*

A Profit and Loss Statement is fairly intuitive. I rarely find a client who does not understand how to read one. The P&L shows revenues and expenses over various time periods. Sounds simple, yes? Not quite. There is more to the P&L than meets the eye. And the P&L represents the beginning, not the end, of the understanding of company performance. We require more than a superficial assessment of revenues, cost, and profit, as you will see later in the chapter.

Using Accrual Accounting

The Profit and Loss Statement is normally developed using an accrual accounting approach. What does this mean? It means that the numbers shown on the P&L do not represent actual cash coming in and going out the door of the company. Said another way, the profit or loss shown at the bottom of the statement does not represent actual cash profit or a cash loss. Yes, the P&L is truly a representation of the operations of the company, but it must be reconciled to the Statement of Cash Flows in order to understand the actual cash status of the company.

Let's begin our understanding of this reconciliation with a definition. *Accrual accounting* is an accounting method that recognizes income when it is earned and expenses when they are incurred, rather than when they are received or paid. For example, the sale of an item and the sales commission paid on the sale may both be shown on the P&L in the same month, regardless of the fact that the cash collected for the sale and the commission paid occurs in the next month. The revenues and costs are aligned and related (accrued) to one time period.

Revenue and corresponding expenditures required to generate revenue are recognized in the same period regardless of actual cash inflows or outflows.

■**Note** If you are not using accrual accounting, you may be practicing one of several other accounting methodologies, such as cash basis, modified cash basis, or tax basis accounting. For example, in *cash basis accounting*, you recognize income when payment is received and expenses when the bills are actually paid.

The P&L represents revenues and expenses as they are incurred from an operational perspective but does not necessarily show actual cash flowing in and out of the business.

Interpreting the P&L from an Accrual Point of View

In this section, we will look at the major line items that make up a P&L and discuss how they are viewed from the standpoint of accrual accounting and their relationship to cash flow. Once we have done this, you will be well on your way to understanding the reconciliation between the P&L and cash flow needed to develop the true cash position of the company.

The following discussion and examples are generic and conceptual. We will discuss specific company financial model assumptions and implementation later in this chapter within the context of the Company business case.

Let's first begin with a sample P&L (see Figure 10-1). Month 1 and Month 2 represent the first months of operation for the company. Sales in Month 1 are $15,000 and Cost of Goods Sold is $3,500. Gross Margin is $11,500. Profit after all other expenses is $4,500. Note the corresponding data for Month 2.

Viewing Sales in Terms of Accounts Receivable

Let's think of sales in the context of accounts receivable (AR), as shown in Figure 10-2. In this example, the company has shown $15,000 in sales in Month 1 on the P&L. Let's assume it collects payments on the sales of $2,500 in the same month. The beginning AR balance is $0, since the company is just getting started. The ending AR balance is $12,500 calculated as follows: Beg Balance *plus* Sales *minus* Collections *equals* Ending Balance.

■**Note** Located just below the AR account, we have noted that the "Direct Method – Cash" (in) was $2,500 and that the "Indirect - Change in AR" (balance) is $12,500 (changed from $0 to $12,500). We will use this data at the end of this example to derive a cash impact of these operating activities shown on the P&L. At the bottom of each figure, the direct and indirect methods of looking at the data in the figure are shown. The reason for this will become clear later in this chapter.

F	G	H
Accounts Receivable (AR)		
	Month 1	**Month 2**
Beg Balance	$ -	$ 12,500
Sales	$ 15,000	$ 25,000
Collections	$ 2,500	$ 9,000
Ending Balance	$ 12,500	$ 28,500
Direct Method - Cash	$ 2,500	$ 9,000
Indirect - Change in AR	$ 12,500	$ 16,000

Figure 10-2. *P&L Revenue (Sales) from an AR point of view*

Cost of Goods Sold as Inventory and Accounts Payable

Let's now look at cost of goods sold and inventory. First, we will make an assumption that the product being sold is a hardware product that must be purchased and placed in inventory before it can be sold. We must think about the cost of goods sold in two ways:

- Before the product can be sold, it has to be purchased from a supplier and put into inventory (see Figure 10-3). When products are sold, we move them out of inventory and book them as a cost of goods sold. This accounting transaction reduces the amount of inventory by the amount of the cost of goods sold but does not result in a cash outlay. However, the cost of goods sold does reduce the amount of profit on the P&L.

- The purchased inventory must be paid for. If the company does not completely pay for all inventory each month, there will be a cost of goods sold accounts payable balance due. Paying for the inventory results in a cash outlay.

The net effect of these two transactions is reconciled between the P&L and Statement of Cash Flows. Both transactions are used to adjust Net Income from the P&L to the Statement of Cash Flows.

See Figure 10-3 for the inventory transaction related to the cost of goods sold. In this example, the company has a beginning inventory balance of $0. The company purchases $4,000 of inventory in the first month. In the same month, it consumes $3,500 worth of the inventory and books $3,500 to cost of goods sold (see Figure 10-1) for the current month's sales.

■**Note** The consumption of the inventory (booking or moving it into Cost of Goods Sold) is not the same thing as paying for the inventory. Figure 10-4 shows that the effect on cash will be compensated through the change in accounts payable.

In Figure 10-3, you can see that the ending inventory balance is $500 calculated as follows: Beg Balance *plus* Inventory Purchased *minus* Inventory Used (COGS) *equals* Ending Balance. Note the "Direct Method – Cash" (no impact) and "Indirect - Change in Inventory" notations in the figure.

Inventory		
	Month 1	Month 2
Beg Balance	$ -	$ 500
Inventory Purchased	$ 4,000	$ 6,000
Inventory Used (COGS)	$ 3,500	$ 5,000
Ending Balance	$ 500	$ 1,500
Direct Method - Cash	$ -	$ -
Indirect - Change in Inventory	$ 500	$ 1,000

Figure 10-3. *Inventory reporting format showing inventory usage that reduces physical inventory and is booked to cost of goods sold*

See Figure 10-4 for the Accounts Payable (AP) - Inventory view. The company has a beginning inventory AP balance of $0. It purchased $4,000 of inventory (see Figure 10-3) in the first month. In the same month, it paid $3,000 to the vendor of the inventory for the current month's purchase of inventory. The ending inventory AP balance is $1,000 calculated as follows: Beg Balance *plus* Inventory Purchased *minus* Inventory Payment *equals* Ending Balance. Note the "Direct Method - Cash" and "Indirect - Change in Inventory AP" notations.

Accounts Payable (AP) - Inventory				
	Month 1		Month 2	
Beg Balance	$	-	$	1,000
Inventory Purchased	$	4,000	$	6,000
Inventory Payment	$	3,000	$	4,800
Ending Balance	$	1,000	$	2,200
Direct Method - Cash	$	(3,000)	$	(4,800)
Indirect - Change in Inventory AP	$	1,000	$	1,200

Figure 10-4. *The Accounts Payable (AP) - Inventory view shows the impact on AP of payments for inventory.*

Calculating Gross Margin

Gross margin is calculated as follows: Sales *minus* Cost of Goods Sold *equals* Gross Margin.

Operating Expenses as Accounts Payable

As in inventory, if we don't pay what we owe in the current month for other operating expenses, we will have an operating expense account payable. In our current example, we will combine all other operating expenses to create one example of an operating expense account payable. Any expense incurred by a company, whether related to sales support, product development, or salaries and benefits, can be viewed from the standpoint of accounts payable.

Operating expenses can be paid for in full in the current period, partially paid, or accrued. For example, an employee may earn sick days each month that are not paid for in the current month, but the expense is booked in the current month as an accrued expense by the company. Another example is that Web design services for sales and marketing may be paid for over an extended period based on terms given by the Web designer. In both cases, an account payable (sometimes called an accrued expense) is created.

In this example, we have combined expenses for the following costs:

- Sales and marketing
- Product development
- Salaries, wages, and benefits
- Other operating expenses

See Figure 10-5 for the Accounts Payable (AP) Expenses view. The company has a beginning AP expense balance of $0. Expenses in Month 1 total $6,500. In the same month, the company outlays a total of $4,875 to pay these expenses. The ending expense AP balance is $1,625 calculated as follows: Beg Balance *plus* Expense Incurred *minus* Expenses Paid *equals* Ending Balance. Note the "Direct Method – Cash" and "Indirect - Change in Expense AP" notations.

Accounts Payable (AP) Expenses				
	Month 1		Month 2	
Beg Balance	$	-	$	1,625
Expense Incurred	$	6,500	$	8,000
Expenses Paid	$	4,875	$	6,000
Ending Balance	$	1,625	$	3,625
Direct Method - Cash	$	(4,875)	$	(6,000)
Indirect - Change in Expense AP	$	1,625	$	2,000

Figure 10-5. *Accounts Payable (AP) Expenses view*

Calculating Depreciation

The depreciation expense shown on the P&L is derived from a calculation of depreciation on the fixed assets of the company. In this example, we assume that the company has purchased one piece of capital equipment for $30,000. The equipment has a useful life of five years and is depreciated in a straight line over 60 months. The monthly depreciation cost of $500 is calculated as follows: $30,000 purchase price *divided by* 60 months *equals* $500 of depreciation per month for 60 months.

In accrual accounting theory, the rationale is that the investment in the asset is spread over the useful life of the asset. Depreciation is a noncash accounting entry. It reduces profit on the P&L by $500 but does not increase cash outlay. The cash outlay for the equipment is shown on the Statement of Cash Flows as an investment activity, and an adjustment for depreciation is shown as an operating activity adjustment.

Understanding the Statement of Cash Flows

The purpose of the Statement of Cash Flows is to provide an understanding of the financial consequences of business activities by providing a detailed look at the sources and uses of cash.

■**Note** The Statement of Cash Flows can be extraordinarily revealing if you know how to read it. You can see, on a line-by-line basis, how the company cash position has been affected in operating, investment, and financing activities.

When assessing a company's performance, you not only need to know the overall cash position, but where the cash is coming from and how it is being used. As we said in Chapter 1, "Cash is king!" The smart entrepreneur knows to focus on cash and uses a financial model as the primary cash-forecasting tool, providing analysis of margin contributions, cash flows, and break-even points. The single most important value event that an early-stage company attains is cash flow positive.

To manage anything, you have to understand it. To manage cash, you have to understand where it is coming from and how it is being used. The primary challenge in preparing and understanding the Statement of Cash Flows is understanding the relationship between it and the other financial statements.

Let's now begin a review of the Statement of Cash Flows so that you can understand how to read it and use it in managing the cash within your enterprise.

The Statement of Cash Flows has three sections:

- Operating
- Investing
- Financing

Each section provides detailed information related to cash flow from these activities. Under generally accepted accounting principles (GAAP), there are two ways to present a cash flow: the indirect method and the direct method. The only difference between these two methods lies within the presentation of the operating activities section of the statement.

Direct method: The direct method directly lists cash receipts and disbursements related to operations to arrive at cash flow from operating activities (CFO). Direct cash receipts and disbursements derived from our analysis of the P&L are shown in Figure 10-7. This is an example of a direct listing of cash as used in this method.

Indirect method: The indirect method starts with the net income figure from the P&L and adjusts it for items that reflect differences between the net income and actual cash flows from operations. There are two types of adjustments that convert net income into CFO using this method:

- Adjust for noncash revenues and expenses that were included under accrual accounting. One common example of a noncash expense is depreciation.

- Adjust for changes in operating assets and operating liabilities, those assets and liabilities that are normally considered current assets and current liabilities. Examples include AR and AP.

A company can choose either method, but there is a catch. If you choose the direct method, you must provide backup for it by providing the same detail that would be used in the indirect method. Most companies use the indirect method. We will use the indirect method in this example and in the financial model for the example company business case.

You can see from the reconciliation shown in Figure 10-6 that the P&L is not a great indicator of cash flow for the company. To further understand the full picture, we must now create the Statement of Cash Flows. We will use the *indirect method* to develop this statement.

Creating the Statement of Cash Flows

We will now create the Statement of Cash Flows, making necessary adjustments to operating activities, accounting for investment activities, and recognizing financing activities.

Accounting for Operating Activities

We begin by adjusting the Net Income from the P&L for noncash revenues and expenses and for changes in operating assets and liabilities, as shown in Figure 10-6. The adjustments to net income are as follows and refer to Month 1:

Depreciation: Add back Depreciation of $500, since it is a noncash expense.

(Increase) decrease in A/R+Other Assets: See Figure 10-2. AR increased by $12,500. The adjustment is a negative $12,500. When receivables increase, the adjustment to P&L net income is negative.

(Increase) decrease in Inventory: See Figure 10-3. Inventory increased by $500. The adjustment is a negative $500. When inventory increases, the adjustment to P&L net income is negative.

Increase (decrease) in AP- COGS/Inventory: See Figure 10-4. The inventory AP balance increased by $1,000. The adjustment is $1,000. When AP increases, the adjustment to P&L net income is positive.

Increase (decrease) in AP- Other Expenses: See Figure 10-5. The AP balance for other expenses AP increased by $1,625. The adjustment is $1,625. When AP increases, the adjustment to P&L net income is positive.

Statement of Profit and Loss	Month 1	Month 2
Sales	$ 15,000	$ 25,000
Cost of Goods Sold (COGS)	$ 3,500	$ 5,000
Gross Margin	$ 11,500	$ 20,000
Total Expenses	$ 7,000	$ 8,500
Net Income	$ 4,500	$ 11,500
Statement of Cash Flows		
	↓	↓
Operating Activities		
Net Income	$ 4,500	$ 11,500
Adjustment to Cash used by operating activities		
Depreciation	$ 500	$ 500
(Increase) decrease in A/R+Other Assets	$ (12,500)	$ (16,000)
(Increase) decrease in Inventory	$ (500)	$ (1,000)
Increase (decrease) in AP- COGS/Inventory	$ 1,000	$ 1,200
Increase (decrease) in AP- Other Expenses	$ 1,625	$ 2,000
Total Adjustments	$ (9,875)	$ (13,300)
Net Cash Provided (Used In) Operating Activities	$ (5,375)	$ (1,800)
Investment Activities		
Purchase of Capital Assets and Other Assets	$ (30,000)	$ -
Net Cash Used in Investing	$ (30,000)	$ -
Financing Activities		
Stockholders Contribution	$ 50,000	$ -
Net Cash Provided by Financing Activities	$ 50,000	$ -
Net increase <decrease> in cash	$ 14,625	$ (1,800)
Cash Balance at Beg of Period	$ -	$ 14,625
Cash Balance at End of Period	$ 14,625	$ 12,825

Figure 10-6. *This example Statement of Cash Flows shows its relationship to the Profit and Loss Statement. See Profit and Loss Statement in Figure 10-1.*

The total adjustments are negative $9,875. When this adjustment is added to net income from the P&L of $4,500, the net effect is a cash outflow from Operating Activities of $5,375. This completes the operating activities portion of the Statement of Cash Flows.

Accounting for Investment Activities

If the company invests in property, plants, or equipment, the investment is recorded in the Investment Activities section. In our example, the company has invested $30,000 in new equipment, so this cash outlay is recorded in Investment Activities. Net cash used in investing is $30,000 (see Figure 10-6). If the company loans money, the notes receivable amount would show in this section of the report.

Accounting for Financing Activities

Financing activities are activities related to the financing of the company. Notes payable, shareholder investment, dividends paid to stockholders, or capital leases may be included in the section. In our example (see Figure 10-6), the owners have invested $50,000 into the business.

Accounting for Net Increases (Decreases in Cash)

The bottom line of the Statement of Cash Flows is the net increase or decrease in cash. This is computed as follows: net cash used in operating activities *minus* net cash used in investing activities *plus* net cash provided by financing activities. The net *increase* or *decrease* in cash is *added* to the cash balance at the beginning of the period to derive the cash balance at the end of the period.

Reading and Interpreting the Statement of Cash Flows

You can now read the P&L and Statement of Cash Flows and interpret the operating results. In the example shown in Figure 10-6, we interpret the statement as follows:

- In Month 1 on sales of $15,000, the company had a net profit of $4,500.

- At the end of the month, the company's net cash position was $14,625. This cash position resulted from the combination of Net Cash from Operating Activities of ($5,375), Net Cash Used in Investing of ($30,000), and Stockholders Contribution of Cash of $50,000.

- We also know, from our previous detailed look at accrual impacts on AR and AP inventory and AP expense, that on sales of $15,000 only $2,500 was collected, $4,000 in inventory was purchased, and $3,000 was paid for it. Payments of $4,875 were made on total operating expenses of $6,500.

Checking Our Work Using the Direct Method

We reviewed each line item of the P&L from an accrual viewpoint. As we investigated the transactions behind each line item, we also established an actual cash impact associated with the transaction. The summary of these impacts is shown in Figure 10-7. Our analysis shows that during Month 1, which shows a P&L operating profit of $4,500, the company experienced a cash outflow from operating activities of $5,375. Month 2 shows an operating profit of $11,500, and the company experienced a net outflow of cash of $1,800. The total cash outflow in Month 1 of $5,375 consists of the following transactions:

- $2,500 cash in from sales (See Figure 10-2.)

- No cash out from reducing inventory and booking it as cost of goods sold (See Figure 10-3.)

- $3,000 cash out from the purchase of inventory (See Figure 10-4.)

- $4,875 cash out for the payment of operating expenses (See Figure 10-5.)

Direct Method		Cash		
		Month 1		Month 2
AR	$	2,500	$	9,000
AP COGS	$	(3,000)	$	(4,800)
Inventory	$	-	$	-
AP Other Exp	$	(4,875)	$	(6,000)
Total Cash In (Out)	$	(5,375)	$	(1,800)

Figure 10-7. *A direct method listing of cash receipts and disbursements from analysis of the P&L statement*

■**Note** The adjustments we have made to Operating Activities using the indirect method result in the identical cash impact that was previously computed using the direct method shown in Figure 10-7.

We can garner a great deal of detail regarding what actually happened in the business during the month. This level of detail can be utilized to assess the performance and day-to-day decisions being made by the company. Analyzing the Statement of Cash Flows with a knowledgeable eye can expose actual cash expenditure impacts that are sometimes masked by the accrual-based Profit and Loss Statement. The Profit and Loss Statement and the Statement of Cash Flows, viewed in tandem, can reveal the fundamentals of company business operations. Viewed separately, they have much less value.

We have completed our business thinking about the P&L and Statement of Cash Flows. Now, we will consider the FIN model and its application to the following company business case. The business case for this chapter will be stated in a context that relates to our previous analysis, that is, operating activities, investment activities, and financing activities.

Exploring Cash Flow Impacts of the Product Development Strategy Business Case

Green Devil Control Systems (the Company) is an early-stage technology startup. The Company develops energy monitoring and control systems for the residential markets. Specifically, it builds and sells the Green Devil Energy Control System (ECS). The Company president is well known and has extensive experience and contacts in the home building industry. His partner is a graduate level electrical engineer, and she has extensive experience in developing smart control systems.

Defining the Product

ECS is a patent-pending programmable hardware and software device that monitors and controls electricity usage on a circuit-by-circuit basis within a facility. ECS is installed on the facility side of the electrical breaker box and provides Internet-based, secure, and remote setup, programming control, and diagnostics. ECS also provides a suite of analysis tools and system setup tools for optimizing electricity usage. ECS comes with two software options: Local Services (LS) or Extended Services (ES). LS and ES web browser user interfaces are highly intuitive, attractive, and easy to use.

Planning Operating Activities

The Company will pursue an aggressive schedule to develop, manufacture, and sell ECS. Figure 10-8 is a graphical rendering of the major operating activities of the Company. It should be noted that this type of schedule will ideally be created in Microsoft Project or some other scheduling tool. I have used this graphical example to demonstrate what planning software output would produce in terms of a high-level schedule.

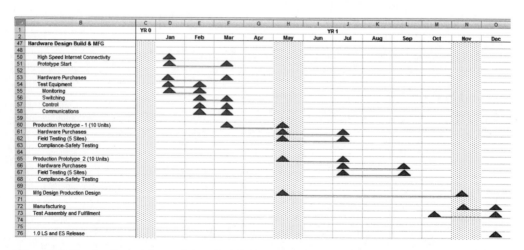

Figure 10-8. *Top-level operating activity schedule from FIN-MSCHEDULE_DB*

The major operating milestones follow, in sequence of their planned performance:

1. *Prototype development*: Low-level breadboard prototype development and testing will be completed by March of YR 1.

2. *Production prototype development*: Ten production prototypes will be built and completed by May of YR 1. Five production prototypes will be used for field testing and five prototypes for compliance (lab) and safety testing.

3. *Field, compliance, and safety testing*: There will be two iterations of field and compliance testing, which will include final modifications to the production prototype. Testing will be completed by September of YR 1.

4. *Manufacturing design*: Manufacturing design will begin in May of YR 1 and be completed in November of YR 1.

5. *Manufacturing*: Manufacturing will be outsourced and will begin in November of YR 1.

6. *Product release*: The ECS product (with both software options) will be available in December of YR 1.

7. *Software*: LS software and ES software will be developed in an integrated plan with product development.

8. *Staffing*: The Company will aggressively hire the staff required to implement the product development and sales strategy of the Company.

9. *Product availability*: The Company projects commercial release and product availability in December of YR 1.

10. *Inventory*: The manufacturer will ship components to the Company, where they will be inventoried, assembled, and tested prior to shipment to the customer. The Company plans to order and keep in stock (in inventory) a three-month supply of ECS units.

Charting Investment Activities

In support of operating activities, the Company will invest in capital equipment as set forth in its capital expenditure plan. In Figure 10-9, Company capital expenditures (CAPEX) are shown. These capital expenditures represent the investment activities of the Company. Notice in Figure 10-11 that these amounts are shown under investment activities on the Statement of Cash Flows.

	B	C	D	E	F	G	H
3		YR 0	YR 1	YR 2	YR 3	YR 4	YR 5
4							
5	Fixed Assets- Beginning	$ -	$ 11,000	$ 136,250	$ 165,000	$ 181,500	$ 208,500
6	CAPEX	$ 11,000	$ 125,250	$ 28,750	$ 16,500	$ 27,000	$ -
7	Fixed Assets - Ending	$ 11,000	$ 136,250	$ 165,000	$ 181,500	$ 208,500	$ 208,500
8	Change in Assets	$ 11,000	$ 125,250	$ 28,750	$ 16,500	$ 27,000	$ -
9	Depreciation	$ (183)	$ (24,338)	$ (31,913)	$ (36,300)	$ (41,700)	$ (41,517)
10	Accumulated Depreciation	$ (183)	$ (24,521)	$ (56,433)	$ (92,733)	$ (134,433)	$ (175,950)
11		$ -					
12	Net Fixed Assets	$ 10,817	$ 111,729	$ 108,567	$ 88,767	$ 74,067	$ 32,550

Figure 10-9. *CAPEX-FA_CWS, the Company's fixed assets summary*

Capital expenditures and depreciation are plotted in Figure 10-10.

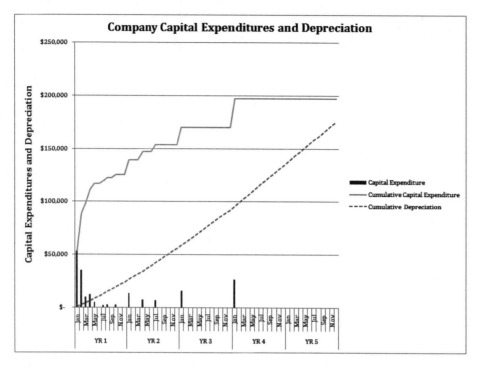

Figure 10-10. *CAPEX_CHART shows Company investment activity (capital expenditures and depreciation).*

Reflecting Financing Activities

As shown in the Company Statement of Cash Flows (see Figure 10-11), Company founders have invested $870,906 into the Company in YR 0 and $1,709,773 in YR 1. These investments, amounts, and timing are based on analysis and strategies that are developed in detail in Chapter 11.

■**Note** As opposed to the previous generic example given in this chapter, the Company is assuming no accounts payable associated with other operating expenses, for simplicity. The Company has AR associated with sales and AP associated with inventory only.

	B	C	D
		YR 0	YR 1
1			
2	STATEMENT OF CASH FLOWS		
3			
4	OPERATING ACTIVITIES		
5	Net Income	$ (57,757)	$ (1,882,868)
6			
7	Adjustments to Cash used by operating activities		
8	Depreciation	$ 183	$ 24,338
9	(Increase) decrease in A/R+Other Assets	$ -	$ (53,055)
10	(Increase) decrease in Inventory	$ -	$ (109,500)
11	Increase (decrease) in AP+Other Liabilities	$ -	$ 87,750
12			
13	Total Adjustments	$ 183	$ (50,468)
14			
15	Net Cash Used In Operating Activities	$ (57,574)	$ (1,933,336)
16			
17	INVESTMENT ACTIVITIES		
18	Purchase of Capital Assets and Other Assets	$ (11,000)	$ (125,250)
19			
20	Net Cash Used In Investing Activities	$ (11,000)	$ (125,250)
21			
22	FINANCING ACTIVITIES		
23	Stockholders Contribution	$ 870,906	$ 1,709,773
24			
25	Net increase <decrease> in cash	$ 802,333	$ (348,813)
26			
27	Cash Balance at Beg of Period	$ -	$ 802,333
28	Cash Balance at End of Period	$ 802,333	$ 453,519

Figure 10-11. *FIN-CASHFLOW_CWS shows Company financing activities including stockholders' (founders') investments in YR 0 and other investments in YR 1.*

Planning the FIN Model

The purpose of the FIN model (see Figure 10-12) is to consolidate the outputs from all operating models and present them in three key financial statements:

- Profit and Loss Statement
- Statement of Cash Flows
- Balance Sheet

In this section, we will focus on the profit and loss and cash flows reports. Chapter 12 will cover the Balance Sheet in more detail. The primary purpose of the FIN model is generating and formatting standard financial statements and reports.

Planning the Profit and Loss Statement: Review the output from all operating models that generate data for the P&L. Plan the report format for the P&L including the order of presentation and the level of detail that you require. The format is important, because it provides an opportunity to emphasize the categories and summations of revenue and expense that you deem to be important to a reviewer.

Planning the Statement of Cash Flows: Review the output from all operating models that generate data for the Statement of Cash Flows. The report format is standard, so spend your time making sure that you understand all of the linking and relationships necessary to build the report.

Understanding the Building Blocks of the FIN Model

When the planning is complete, build and test the model. This section provides an overview of FIN and the functionality of the model components, shown in Figure 10-12. As previously stated, the emphasis on this chapter is on the Profit and Loss and the Statement of Cash Flows reports.

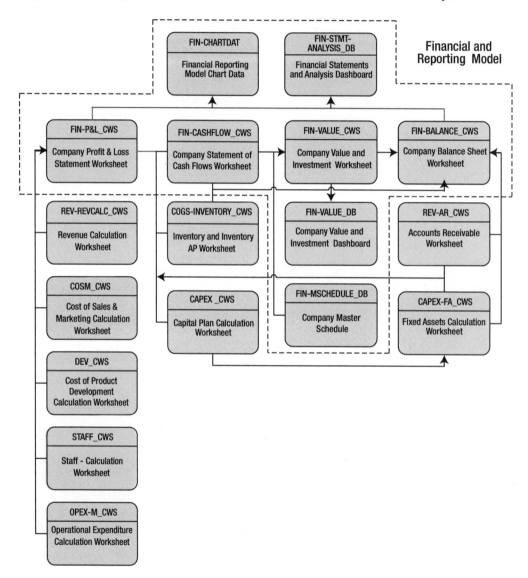

Figure 10-12. *Top-level design and process flow of the FIN model. Within the dotted lines are the core modules of FIN, and arrows represent major data and process flows between modules.*

Understanding the Profit & Loss Statement Worksheet

The Profit & Loss Statement Worksheet, FIN-P&L_CWS, creates the Company's Profit and Loss Statement, as shown in Figure 10-13. The major line items of the P&L and the source worksheets for the data follow:

- *Product, software, and service revenues and cost of goods sold*: REVCALC_CWS, the Revenue Calculation Worksheet

- *Sales and marketing costs*: COSM_CWS, the Cost of Sales & Marketing Calculation Worksheet

- *Technical operations and product development costs*: DEV_CWS, the Cost of Product Development Calculation Worksheet

- *Salaries, wages, bonuses, and commissions*: STAFF_CWS, the Staff Calculation Worksheet

- *Operating expenses*: OPEX-M_CWS, the Operational Expenditure Calculation Worksheet

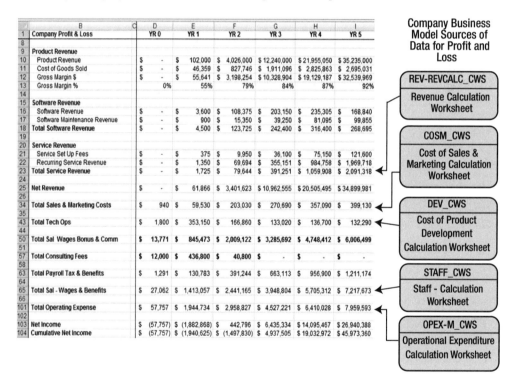

Figure 10-13. *FIN-P&L_CWS, the Company Profit & Loss Statement Worksheet*

Creating the Company Profit & Loss Statement Worksheet, FIN-P&L_CWS, is a fairly straight-forward task of linking the data from the source models into the P&L format. Figure 10-14 shows a formula view of the Revenue section of the P&L. Note that all revenue data has been previously developed within REV-REVCALC_CWS, and to create the P&L, all that is required is to link to the data. As stated before, the primary thinking about this report regards organization and format.

	B	E	F
108		Jan	Feb
109			
110			
111	Unit Sales	='REV-REVCALC_CWS'!E6	='REV-REVCALC_CWS'!F6
112			
113	Product Revenue		
114	Product Revenue	='REV-REVCALC_CWS'!E10	='REV-REVCALC_CWS'!F10
115	Cost of Goods Sold	='REV-REVCALC_CWS'!E19	='REV-REVCALC_CWS'!F19
116	Gross Margin $	='REV-REVCALC_CWS'!E21	='REV-REVCALC_CWS'!F21
117	Gross Margin %	='REV-REVCALC_CWS'!E22	='REV-REVCALC_CWS'!F22
118			
119	Software Revenue		
120	Software Revenue	='REV-REVCALC_CWS'!E34	='REV-REVCALC_CWS'!F34
121	Software Maintenance Revenue	='REV-REVCALC_CWS'!E35	='REV-REVCALC_CWS'!F35
122	Total Software Revenue	=SUM(E120:E121)	=SUM(F120:F121)
123			
124	Service Revenue		
125	Service Set Up Fees	='REV-REVCALC_CWS'!E38	='REV-REVCALC_CWS'!F38
126	Recurring Service Revenue	='REV-REVCALC_CWS'!E39	='REV-REVCALC_CWS'!F39
127	Total Service Revenue	=SUM(E125:E126)	=SUM(F125:F126)
128			
129	Net Revenue	=E127+E122+E116	=F127+F122+F116

Figure 10-14. *The formula view of the Product Revenue section of FIN-P&L_CWS, the Company Profit & Loss Statement Worksheet*

Understanding the Statement of Cash Flows Worksheet

The Statement of Cash Flows Worksheet, FIN-CASHFLOW_CWS, creates the Company Statement of Cash Flows and is shown in Figure 10-15. It utilizes inputs from the following worksheets:

- *Net Income*: FIN-P&L_CWS, the Profit & Loss Statement Worksheet
- *Depreciation*: FIN-P&L_CWS, the Profit & Loss Statement Worksheet
- *(Increase) decrease in A/R+Other Assets*: REV-AR_CWS, the Accounts Receivable Worksheet
- *(Increase) decrease in Inventory*: COGS-INVENTORY_CWS, the Inventory and Inventory AP Worksheet
- *Increase (decrease) in AP+Other Liabilities*: COGS-INVENTORY_CWS, the Inventory and Inventory AP Worksheet
- *Purchase of Capital Assets and Other Assets*: CAPEX _CWS, the Capital Plan Calculation Worksheet
- *Stockholders Contribution*: FIN-VALUE_CWS, the Company Value and Investment Worksheet

■**Note** See Exercise 10-1 for a detailed explanation of creating this report.

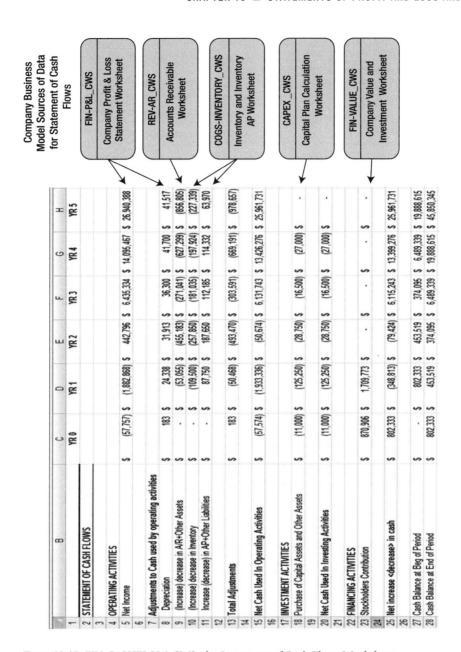

Company Business Model Sources of Data for Statement of Cash Flows

- **FIN-P&L_CWS** — Company Profit & Loss Statement Worksheet
- **REV-AR_CWS** — Accounts Receivable Worksheet
- **COGS-INVENTORY_CWS** — Inventory and Inventory AP Worksheet
- **CAPEX_CWS** — Capital Plan Calculation Worksheet
- **FIN-VALUE_CWS** — Company Value and Investment Worksheet

B	C — YR 0	D — YR 1	E — YR 2	F — YR 3	G — YR 4	H — YR 5
STATEMENT OF CASH FLOWS						
OPERATING ACTIVITIES						
Net Income	$ (57,757)	$ (1,882,868)	$ 442,796	$ 6,435,334	$ 14,095,467	$ 26,940,388
Adjustments to Cash used by operating activities						
Depreciation	$ 183	$ 24,338	$ 31,913	$ 36,300	$ 41,700	$ 41,517
(Increase) decrease in AR+Other Assets	$ -	$ (53,055)	$ (455,183)	$ (271,041)	$ (627,299)	$ (856,805)
(Increase) decrease in Inventory	$ -	$ (109,500)	$ (257,850)	$ (181,035)	$ (197,924)	$ (227,339)
Increase (decrease) in AP+Other Liabilities	$ -	$ 87,750	$ 187,650	$ 112,185	$ 114,332	$ 63,970
Total Adjustments	$ 183	$ (50,468)	$ (493,470)	$ (303,591)	$ (669,191)	$ (978,657)
Net Cash Used In Operating Activities	$ (57,574)	$ (1,933,336)	$ (50,674)	$ 6,131,743	$ 13,426,276	$ 25,961,731
INVESTMENT ACTIVITIES						
Purchase of Capital Assets and Other Assets	$ (11,000)	$ (125,250)	$ (28,750)	$ (16,500)	$ (27,000)	$ -
Net Cash Used In Investing Activities	$ (11,000)	$ (125,250)	$ (28,750)	$ (16,500)	$ (27,000)	$ -
FINANCING ACTIVITIES						
Stockholders Contribution	$ 870,906	$ 1,709,773	$ -	$ -	$ -	$ -
Net increase <decrease> in cash	$ 802,333	$ (348,813)	$ (79,424)	$ 6,115,243	$ 13,399,276	$ 25,961,731
Cash Balance at Beg of Period	$ -	$ 802,333	$ 453,519	$ 374,095	$ 6,469,339	$ 19,868,615
Cash Balance at End of Period	$ 802,333	$ 453,519	$ 374,095	$ 6,469,339	$ 19,868,615	$ 45,850,345

Figure 10-15. *FIN-CASHFLOW_CWS, the Statement of Cash Flows Worksheet*

Note that in Figure 10-15 the Statement of Cash Flows shows a Stockholders Contribution of $870,906 in YR 0 and another of $1,709,773 in YR 1 for a total of $2,580,679 or roughly $2.6 million. On what basis were these investments made?

Figure 10-16 shows a graph of the cash position of the Company forecast by the Statement of Cash Flows *before* any investment. The lowest point of the curve, shows that the maximum cash needs of the Company as forecast in the CBM is $2.6 million, occurring in March of YR 2. The Statement of Cash Flows shows that $2.6 million in stockholder investment has been made to solve the cash shortfall shown in Figure 10-16. We will cover the rationale for the amounts and timing of these investments in detail in Chapter 11.

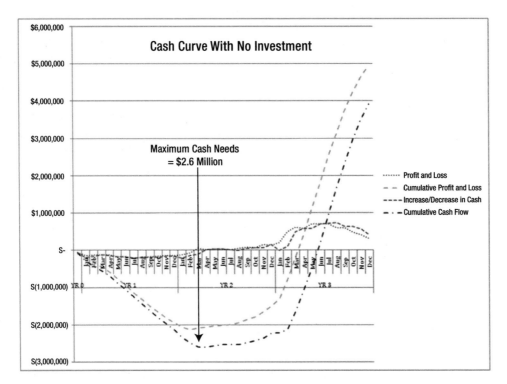

Figure 10-16. *FIN_CHART, the Cash Curve with No Investment chart, shows maximum cash needs of $2.6 million by March of YR 2.*

Understanding the Value and Investment Worksheet

The Value and Investment Worksheet, FIN-VALUE_CWS, is a company valuation model that utilizes risk factors or discount rates applied to cash flows generated within the FIN model to demonstrate investment options and company valuation scenarios. This model is the primary workhorse that develops the rationale for the Stockholders Contribution as shown in Figure 10-15. This model will be covered in detail in Chapter 11.

Understanding the Value and Investment Dashboard

The Value and Investment Dashboard, FIN-VALUE_DB, provides a management overview and worksheet for the calculation of risk factors and the display of resulting valuations calculated in FIN-VALUE_CWS. This dashboard will be covered in detail in Chapter 11.

Understanding the Company Balance Sheet Worksheet

The Balance Sheet Worksheet, FIN-BALANCE_CWS, creates the Company's Balance Sheet. This worksheet will be covered in great detail in Chapter 12.

Understanding Financial Reporting Model Chart Data

Financial Reporting Model Chart Data, FIN-CHARTDAT, preformats data from FIN model components in support of the development of management charts.

EXERCISE 10-1. USING MICROSOFT EXCEL TO DEVELOP THE COMPANY STATEMENT OF CASH FLOWS

The Company has developed major operational component forecast models.

- *Problem*: The Company now needs to develop standard financial reports from this data. One of the reports required is the Statement of Cash Flows.

- *Solution*: Develop a Statement of Cash Flows from the data generated by operations component models of the CBM.

FIN-CASHFLOW_CWS Model Overview

FIN-CASHFLOW_CWS, the Statement of Cash Flows Worksheet, develops a cash flow analysis for the Company from component model inputs using the following concepts:

- *Structure of the model*: Referring to Figure 10-17, note the structure of the cash flow model and its relationship to the P&L. Figure 10-18 provides a formula view of the fairly straightforward cash flow model. Each line item is taken (linked) from an input source in another model.

- *Concept of the model*: We are using the indirect method to adjust income from operating activities to a cash basis. The indirect method starts with the net income figure from the P&L and adjusts it for items that reflect differences between the net income and actual cash operating flows. There are two types of adjustments that convert net income into cash from operating activities using this method:

  - Noncash revenues and expenses that were included under accrual accounting, for example, depreciation

  - Changes in operating assets and operating liabilities—those assets and liabilities that are normally considered current assets and current liabilities, including AR and AP

We are also quantifying the amount of cash spent on investments and the amount of cash financing the Company. The net of these numbers gives us the current month cash position of the Company. We will now discuss each line item in the Statement of Cash Flows. See Figure 10-17.

	B	D	E	F	G	H	I
1	COMPANY PROFIT & LOSS	YR 0	YR 1	YR 2	YR 3	YR 4	YR 5
24							
25	Net Revenue	$ -	$ 61,866	$ 3,401,623	$ 10,962,555	$ 20,505,495	$ 34,899,981
26							
27	Sales & Marketing Costs						
34	Total Sales & Marketing Costs	$ 940	$ 59,530	$ 203,030	$ 270,690	$ 357,090	$ 399,130
35							
43	Total Tech Ops	$ 1,800	$ 353,150	$ 166,860	$ 133,020	$ 136,700	$ 132,290
44							
65	Total Sal - Wages & Benefits	$ 27,062	$ 1,413,057	$ 2,441,165	$ 3,948,804	$ 5,705,312	$ 7,217,673
101	Total Operating Expense	$ 57,757	$ 1,944,734	$ 2,958,827	$ 4,527,221	$ 6,410,028	$ 7,959,593
102							
103	Net Income	$ (57,757)	$ (1,882,868)	$ 442,796	$ 6,435,334	$ 14,095,467	$ 26,940,388

	B	C	D	E	F	G	H
1		YR 0	YR 1	YR 2	YR 3	YR 4	YR 5
2	STATEMENT OF CASH FLOWS						
3							
4	OPERATING ACTIVITIES						
5	Net Income	$ (57,757)	$ (1,882,868)	$ 442,796	$ 6,435,334	$ 14,095,467	$ 26,940,388
6							
7	Adjustments to Cash used by operating activities						
8	Depreciation	$ 183	$ 24,338	$ 31,913	$ 36,300	$ 41,700	$ 41,517
9	(Increase) decrease in A/R+Other Assets	$ -	$ (53,055)	$ (455,183)	$ (271,041)	$ (627,299)	$ (856,805)
10	(Increase) decrease in Inventory	$ -	$ (109,500)	$ (257,850)	$ (181,035)	$ (197,924)	$ (227,339)
11	Increase (decrease) in AP+Other Liabilities	$ -	$ 87,750	$ 187,650	$ 112,185	$ 114,332	$ 63,970
12							
13	Total Adjustments	$ 183	$ (50,468)	$ (493,470)	$ (303,591)	$ (669,191)	$ (978,657)
14							
15	Net Cash Used In Operating Activities	$ (57,574)	$ (1,933,336)	$ (50,674)	$ 6,131,743	$ 13,426,276	$ 25,961,731
16							
17	INVESTMENT ACTIVITIES						
18	Purchase of Capital Assets and Other Assets	$ (11,000)	$ (125,250)	$ (28,750)	$ (16,500)	$ (27,000)	$ -
19							
20	Net Cash Used In Investing Activities	$ (11,000)	$ (125,250)	$ (28,750)	$ (16,500)	$ (27,000)	$ -
21							
22	FINANCING ACTIVITIES						
23	Stockholders Contribution	$ 870,906	$ 1,709,773	$ -	$ -	$ -	$ -
24							
25	Net increase <decrease> in cash	$ 802,333	$ (348,813)	$ (79,424)	$ 6,115,243	$ 13,399,276	$ 25,961,731
26							
27	Cash Balance at Beg of Period	$ -	$ 802,333	$ 453,519	$ 374,095	$ 6,489,339	$ 19,888,615
28	Cash Balance at End of Period	$ 802,333	$ 453,519	$ 374,095	$ 6,489,339	$ 19,888,615	$ 45,850,345

Figure 10-17. *Company model P&L and Statement of Cash Flows data shown together*

	B	C	D	E
32	STATEMENT OF CASH FLOWS			
33		YR 0	Jan	Feb
34	OPERATING ACTIVITIES			
35	Net Income	='FIN-P&L_CWS'!D207	='FIN-P&L_CWS'!E207	='FIN-P&L_CWS'!F207
36				
37	Adjustments to Cash used by operating activities			
38	Depreciation	='FIN-P&L_CWS'!D203	='FIN-P&L_CWS'!E203	='FIN-P&L_CWS'!F203
39	(Increase) decrease in A/R+Other Assets	='REV-AR_CWS'!C20*-1	='REV-AR_CWS'!D20*-1	='REV-AR_CWS'!E20*-1
40	(Increase) decrease in Inventory	='COGS-INVENTORY_CWS'!C43*-1	='COGS-INVENTORY_CWS'!D43*-1	='COGS-INVENTORY_CWS'!E43
41	Increase (decrease) in AP+Other Liabilities	='COGS-INVENTORY_CWS'!C70	='COGS-INVENTORY_CWS'!D70	='COGS-INVENTORY_CWS'!E7(
42				
43	Total Adjustments	=SUM(C38:C42)	=SUM(D38:D42)	=SUM(E38:E42)
44				
45	Net Cash Used In Operating Activities	=C35+C43	=D35+D43	=E35+E43
46				
47	INVESTMENT ACTIVITIES			
48	Purchase of Capital Assets and Other Assets	='CAPEX_CWS '!E40*-1	='CAPEX_CWS '!F40*-1	='CAPEX_CWS '!G40*-1
49				
50	Net Cash Used In Investing	=SUM(C48:C49)	=SUM(D48:D49)	=SUM(E48:E49)
51				
52	FINANCING ACTIVITIES			
53	Stockholders Contribution	='FIN-VALUE_CWS'!C13	='FIN-VALUE_CWS'!D13	='FIN-VALUE_CWS'!E13
54				
55	Net increase <decrease> in cash	=+C45+C50+C53	=+D45+D50+D53	=+E45+E50+E53
56				
57	Cash Balance at Beg of Period	0	=C58	=D58
58	Cash Balance at End of Period	=C55	=D57+D55	=E57+E55
59				
60	Cumulative Stockholders Contribution	=C53	=D53+C60	=E53+D60

Figure 10-18. *Formula view of FIN-CASHFLOW_CWS, the Company's Statement of Cash Flows Worksheet*

Operating Activities

The following list is a further explanation of each line item in the Operating Activities section of the Statement of Cash Flows:

- *Net Income*: The source of Net Income data is FIN-P&L_CWS, the Profit & Loss Statement Worksheet.

- *Depreciation*: The source of depreciation data is FIN-P&L_CWS, the Profit & Loss Statement Worksheet. Depreciation is a noncash expense and is added back to operating income in recognition that the expense taken on the P&L did not affect cash.

- *(Increase) decrease in A/R+Other Assets*: The source of this data is REV-AR_CWS, the Accounts Receivable Worksheet. Note that we have reversed the sign of data in cell C39 by multiplying the link in cell C39 by a negative 1 (-1). Why? If Accounts Receivable has increased (shows as a positive number in REV-AR_CWS), we must have not collected all cash due on the sales shown on the P&L, thus we must adjust net income downward. If it has decreased (shows as a negative number in REV-AR_CWS), we have collected more money than is shown on the P&L and need to adjust the net income upward.

- *(Increase) decrease in Inventory*: The source of Inventory data is COGS-INVENTORY_CWS, the Inventory and Inventory AP Worksheet. Note that we have reversed the sign of data in cell C40 by multiplying the link in cell C40 by a minus 1 (=*-1). Why? If our change in inventory is a positive number in COGS-INVENTORY_CWS, we have increased inventory, thus we must adjust net income downward. If inventory has been reduced (shows as a negative number in COGS-INVENTORY_CWS), we must have consumed more inventory, so we adjust net income upward.

- *Increase (decrease) in AP+Other Liabilities*: The source of this data is COGS-INVENTORY_CWS, the Inventory and Inventory AP Worksheet. Note that we *do not* reverse the sign in Cell C41. If accounts payable is positive, it is a positive adjustment to net income. If we pay less for expensed items than the expense shown on the P&L, the effect on the bottom line is positive. If accounts payable is negative in COGS-INVENTORY_CWS, we have paid out more than shown as expense and the impact is negative on the bottom line.

Investment Activities

The source of *Purchase of Capital Assets and Other Assets* data is CAPEX _CWS, the Capital Plan Calculation Worksheet. This linkage is fairly simple. This amount shown as investing activity is the amount of capital expenditures made in the current month. In our example, it is assumed that 100 percent of the expenditure for the item is made in the current month, that is, there is no accounts payable generated. Note that we multiply this value by a negative 1 (=*-1) to display it as a negative number (outflow) on the statement.

Financing Activities

The source of *Stockholders Contribution* data is the link entry or formula ='FIN-VALUE_CWS'!C13, which brings across the actual or planned contribution by stockholders as computed in FIN-VALUE_CWS.

Cash Position

Finally, we look at the line items that present the cash position of the company at the bottom of the Statement of Cash Flows:

- *Net increase (decrease) in cash*: The net increase or decrease in cash in the current month is calculated in cell C55 as follows: Net Income *plus* Total Adjustments *minus* Net Cash used in Investing *plus* Stockholders Contribution.

- *Cash Balance at Beg of Period*: Cash Balance at the Beg of Period is carried forward from the previous month.

- *Cash Balance at End of Period*: Cash Balance at the End of the Period is computed as follows: Cash Balance at the Beg of Period *plus* Net increase (decrease) in cash.

Summary

This is the first of three chapters (Chapter 10, 11, and 12) that deal with the financial and financial reporting aspects of modeling the startup technology company. In previous chapters, we have built financial models of operational components of the Company to plan and quantify key operating aspects of a technology company.

In this chapter, we created a consolidated view of the operations and financial performance of the Company by developing two key financial statements: the Profit and Loss Statement and the Statement of Cash Flows.

Business thinking about profit, loss, and cash flow is essentially about company performance. To understand company performance, you must understand and be able to read and interpret the Profit and Loss Statement and the Statement of Cash Flows. These two statements must be created and viewed together in order to fully understand the operating performance picture.

The P&L shows revenues and expenses over various time periods, and it represents the beginning, not the end, of understanding company performance. More than a superficial assessment of revenues, cost, and profit is required in effective financial planning.

The purpose of the Statement of Cash Flows is to provide an understanding of the financial consequences of business activities by providing a detailed look at the sources and uses of cash. When assessing a company's performance, you need to know not only the overall cash position but also where the cash is coming from and how it is being used.

Here's the question to ask yourself regarding the Profit and Loss Statement and Statement of Cash Flows: what can you say about the operations of your company by interpreting these two statements?

■ ■ ■

CHAPTER 11

Modeling Valuation and Investment with the FIN Model

Our emphasis in this chapter is on the financial analysis that is required to raise working capital needed to fund company operations. This analysis and the modeling that accompanies it will create a valuation and investment strategy. The Statement of Cash Flows, covered in the previous chapter, is a primary contributor to this analysis since it generates a time-phased cash flow forecast based on the outputs of the operating models that we have developed thus far in this book.

In this chapter, you will learn how to plan, create, and use key components of the Financial and Reporting (FIN) model to develop a valuation and investment strategy. In addition you will learn how to

- Understand concepts of valuation and investment as they apply to high-tech startups.

- Use the discounted cash flow method for company valuations.

- Use the build-up method to develop risk profiles.

- Identify value events, reduce risk, and make your company worth more.

- Develop a valuation and investment model that can serve as the basis for your investment strategy.

Business Thinking about Valuation and Investment

High-tech startup companies, in the initial stages, must incur large costs to create the technological capability, intellectual property, business processes, and customer relationships needed to implement their business concept. These assets are required in order to generate cash flows in subsequent periods. Usually, the assets are not capitalized but are expensed, explaining the high losses that are posted by high-tech firms in the early stages of their development.

High-tech startups are characterized by high uncertainty and high losses in the early stages. There is an expectation, however, that their technologies will provide a competitive advantage and they will experience higher growth rates than traditional companies and generate significantly higher margins. This model inevitably results in the entrepreneur standing in front of investors, seeking working capital. From the first chapter of this book, you know that this process usually begins with three fundamental questions from potential investors and lenders:

- Cool idea, how do you make money with it?

- How much do you need, and why and when?

- What do you think your company is worth?

These fairly straightforward questions are the starting point from which the investor or lender proceeds to assess the risk/opportunity profile of the company. They are the same questions anyone asks when they are thinking about purchasing or investing in anything. Does it work like you say it does? How much do you want for it? What makes you think it's worth that? How much cash is needed and when?

If you have developed a financial model, as we have in the previous chapters, you will be able to answer these questions, and more.

- Cool idea, how do you make money with it?

  - *Answer*: The financial model provides the ability to explain and document, in detail, how you make money.

- How much do you need and why and when?

  - *Answer*: The financial model provides you with an exact, time-phased answer for how much and when. The "why" and "when" questions are implicit to the structure of the model and can be explicitly explained.

- What do you think your company is worth?

  - *Answer*: The valuation of your company is a primary subject of this chapter.

■**Caution** Company valuation and investment are very broad, highly complex subjects and deserve extensive study. This chapter provides a conceptual framework for understanding this subject in the context of high-tech startups and financial modeling. Use it as a starting point for your studies on the subject.

Understanding Valuation and Investment

Any financial transaction must include an agreement on value. The following discussion of value and investment is presented within the context of valuation and investment for high-tech startups.

There are several standard methods for valuing companies. Examples are the *cost approach*, measuring company value in terms of the replacement cost of company capabilities, and the *market approach*, valuing a company based on comparisons to like companies in the industry. High-tech startups are usually not capital intensive and have insignificant tangible assets that can be valued. Their uniqueness often precludes comparison methods to establish value. There is, however, one widely used valuation approach for valuing technology startups, the *income approach*.

■**Note** The *income approach* employs the discounted cash flow (DCF) method of valuation. DCF derives the present value of expected cash flows based on a discount rate that is itself based on the unique risk profile for the company.

The financial model provides an ideal environment within which to apply the income approach to determine a baseline valuation.

Optimizing the Cost of Capital

Capital is *necessary* to build the assets needed to generate future cash flows. The *objective* is to raise capital at the *lowest possible cost of capital*. The cost of capital for any transaction always represents the economic cost of attracting it in a competitive environment where investors are carefully analyzing and comparing investment opportunities. The cost of capital can be thought of as an *opportunity cost*, that is, the cost of foregoing the next best alternative investment of similar risk. The cost of capital is market driven, comparable to other investments of similar risk.

The entrepreneur seeks to raise capital at the lowest possible cost, because the cost of capital translates directly into the amount of company ownership that must be sold to raise the capital. The strategy for accomplishing this objective requires balancing the factors that ultimately drive or determine the cost of the capital needed. As you will see later, a primary strategy is to mitigate risk.

Also, later in this chapter, we will develop a financial model to analyze and balance these factors, but first, let's look at the simple, mathematical relationship of how company value and the amount of investment needed equate to ownership.

In our first example (see Figure 11-1), the amount of cash needed is $650,000. If the company is valued at $1,000,000, the investor would expect 65 percent ownership of the company to make the investment. In our example, % Ownership equals Cash Needed divided by Company Value. At a valuation of $1,500,000, the investor would expect 43.33 percent ownership of the company. At a valuation of $2,000,000, the investor would expect 32.5 percent ownership of the company.

Under this simplified valuation approach, the various company valuations have been determined assuming the necessary funding will be provided. Thus the new investment of $650,000 is not considered to add value to the company; rather, it is necessary to achieve the current valuation.

■**Note** The higher the company valuation, the lower the cost of the investment to the entrepreneur and less of the company given away.

Cash Needed	Company Value	% Ownership
$ 650,000		
	$ 1,000,000	65.00%
	$ 1,500,000	43.33%
	$ 2,000,000	32.50%

Figure 11-1. *Basic mathematical relationship between Cash Needed and Company Value*

Referring to Figure 11-2, let's look at another scenario and the beginnings of a strategic approach to financing. The cash needed is still $650,000. In Strategy 1, the entrepreneur gives up control of the company. The investor gains 65 percent ownership, because the entrepreneur is only able to justify a valuation of $1,000,000. In Strategy 2, however, the entrepreneur raises cash needed in increments and, in the later two increments, has justified a higher valuation of the company. The second increment of financing, $350,000, is raised at a valuation of $1,500,000. The entrepreneur gives up 23.33 percent for this increment. The final increment of $200,000 is raised at a valuation of $2,000,000 and costs 10 percent. In Strategy 2, total financing will cost 43.33 percent of the company.

■**Note** The ability to time the raising of cash with increases in company valuation results in a lower cost of financing.

	Period	Cash Needed	Company Value	% Ownership
Strategy 1	YR 1	$ 650,000	$ 1,000,000	65.00%
Strategy 2	YR 1	$ 100,000	$ 1,000,000	10.00%
	YR 1	$ 350,000	$ 1,500,000	23.33%
	YR 2	$ 200,000	$ 2,000,000	10.00%
				43.33%

Figure 11-2. *Another view of the mathematical relationship between Cash Needed and Company Value showing the application of investment strategy to reduce the cost of capital.*

The foregoing example begs the question of how one increases company value. Before we answer this question, let's look closer at the components of the equation in more detail:

- Cash needs
- Company value

Defining Cash Needs

The FIN model, specifically the Statement of Cash Flows, provides a detailed, time-phased report of the cash needs of the company based on the modeling assumptions built into the operating models that we have discussed in previous chapters. Chapter 10 provides a detailed explanation of the Statement of Cash Flows, showing how they are derived.

Now, look at Figure 11-3. This cash curve was developed from FIN model's Profit and Loss Statement and Statement of Cash Flows data. Note that in March of YR 2, cumulative cash needs (assuming no outside investment) are $2.6 million. Note also that the cumulative cash curve begins to improve (slope upward) at the same time that the company begins to break even or achieves positive cash flow. As you can see, FIN model provides month-by-month cash requirements, the cash needs of the company.

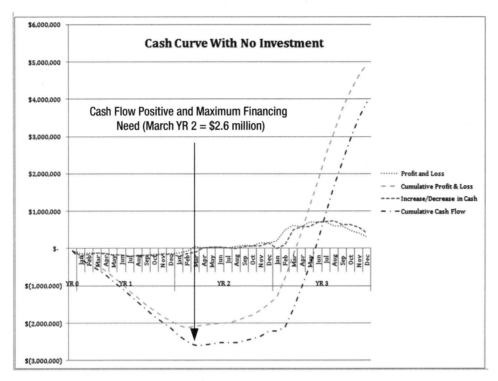

Figure 11-3. *FIN_CHART-NO-INVEST shows the point of cash flow positive and maximum financing needs.*

This cash profile is typical of a high-tech startup. High front-end costs and negative cash flows are followed by rapid growth.

■Note One perception of the value of any operating asset or investment is that it equals the present value of its expected future economic benefit stream.

Any valuation must consider future cash flows discounted for the opportunity cost of capital (what could be made with another investment) and also discounted for the specific risk associated with investing in the company.

Defining the Company Value

What is the company worth? The answer to this question is the *valuation* of the company. In reality, value is determined by the investor. It is the investor's valuation of the company, not the entrepreneur's opinion, however passionate, that determines the valuation of the company and the basis on which the investment is made. Herein begins what I call the valuation dance.

■**Note** The *valuation dance* is the process whereby the entrepreneur and the investor reach agreement on a valuation that will serve as the basis for the terms and conditions on which the investment is made.

Financing of early-stage technology companies is, in my opinion, primarily a subjective investor decision. The decision is made within a framework of empirical data and analysis of varying quality, but in the end, it is the investor's subjective assessment of the risk and reward of the deal that determines the final terms and conditions of the investment.

The decision process is more art than science, but it has solid underpinnings in accepted business practices. The process incorporates both quantitative and qualitative components and is also highly influenced by the human factor, the nature of the parties involved.

The primary finding from this process and the primary factor in assessing value for technology startups is, again, an assessment of risk. Risk is the primary factor in determining value using the income approach. Value will vary inversely with the riskiness of the anticipated future cash flows, because increased risk demands a higher return. Higher risk means that a higher discount rate will be used to value the anticipated cash generated by the company. The higher the discount rate used, the lower the value and vice versa.

■**Note** Reducing risk factors of a business will increase its value.

Understanding Investor Expectations

An investment requires a commitment of dollars that the investor currently holds in exchange for the expectation that the investor will receive some greater amount of dollars at some point in the future. This premise is basic to all investment decisions and business valuations.

Investor expectations are captured in the cost of capital. The cost of capital includes but is not limited to the following:

- Rate of return that investors expect for letting the entrepreneur use their money on a risk-free basis

- Expected inflation, that is, the expected depreciation in purchasing power while the money is tied up

- Risk, the uncertainty about how much cash flow and other benefits will be realized

The cost of capital is also referred to as a discount or capitalization (cap) rate. It equals the total expected rate of return on the investment (total net return) taking into consideration all the afore-mentioned factors.

Using the Discounted Cash Flow Method

The core of the income approach to valuation is the DCF method. DCF consists of two steps:

1. *Define the future benefits stream.* In company valuations where there is an actual track record of performance, the future income stream must be adjusted or normalized for factors like nonrecurring or unusual items, accounting departures, and ownership characteristics. We are relying entirely on the future benefit stream as forecasted in the FIN model's State-ment of Cash Flows. We will not adjust our forward-looking revenue stream, because all critical known factors are built into the model.

2. *Apply a discount factor to the stream to determine its net present value.* When calculating the net present value (NPV) of the future benefits stream, use the NPV formula in Figure 11-4.

$$NPV = \sum_{t=0}^{n} \frac{(\text{Future Benefit Stream})_t}{(1+r)^t}$$

r = Discount rate
n = Last period of expected return
t = Period (usually in years)

Figure 11-4. *In the Net Present Value (NPV) formula, note the numerator, which is the future benefit stream, and the denominator, which is the discount rate.*

The key to this formula is the discount rate. How is this rate established? Let's remember that the discount rate embodies all risk factors. It represents the rate of return expected based on the specific market factors and risks associated with the deal. One way of establishing this rate is by using an approach called the *build-up method*. The next section will discuss this approach.

Using the Build-Up Method

The *build-up method* creates a discount rate by adding incremental risk factors to a riskless rate of return. In other words, you start with a rate of return that you would expect from a virtually risk-free investment (historically, this has been 20-year Treasury bonds) and then add incremental risk factors to it in order to arrive at a discount rate that considers all factors associated with the investment.

In this method, there are two basic categories of risk that are added to the riskless rate: systemic risk and unsystemic risk. *Systemic risk* is risk associated with macroeconomic factors that effect economic conditions. Examples are political climate and international, socio-cultural, and demographic issues. *Unsystemic risk* is risk directly associated with the investment opportunity. Examples are the size of the company and specific risk factors such as direct competition, product development, and technical risk.

The build-up method can be structured as follows: riskless rate *plus* systemic risk *plus* unsystemic risk *equals* discount rate.

Let's now tie the previous discussion together with an example called Company A.

An Investment Optimization Strategy for Company A

Company A has finished its first financial model and has developed an investment and valuation strategy (see Figure 11-5). It forecasts a cash deficit of $150,000 and $250,000 in YR 1 and YR 2 of operations, respectively, and positive cash flow totaling $9,000,000 over the next three years (see Figure 11-5, section A). Company A must raise working capital to cover this shortfall in YR 1 and YR 2. The company and an investor negotiate a discount rate to value the company. The founder asserts that an investment of $150,000 in YR 1 will allow the company to leverage significant assets necessary to generate future benefits.

Using the build-up method, the founder and investor agree on a discount rate of 71 percent for this very risky investment, which is composed of a risk-free rate of 6 percent, a systemic risk factor of 15 percent, and an unsystemic risk of 50 percent (see Figure 11-5, section B).

The resulting valuation of the company of $785,408 is shown in Figure 11-5, section C. The valuation is made by computing the NPV of the forecasted revenue stream. The first investment of $150,000 is made and the entrepreneur gives up 19 percent ownership of the company to the investor, as shown in Figure 11-5, section D.

Company A performs perfectly in YR 1, using the investment to build its ability to earn future benefits. The entrepreneur and investor meet again to fund the second year of cash shortfall. They agree on a discount rate of 46 percent, since excellent company performance has reduced risk. The YR 2 investment of $250,000 is made at a valuation of $2,486,810 and the entrepreneur gives up another 10 percent of ownership to the investor. The investor now owns 27 percent of the company, as shown in section D of Figure 11-5.

What is the investor's expectation of return on his investment? The entrepreneur contends and the investor agrees that, given funding and performance to plan, that the company will be in full operating capability at the beginning of YR 3. At that point, it is possible that the company could be sold to a strategic buyer, and the future value of the company computed at a discount of 25 percent would be $5,424,000. The lower 25 percent discount rate takes into consideration that significant risk has been taken out of the equation and the company is at full operating capability. This is the projected exit value of the company. If the company is sold at the beginning of YR 3, the investor, owning 27 percent of the company, will receive $931,756 for the first $150,000 investment or a return of 6.21 times the initial investment and also would receive $545,277 from the second investment of $250,000, or a return of 2.18 times the investment.

■**Note** See Exercise 11-1 for a detailed explanation of NPV computations used in valuation.

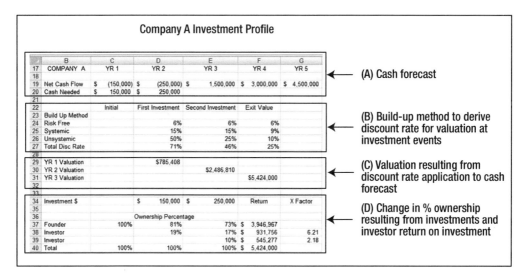

Figure 11-5. *Company A's investment profile*

■**Note** In this chapter, I am not rounding valuations or the amount of cash invested so that you can better follow the formulas and their results. In reality, valuations and investment amounts would be rounded in some manner. No one is going to claim, using the previous example, that a company is valued at exactly $785,408.

Assessing the Value of Events and Risk

You can see from the Company A example that the investor's assessment of risk, as reflected in the discount rate, drives the terms and conditions of the investment. Why does the discount rate decrease? Evidently, Company A has achieved critical milestones or value events and the achievement of these value events signals a significant reduction in the risk profile of the company. To put it simply, lower risk equals higher value.

We discussed value events in Chapter 1. Now, let's relate them directly to risk and valuation. As the company executes its operating plan and achieves value events (see Figure 11-6), it builds credibility and its value grows because risk is reduced. As risk declines, it becomes more attractive to investors and the cost of raising capital decreases.

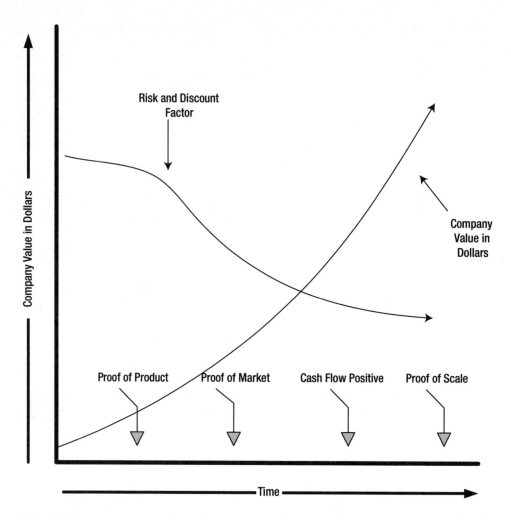

Figure 11-6. *As a company achieves value events, risk and discount factors are reduced, and the value of the company increases.*

Reducing Risk with Value Events

When achieved, the following four value events of early-stage technology development, as discussed in detail in Chapter 1, can result in a significant reduction in the risk profile of a company.

- *Proof of product*: When the product is developed and proven in the field, the company has overcome the significant technical risk involved in new product development.

- *Proof of market*: When the product is selling at a profitable price, the company has overcome the significant risk that its product's value proposition is not compelling to the customer.

- *Proof of scale*: When the company is operationally positioned to move to the next level of growth, while maintaining profitability and quality, it has proven its ability to evolve from a startup into an operating company, and the risk of not attaining future cash flows is reduced.

- *Cash flow positive*: When the company is generating free cash equal to or exceeding cash needs, the risk of not being able to raise operating capital is significantly mitigated.

Exploring the Valuation and Investment Strategy Business Case

Green Devil Control Systems (the Company) is an early-stage technology startup that develops energy monitoring and control systems for residential markets. The Company builds and sells the Green Devil Energy Control System (ECS). The Company president is well known and has extensive experience and contacts in the home building industry. His partner is a graduate-level electrical engineer, and she has extensive experience in developing smart control systems.

Defining the Product

ECS is a patent-pending, programmable hardware and software device that monitors and controls electricity usage on a circuit-by-circuit basis within a facility. ECS is installed on the facility side of the electrical breaker box.

ECS allows for the mapping of all electric circuits extending into and utilized by the facility. It is particularly targeted for the smart home market. ECS is programmable and provides switching and control capabilities (like a programmable thermostat) for all individual electrical circuits within a facility. Electrical usage, at the appliance level, can be programmed, controlled, and monitored. ECS is a network addressable device and is designed to work seamlessly with wireless or wired LANs and to support Internet access.

ECS comes with two software options: Local Services (LS) or Extended Services (ES). The LS software is the default software option with each installation of ECS and provides for a local web browser user interface to enable local setup and programming, as well as one month of electricity usage diagnostics.

The ES software provides Internet-based, secure, remote setup, programming control, and diagnostics. ES also provide a suite of analysis tools and system set up tools for optimizing electricity usage, along with demographic comparison data and unlimited usage data and statistics.

LS and ES web browser user interfaces are highly intuitive, attractive, and easy to use.

Creating a Strategy to Build Value and Credibility

The two founding entrepreneurs have completed their CBM. They are confident that they have created a realistic operating model and have a solid estimate of their cash needs to implement their strategies. Their forecast (see Figure 11-3) shows that they will need $2.6 million to bring their business into full operating capability. They must raise working capital. They have read the first chapter of this book and know that the key to success is to implement a strategy that builds value and credibility. They are prepared to answer the three big questions, and they have planned a specific success strategy with the following characteristics:

- Performance and execution characteristics

  - *Getting there fast*: The Company has committed to an aggressive development schedule, moving into manufacturing ECS by November of YR 1.

  - *Taking early action*: The founders aggressively researched their market during the feasibility study phase, targeted smart home owners, and are confident they are building a product that will be readily accepted by their market.

  - *Establishing the feedback loop and rapid response times*: The Company has implemented a specific feedback loop process that includes the aggressive gathering of customer data from field tests and compliance testing. Rapid improvements and modifications of the ECS product based on this input are built into their product development strategy.

- *Using prototypes for simultaneous research and selling*: The Company's strategy is highly dependent on placing working prototypes into the hands of target customers as quickly as possible.

- *Implementing agile technology development*: The Company's product development strategy is built around agile technology development techniques.

- *Focusing on cash management*: The Company is using the financial model as the primary cash forecasting tool and using it to derive investment strategy.

- People and processes

  - *Securing the team*: The Company has hired visionary and pathfinder developers that are capable of developing their product quickly and with innovation and responsiveness to customer feedback.

  - *Demonstrating skin in the game*: The founders are demonstrating *skin in the game* by making personal investments in the Company.

- Corporate structure

  - *Structuring for cash investments*: The Company will implement a corporate structure that will only accept cash investments in return for stock in the Company. They assume that all net cash flow generated is available for dividend distribution.

Devising the Investment and Valuation Strategy

The founders know that the Company will require $2.6 million. Their strategy is to acquire the necessary funding at as low a cost of capital as possible. They know they must personally fund part of the cash needs and that the amount needed and the size of the Company puts them in the investment range of angel investors. They are probably not big enough to attract venture capitalists.

Their strategy is fairly simple. From their model, they know how much cash is required. They have clearly identified key operational milestones or value events that, when achieved, significantly increase the credibility of the Company and significantly reduce the risk profile of the venture. They will raise money in increments that allow the Company to attain these value events, each round being less expensive than the previous, due to the fact that they have achieved the value events (see Figure 11-7). These value events and the dates they are planned follow:

- *Prototype complete*: May of YR 1

- *Proof of product*: November of YR 1

- *Proof of market*: April of YR 2

- *Cash flow positive*: April of YR 2

- *Proof of scale*: July of YR 2

	C	D	E	F	G	H	I	J	K	L	M	N	O	P	Q	R	S	T	U	V
	YR 0					YR 1										YR 2			
		Jan	Feb	Mar	Apr	May	Jun	Jul	Aug	Sep	Oct	Nov	Dec	Jan	Feb	Mar	Apr	May	Jun	Jul
Value Events																				
Prototype Complete						▲														
Proof of Product												▲								
Proof of Market																	▲			
Cash Flow Positive																	▲			
Proof of Scale																				▲
Investment Rounds	Founder					Round 1						Round 2					No Round			Exit
Investment Amount	$ 870,906					$ 1,096,803						$ 612,970								
Discount Factor	na					75.5%						48.0%								25.0%
Valuation	$ 870,906					$ 2,672,187						$ 10,333,757								$ 25,025,373
Cumulative Investment	$ 870,906					$ 1,967,709						$ 2,580,679								

Figure 11-7. *Company strategy summary showing key value events and investment rounds and amounts*

Figure 11-8 shows a monthly view of the Profit and Loss Statement and Statement of Cash Flows showing that cash flow positive is attained in April of YR 2. Figure 11-9 shows the impact of the investment strategy on the cash position of the Company: the Company maintains a positive cash position as it attains its objectives with respect to each value event.

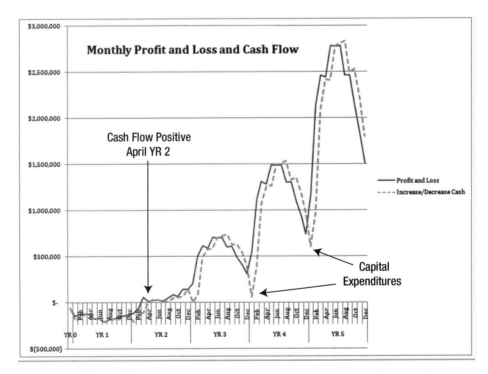

Figure 11-8. *FIN_CHART, Cash Curve Monthly, showing a monthly chart of cash position. Note that the sum of the montly negative cash positions prior to April of YR 2 equals $2.6 million as shown in Figure 11-9.*

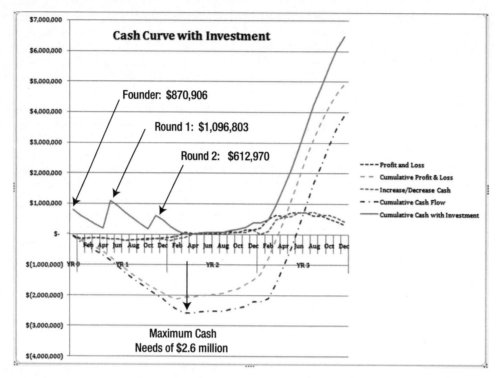

Figure 11-9. *FIN_CHART-YES-INVEST is the cash curve summary; it shows a cash deficit with no investment as well as the impact on cash from the investments.*

Cash needs, shown in Figure 11-10, are as follows:

- *YR 0 to May of YR 1*: $870,906 in cash is needed. The value event to achieve is the completion of the first prototype.

- *June YR 1 to November YR 1*: $1,096,803 in cash is needed. The value event to achieve is proof of product.

- *December YR 1 to April YR 2*: $612,970 in cash is needed. The value events to achieve are cash flow positive and proof of market.

	B	C	D	E
21	Cash Requirements w/ No Investment	Founders	First Round	Second Round
22	Investment Date	YR 0	May YR 1	Nov YR 1
23	From	YR 0	Jun YR 1	Dec YR 1
24	Through	May YR 1	Nov YR 1	Apr YR 2
25	Value Event at end of period	Proto Complete	POP	POM and CF+
26				
27	Beg Cash Balance	$ -	$ (870,906)	$ (1,967,709)
28	Cash Expenditure	$ (870,906)	$ (1,096,803)	$ (612,970)
29	Ending Cash Balance	$ (870,906)	$ (1,967,709)	$ (2,580,679)
30				
31				
32		Discount Rate	Value	Cash needed
33				
34	First Round - NPV from June YR 1	75.50%	$ 2,672,187	$ 1,096,803
35	Second Round - NPV from Dec YR 1	48.00%	$ 10,333,757	$ 612,970
36	Exit Valuation - NPV from Jul YR 2	25.00%	$ 25,025,373	

Figure 11-10. *FIN-VALUE_CWS, the Value and Investment Worksheet*

The following valuation and investment strategy (see Figures 11-11 and 11-12) was developed:

Founders will personally invest $870,906 to cover the period YR 0 to May of YR 1. Each will invest $435,453 and receive a 50 percent ownership share based on an initial Company valuation of $870,906. 100,000 shares will be issued, split evenly between the founders.

Round One of investment will be acquired in May of YR 1 and will require $1,096,803 on a Company valuation of $2,672,187. The valuation will be based on an NPV calculation of future cash using a discount rate of 75.5 percent. This rate is derived from a build-up method that recognizes that the Company has completed its prototype. Additional shares totaling 69,621 will be issued to the investor representing a purchase of 41 percent of the Company. Total shares outstanding will be 169,621. Each of the founder's ownership positions will be diluted to 29.5 percent.

Round Two of investment will be acquired in November of YR 1 and will require $612,970. It will be offered on the basis of Company valuation of $10,333,757. The valuation will be based on a NPV calculation of future cash using a discount rate of 48 percent derived from a build-up method recognizing that the Company has achieved proof of product. Additional shares totaling 10,696 will be issued to the investor representing a purchase of 5.9 percent of the Company. This will bring shares outstanding to 180,317. The founder's ownership positions will be diluted to 27.7 percent each. The first investor's ownership position will be diluted to 38.6 percent.

After Round Two no further investment is required since the Company achieves cash flow positive in April of YR 2.

	B	C	D	E	F	G	H
39	Investment and Valuation Stategy WS	Date	Investment	Valuation		Ownership %	
40					Founder	First Round	Second Round
41	Founders Investment						
42	Founder 1	YR 0	$ 435,453		50%	29.5%	27.7%
43	Founder 2	YR 0	$ 435,453		50%	29.5%	27.7%
44	Company Value			$ 870,906			
45	Founder 1 - Shares Issued		50,000				
46	Founder 2 - Shares Issued		50,000				
47	Total Shares Issued		100,000				
48	Value Per Share		$ 8.71				
49	Total Ownership				100%		
50							
51	Round One						
52	Investor 1	May YR 1	$ 1,096,803			41.0%	38.6%
53	Company Value			$ 2,672,187			
54	Investor 1 - Shares Issued		69,621				
55	Total Shares Issued		169,621				
56	Value Per Share		$ 15.75				
57	Total Ownership					100.0%	
58							
59	Round One						
60	Investor 2	Nov YR 1	$ 612,970				5.9%
61	Company Value			$ 10,333,757			
62	Investor 2 - Shares Issued		10,696				
63	Total Shares Issued		180,317				
64	Value Per Share		$ 57.31				
65	Total Ownership						100.0%

Figure 11-11. *FIN-VALUE_CWS, the Value and Investment Worksheet section, shows the impact of investment on ownership.*

■**Note** See Exercise 11-1 for a detailed explanation of the computations underlying this model.

Investor expectations regarding return on investment are based on a Company valuation that is made as of July YR 2 (see Figure 11-12). The Company is valued at $25,025,373 using a discount rate of 25 percent. This discount rate represents the rate of return that buyers of the Company would expect based on the assumption that the Company is at full operating capability and has achieved the proof of scale value event. Referring to Figure 11-12, if a sale of the Company was completed at this valuation in July of YR 2, the founders would receive a return of 15.94 times their investment. The first investor would receive a return of 8.81 times the investment, and the second investor would receive a return of 2.42 times the investment.

The founders now have all the data necessary to create a business plan and start their business. The business plan will be written to explain the assumptions, relationships, and amounts that have been developed utilizing the CBM.

	B	C	D	E	F
67	Investor Returns	$ Investment	% Ownership	$ Value	ROI (X)
68					
69	July YR 2 - First Exit Value	$ 25,025,373			
70	Founder 1	$ 435,453	27.7% $	6,939,264	15.94
71	Founder 2	$ 435,453	27.7% $	6,939,264	15.94
72	Investor 1	$ 1,096,803	38.6% $	9,662,409	8.81
73	Investor 2	$ 612,970	5.9% $	1,484,436	2.42
74					
75	Total Invested	$ 2,580,679	100.0% $	25,025,373	9.70

Figure 11-12. *FIN-VALUE_CWS, the Value and Investment Worksheet, showing anticipated investor returns on investments*

Planning the FIN Model

The primary purpose of the FIN model is to consolidate the outputs from all operating models and present them in three key financial statements: Profit and Loss Statement, Statement of Cash Flows, and Balance Sheet.

In this chapter, we will focus on creating the Company's Value and Investment Worksheet and Value and Investment Dashboard. We will develop these two worksheets and use them in conjunction with the Company's Statement of Cash Flow Worksheet to develop a valuation and investment strategy for the Company.

We begin our planning by reviewing the Company's Master Schedule, FIN-M-SCHEDULE_DB. This worksheet is a graphic depiction of the Company's operational master schedule, which is important because it shows the planned achievement of operational milestones or value events.

Next, we will review the Company's Statement of Cash Flows and assess the cash requirements. This review provides us with a map of cash requirements against Company value events. In other words, we are able to tell how much cash it will take for the Company to achieve critical planned value events.

Look at the Company Master schedule shown in Figure 11-14, and notice a value event, like proof of product. Notice which month that event is achieved. You can determine the cumulative cash required to get to that point by looking at the same month on the Cash Balance at End of Period line of the monthly Statement of Cash Flows. This analysis sets the stage for developing the investment and valuation models, the Company's Value and Investment Worksheet and the Value and Investment Dashboard.

Understanding the Building Blocks of the FIN Model

The following section provides an overview of FIN and the top-level functionality of model components (see Figure 11-13). As previously stated, the emphasis in this chapter is on the valuation and investment strategy and the model components that support this functionality.

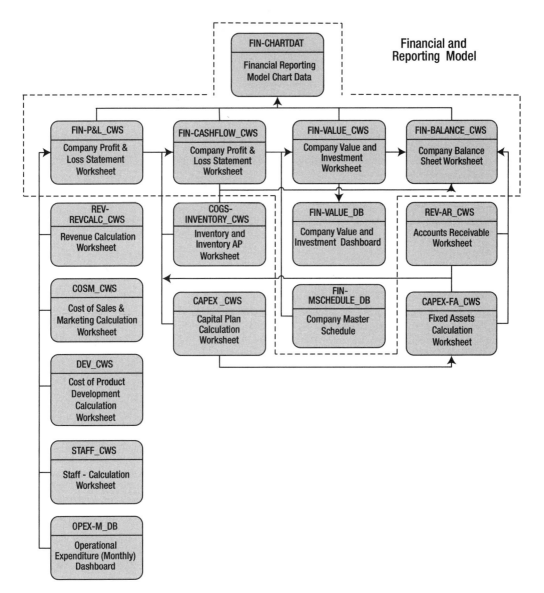

Figure 11-13. *This is the top-level design and process flow of the Financial and Reporting (FIN) model. Within the dotted lines are the core modules of FIN. Arrows represent major data and process flows between modules.*

Understanding the Profit & Loss Statement Worksheet

The Company Profit & Loss Statement Worksheet, FIN-P&L_CWS, creates the Company Profit and Loss Statement.

Understanding the Balance Sheet Worksheet

The Balance Sheet Worksheet, FIN-BALANCE_CWS, creates the Company Balance Sheet. This worksheet will be covered in greater detail in Chapter 12.

Understanding the Financial Reporting Model Chart Data Worksheet

The Financial Reporting Model Chart Data Worksheet, FIN_CHARTDAT, preformats data from FIN model components in support of the development of management charts.

Understanding the Company Master Schedule

FIN-M-SCHEDULE_DB is a graphical representation of the Company's Master Schedule (see Figure 11-14). This schedule represents the top-level operating assumptions that are built into the various operational models of the CBM. It is important to note that this schedule reflects the timing assumptions within the underlying operational model components of the CBM.

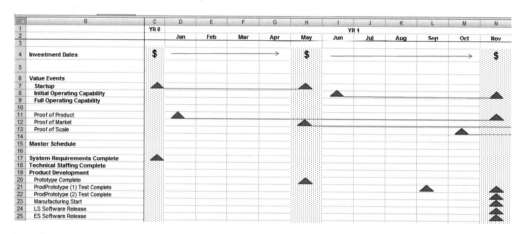

Figure 11-14. *FIN-M-SCHEDULE_DB, the Master Schedule, showing the achievement of a major value event, proof of product by November of YR 1*

Understanding the Statement of Cash Flow Worksheet

FIN-CASHFLOW_CWS creates the Company's Statement of Cash Flows. It utilizes inputs from the following worksheets:

- *Net Income*: FIN-P&L_CWS, the Profit & Loss Statement Worksheet
- *Depreciation*: CAPEX _CWS, the Capital Plan Calculation Worksheet
- *(Increase) decrease in A/R+Other Assets*: REV-AR_CWS, the Accounts Receivable Worksheet
- *(Increase) decrease in Inventory*: COGS-INVENTORY_CWS, the Inventory and Inventory AP Worksheet
- *Increase (decrease) in AP+Other Liabilities*: COGS-INVENTORY_CWS, the Inventory and Inventory AP Worksheet
- *Purchase of Capital Assets and Other Assets*: CAPEX _CWS, the Capital Plan Calculation Worksheet

■**Note** See Exercise 10-1 for a detailed explanation of creating the Statement of Cash Flows.

The Statement of Cash Flows is critical to the development of the valuation and investment strategy of the Company. This report is the source for the expected future benefits (cash flows) that are the basis for the valuation of the Company. Figure 11-15 shows that the Company is in a negative cash position until YR 3, after which it experiences a rapid growth in profits, or positive cash flow.

B	C	D	E	F	G	H
	YR 0	YR 1	YR 2	YR 3	YR 4	YR 5
STATEMENT OF CASH FLOWS						
OPERATING ACTIVITIES						
Net Income	$ (57,757)	$ (1,882,868)	$ 442,796	$ 6,435,334	$ 14,095,467	$ 26,940,388
Adjustments to Cash used by operating activities						
Depreciation	$ 183	$ 24,338	$ 31,913	$ 36,300	$ 41,700	$ 41,517
(Increase) decrease in A/R+Other Assets	$ -	$ (53,055)	$ (455,183)	$ (271,041)	$ (627,299)	$ (856,805)
(Increase) decrease in Inventory	$ -	$ (109,500)	$ (257,850)	$ (181,035)	$ (197,924)	$ (227,339)
Increase (decrease) in AP+Other Liabilities	$ -	$ 87,750	$ 187,650	$ 112,185	$ 114,332	$ 63,970
Total Adjustments	$ 183	$ (50,468)	$ (493,470)	$ (303,591)	$ (669,191)	$ (978,657)
Net Cash Used In Operating Activities	$ (57,574)	$ (1,933,336)	$ (50,674)	$ 6,131,743	$ 13,426,276	$ 25,961,731
INVESTMENT ACTIVITIES						
Purchase of Capital Assets and Other Assets	$ (11,000)	$ (125,250)	$ (28,750)	$ (16,500)	$ (27,000)	$ -
Net Cash Used In Investing Activities	$ (11,000)	$ (125,250)	$ (28,750)	$ (16,500)	$ (27,000)	$ -
FINANCING ACTIVITIES						
Stockholders Contribution	$ 870,906	$ 1,709,773	$ -	$ -	$ -	$ -
Net increase <decrease> in cash	$ 802,333	$ (348,813)	$ (79,424)	$ 6,115,243	$ 13,399,276	$ 25,961,731
Cash Balance at Beg of Period	$ -	$ 802,333	$ 453,519	$ 374,095	$ 6,489,339	$ 19,888,615
Cash Balance at End of Period	$ 802,333	$ 453,519	$ 374,095	$ 6,489,339	$ 19,888,615	$ 45,850,345

Figure 11-15. *In FIN-CASHFLOW_CWS, the Statement of Cash Flow Worksheet, note that this cash flow statement is shown before any member contribution investment.*

Understanding the Value and Investment Worksheet

FIN-VALUE_CWS is the Value and Investment Worksheet. In this model (see Figure 11-16), we derive the valuation and investment strategy as set forth in the business case. Specifically, we determine the cash required to take the Company forward to the accomplishment of value events that, by definition, reduce its overall risk profile. We then calculate Company valuation using the build-up method at a discount rate that is appropriate for each forward round of financing, under the assumption that the previous financing has been obtained and the value events achieved.

The valuation model that is derived becomes the basis for the Company valuation and investment strategy. The model demonstrates an approach to minimizing the cost of capital by computing cash requirements and their relationship to value events that reduce risk, thus reducing the discount rates used for valuation. It is not totally automated but works quite well using the Statement of Cash Flows to drive out cash needs as the model is manipulated in other areas to adjust for operational assumptions.

	B	C	D	E
21	Cash Requirements w/ No Investment	Founders	First Round	Second Round
22	Investment Date	YR 0	May YR 1	Nov YR 1
23	From	YR 0	Jun YR 1	Dec YR 1
24	Through	May YR 1	Nov YR 1	Apr YR 2
25	Value Event at end of period	Proto Complete	POP	POM and CF+
26				
27	Beg Cash Balance	$ -	$ (870,906)	$ (1,967,709)
28	Cash Expenditure	$ (870,906)	$ (1,096,803)	$ (612,970)
29	Ending Cash Balance	$ (870,906)	$ (1,967,709)	$ (2,580,679)
30				
31				
32		Discount Rate	Value	Cash needed
33				
34	First Round - NPV from June YR 1	75.50%	$ 2,672,187	$ 1,096,803
35	Second Round - NPV from Dec YR 1	48.00%	$ 10,333,757	$ 612,970
36	Exit Valuation - NPV from Jul YR 2	25.00%	$ 25,025,373	

Figure 11-16. *FIN-VALUE_CWS, the Value and Investment Worksheet*

Understanding the Value and Investment Dashboard

FIN-VALUE_DB is the build-up model to determine the discount rate applied to financing rounds. This model provides a management view of the risk assumptions applied to important operational aspects of the Company. It should be noted that all of these categories are considered *unsystemic* risk, or risk directly associated with the Company and its operating environment.

In Figure 11-17, note the discount rate begins with a risk-free rate of 6 percent after which incremental risk factors are added. The change in risk between columns (financing rounds) is a direct function of the value events that have been achieved and the resulting reduction in risk thereof. As said earlier, this is actually the investor's call. It is up to the entrepreneur to justify the claims of risk reduction.

	B	C	D	E F	G
9					
10	**Build Up Method**	First Round	Second Round	Exit Valuation	**Risk Definition**
11					
12	Rate of Return for a risk free security	6.00%	6.00%	6.00%	Rate of return for a risk free security (historically this has been returns on U.S Treasury Bonds)
13	Risk premium for small size	10.00%	8.00%	2.00%	Small companies are known to be riskier than larger companies for many reasons
14					
15	**Unsystemic risk (specific company risk)**				
16	Founder Risk	2.00%	2.00%	0.00%	Founders may leave or not be able to participate
17	Capital Risk	5.00%	2.50%	0.00%	Capital in subsequent rounds cannot be obtained
18	Technology Risk				
19	Team	5.00%	1.00%	0.00%	Technical team cannot be acquired in required time frame
20	Hardware Design	5.00%	0.00%	0.00%	Hardware design is new and untested
21	Embedded Software Design	3.00%	0.00%	0.00%	Embedded software design is new and untested
22	Compliance	5.00%	0.00%	0.00%	Production prototypes will fail compliance and standards testing
23	Application software risk	2.00%	1.00%	0.00%	Application software is new and untested
24	Value Proposition	5.00%	5.00%	2.00%	Value proposition (ROI) not proved in field tests or lower than anticipated
25	Manufacturing				
26	Manufacturing design	5.00%	2.50%	0.00%	Manufacturing design is new and untested and dependent on successful production prototype
27	Manufacturing	2.50%	2.50%	2.50%	Manufacturing is outsourced - risk of outsourcing
28	Supplier Risk - Price	2.50%	2.50%	2.50%	Risk that powerful suppliers will adversely affect price
29	Supplier Risk - Availability	1.00%	1.00%	1.00%	Risk that powerful suppliers will adversely affect component availability
30	Market Risk				
31	Threat of New Entrants	1.00%	1.00%	4.50%	Threat of entry of new competitors into marketplace
32	Established Rivals	1.00%	1.00%	2.50%	Threat of established rivals that can immediately compete
33	Suppliers	2.00%	2.00%	1.00%	Threat of powerful suppliers of components, or labor required to support implementation
34	Customers	5.00%	5.00%	1.00%	Threat of powerful customers that can control access to markets and demand price concessions
35	Substitute Products or Services	7.50%	5.00%	2.50%	Threat of substitute products services or other methods to achieve same result
36	Industry Growth Rate	2.50%	2.50%	2.50%	Industry growth rate can affect product acceptance speed and pricing
37	Technology and Innovation	5.00%	5.00%	2.50%	Technology adoption characteristic of target market (are they early or slow adopters of new technology?)
38	Government	-5.00%	-5.00%	-5.00%	Effect of government regulatory environment on all aforementioned risk categories
39	Complementary Products and Services	-2.50%	-2.50%	-2.50%	Effect of the existence of complementary products and services that could positively affect sales
40					
41	**Summary Discount Rate (CAP RATE)**	**75.50%**	**48.00%**	**25.00%**	**Discount rate 'built up' from risk factors and used for valuation of future stream of cash flows**

Figure 11-17. *FIN-VALUE_DB, the Value and Investment Dashboard, showing the build-up method used to derive the discount rate applied to each round of financing*

EXERCISE 11-1. USING MICROSOFT EXCEL TO DEVELOP THE COMPANY VALUATION AND INVESTMENT MODEL

The Company has completed its CBM and is now ready to develop a Company valuation and investment strategy.

- *Solution:* Develop a Valuation and Investment model to determine investment needs. Determine valuation and investment scenarios resulting in an optimized investment strategy for the Company.

- *Model overview and concept:* The following three worksheets are utilized to determine cash needs, develop Company valuation, and model an investment strategy that mitigates the total cost of raising the cash needed for operations: FIN-VALUE_CWS, the Value and Investment Worksheet; FIN-VALUE_DB, the Value and Investment Dashboard; and FIN-CASHFLOW_CWS, the Statement of Cash Flows.

Cash flows from FIN-CASHFLOW_CWS are parsed into increments of cash that are needed to attain important value events. In other words, the Statement of Cash Flows, used in conjunction with dates from the Company Master Schedule (FIN-M-SCHEDULE_DB), help determine how much it costs for the Company to attain major value events. We define these increments of cash requirements as "rounds" of funding. The rounds of funding become less and less expensive as the Company achieves its value events.

The model supports the following steps, which are completed in sequence:

1. *Determine total cash needs* of the Company.

2. *Determine incremental cash needed* to attain specific value events and how much cash will be raised in each round.

3. *Develop a discount rate* that reflects the change in risk as the Company attains funding.

4. *Compute valuations* of the future benefits (cash flows) from the point of each round of funding.

5. *Compute percentage ownership* that each round of financing represents.

6. *Develop an interactive model* of the aforementioned steps that allows for the iterative analysis of various investment scenarios.

7. *Determine an exit valuation* to set investor expectations.

The following sections will provide details on how to use Microsoft Excel 2007 to accomplish these steps. Refer to FIN-CASHFLOW_CWS, the Statement of Cash Flow Worksheet, in the following section for more detailed instructions on determining cash needs of the Company.

Determine Total Cash Needs

In Figure 11-18 (data view) and Figure 11-19 (formula view), note that we have linked to the Net increase (decrease) in Cash section of FIN-CASHFLOW_CWS to create a Cash Flow NO Financing baseline that replicates the data in the Statement of Cash Flows. Below that is a Cash Flow WITH Financing section that provides for adding investments (values on row 13) to the cash flow pulled from above (see the formulas in the range C13:18). Here, we add our scenarios of cash investment into our cash flow data to see the effect on total cash flow. The total cash needs of the Company are represented by the highest negative number of cash flow from the Statement of Cash Flows. For example, in this scenario, cell R9, which is March of YR 2, shows a negative cash position of –$2,586,874, which is the highest negative cash position that the Company reaches.

	B	C	D	E	F	G	H	I	J
1								YR 1	
2	Cash Flow NO Financing	YR 0	Jan	Feb	Mar	Apr	May	Jun	Jul
3									
4	Stockholders Contribution	$ -	$ -	$ -	$ -	$ -	$ -	$ -	$ -
5									
6	Net increase <decrease> in cash	$ (68,574)	$ (199,487)	$ (153,207)	$ (130,597)	$ (139,693)	$ (179,350)	$ (174,580)	$ (211,289)
7									
8	Cash Balance at Beg of Period	$ -	$ (68,574)	$ (268,061)	$ (421,267)	$ (551,864)	$ (691,556)	$ (870,906)	$ (1,045,486)
9	Cash Balance at End of Period	$ (68,574)	$ (268,061)	$ (421,267)	$ (551,864)	$ (691,556)	$ (870,906)	$ (1,045,486)	$ (1,256,776)
10									
11	Cash Flow WITH Financing								
12									
13	Stockholders Contribution	$ 870,906	$ -	$ -	$ -	$ -	$ 1,096,803	$ -	$ -
14									
15	Net increase <decrease> in cash	$ (68,574)	$ (199,487)	$ (153,207)	$ (130,597)	$ (139,693)	$ 917,453	$ (174,580)	$ (211,289)
16									
17	Cash Balance at Beg of Period	$ 870,906	$ 802,333	$ 602,846	$ 449,639	$ 319,043	$ 179,350	$ 1,096,803	$ 922,223
18	Cash Balance at End of Period	$ 802,333	$ 602,846	$ 449,639	$ 319,043	$ 179,350	$ 1,096,803	$ 922,223	$ 710,934

Figure 11-18. *Data view of FIN-VALUE_CWS, the Company's Value and Investment Worksheet, showing Cash Flow NO Financing and Cash Flow WITH Financing*

	B	C	D	E
1				
2	Cash Flow NO Financing	YR 0	Jan	Feb
3				
4	Stockholders Contribution	=FIN-CASHFLOW_CWS'!C65	='FIN-CASHFLOW_CWS'!D65	=FIN-CASHFLOW_CWS'!E65
5				
6	Net increase <decrease> in cash	=FIN-CASHFLOW_CWS'!C67	='FIN-CASHFLOW_CWS'!D67	=FIN-CASHFLOW_CWS'!E67
7				
8	Cash Balance at Beg of Period	=FIN-CASHFLOW_CWS'!C69	='FIN-CASHFLOW_CWS'!D69	=FIN-CASHFLOW_CWS'!E69
9	Cash Balance at End of Period	=FIN-CASHFLOW_CWS'!C70	='FIN-CASHFLOW_CWS'!D70	='FIN CASHFLOW_CWS'!E70
10				
11	Cash Flow WITH Financing			
12				
13	Stockholders Contribution	=C28*-1	0	0
14				
15	Net increase <decrease> in cash	=C6	=D6+D13	=E6+E13
16				
17	Cash Balance at Beg of Period	=C13	=C18	=D18
18	Cash Balance at End of Period	=C13+C15	=D15+D17	=E15+E17

Figure 11-19. *Formula view of FIN-VALUE_CWS, the Company's Value and Investment Worksheet, showing Cash Flow NO Financing and Cash Flow WITH Financing*

Determine Incremental Cash Needs

This next step begins with some management thought. After scanning the month-by-month negative cash flows and examining the Company's Master Schedule, we can figure out how much cash is needed between major value events. We compute cash needed between events by linking to the ending cash balance in the month in which the value event occurred.

In Figures 11-20 and 11-21, in row 29, observe cell references H9, N9, and S9. These references refer to ending cash balances in May of YR 1, November of YR 1, and April of YR 2 respectively, which are the dates of the planned attainment of the value events Proto Complete (prototype complete), POP (proof of product), and "POM and CF+" (proof of market and cash flow positive). We have now determined the amount of cash required for the Company to attain each of these important value events. This assumes, of course, that each round of funding is successful.

	B	C	D	E
21	Cash Requirements w/ No Investment	Founders	First Round	Second Round
22	Investment Date	YR 0	May YR 1	Nov YR 1
23	From	YR 0	Jun YR 1	Dec YR 1
24	Through	May YR 1	Nov YR 1	Apr YR 2
25	Value Event at end of period	Proto Complete	POP	POM and CF+
26				
27	Beg Cash Balance	$ -	$ (870,906)	$ (1,967,709)
28	Cash Expenditure	$ (870,906)	$ (1,096,803)	$ (612,970)
29	Ending Cash Balance	$ (870,906)	$ (1,967,709)	$ (2,580,679)

Figure 11-20. *Data view of FIN-VALUE_CWS, the Value and Investment Worksheet, showing cash requirements assuming no investment*

B	C	D	E
21 Cash Requirements w/ No Investment	Founders	First Round	Second Round
22 Investment Date	YR 0	May YR 1	Nov YR 1
23 From	YR 0	Jun YR 1	Dec YR 1
24 Through	May YR 1	Nov YR 1	Apr YR 2
25 Value Event at end of period	Proto Complete	POP	POM and CF+
26			
27 Beg Cash Balance	=C4	=C29	=D29
28 Cash Expenditure	=C29-C27	=D29-D27	=E29-E27
29 Ending Cash Balance	=H9	=N9	=S9

Figure 11-21. *Formula view of FIN-VALUE_CWS, the Value and Investment Worksheet, showing cash requirements assuming no investment*

Develop a Discount Rate

Now that we have determined when the rounds of funding should occur based on when value events are achieved, we must develop discount rates that reflect the relative risk of each round or increment of financing. Again, this is a subjective exercise, but it can be developed using the build-up method. FIN-VALUE_DB, the Value and Investment Dashboard (see Figure 11-22), is used to develop discount rates using the build-up method. Note that the founders' round is excluded.

The Round One and Round Two discount rates are built up by adding incremental risk factors to a beginning rate of return for a risk-free security that is set at 6 percent (wishful thinking, perhaps). The risk at Round One is based on an assumption that the founders have funded the Company through the first value event, that is, the development of the prototype. The change in the risk factors (they decrease) between Rounds One and Two is based on the assumption that Round One has financed the Company through its attainment of proof of product.

The Exit Valuation discount rate is based on the assumption that both rounds have been successful and that the Company is at full operating capability and has attained the value event proof of scale. In effect, this is the rate at which the Company is assumed to be valued if it were to be sold. A formula view of this spreadsheet (see Figure 11-23) shows that the discount rate is a simple sum of all the individual rates.

B	C	D	E	G
10 **Build Up Method**	**First Round**	**Second Round**	**Exit Valuation**	**Risk Definition**
11				
12 Rate of Return for a risk free security	6.00%	6.00%	6.00%	Rate of return for a risk free security (historically this has been returns on U.S Treasury Bonds)
13 Risk premium for small size	10.00%	8.00%	2.00%	Small companies are known to be riskier than larger companies for many reasons
14				
15 **Unsystemic risk (specific company risk)**				
16 Founder Risk	2.00%	2.00%	0.00%	Founders may leave or not be able to participate
17 Capital Risk	5.00%	2.50%	0.00%	Capital in subsequent rounds cannot be obtained
18 Technology Risk				
19 Team	5.00%	1.00%	0.00%	Technical team cannot be acquired in required time frame
20 Hardware Design	5.00%	0.00%	0.00%	Hardware design is new and untested
21 Embedded Software Design	3.00%	0.00%	0.00%	Embedded software design is new and untested
22 Compliance	5.00%	0.00%	0.00%	Production prototypes will fail compliance and standards testing
23 Application software risk	2.00%	1.00%	0.00%	Application software is new and untested
24 Value Proposition	5.00%	5.00%	2.00%	Value proposition (ROI) not proved in field tests or lower than anticipated
25 Manufacturing				
26 Manufacturing design	5.00%	2.50%	0.00%	Manufacturing design is new and untested and dependent on successful production prototype
27 Manufacturing	2.50%	2.50%	2.50%	Manufacturing is outsourced - risk of outsourcing
28 Supplier Risk - Price	2.50%	2.50%	2.50%	Risk that powerful suppliers will adversely affect price
29 Supplier Risk - Availability	1.00%	1.00%	1.00%	Risk that powerful suppliers will adversely affect component availability
30 Market Risk				
31 Threat of New Entrants	1.00%	1.00%	4.50%	Threat of entry of new competitors into marketplace
32 Established Rivals	1.00%	1.00%	2.50%	Threat of established rivals that can immediately compete
33 Suppliers	2.00%	2.00%	1.00%	Threat of powerful suppliers of components, or labor required to support implementation
34 Customers	5.00%	5.00%	1.00%	Threat of powerful customers that can control access to markets and demand price concessions
35 Substitute Products or Services	7.50%	5.00%	2.50%	Threat of substitute products services or other methods to achieve same result
36 Industry Growth Rate	2.50%	2.50%	2.50%	Industry growth rate can affect product acceptance speed and pricing
37 Technology and Innovation	5.00%	5.00%	2.50%	Technology adoption characteristic of target market (are they early or slow adopters of new technology?)
38 Government	-5.00%	-5.00%	-5.00%	Effect of government regulatory environment on all aforementioned risk categories
39 Complementary Products and Services	-2.50%	-2.50%	-2.50%	Effect of the existence of complementary products and services that could positively affect sales
40				
41 **Summary Discount Rate (CAP RATE)**	**75.50%**	**48.00%**	**25.00%**	**Discount rate 'built up' from risk factors and used for valuation of future stream of cash flows**

Figure 11-22. *Data view of FIN-VALUE_DB, the Value and Investment Dashboard, showing the build-up method used to develop discount rates for investment rounds*

	B	C	D	E
9				
10	**Build Up Method**	**First Round**	**Second Round**	**Exit Valuation**
11				
12	Rate of Return for a risk free security	0.06	0.06	0.06
13	Risk premium for small size	0.1	0.08	0.02
14				
15	**Unsystemic risk (specific company risk)**			
16	Founder Risk	0.02	0.02	0
17	Capital Risk	0.05	0.025	0
18	Technology Risk			
19	Team	0.05	0.01	0
20	Hardware Design	0.05	0	0
21	Embedded Software Design	0.03	0	0
22	Compliance	0.05	0	0
23	Application software risk	0.02	0.01	0
24	Value Proposition	0.05	0.05	0.02
25	Manufacturing			
26	Manufacturing design	0.05	0.025	0
27	Manufacturing	0.025	0.025	0.025
28	Supplier Risk - Price	0.025	0.025	0.025
29	Supplier Risk - Availability	0.01	0.01	0.01
30	**Market Risk**			
31	Threat of New Entrants	0.01	0.01	0.045
32	Established Rivals	0.01	0.01	0.025
33	Suppliers	0.02	0.02	0.01
34	Customers	0.05	0.05	0.01
35	Substitute Products or Services	0.075	0.05	0.025
36	Industry Growth Rate	0.025	0.025	0.025
37	Technology and Innovation	0.05	0.05	0.025
38	Government	-0.05	-0.05	-0.05
39	Complementary Products and Services	-0.025	-0.025	-0.025
40				
41	**Summary Discount Rate (CAP RATE)**	=SUM(C12:C40)	=SUM(D12:D40)	=SUM(E12:E40)

Figure 11-23. *Formula view of FIN-VALUE_DB, the Value and Investment Dashboard, showing the build-up method used to develop discount rates for investment rounds*

Compute Valuations

We have the components necessary to compute valuations: the timing of the investment rounds, the cash needed, and a discount rate. We will now use the DCF to compute Company valuation. We will utilize the Excel NPV function to derive the valuation for each funding round. See Figure 11-24 for a data view of our value calculation and Figure 11-25 for a formula view.

Note the formulas in range D34:36 of Figure 11-25. The NPV function requires two inputs: a discount rate and a range of values representing the future cash flow to be discounted. In cell C34, we link to the first round discount rate that we computed in FIN-VALUE_DB (see Figure 11-22). The formula is =NPV(+C34/12,I6:BK6).

Figure 11-26 shows how Excel helps us to build this formula using the NPV function input screen: the discount rate is the value in C34, which is 75.5 percent. Note that we divide this number by 12. Why? The range of values that we are providing to the NPV function is in months. NPV is expecting yearly values. When we divide by 12, we allow NPV to discount the cash flows on a monthly basis. The range of values being discounted is I6:BK6 (refer again to Figure 11-22). Note that the range beginning with column I (see the downloaded sample file) is the next period after the financing in Round One. In other words, the range I6:BK6 is the range of values (expected benefits) accruing to the Company from the time immediately after Round One is completed through the end of the period of performance of the model, which is found in column BK.

To summarize, the net present value of the range of cash values from column I (June of YR 1) to the end of the period of performance (December of YR 5), discounted at 75.5 percent, is $2,672,187. This is the valuation of the Company under which Round One investment is made. We use this same methodology to compute the valuation for Round Two and for the exit value of the Company.

	B	C	D	E	F
32		Discount Rate	Value	Cash needed	% Ownership
33					
34	First Round - NPV from June YR 1	75.50%	$ 2,672,187	$ 1,096,803	41.05%
35	Second Round - NPV from Dec YR 1	48.00%	$ 10,333,757	$ 612,970	5.93%
36	Exit Valuation - NPV from Jul YR 2	25.00%	$ 25,025,373		0.00%

Figure 11-24. *Data view of FIN-VALUE_CWS, the Value and Investment Worksheet, showing computation of Company value for rounds of financing*

	B	C	D	E	F
32		Discount Rate	Value	Cash needed	% Ownership
33					
34	First Round - NPV from June YR 1	='FIN-VALUE_DB'!C41	=NPV(+C34/12,I6:BK6)	=D28*-1	=E34/D34
35	Second Round - NPV from Dec YR 1	='FIN-VALUE_DB'!D41	=NPV(+C35/12,N6:BK6)	=E28*-1	=E35/D35
36	Exit Valuation - NPV from Jul YR 2	='FIN-VALUE_DB'!E41	=NPV(+C36/12,V6:BK6)		=E36/D36

Figure 11-25. *Formula view of FIN-VALUE_CWS, the Value and Investment Worksheet, showing computation of Company value for rounds of financing*

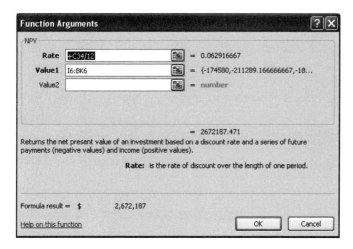

Figure 11-26. *Microsoft input template for NPV function*

Compute Percentage of Ownership

Percentage of ownership is calculated as cash investment divided by valuation. Refer to Figure 11-24, cells F34 and F35; we have computed ownership of 41.05 percent and 5.93 percent, respectively, for the first and second rounds of funding. Figure 11-25 provides a formula view of cells F34 and F35 showing this computation. Note also that we are multiplying cash needed by −1 to make the value a positive number, since we are taking it from our cash needs forecast that computes it as a negative number.

Develop an Interactive Model

Figure 11-27 shows a data view of one type of format that can be used to summarize and model the data that we have previously created. Figure 11-28 provides a formula view of the same. Rather than go through an exhaustive explanation of each formula, I'll ask you to please note the following points:

- Founders

    - *Cell E44*: The initial valuation of the Company is equal to the amount of the investment that the founders will make.

    - *Cells F42 and F43*: Each founder owns 50 percent of the Company immediately after the founders' investments.

    - *Cells D45 and D46*: The Company issues 100,000 shares of stock; each founder is issued 50,000 shares.

    - *Cell D48*: The value of each share is computed as Company value divided by the number of shares.

- Round One

    - *Cell E53*: The valuation of the Company is as previously calculated, $2,672,187.

    - *Cell D52*: The investment of $1,096,803 yields an ownership percentage of 41 percent for the investor (cell G52).

    - *Cell D54*: The total number of shares is increased by 69,621, which is computed by dividing the total number of shares outstanding (100,000) by 1–41 percent (dilution factor) minus the total number of shares outstanding (100,000). Cell D55 shows that Total Shares Issued equals 169,621.

    - *Cells G42 and G43*: Founder shares (ownership) are diluted to 29.5 percent. This is calculated by multiplying their respective share percentages after Round One by 1–41 percent, which has the effect of reducing their respective 50 percent ownership by 41 percent. Notice that Total Ownership in cell G57 is 100 percent.

- Round Two follows the same logic as Round One.

	B	C	D	E	F	G	H
						Ownership %	
39	Investment and Valuation Stategy WS	Date	Investment	Valuation			
40					Founder	First Round	Second Round
41	Founders Investment						
42	Founder 1	YR 0	$ 435,453		50%	29.5%	27.7%
43	Founder 2	YR 0	$ 435,453		50%	29.5%	27.7%
44	Company Value			$ 870,906			
45	Founder 1 - Shares Issued		50,000				
46	Founder 2 - Shares Issued		50,000				
47	Total Shares Issued		100,000				
48	Value Per Share		$ 8.71				
49	Total Ownership				100%		
50							
51	Round One						
52	Investor 1	May YR 1	$ 1,096,803			41.0%	38.6%
53	Company Value			$ 2,672,187			
54	Investor 1 - Shares Issued		69,621				
55	Total Shares Issued		169,621				
56	Value Per Share		$ 15.75				
57	Total Ownership					100.0%	
58							
59	Round One						
60	Investor 2	Nov YR 1	$ 612,970				5.9%
61	Company Value			$ 10,333,757			
62	Investor 2 - Shares Issued		10,696				
63	Total Shares Issued		180,317				
64	Value Per Share		$ 57.31				
65	Total Ownership						100.0%

Figure 11-27. *Data view of FIN-VALUE_CWS, the Company's Value and Investment Worksheet, showing a model of valuation and investment strategy*

	B	C	D	E	F	G		H
39	Investment and Valuation Stategy WS	Date	Investment	Valuation		Ownership %		
40					Founder	First Round		Second Round
41	Founders Investment							
42	Founder 1	YR 0	=C13/2		=D42/E44	=F42*(1-G52)		=G42*(1-H60)
43	Founder 2	YR 0	=C13/2		=D43/E44	=F43*(1-G52)		=G43*(1-H60)
44	Company Value			=D43+D42				
45	Founder 1 - Shares Issued		50000					
46	Founder 2 - Shares Issued		50000					
47	Total Shares Issued		=SUM(D45:D46)					
48	Value Per Share		=E44/D47					
49	Total Ownership				=SUM(F42:F48)			
50								
51	Round One							
52	Investor 1	May YR 1	=E34			=D52/E53		=G52*(1-H60)
53	Company Value			=D34				
54	Investor 1 - Shares Issued		=D47/(1-G52)-D47					
55	Total Shares Issued		=D47+D54					
56	Value Per Share		=E53/D55					
57	Total Ownership					=SUM(G42:G56)		
58								
59	Round One							
60	Investor 2	Nov YR 1	=E35					=D60/E61
61	Company Value			=D35				
62	Investor 2 - Shares Issued		=D66/(1-H60)-D55					
63	Total Shares Issued		=D55+D62					
64	Value Per Share		=E61/D63					
65	Total Ownership							=H60+H52+H43+H42

Figure 11-28. *Formula view of FIN-VALUE_CWS, the Company's Value and Investment Worksheet, showing a model of valuation and investment strategy*

Determine an Exit Valuation

Investors must have an expectation of return on their investment. Figures 11-29 and 11-30 show data and formula views of the computation of an exit value for the Company. The computation is made using the same NPV formula previously discussed in this exercise. Cell C69 of Figure 11-29 shows that the Company value is $25,025,373 based on the NPV of future cash streams beginning in July of YR 2 using a discount rate of 25 percent. Cell E72 shows that the value of Investor 1's 38.6 percent ownership of the Company is $9,662,409. Based on the investment of $1,096,803 shown in cell C72, a return of 8.81 times the initial investment can be expected, as shown in cell F72.

	B	C	D	E	F
67	Investor Returns	$ Investment	% Ownership	$ Value	ROI (X)
68					
69	July YR 2 - First Exit Value	$ 25,025,373			
70	Founder 1	$ 435,453	27.7% $	6,939,264	15.94
71	Founder 2	$ 435,453	27.7% $	6,939,264	15.94
72	Investor 1	$ 1,096,803	38.6% $	9,662,409	8.81
73	Investor 2	$ 612,970	5.9% $	1,484,436	2.42
74					
75	Total Invested	$ 2,580,679	100.0% $	25,025,373	9.70

Figure 11-29. *Data view of FIN-VALUE_CWS, the Value and Investment Worksheet, showing model of investor returns*

	B	C	D	E	F
67	Investor Returns	$ Investment	% Ownership	$ Value	ROI (X)
68					
69	July YR 2 - First Exit Value	=D36			
70	Founder 1	=D42	=H42	=$C$69*D70	=E70/C70
71	Founder 2	=D43	=H43	=$C$69*D71	=E71/C71
72	Investor 1	=D52	=H52	=$C$69*D72	=E72/C72
73	Investor 2	=D60	=H60	=$C$69*D73	=E73/C73
74					
75	Total Invested	=SUM(C70:C73)	=SUM(D70:D73)	=SUM(E70:E73)	=E75/C75

Figure 11-30. *Formula view of FIN-VALUE_CWS, the Value and Investment Worksheet, showing model of investor returns*

Summary

In this chapter, you have learned how to plan, create, and use key components of the Financial Reporting (FIN) model to develop a valuation and investment strategy. This chapter covered concepts of valuation and investment as they apply to high-tech startups, how to use the discounted cash flow (DCF) method for company valuations, how to use the build-up method to develop risk profiles, how value events reduce risk and make your company worth more, and how to develop a valuation and investment model that can serve as the basis for your investment strategy.

High-tech startup companies, in the initial stages, must incur large costs to create the technological capability and intellectual property. Early losses, regardless of downstream gains, naturally lead to a requirement to raise operating capital. The entrepreneur inevitably must seek working capital from investors. With a financial model, as we have in the previous chapters, the entrepreneur will be well prepared to answer the three fundamental questions from potential investors and lenders:

- Cool idea, how do you make money with it?

- How much do you need and why and when?

- What do you think your company is worth?

There are several standard methods for valuing companies. High-tech startups are usually not capital intensive and have insignificant tangible assets that can be valued. Their uniqueness precludes comparison methods to establish value, so the income approach is an often-used valuation approach for technology startups. It measures the present value of expected cash flows based on a discount rate that is determined on the basis of the unique risk profile for the company. The financial model provides an ideal environment within which to apply the income approach to determine a baseline valuation.

The cost of capital for any transaction always represents the economic cost of attracting it in a competitive environment where investors are carefully analyzing and comparing investment opportunities. The cost of capital can be thought of as an opportunity cost, that is, the cost of foregoing the next best alternative investment of similar risk. The cost of capital is market driven, comparable to other investments of similar risk.

The entrepreneur seeks to raise capital at the lowest possible cost, because the cost of capital translates directly into the amount of company ownership that must be sold to raise the capital. The strategy for accomplishing this objective requires balancing the factors that ultimately drive or determine the cost of the capital needed. This chapter provides tools and methods to model valuation and investment strategies to acquire capital at the lowest possible cost.

Here are the key questions to consider for this chapter: What is your company's investment strategy? How much capital do you need and when? What is your company worth? How will you leverage your company's value events achievements to optimize the cost of raising capital?

■■■

CHAPTER 12

Financial Reporting and Analysis Using the FIN Model

In Chapters 10 and 11, we created and then utilized the Statement of Profit and Loss and the Statement of Cash Flows to determine cash needs and to develop an investment and valuation strategy for a company. In this chapter, we continue to examine the data presented by these operating statements, and I'll introduce the third essential financial statement, the Balance Sheet. We will further examine the relationship among these three key financial statements and discuss methods to analyze the data presented by them. This will take some of the mystery out of profit, loss, cash flow, and the Balance Sheet.

In addition, you will learn how to plan, create, and use key components of the Financial Reporting (FIN) model. You will learn how to:

- Develop a Balance Sheet for the company

- Develop, select, and use financial ratios to analyze company data

- Understand the relationships among the three primary operating statements

Business Thinking About Financial Reporting and Analysis

There is always a reason that someone picks up financial statements and begins to analyze them. In the case of high-tech startups, often a potential investor is doing the analysis. Business thinking about financial analysis centers on what the financial statements reveal about the current and future financial condition of the company.

Financial analysis often involves comparisons between companies, comparisons against external benchmarks, and analysis of internal performance trends. Analysis usually includes *pro forma* forecasts that are based on historical data and relationships.

I stated in previous chapters that high-tech startups, in many cases, are difficult to compare to other companies. Their uniqueness often precludes comparisons, and their lack of operational performance data precludes analysis based on past performance. Since this book primarily deals with forecasting operational and financial performance, we should tee up our discussion with the questions: What types of financial analysis are meaningful in the context of a startup that has developed *pro forma* forecasts with a financial model? What type of analysis should we perform on the data that is generated by the model? In other words, what should we be looking for?

I believe the answer to these questions is this: our financial analysis should focus on metrics that directly demonstrate the company's ability to generate and manage working capital.

Financial analysts have a wide array of analysis tools at their disposal. Financial ratios are fundamental analytical tools for interpreting financial statements. Financial ratio analysis relates items in the financial statements in a manner that *drives out* performance information about the company. Financial ratios fall into groupings that appraise various aspects of the financial condition of the company. These ratio groupings include the following:

- Liquidity ratios

- Profitability ratios

- Debt ratios

- Operation performance ratios

- Cash flow indicator ratios

- Investor valuation ratios

Later in this chapter, we will select several financial ratios from these categories and utilize them to analyze the company. We are primarily interested in analysis that demonstrates the company's ability to generate and manage working capital. Before we can perform this analysis, however, we must first complete our discussion of financial statements with a review of the Balance Sheet. After that, we will return to the subject of financial analysis and apply it to our financial statements.

Understanding the Balance Sheet

A Balance Sheet is a summary of the financial position of a business at a specific point in time, showing all assets, liabilities, and equity. It represents the accounting equation: assets *equals* liabilities *plus* shareholders' equity.

How does it balance? Assets are the means utilized to operate the company and are balanced by a company's financial obligations plus equity investment brought into the business and retained earnings. Here is a very simple example: For your small business, you buy an office building (asset) for $100,000 with a down payment of $20,000 (equity) that comes from your own pocket. Your mortgage is $80,000, which is a loan or liability. (Assume you've obtained a no-interest loan from your Uncle Bob.) Your balance sheet is as shown in Table 12-1.

Table 12-1. *A Simple Balance Sheet*

Financial Obligation	Value
Assets	
Office	$100,000
Total Assets	**$100,000**
Liabilities	
Loans Outstanding	$80,000
Owner's Equity	$20,000
Total Liabilities and Equity	**$100,000**

What the company utilizes for operations (the office) is offset by and exactly equal to what the company owes (for the office) plus the equity of the owner.

■**Note** Just like in Accounting 101, anything that the business owns and that has value is an asset. Anything that the business owes is a liability.

The balance sheet normally takes the form shown in Table 12-2.

Table 12-2. *A Standard Balance Sheet Format*

Asset and Liability Categories	Examples and Explanation
Assets	
Current assets	Examples include cash, marketable securities, accounts receivable, and prepaid expenses.
Long-term investments and other assets	Examples include investments in other companies and loan costs being amortized.
Property, plant, and equipment	Examples include fixed assets and machinery.
Intangible assets	Examples include goodwill and patents.
Total assets	Total of all current, long-term and intangible assets.
Liabilities and Equity	
Current liabilities	Examples include accounts payable and short-term debt.
Long-term liabilities	For example, long-term debt.
Total liabilities	Total of all current and long-term liabilities.
Equity	
Retained earnings	Cumulative company net income or loss.
Owner equity	Examples include owner contributions and investments.
Total equity	Total of retained earnings and owner equity.
Total liabilities and equity	Total of liabilities and equity.

Assets and the sum of total liabilities and equity must always be equal, or balance, hence the term "balance sheet."

Like the Profit and Loss Statement, the Balance Sheet is most often developed using an accrual accounting approach. What does this mean? It means that the numbers shown on the Balance Sheet represent the status of the company at a given point in time, taking into account that revenues and expenses have been accrued through that period. In other words, the Balance Sheet does not represent an actual cash view of the enterprise (unless you are using a cash basis for your accounting). The Statement of Cash Flows provides an understanding of the actual cash status of the company. For a more detailed explanation of accrual accounting, see Chapter 10.

Creating the Balance Sheet

In Chapter 10, as we created the Profit and Loss Statement and Statement of Cash Flows, we were also creating the building blocks necessary to build the Balance Sheet. The one building block for the Balance Sheet that we did not cover is the Fixed Assets Summary (see Figure 12-2). Figure 12-1 shows the Balance Sheet that is derived from our exercises in Chapter 10. For easy reference, Figure 12-3 is a repeat of the summary of the Statement of Cash Flows and Profit and Loss Statement from the Chapter 10 examples.

In the following sections we will review each line item of the Balance Sheet shown in Figure 12-1. After this we will review the Green Devil Control Systems business case, and then we will create the Green Devil Control Systems Balance Sheet using components from its Profit and Loss Statement and the Statement of Cash Flows. By the end of this chapter we will have reviewed the interrelationships between the three key financial statements.

■Note Assets on the Balance Sheet are presented in order of liquidity and liabilities are in the order of potential call or due date.

BALANCE SHEET

	Month 1	Month 2	Source of Data	Figure
ASSETS				
Current Assets				
Cash	$ 14,625	$ 12,825	Statement of Cash Flows	Figure 12-3
Accounts Receivable	$ 12,500	$ 28,500	Accounts Receivable (AR)	Figure 10-2
Inventory	$ 500	$ 1,500	Inventory	Figure 10-3
Total Current Assets	$ 27,625	$ 42,825		
Property and Equipment				
Fixed Assets	$ 30,000	$ 30,000	Fixed Assets Summary	Figure 12-2
Accumulated Depreciation	$ 500	$ 1,000	Fixed Assets Summary	Figure 12-2
Total Property and Equipment	$ 29,500	$ 29,000		
TOTAL ASSETS	$ 57,125	$ 71,825		
LIABILITIES AND EQUITY				
Current Liabilities				
Accounts Payable	$ 2,625	$ 5,825	Accounts Payable - Inv + Exp	Figure 10-4 &10-5
Total Current Liabilities	$ 2,625	$ 5,825		
Long-Term Liabilities				
Total Long-Term Liabilities	$ -	$ -	n/a - none in example	n/a - none in exercise
Total Liabilities	$ 2,625	$ 5,825		
Equity				
Stockholders Contribution	$ 50,000	$ 50,000	Statement of Cash Flows	Figure 12-3
Retained Earnings		$ 4,500	Statement of Profit and Loss	Figure 12-3
Net Income	$ 4,500	$ 11,500	Statement of Profit and Loss	Figure 12-3
Total Equity	$ 54,500	$ 66,000		
TOTAL LIABILITIES & EQUITY	$ 57,125	$ 71,825		

Figure 12-1. *Example of Balance Sheet derived from previous Chapter 10 exercises and with the addition of the Fixed Assets Summary shown in Figure 12-2*

Fixed Assets Summary	Month 1	Month 2
Fixed Assets	$ -	$ 30,000
CAPEX	$ 30,000	$ -
Cumulative Fixed Assets	$ 30,000	$ 30,000
Change in Assets	$ 30,000	$ -
Depreciation	$ 500	$ 500
Accumulated Depreciation	$ 500	$ 1,000
Net Fixed Assets	$ 29,500	$ 29,000

Figure 12-2. *Fixed Assets Summary*

Statement of Profit and Loss	Month 1	Month 2
Sales	$ 15,000	$ 25,000
Cost of Goods Sold (COGS)	$ 3,500	$ 5,000
Gross Margin	$ 11,500	$ 20,000
Total Expenses	$ 7,000	$ 8,500
Net Income	$ 4,500	$ 11,500
Statement of Cash Flows		
Operating Activities		
Net Income	$ 4,500	$ 11,500
Adjustment to Cash used by operating activities		
Depreciation	$ 500	$ 500
(Increase) decrease in A/R+Other Assets	$ (12,500)	$ (16,000)
(Increase) decrease in Inventory	$ (500)	$ (1,000)
Increase (decrease) in AP- COGS/Inventory	$ 1,000	$ 1,200
Increase (decrease) in AP- Other Expenses	$ 1,625	$ 2,000
Total Adjustments	$ (9,875)	$ (13,300)
Net Cash Provided (Used In) Operating Activities	$ (5,375)	$ (1,800)
Investment Activities		
Purchase of Capital Assets and Other Assets	$ (30,000)	$ -
Net Cash Used in Investing	$ (30,000)	$ -
Financing Activities		
Stockholders Contribution	$ 50,000	$ -
Net Cash Provided by Financing Activities	$ 50,000	$ -
Net increase <decrease> in cash	$ 14,625	$ (1,800)
Cash Balance at Beg of Period	$ -	$ 14,625
Cash Balance at End of Period	$ 14,625	$ 12,825

Figure 12-3. *Example of Statement of Cash Flows showing its relationship to the Profit and Loss Statement from discussions in Chapter 10*

Current Assets

Current assets are expected to be consumed, sold, or converted to cash either in one year or in the operating cycle or accounting period, whichever is longer. They might include the following:

- *Cash*: The source is Cash Balance at End of Period from the Statement of Cash Flows. This is the actual amount of cash on hand for the company (see Figure 12-3).

- *Accounts Receivable*: The source is the Accounts Receivable Ending Balance. This is the amount owed to the company for sales of products and services (see Figure 10-2).

- *Inventory*: The source is the Inventory Ending Balance on hand (see Figure 10-3).

Property and Equipment Assets

Property and equipment are fixed assets that have a useful life of more than one year and have been capitalized rather than expensed. The amount of property and equipment is shown at book value *minus* accumulated depreciation on the Balance Sheet and is calculated as follows: Fixed Assets *minus* Accumulated Depreciation *equals* Net Property and Equipment.

See Chapter 8 for a more detailed discussion of capitalizing and expensing assets. The following property and equipment assets are listed on the Balance Sheet in Figure 12-1:

- *Fixed Assets*: The source is the Fixed Assets Summary (see Figure 12-2). The Fixed Assets summary is a summary report of the book value of fixed assets of the company and shows accumulated depreciation of the assets.

- *Accumulated Depreciation*: The source is the Fixed Assets Summary (see Figure 12-2). Accumulated depreciation is the cumulative amount of depreciation that has been applied to the original book value of the asset through the end of the current accounting period.

- *Total Property and Equipment*: The source is the Fixed Assets Summary (see Figure 12-2). The Total Property and Equipment amount is the net book value, after depreciation, of Property and Equipment as shown on the Fixed Asset Summary.

Total Assets

The Total Assets amount is computed as follows: Total Current Assets *plus* Total Property and Equipment.

Note that, in our example, we have *no* Long-Term Assets like stocks, bonds, or investments in other companies nor do we have any Intangible Assets like goodwill or patents (intangible assets are a broad subject and beyond the scope of this book).

Current Liabilities

Current Liabilities are liabilities that are expected to be addressed within the current operating period, usually one calendar or fiscal year.

- *Accounts Payable*: The source is the Accounts Payable Ending Balance (see Figure 10-4) and the Accounts Payable Expenses Ending Balance (See Figure 10-5).

Long-Term Liabilities

We do not have any Long-Term Liabilities in our example. An example of a long-term liability would be a long-term note payable, like a mortgage.

Components of Equity

Equity is made up of retained earnings and stockholders' contributions. Stockholders' contributions are the funds invested by the owners of the corporation. Retained earnings are the cumulative net income or loss of the company. Note that stockholders' contributions and net income are carried as cumulative numbers on the Balance Sheet. Here are the Balance Sheet's Equity section details:

- *Stockholders Contribution*: The source is Stockholders Contribution from the Statement of Cash Flows. This is the actual amount of cash invested in the company by investors (see Figure 12-1).

- *Net Income*: The source is Net Income from the Profit and Loss Statement. This is the net income shown by the company from the P&L (see Figure 12-1).

- *Retained Earnings*: This is computed as the cumulative total of Net Income in prior periods and is the cumulative net income earned by the company (see Figure 12-1).

- *Total Equity*: Total Equity is the sum of Stockholders Contribution, Net Income, and Retained Earnings.

- *Total Liabilities & Equity*: Total Liabilities & Equity contains the sum of Total Equity and Total Liabilities.

This concludes our review of the three key financial statements and their relationship to one another in the context of creating the Balance Sheet. Next, we will look at tools to analyze this data, financial ratios.

Using Financial Ratios to Analyze Financial Statements

We have developed the three key financial statements using the CBM. Financial ratio analysis is a standard method for analyzing data in the statements. I have previously stated, "Our financial analysis should focus on metrics that directly demonstrate the company's ability to generate and manage working capital."

Financial ratios fall into four classes: liquidity, solvency, cash management, and profitability. Within these categories, a variety of financial ratios can be utilized to analyze a company. Since we are primarily interested in financial analysis that will demonstrate our company's ability to generate and manage working capital, we will select and utilize the following ratios:

- Liquidity ratios

    - *Current ratio*: Typically the higher the ratio, the more protection a company has against liquidity problems. If the ratio is growing, the company is more liquid and vice versa. The formula for this ratio is current assets *divided by* current liabilities.

    - *Quick (acid test) ratio*: The quick ratio measures a company's ability to use its "near cash" or quick assets to immediately extinguish near-term liabilities. To compute this ratio, add cash *plus* accounts receivable and *divide* that total by current liabilities.

- Cash management ratios

    - *Accounts receivable turnover*: This ratio measures the number of times a year that receivables turn over. Increase in the ratio indicates improved performance and better management, and usually faster collection, of receivables. It can also be an indicator of a company's credit policies. The formula for this ratio is net accounts receivables *divided by* net sales.

    - *Inventory turnover*: The inventory turnover ratio measures how fast inventory items move through a business. It is an indicator of how well the funds invested in inventory are being managed. The formula for this ratio is cost of goods sold *divided by* average inventory (during the current period).

    - *Accounts payable turnover*: This ratio measures how many times per period the company pays its average payable amount. A turnover ratio that falls from one period to another is a sign that the company is taking longer to pay off its suppliers than it was before. The opposite is true when the turnover ratio is increasing; the company is paying off suppliers at a faster rate. The formula for this ratio is cost of goods sold *divided by* average accounts payable (during the current period).

- Profitability ratios

    - *Profit margin*: This measures the total operating and financial ability of management to generate income on the assets at their disposal, or how well it manages cost against revenue. The formula for this ratio is net income *divided by* net sales.

    - *Return on equity*: This is a measure of how well management has managed the company with the permanent funds (equity) at its disposal. The formula for this ratio is net income *divided by* average equity (during current period).

■**Caution** Ratio analysis used exclusively with forecast model data can result in self-fulfilling results. For example, if your model incorporates cash collection and inventory assumptions, the applicable ratios will mirror these assumptions. Make sure you know what you are looking at because these self-fulfilling results may give you reason to change your modeling assumptions.

We have completed our discussion of the three key financial statements and ratio analysis that may be utilized to analyze operating results. Now, we will apply these methods to the terms of the Company business case.

Understanding the Business Case Impact on Financial Results

Green Devil Control Systems (the Company) is an early-stage technology startup. The Company develops energy monitoring and control systems for the residential markets; specifically, it builds and sells the Green Devil Energy Control System (ECS). ECS is a patent-pending, programmable hardware and software device that monitors and controls electricity usage on a circuit-by-circuit basis within a facility.

ECS comes with two software options: Local Services (LS) or Extended Services (ES). The LS software is the default each installation for ECS and provides for a local web browser user interface to enable local setup and programming. LS provide one month of electricity usage diagnostics. ES also provide demographic comparison data and unlimited usage data and statistics. The LS and ES web browser user interfaces are highly intuitive, attractive, and easy to use.

Impact of Operating Activities

The Company will pursue an aggressive schedule to develop, manufacture, and sell ECS. These operating activities are primary drivers of cash requirements. A summary of the major operating activities of the Company follows. It is important to be able to explain the timing, purpose, and importance of operating activities to justify the cash needs of the Company. Here's a brief review of the major operating activities, which are covered in more detail in Chapter 7:

- Prototype development
- Production prototype development
- Field, compliance, and safety testing
- Manufacturing design
- Manufacturing
- Product release
- Software development
- Staffing
- Product release
- Inventory

Planned Investment Activities

In support of operating activities, the Company will invest in capital equipment as set forth in its capital expenditure plan. In the Fixed Assets Summary (see Figure 12-4), Company capital expenditures (CAPEX) are shown. These capital expenditures represent the investment activities of the Company. Capital expenditures and depreciation are plotted in Figure 12-5. Refer to Chapter 9 for a more detailed discussion of capital expenditures.

	B	C	D	E	F	G	H
3		YR 0	YR 1	YR 2	YR 3	YR 4	YR 5
4							
5	Fixed Assets- Beginning	$ -	$ 11,000	$ 136,250	$ 165,000	$ 181,500	$ 208,500
6	CAPEX	$ 11,000	$ 125,250	$ 28,750	$ 16,500	$ 27,000	$ -
7	Fixed Assets - Ending	$ 11,000	$ 136,250	$ 165,000	$ 181,500	$ 208,500	$ 208,500
8	Change in Assets	$ 11,000	$ 125,250	$ 28,750	$ 16,500	$ 27,000	$ -
9	Depreciation	$ (183)	$ (24,338)	$ (31,913)	$ (36,300)	$ (41,700)	$ (41,517)
10	Accumulated Depreciation	$ (183)	$ (24,521)	$ (56,433)	$ (92,733)	$ (134,433)	$ (175,950)
11		$ -					
12	Net Fixed Assets	$ 10,817	$ 111,729	$ 108,567	$ 88,767	$ 74,067	$ 32,550

Figure 12-4. *The Company's Fixed Assets Summary, CAPEX-FA_CWS*

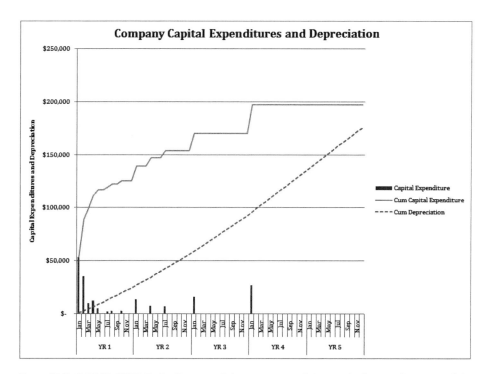

Figure 12-5. *CAPEX_CHART, the Company's investment activity (capital expenditures) and depreciation chart*

Targeted Financing Activities

As explained in Chapter 11, the Company has developed an investment and valuation strategy that will result in raising $2.6 million. An investment of this amount will keep the Company in a cash-positive position until operations begin generating enough cash to cover operating expenses in April of YR 2. In Figure 12-6, the Statement of Cash Flows Stockholders Contribution row shows an initial investment of $870,906 made by the founders in YR 0. This is followed by two investment rounds totaling $1,709,773 in YR 1. See Chapter 11 for a detailed discussion of the financing activities of the Company.

	B	C	D	E	F	G	H
1		YR 0	YR 1	YR 2	YR 3	YR 4	YR 5
2	STATEMENT OF CASH FLOWS						
3							
4	OPERATING ACTIVITIES						
5	Net Income	$ (57,757)	$ (1,882,868)	$ 442,796	$ 6,435,334	$ 14,095,467	$ 26,940,388
6							
7	Adjustments to Cash used by operating activities						
8	Depreciation	$ 183	$ 24,338	$ 31,913	$ 36,300	$ 41,700	$ 41,517
9	(Increase) decrease in A/R+Other Assets	$ -	$ (53,055)	$ (455,183)	$ (271,041)	$ (627,299)	$ (856,805)
10	(Increase) decrease in Inventory	$ -	$ (109,500)	$ (257,850)	$ (181,035)	$ (197,924)	$ (227,339)
11	Increase (decrease) in AP+Other Liabilities	$ -	$ 87,750	$ 187,650	$ 112,185	$ 114,332	$ 63,970
12							
13	Total Adjustments	$ 183	$ (50,468)	$ (493,470)	$ (303,591)	$ (669,191)	$ (978,657)
14							
15	Net Cash Used In Operating Activities	$ (57,574)	$ (1,933,336)	$ (50,674)	$ 6,131,743	$ 13,426,276	$ 25,961,731
16							
17	INVESTMENT ACTIVITIES						
18	Purchase of Capital Assets and Other Assets	$ (11,000)	$ (125,250)	$ (28,750)	$ (16,500)	$ (27,000)	$ -
19							
20	Net Cash Used In Investing Activities	$ (11,000)	$ (125,250)	$ (28,750)	$ (16,500)	$ (27,000)	$ -
21							
22	FINANCING ACTIVITIES						
23	Stockholders Contribution	$ 870,906	$ 1,709,773	$ -	$ -	$ -	$ -
24							
25	Net increase <decrease> in cash	$ 802,333	$ (348,813)	$ (79,424)	$ 6,115,243	$ 13,399,276	$ 25,961,731
26							
27	Cash Balance at Beg of Period	$ -	$ 802,333	$ 453,519	$ 374,095	$ 6,489,339	$ 19,888,615
28	Cash Balance at End of Period	$ 802,333	$ 453,519	$ 374,095	$ 6,489,339	$ 19,888,615	$ 45,850,345

Figure 12-6. *FIN-CASHFLOW_CWS showing the yearly format of the Statement of Cash Flows*

Planning the FIN Model

We are still working within the capabilities of the FIN model. To review, the purpose of the FIN model is to consolidate the outputs from all operating models and present them in three key financial statements: the Statement of Profit and Loss, the Statement of Cash Flows, and the Balance Sheet. In this chapter, we've reviewed the Profit and Loss Statement and Statement of Cash Flows and we will also create the Balance Sheet. We will also apply financial ratios to the data in these statements to perform analysis on the Company. Planning the FIN model in this context requires the following thought process:

- *Planning the Profit and Loss Statement:* Review the output from all operating models that generate data for the P&L. Plan the report format for the P&L including the order of presentation and the level of detail that you require for the report.

- *Planning the Statement of Cash Flows:* Review the output from all operating models that generate data for the Statement of Cash Flows. The report format is standard, so spend your time making sure that you understand all of the linking and relationships necessary to build the report.

- *Planning the Balance Sheet:* Review the location of all data required to build the Balance Sheet. The report format is standard, so spend your time making sure that you understand all of the linking and relationships necessary to build the report.

Understanding the Building Blocks of the FIN Model

This section provides an overview of the FIN model and the top-level functionality of model components. As previously stated, the emphasis in this chapter is a review of the Profit and Loss Statement and the Statement of Cash Flows, building the Balance Sheet, and applying financial analysis to these statements. Referring to Figure 12-7, read the following sections to glean an overview of the major building blocks of the FIN model and detailed description of the functionality and workings of each of its major components.

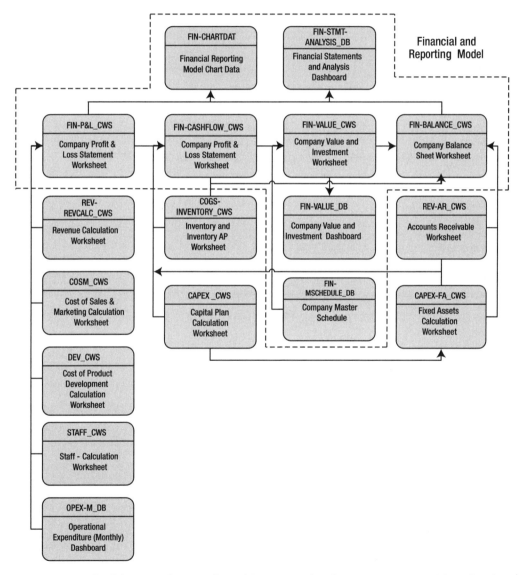

Figure 12-7. *Top-level design and process flow of the Financial and Reporting (FIN) model. Within the dotted line are the core modules of the FIN model, and arrows represent major data and process flows between modules. FIN-M-SCHEDULE_DB is a graphical representation of the Company master schedule and is used as a primary reference for the timing of value events that are developed in operational worksheets.*

Understanding the Profit & Loss Statement Worksheet

The Profit & Loss Statement Worksheet, FIN-P&L_CWS, creates the Company's Profit and Loss Statement. It utilizes inputs from the following worksheets. The following are the major line items of the P&L and the source worksheets for the data:

- *Product Revenue, Software Revenue, Service Revenue, and Cost of Goods Sold*: Source is REVCALC_CWS, the Revenue Calculation Worksheet

- *Total Sales and Marketing Costs*: Source is COSM_CWS, the Cost of Sales & Marketing Calculation Worksheet

- *Total Technical Operations (Product Development Costs)*: Source is DEV_CWS, the Cost of Product Development Calculation Worksheet

- *Total Sal Wages Bonus & Comm*: Source is STAFF_CWS, the Staff Calculation Worksheet

- *Total Operating Expenses*: Source is OPEX-M_DB, the Operational Expenditure (Monthly) Dashboard

Creating FIN-P&L_CWS, the Profit & Loss Statement Worksheet shown in Figure 12-8, is a fairly straightforward task of linking the data from the source data models into the FIN-P&L_CWS format. Figure 12-9 shows a formula view of the revenue sections of the P&L. Note that all revenue data has been previously developed within REV-REVCALC_CWS, and to create the P&L, all that is required is to link to the data. As stated before, the primary thinking about this report regards organization and format.

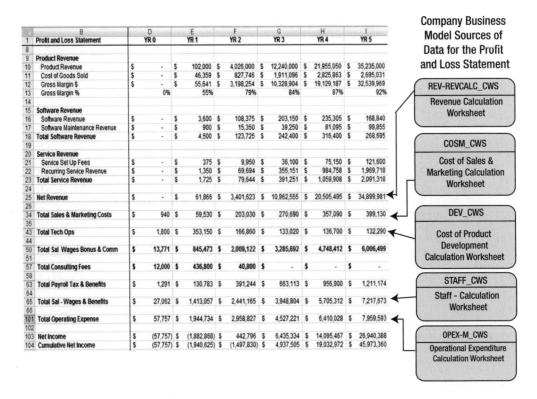

Figure 12-8. *FIN-P&L_CWS, the Profit & Loss Statement Worksheet*

B	E	F
108	Jan	Feb
109		
110		
111 Unit Sales	='REV-REVCALC_CWS'!E6	='REV-REVCALC_CWS'!F6
112		
113 **Product Revenue**		
114 Product Revenue	='REV-REVCALC_CWS'!E10	='REV-REVCALC_CWS'!F10
115 Cost of Goods Sold	='REV-REVCALC_CWS'!E19	='REV-REVCALC_CWS'!F19
116 Gross Margin $	='REV-REVCALC_CWS'!E21	='REV-REVCALC_CWS'!F21
117 Gross Margin %	='REV-REVCALC_CWS'!E22	='REV-REVCALC_CWS'!F22
118		
119 **Software Revenue**		
120 Software Revenue	='REV-REVCALC_CWS'!E34	='REV-REVCALC_CWS'!F34
121 Software Maintenance Revenue	='REV-REVCALC_CWS'!E35	='REV-REVCALC_CWS'!F35
122 **Total Software Revenue**	=SUM(E120:E121)	=SUM(F120:F121)
123		
124 **Service Revenue**		
125 Service Set Up Fees	='REV-REVCALC_CWS'!E38	='REV-REVCALC_CWS'!F38
126 Recurring Service Revenue	='REV-REVCALC_CWS'!E39	='REV-REVCALC_CWS'!F39
127 **Total Service Revenue**	=SUM(E125:E126)	=SUM(F125:F126)
128		
129 **Net Revenue**	=E127+E122+E116	=F127+F122+F116

Figure 12-9. *Formula view of the Product Revenue section of FIN-P&L_CWS, the Profit & Loss Statement Worksheet*

Understanding the Statement of Cash Flow Worksheet

The Statement of Cash Flow Worksheet, FIN-CASHFLOW_CWS, creates the Company's Statement of Cash Flows (see Figure 12-10). It utilizes inputs from the following worksheets:

- *Net Income*: Source is FIN-P&L_CWS, the Profit & Loss Statement Worksheet

- *Depreciation*: Source is FIN-P&L_CWS, the Profit & Loss Statement Worksheet

- *(Increase) decrease in A/R+Other Assets*: Source is REV-AR_CWS, the Accounts Receivable Worksheet

- *(Increase) decrease in Inventory*: Source is COGS-INVENTORY_CWS, the Inventory and Inventory AP Worksheet

- *Increase (decrease) in AP+Other Liabilities*: Source is COGS-INVENTORY_CWS, the Inventory and Inventory AP Worksheet

- *Purchase of Capital Assets and Other Assets*: Source is CAPEX _CWS, the Capital Plan Calculation Worksheet

---

■**Note** See Exercise 10-1 for a detailed explanation of creating the Company's Statement of Cash Flows.

As shown in Figure 12-11, the first two years of Company performance using P&L data and Cash Flow data show that there is a cash problem: the Company forecasts a cash shortfall of $2.6 million in the first two years of operation. The Company strategy (fully developed in Chapter 11) is to raise this money from a founder's investment of $870,906 in YR 0 and two rounds of additional funding totaling $1,709,773 in YR 1. See Figure 12-10, the Statement of Cash Flows, for the cash impact of this strategy and Figure 12-12 for a graphical look at the same strategy.

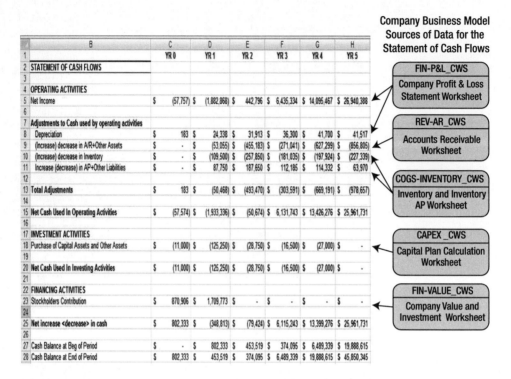

Figure 12-10. *FIN-CASHFLOW_CWS, the Statement of Cash Flow Worksheet*

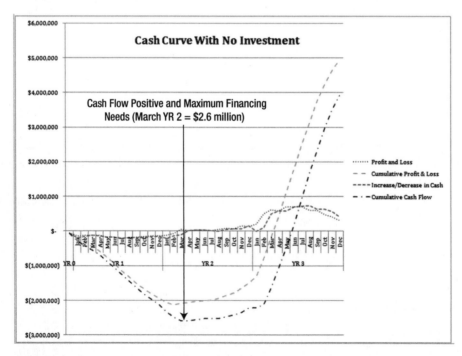

Figure 12-11. *FIN_CHART-NO-INVEST charts monthly profit and loss, cumulative profit and loss, and cumulative cash needs.*

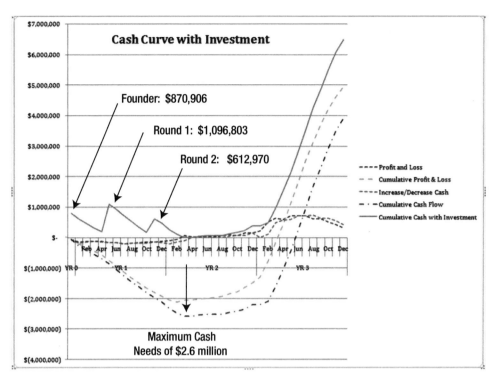

Figure 12-12. *FIN_CHART-YES-INVEST charts monthly profit and loss versus cumulative profit and loss and cumulative cash needs.*

Understanding the Balance Sheet Worksheet

The Balance Sheet Worksheet shown in Figure 12-13, FIN-BALANCE_CWS, creates the Company's Balance Sheet from data developed in the Profit and Loss Statement and the Statement of Cash Flows.

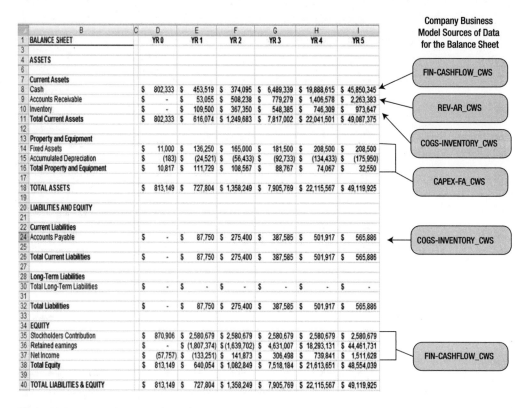

B	C	D	E	F	G	H	I
1 BALANCE SHEET		YR 0	YR 1	YR 2	YR 3	YR 4	YR 5
3							
4 ASSETS							
6							
7 Current Assets							
8 Cash		$ 802,333	$ 453,519	$ 374,095	$ 6,489,339	$ 19,888,615	$ 45,850,345
9 Accounts Receivable		$ -	$ 53,055	$ 508,238	$ 779,279	$ 1,406,578	$ 2,263,383
10 Inventory		$ -	$ 109,500	$ 367,350	$ 548,385	$ 746,309	$ 973,647
11 Total Current Assets		$ 802,333	$ 616,074	$ 1,249,683	$ 7,817,002	$ 22,041,501	$ 49,087,375
12							
13 Property and Equipment							
14 Fixed Assets		$ 11,000	$ 136,250	$ 165,000	$ 181,500	$ 208,500	$ 208,500
15 Accumulated Depreciation		$ (183)	$ (24,521)	$ (56,433)	$ (92,733)	$ (134,433)	$ (175,950)
16 Total Property and Equipment		$ 10,817	$ 111,729	$ 108,567	$ 88,767	$ 74,067	$ 32,550
17							
18 TOTAL ASSETS		$ 813,149	$ 727,804	$ 1,358,249	$ 7,905,769	$ 22,115,567	$ 49,119,925
19							
20 LIABILITIES AND EQUITY							
21							
22 Current Liabilities							
24 Accounts Payable		$ -	$ 87,750	$ 275,400	$ 387,585	$ 501,917	$ 565,886
25							
26 Total Current Liabilities		$ -	$ 87,750	$ 275,400	$ 387,585	$ 501,917	$ 565,886
27							
28 Long-Term Liabilities							
30 Total Long-Term Liabilities		$ -	$ -	$ -	$ -	$ -	$ -
31							
32 Total Liabilities		$ -	$ 87,750	$ 275,400	$ 387,585	$ 501,917	$ 565,886
33							
34 EQUITY							
35 Stockholders Contribution		$ 870,906	$ 2,580,679	$ 2,580,679	$ 2,580,679	$ 2,580,679	$ 2,580,679
36 Retained earnings		$ -	$ (1,807,374)	$ (1,639,702)	$ 4,631,007	$ 18,293,131	$ 44,461,731
37 Net Income		$ (57,757)	$ (133,251)	$ 141,873	$ 306,498	$ 739,841	$ 1,511,628
38 Total Equity		$ 813,149	$ 640,054	$ 1,082,849	$ 7,518,184	$ 21,613,651	$ 48,554,039
39							
40 TOTAL LIABILITIES & EQUITY		$ 813,149	$ 727,804	$ 1,358,249	$ 7,905,769	$ 22,115,567	$ 49,119,925

Company Business Model Sources of Data for the Balance Sheet

FIN-CASHFLOW_CWS
REV-AR_CWS
COGS-INVENTORY_CWS
CAPEX-FA_CWS
COGS-INVENTORY_CWS
FIN-CASHFLOW_CWS

Figure 12-13. *FIN-BALANCE_CWS, the Company Balance Sheet*

■**Note** See Exercise 12-1 for a detailed explanation of creating the Company's Balance Sheet.

Understanding the Value and Investment Worksheet

The Value and Investment Worksheet shown in Figure 12-14, FIN-VALUE_CWS, is a Company valuation model that utilizes risk factors or discount rates applied to cash flows generated within the FIN model in order to assess investment options and Company valuation scenarios. This model is reviewed in detail in Chapter 11.

	B	C	D	E
21	Cash Requirements w/ No Investment	Founders	First Round	Second Round
22	Investment Date	YR 0	May YR 1	Nov YR 1
23	From	YR 0	Jun YR 1	Dec YR 1
24	Through	May YR 1	Nov YR 1	Apr YR 2
25	Value Event at end of period	Proto Complete	POP	POM and CF+
26				
27	Beg Cash Balance	$ -	$ (870,906)	$ (1,967,709)
28	Cash Expenditure	$ (870,906)	$ (1,096,803)	$ (612,970)
29	Ending Cash Balance	$ (870,906)	$ (1,967,709)	$ (2,580,679)
30				
31				
32		Discount Rate	Value	Cash needed
33				
34	First Round - NPV from June YR 1	75.50%	$ 2,672,187	$ 1,096,803
35	Second Round - NPV from Dec YR 1	48.00%	$ 10,333,757	$ 612,970
36	Exit Valuation - NPV from Jul YR 2	25.00%	$ 25,025,373	

Figure 12-14. *FIN-VALUE_CWS showing cash requirements between value events and valuations created using varying discount rates*

Understanding the Value and Investment Dashboard

The Value and Investment Dashboard shown in Figure 12-15, FIN-VALUE_DB, provides a management view of the build-up method of deriving the discount rate used in Company valuation computations. This spreadsheet and its methodology are covered in detail in Chapter 11.

	B	C	D	E	F	G
10	**Build Up Method**	**First Round**	**Second Round**	**Exit Valuation**		**Risk Definition**
11						
12	Rate of Return for a risk free security	6.00%	6.00%	6.00%		Rate of return for a risk free security (historically this has been returns on U.S Treasury Bonds)
13	Risk premium for small size	10.00%	8.00%	2.00%		Small companies are known to be riskier than larger companies for many reasons
14						
15	**Unsystemic risk (specific company risk)**					
16	Founder Risk	2.00%	2.00%	0.00%		Founders may leave or not be able to participate
17	Capital Risk	5.00%	2.50%	0.00%		Capital in subsequent rounds cannot be obtained
18	Technology Risk					
19	Team	5.00%	1.00%	0.00%		Technical team cannot be acquired in required time frame
20	Hardware Design	5.00%	0.00%	0.00%		Hardware design is new and untested
21	Embedded Software Design	3.00%	0.00%	0.00%		Embedded software design is new and untested
22	Compliance	5.00%	0.00%	0.00%		Production prototypes will fail compliance and standards testing
23	Application software risk	2.00%	1.00%	0.00%		Application software is new and untested
24	Value Proposition	5.00%	5.00%	2.00%		Value Proposition (ROI) not proved in field tests or lower than anticipated
25	Manufacturing					
26	Manufacturing design	5.00%	2.50%	0.00%		Manufacturing design is new and untested and dependent on successful production prototype
27	Manufacturing	2.50%	2.50%	2.50%		Manufacturing is outsourced - risk of outsourcing
28	Supplier Risk - Price	2.50%	2.50%	2.50%		Risk that powerful suppliers will adversely affect price
29	Supplier Risk - Availability	1.00%	1.00%	1.00%		Risk that powerful suppliers will adversely affect component availability
30	Market Risk					
31	Threat of New Entrants	1.00%	1.00%	4.50%		Threat of entry of new competitors into marketplace
32	Established Rivals	1.00%	1.00%	2.50%		Threat of established rivals that can immediately compete
33	Suppliers	2.00%	2.00%	1.00%		Threat of powerful suppliers of components, or labor required to support implementation
34	Customers	5.00%	5.00%	1.00%		Threat of powerful customers that can control access to markets and demand price concessions
35	Substitute Products or Services	7.50%	5.00%	2.50%		Threat of substitute products services or other methods to achieve same result
36	Industry Growth Rate	2.50%	2.50%	2.50%		Industry growth rate can affect product acceptance speed and pricing
37	Technology and Innovation	5.00%	5.00%	2.50%		Technology adoption characteristic of target market (are they early or slow adopters of new technology?)
38	Government	-5.00%	-5.00%	-5.00%		Effect of government regulatory environment on all aforementioned risk categories
39	Complementary Products and Services	-2.50%	-2.50%	-2.50%		Effect of the existence of complementary products and services that could positively affect sales
40						
41	**Summary Discount Rate (CAP RATE)**	**75.50%**	**48.00%**	**25.00%**		**Discount rate 'built up' from risk factors and used for valuation of future stream of cash flows**

Figure 12-15. *FIN-VALUE_DB showing the build-up method for determining discount rates for rounds of funding*

Understanding the Financial Statements and Analysis Dashboard

The Financial Statements and Analysis Dashboard shown in Figure 12-16, FIN-STMT-ANALYSIS_DB, presents the three key financial statements—the Profit and Loss Statement, the Statement of Cash Flows, and the Balance Sheet—in one worksheet. At the top of the worksheet are financial ratios developed for the purpose of analysis of the data in the three key statements.

	B	C	D	E	F	G	H	I	J
		YR 0	YR 1	YR 2	YR 3	YR 4	YR 5		
2	Ratio Analysis								Ratio Computation Formula
3									
4	Liquidity Ratios								
5	Current Ratio	na	7.02	4.54	20.17	43.91	86.74		Current assets / current liabilities
6	Quick (ACID TEST) Ratio	na	5.77	3.20	18.75	42.43	85.02		Cash + AR / Current liabilities
7									
8	Cash Management Ratios								
9	Accounts Receivable Turnover	na	2.04	8.32	16.52	16.59	16.61		Sales / AR
10	Inventory turnover	na	0.85	3.47	4.17	4.37	3.13		Cost of Goods Sold / Average Inventory
11	Accounts Payable turnover		1.06	4.56	5.77	6.35	5.05		Cost of Goods Sold / Average AP
12									
13	Profitability Ratios								
14	Profit Margin	na	-1740%	10%	50%	60%	72%		Net income / Net revenue
15	Return on Equity	na	-588%	51%	150%	97%	77%		Net income / average equity
16									
17	STATEMENT OF PROFIT & LOSS								
18									
19	Product Revenue								
20	Product Revenue	$ -	$ 102,000	$ 4,026,000	$ 12,240,000	$ 21,955,050	$ 35,235,000		
21	Cost of Goods Sold	$ -	$ 46,359	$ 827,746	$ 1,911,096	$ 2,825,863	$ 2,695,031		
22	Gross Margin $	$ -	$ 55,641	$ 3,198,254	$ 10,328,904	$ 19,129,187	$ 32,539,969		
23	Gross Margin %	0%	55%	79%	84%	87%	92%		
24									
25	Software Revenue								
26	Software Revenue	$ -	$ 3,600	$ 108,375	$ 203,150	$ 235,305	$ 168,840		
27	Software Maintenance Revenue	$ -	$ 900	$ 15,350	$ 39,250	$ 81,095	$ 99,855		
28	Total Software Revenue	$ -	$ 4,500	$ 123,725	$ 242,400	$ 316,400	$ 268,695		

Figure 12-16. *FIN-STMT-ANALYSIS_DB showing ratio analysis performed on financial statements*

■Note See Exercise 12-2 for a detailed explanation of using financial ratios in conjunction with financial statements.

Understanding the Financial Reporting Model Chart Data Worksheet

The Financial Reporting Model Chart Data Worksheet shown in Figure 12-17, FIN_CHARTDAT, preformats data from FIN model components in support of the development of management charts.

	B	C	D	E	F	G	H	I	J
40	Cash Curve W No Investment	YR 0							YR 1
41			Jan	Feb	Mar	Apr	May	Jun	Jul
42	Profit and Loss	$ (57,757)	$ (147,062)	$ (119,373)	$ (122,430)	$ (128,988)	$ (175,988)	$ (176,718)	$ (210,968)
43	Cum Profit & Loss	$ (57,757)	$ (204,819)	$ (324,192)	$ (446,622)	$ (575,611)	$ (751,598)	$ (928,316)	$ (1,139,284)
44	Increase/Decrease Cash	$ (68,574)	$ (199,487)	$ (153,207)	$ (130,597)	$ (139,693)	$ (179,350)	$ (174,580)	$ (211,289)
45	Cum Cash Flow	$ (68,574)	$ (268,061)	$ (421,267)	$ (551,864)	$ (691,556)	$ (870,906)	$ (1,045,486)	$ (1,256,776)
46									
47	Profit and Cash Monthly	YR 0							YR 1
48			Jan	Feb	Mar	Apr	May	Jun	Jul
49	Profit and Loss	$ (57,757)	$ (147,062)	$ (119,373)	$ (122,430)	$ (128,988)	$ (175,988)	$ (176,718)	$ (210,968)
50	Increase/Decrease Cash	$ (68,574)	$ (199,487)	$ (153,207)	$ (130,597)	$ (139,693)	$ (179,350)	$ (174,580)	$ (211,289)
51									
52	Cash Curve WITH Investment								
53		YR 0							YR 1
54			Jan	Feb	Mar	Apr	May	Jun	Jul
55	Profit and Loss	$ (57,757)	$ (147,062)	$ (119,373)	$ (122,430)	$ (128,988)	$ (175,988)	$ (176,718)	$ (210,968)
56	Cum Profit & Loss	$ (57,757)	$ (204,819)	$ (324,192)	$ (446,622)	$ (575,611)	$ (751,598)	$ (928,316)	$ (1,139,284)
57	Increase/Decrease Cash	$ (68,574)	$ (199,487)	$ (153,207)	$ (130,597)	$ (139,693)	$ (179,350)	$ (174,580)	$ (211,289)
58	Cum Cash Flow	$ (68,574)	$ (268,061)	$ (421,267)	$ (551,864)	$ (691,556)	$ (870,906)	$ (1,045,486)	$ (1,256,776)
59	Cum Cash W Investment	$ 802,333	$ 602,846	$ 449,639	$ 319,043	$ 179,350	$ 1,096,803	$ 922,223	$ 710,934

Figure 12-17. *FIN_CHARTDAT showing data used to develop cash curve charts*

EXERCISE 12-1. USING MICROSOFT EXCEL TO DEVELOP THE COMPANY BALANCE SHEET

The Company has a Profit and Loss Statement and a Statement of Cash Flow. It now needs to complete its suite of financial statements by developing a Balance Sheet. All data necessary to create the Balance Sheet is found in the previously mentioned financial statements.

- *Problem*: The Company has a view of profit and loss and cash flow, now it needs to create a view of the assets and liabilities of the Company. It must create a Balance Sheet.

- *Solution*: Develop a Balance Sheet Model and link it to the profit and loss and the cash flow models that are part of the Company Business Model (CBM).

Model Overview

FIN-BALANCE_CWS, the Company's Balance Sheet Worksheet, creates a Balance Sheet by linking to data in the FIN-P&L_CWS, the Profit & Loss Statement Worksheet, and FIN-CASHFLOW_CWS, the Statement of Cash Flow Worksheet. The following section provides an overview of the structure and concept of the Balance Sheet model:

- *Structure of the model*: Referring to Figure 12-18, note the data view structure of FIN-BALANCE_CWS. Figure 12-19 presents a formula view of the same spreadsheet.

- *Concept of the model*: The concept of this model is very straightforward. We build the spreadsheet by linking to its various components in other models. If the other models are correct, the Balance Sheet will balance.

	B	C	D	E	F	G	H	I	J	K	L
41											
42	USE INVESTMENT FORECAST ?		Y							YR 1	
44	BALANCE SHEET		YR 0	Jan	Feb	Mar	Apr	May	Jun	Jul	Aug
46											
47	ASSETS										
48											
49	Current Assets										
50	Cash		$ 802,333	$ 602,846	$ 449,639	$ 319,043	$ 179,350	$ 1,096,803	$ 922,223	$ 710,934	$ 525,255
51	Accounts Receivable		$ -	$ -	$ -	$ -	$ -	$ -	$ -	$ -	$ -
52	Inventory		$ -	$ -	$ -	$ -	$ -	$ -	$ -	$ 9,750	$ 19,500
53	Total Current Assets		$ 802,333	$ 602,846	$ 449,639	$ 319,043	$ 179,350	$ 1,096,803	$ 922,223	$ 720,684	$ 544,755
54											
55	Property and Equipment										
56	Fixed Assets		$ 11,000	$ 64,500	$ 100,000	$ 110,000	$ 122,750	$ 128,250	$ 128,250	$ 130,750	$ 133,500
57	Accumulated Depreciation		$ (183)	$ (1,258)	$ (2,925)	$ (4,758)	$ (6,804)	$ (8,942)	$ (11,079)	$ (13,258)	$ (15,483)
58	Total Property and Equipment		$ 10,817	$ 63,242	$ 97,075	$ 105,242	$ 115,946	$ 119,308	$ 117,171	$ 117,492	$ 118,017
59											
60	TOTAL ASSETS		$ 813,149	$ 666,088	$ 546,714	$ 424,284	$ 295,296	$ 1,216,111	$ 1,039,394	$ 838,175	$ 662,772
61											
62	LIABILITIES AND EQUITY										
63											
64	Current Liabilities										
66	Accounts Payable		$ -	$ -	$ -	$ -	$ -	$ -	$ -	$ 9,750	$ 19,500
67											
68	Total Current Liabilities		$ -	$ -	$ -	$ -	$ -	$ -	$ -	$ 9,750	$ 19,500
69											
70	Long-Term Liabilities										
72	Total Long-Term Liabilities		$ -	$ -	$ -	$ -	$ -	$ -	$ -	$ -	$ -
73											
74	Total Liabilities		$ -	$ -	$ -	$ -	$ -	$ -	$ -	$ 9,750	$ 19,500
75											
76	EQUITY										
77	Stockholders Contribution		$ 870,906	$ 870,906	$ 870,906	$ 870,906	$ 870,906	$ 1,967,709	$ 1,967,709	$ 1,967,709	$ 1,967,709
78	Retained Earnings		$ -	$ (57,757)	$ (204,819)	$ (324,192)	$ (446,622)	$ (575,611)	$ (751,598)	$ (928,316)	$(1,139,284)
79	Net Income		$ (57,757)	$ (147,062)	$ (119,373)	$ (122,430)	$ (128,988)	$ (175,988)	$ (176,718)	$ (210,968)	$ (185,153)
80	Total Equity		$ 813,149	$ 666,088	$ 546,714	$ 424,284	$ 295,296	$ 1,216,111	$ 1,039,394	$ 828,425	$ 643,272
81											
82	TOTAL LIABILITIES & EQUITY		$ 813,149	$ 666,088	$ 546,714	$ 424,284	$ 295,296	$ 1,216,111	$ 1,039,394	$ 838,175	$ 662,772

Figure 12-18. *Data view of FIN-BALANCE_CWS*

	B	C	D	E
41				
42	USE INVESTMENT FORECAST ?		Y	
44	BALANCE SHEET		YR 0	Jan
46				
47	ASSETS			
48				
49	Current Assets			
50	Cash		=IF($D42="Y",'FIN-CASHFLOW_CWS'!C58,'FIN-CASHFLOW_CWS'!C70)	=IF($D42="Y",'FIN-CASHFLOW_CWS'!D58,'FIN-CASHFLOW_CWS'!D70)
51	Accounts Receivable		='REV-AR_CWS'!C19	='REV-AR_CWS'!D19
52	Inventory		='COGS-INVENTORY_CWS'!C48	='COGS-INVENTORY_CWS'!D48
53	Total Current Assets		=SUM(D50:D52)	=SUM(E50:E52)
54				
55	Property and Equipment			
56	Fixed Assets		='CAPEX-FA_CWS '!C19	='CAPEX-FA_CWS '!D19
57	Accumulated Depreciation		='CAPEX-FA_CWS '!C22	='CAPEX-FA_CWS '!D22
58	Total Property and Equipment		=SUM(D56:D57)	=SUM(E56:E57)
59				
60	TOTAL ASSETS		=D58+D53	=E58+E53
61				
62	LIABILITIES AND EQUITY			
63				
64	Current Liabilities			
66	Accounts Payable		='COGS-INVENTORY_CWS'!C69	='COGS-INVENTORY_CWS'!D69
67				
68	Total Current Liabilities		=SUM(D66:D67)	=SUM(E66:E67)
69				
70	Long-Term Liabilities			
72	Total Long-Term Liabilities		0	0
73				
74	Total Liabilities		=D72+D68	=E72+E68
75				
76	EQUITY			
77	Stockholders Contribution		=IF($D42="Y",'FIN-CASHFLOW_CWS'!C60,'FIN-CASHFLOW_CWS'!C65)	=IF($D42="Y",'FIN-CASHFLOW_CWS'!D60,'FIN-CASHFLOW_CWS'!D65)
78	Retained Earnings		0	=D78+D79
79	Net Income		='FIN-CASHFLOW_CWS'!C35	='FIN-CASHFLOW_CWS'!D35
80	Total Equity		=SUM(D77:D79)	=SUM(E77:E79)
81				
82	TOTAL LIABILITIES & EQUITY		=D80+D74	=E80+E74

Figure 12-19. *Formula view of FIN-BALANCE_CWS*

■**Note** The Balance Sheet and the Statement of Cash Flows are modeled to either use or ignore the investment strategy set forth in Chapter 11. In other words, we have the ability to create a Statement of Cash Flows and a Balance Sheet assuming no investment or assuming the investment scenarios that are modeled in Chapter 11. If we change the basic assumptions in our operating model, cash needs will change, as will their timing. We need to be able to see this pure-cash position before we develop various investment and valuation strategies. The formulas presented in this exercise reflect this ability to turn on or turn off investment assumptions.

Build the Balance Sheet

Two line items in the Balance Sheet are variable based on the choice of whether or not to use the investment amounts from the Chapter 11 strategy. This section refers to the data structure and formulas shown in Figures 12-18 and 12-19.

Let's first consider the ASSETS rows:

- *Cash*: This is the actual amount of cash on hand for the Company, and it comes from the Statement of Cash Flows (FIN-CASHFLOW). The Balance Sheet can be shown with or without investment. We use an IF statement that chooses between a cash amount that recognizes investment if the value in cell D42 is a "Y" or a cash amount that does not recognize investment if the value in cell D42 is not a "Y". The formula for this selection is in cell D50, which, in either case, links to an ending cash balance from FIN-CASHFLOW_CWS. The formula is =IF($D42="Y",'FIN-CASHFLOW_CWS'!C58,'FIN-CASHFLOW_CWS'!C70).

  See Figure 12-20 showing FIN-CASHFLOW_CWS, which is referenced in this formula.

B	C	D	E	F	G
32 **STATEMENT OF CASH FLOWS**					
33	YR 0	Jan	Feb	Mar	Apr
52 **FINANCING ACTIVITIES**					
53 Stockholders Contribution	$ 870,906 $	- $	- $	- $	-
54					
55 **Net increase <decrease> in cash**	$ 802,333 $	(199,487) $	(153,207) $	(130,597) $	(139,693)
56					
57 Cash Balance at Beg of Period	$ - $	802,333 $	602,846 $	449,639 $	319,043
58 Cash Balance at End of Period	$ 802,333 $	602,846 $	449,639 $	319,043 $	179,350
59					
60 Cumulative Stockholders Contribution	$ 870,906 $	870,906 $	870,906 $	870,906 $	870,906
61					
62 **With No Cash Investment**					
63					
64 **FINANCING ACTIVITIES**					
65 Stockholders Contribution	$ - $	- $	- $	- $	-
66					
67 **Net increase <decrease> in cash**	$ (68,574) $	(199,487) $	(153,207) $	(130,597) $	(139,693)
68					
69 Cash Balance at Beg of Period	$ - $	(68,574) $	(268,061) $	(421,267) $	(551,864)
70 Cash Balance at End of Period	$ (68,574) $	(268,061) $	(421,267) $	(551,864) $	(691,556)

Figure 12-20. *Data view of FIN-CASHFLOW_CWS showing the lower part of the cash flow statement where cash flow WITHOUT investment is calculated*

- *Accounts Receivable*: The source is the end of month AR Balance from REV-AR_CWS. The formula in cell D51 is ='REV-AR_CWS'!C19.

- *Inventory*: The source is the end of month Inventory balance from the Fixed Assets Summary, COGS-INVENTORY_CWS. The formula in cell D52 is ='COGS-INVENTORY_CWS'!C48.

- *Total Current Assets*: the sum of Cash, Accounts Receivable, and Inventory

- *Fixed Assets*: The source is the Fixed Assets Summary of CAPEX-FA_CWS. The formula in cell D56 is ='CAPEX-FA_CWS '!C19.

- *Accumulated Depreciation*: The source is the Fixed Assets Summary of CAPEX-FA_CWS. The formula in cell D57 is ='CAPEX-FA_CWS '!C22.

- *Total Property and Equipment*: the sum of Fixed Assets and Accumulated Depreciation

- *Total Assets* is computed as: Total Current Assets plus Net Property and Equipment.

The following lists outline the data in the LIABILITIES AND EQUITY section of Figure 12-18. In the Current Liabilities section, you'll find the following entry:

- *Accounts Payable*: The source is the month-end Accounts Payable balance for Inventory from COGS-INVENTORY_CWS. The formula in cell D66 is ='COGS-INVENTORY_CWS'!C69.

- *Total Long-Term liabilities*: There are no long-term liabilities in this example.

- *Total Liabilities*: This is computed as Total Accounts Payable plus Total Long-Term liabilities.

With regard to the EQUITY section, capital is the sum of Retained earnings, shown as the cumulative total of the Net Income of the Company, and Stockholders Contribution, the amount invested by the owners of the corporation. Note that Stockholders Contribution and Retained Earnings are carried as cumulative totals on the Balance Sheet.

- *Stockholders Contribution:* This is the amount of investment made into the Company, and the source is the Statement of Cash Flows (FIN-CASHFLOW). We use an IF statement that chooses between a cash amount that recognizes investment if the value in cell D42 is a "Y" or a cash amount that does not recognize investment if the value in cell D42 is not a "Y". The formula for this selection is in cell D77, which, in either case, links the Stockholders Contribution line from FIN-CASHFLOW_CWS. The formula is =IF($D42="Y",'FIN-CASHFLOW_CWS'!C60,'FIN-CASHFLOW_CWS'!C65).

  See Figure 12-20, and note that the cell C60 reference points to a cumulative Stockholders Contribution figure that is computed below the normal cash flow statement format. Also note that the cell C65 reference points to the normal Stockholders Contribution line item. The reason for this is that we need a cumulative Stockholders Contribution for the Balance Sheet (in cell C60), and we know that the C65 will always have values of zero in every cell. Thus we are effectively getting cumulative data depending on the choice of the IF statement.

- *Retained Earnings:* This is computed as the cumulative total of Net Income except in the first month. There are no retained earnings in the first month, only the first's month net income. Beginning in the second month, Retained earnings *equals* the current month's Net Income *plus* the prior month's Retained earnings.

- *Net Income:* The source is Net Income in the Statement of Cash Flows. This is the monthly net income figure. The formula in cell D79 is ='FIN-CASHFLOW_CWS'!C35.

- *Total Equity:* Total Equity is the sum of Stockholders Contribution, Retained earnings, and the current period's Net Income.

The TOTAL LIABILITIES & EQUITY row contains the sum of the Total Equity and Total Liabilities rows.

EXERCISE 12-2. USING MICROSOFT EXCEL TO CREATE FINANCIAL RATIOS

The Company has developed a Company Business Model (CBM) that generates a Profit and Loss Statement, a Statement of Cash Flows, and a Balance Sheet. The founders wish to analyze the outputs of the model using a selection of financial ratios.

- *Problem:* The outputs of a financial model must be tested for validity. How to test financial data presents a problem. For instance, what is a valid and standard way of testing the financial results from operational assumptions?

- *Solution:* Make a selection of relevant financial ratios and apply them against financial statement data for purpose of analysis.

Model Overview

FIN-STMT-ANALYSIS_DB, the Financial Statements and Analysis Dashboard, links to appropriate spreadsheets and displays the Profit and Loss Statement, the Statement of Cash Flows, and the Balance Sheet on one summary worksheet. At the top of this worksheet, we create several applicable ratios and compute the ratios based on the data from the financial statements shown on the worksheet.

The concept of this model is very straightforward. We build the spreadsheet by linking to its various components in other models. We then compute ratios based on the data in the worksheet. Figure 12-21 presents a data view of FIN-STMT-ANALYSIS_DB, and Figure 12-22 presents the formula view.

	B	C YR 0	D YR 1	E YR 2	F YR 3	G YR 4	H YR 5	J
1		YR 0	YR 1	YR 2	YR 3	YR 4	YR 5	Ratio Computation Formula
2	Ratio Analysis							Ratio Computation Formula
3								
4	Liquidity Ratios							
5	Current Ratio	na	7.02	4.54	20.17	43.91	86.74	Current assets / current liabilities
6	Quick (ACID TEST) Ratio	na	5.77	3.20	18.75	42.43	85.02	Cash + AR / Current liabilities
7								
8	Cash Management Ratios							
9	Accounts Receivable Turnover	na	2.04	8.32	16.52	16.59	16.61	Sales / AR
10	Inventory turnover	na	0.85	3.47	4.17	4.37	3.13	Cost of Goods Sold / Average Inventory
11	Accounts Payable turnover		1.06	4.56	5.77	6.35	5.05	Cost of Goods Sold / Average AP
12								
13	Profitability Ratios							
14	Profit Margin	na	-1740%	10%	50%	60%	72%	Net income / Net revenue
15	Return on Equity	na	-588%	51%	150%	97%	77%	Net income / average equity
16								
17	STATEMENT OF PROFIT & LOSS							
18								
19	Product Revenue							
20	Product Revenue	$ -	$ 102,000	$ 4,026,000	$ 12,240,000	$ 21,955,050	$ 35,235,000	
21	Cost of Goods Sold	$ -	$ 46,359	$ 827,746	$ 1,911,096	$ 2,825,863	$ 2,695,031	
22	Gross Margin $	$ -	$ 55,641	$ 3,198,254	$ 10,328,904	$ 19,129,187	$ 32,539,969	
23	Gross Margin %	0%	55%	79%	84%	87%	92%	
24								
25	Software Revenue							
26	Software Revenue	$ -	$ 3,600	$ 108,375	$ 203,150	$ 235,305	$ 168,840	
27	Software Maintenance Revenue	$ -	$ 900	$ 15,350	$ 39,250	$ 81,095	$ 99,855	
28	Total Software Revenue	$ -	$ 4,500	$ 123,725	$ 242,400	$ 316,400	$ 268,695	

Figure 12-21. *Data view of FIN-STMT-ANALYSIS_DB*

	B	C YR 0	D YR 1	E YR 2	J
1		YR 0	YR 1	YR 2	
2	Ratio Analysis				Ratio Computation Formula
3					
4	Liquidity Ratios				
5	Current Ratio	na	=D153/D168	=E153/E168	Current assets / current liabilities
6	Quick (ACID TEST) Ratio	na	=(D150+D151)/D168	=(E150+E151)/E168	Cash + AR / Current liabilities
7					
8	Cash Management Ratios				
9	Accounts Receivable Turnover	na	=(+D20+D28+D33)/D151	=(+E20+E28+E33)/E151	Sales / AR
10	Inventory turnover	na	=D21/(D152/2)	=E21/((D152+E152)/2)	Cost of Goods Sold / Average Inventory
11	Accounts Payable turnover		=D21/(D166/2)	=E21/((D166+E166)/2)	Cost of Goods Sold / Average AP
12					
13	Profitability Ratios				
14	Profit Margin	na	=D113/(D20+D28+D33)	=E113/(E20+E28+E33)	Net income / Net revenue
15	Return on Equity	na	=D113/(+D180/2)	=E113/((D180+E180)/2)	Net income / average equity

Figure 12-22. *Formula view of FIN-STMT-ANALYSIS_DB*

■Caution Ratio analysis on *pro forma* statements should primarily be used to check planning assumptions and trends of data being generated by the model. For example, the Current Ratio of 86.7 shown in YR 5 is very high, because the Company is sitting on $45.9 million in cash (see the Balance Sheet in Figure 12-13). Is this the correct planning assumption? I don't think so. If the Company had that much cash, it would likely pay dividends (make distributions to shareholders) or invest it in additional fixed assets or securities to generate additional revenue. As actual operating results are booked, the ratios take on a new meaning, measuring performance.

Compute Ratios

When computing ratios where an average number is used in the ratio formula (for example, average inventory or average payables), you compute the average as follows: ending inventory balance from last year *plus* the ending inventory balance of the current year *divided by* two. In the first year computation, since beginning balances are (in this model) zero, the computation is ending balance in the current year *divided* by two.

Liquidity Ratios

In the Liquidity Ratios section of Figure 12-21, you'll find the following data:

- *Current Ratio*: Typically, the higher the ratio, the more protection a company has against liquidity problems. If the ratio is growing, the company is more liquid, and vice versa. The general formula for this ratio is current assets *divided by* current liabilities, and the formula in cell D5 is =D153/D168.

- *Quick (ACID TEST) Ratio*: The quick ratio measures a company's ability to use its ready cash or quick assets to immediately extinguish short-term liabilities. The general formula for this ratio is to add the cash *to* accounts receivable and *divide* the sum by the current liabilities, and the formula in cell D6 is =(D150+D151)/D168.

Cash Management Ratios

You'll find the following information in the Cash Management Ratios section of the dashboard:

- *Accounts Receivable Turnover*: This ratio measures the number of times a year that receivables turn over. An increase in the ratio indicates improved performance and better management of receivables, usually indicating faster collection of them. It can also be an indicator of a company's credit policies. The general formula for this ratio is net sales *divided by* net accounts receivables, and the formula in cell D9 is =(D20+D28+D33)/D151.

- *Inventory turnover*: The inventory turnover ratio measures how fast inventory items move through a business. It is an indicator of how well the funds invested in inventory are being managed. The general formula for this ratio is cost of goods sold *divided by* average inventory, and the formulas in the worksheet are as follows:

  - The YR 1 formula in cell D10 is =D21/(D152/2).

  - The YR 2 formula in cell E10 is =E21/((D152+E152)/2).

- *Accounts Payable turnover*: This ratio measures how many times per period the company pays its average payable amount. If the turnover ratio is falling from one period to another, this is a sign that the company is taking longer to pay off its suppliers than it was before. The opposite is true when the turnover ratio is increasing; the company is paying suppliers at a faster rate. The general formula for this ratio is cost of goods sold *divided by* average AP, and the formulas in the worksheet are as follows:

  - The YR 1 formula in cell D11 is =D21/(D166/2).

  - The YR 2 formula in cell E11 is =E21/((D166+E166)/2).

Profitability Ratios

The Profitability Ratios section of the dashboard provides the following data:

- *Profit Margin*: This measures the total operating and financial ability of management to generate income on the assets at its disposal, or how well it manages cost against revenue. The general formula for this ratio is net income *divided by* net revenue, and the formula in cell D14 is =D113/(D20+D28+D33).

- *Return on Equity*: This is a measure of how well management has handled the company with the permanent funds (equity) at its disposal. The general formula for this ratio is net income *divided by* average equity, and the formulas in the worksheet are as follows:

  - The YR 1 formula in cell D15 is = D113/(+D180/2).

  - The YR 2 formula in cell E15 is = E113/((D180+E180)/2).

Summary

In this chapter, we have revisited the creation and use of the Profit and Loss Statement and the Statement of Cash Flows and have discussed in depth one final statement, the Balance Sheet. We have taken some of the mystery out of these reports as well: we have examined the relationship between these three key financial statements and discussed the use of financial ratios to analyze the data presented by them.

Someone always has a reason to pick up financial statements and analyze them. In the case of high-tech startups, often a potential investor is doing the analysis. Business thinking about financial analysis centers on what the financial statements reveal about the current and future financial condition of the company. High-tech startups, in many cases, are difficult to compare to other companies. Their uniqueness often precludes comparisons and their lack of operational performance data precludes analysis based on past performance.

Since this book primarily deals with forecasting operational and financial performance, we should tee up our discussion with these questions: What types of financial analysis are meaningful in the context of a startup that has developed *pro forma* forecasts with a financial model? What type of analysis should be performed on the data that is generated by the model?

Index

W

You Need the Companion eBook

You Need the Companion eBook

Your purchase of this book entitles you to buy the companion PDF-version eBook for only $10. Take the weightless companion with you anywhere.

We believe this Apress title will prove so indispensable that you'll want to carry it with you everywhere, which is why we are offering the companion eBook (in PDF format) for $10 to customers who purchase this book now. Convenient and fully searchable, the PDF version of any content-rich, page-heavy Apress book makes a valuable addition to your programming library. You can easily find and copy code—or perform examples by quickly toggling between instructions and the application. Even simultaneously tackling a donut, diet soda, and complex code becomes simplified with hands-free eBooks!

Once you purchase your book, getting the $10 companion eBook is simple:

❶ Visit **www.apress.com/promo/tendollars/**.

❷ Complete a basic registration form to receive a randomly generated question about this title.

❸ Answer the question correctly in 60 seconds, and you will receive a promotional code to redeem for the $10.00 eBook.

eBookshop

2855 TELEGRAPH AVENUE | SUITE 600 | BERKELEY, CA 94705

Offer valid through 10/2009.